FREEDOM UNDONE

The Assault on Liberal Values
and Institutions in Hong Kong

FREEDOM UNDONE

The Assault on Liberal Values and Institutions in Hong Kong

Michael C. Davis

Published by the Association for Asian Studies
Asia Shorts, Number 17
www.asianstudies.org

The Association for Asian Studies (AAS)

Formed in 1941, the Association for Asian Studies (AAS)—the largest society of its kind, with over 6,000 members worldwide—is a scholarly, non-political, non-profit professional association open to all persons interested in Asia. For further information, please visit www.asianstudies.org.

Published by Association for Asian Studies, 825 Victors Way, Suite 310, Ann Arbor, MI 48108 USA

Cover by Hana Meihan Davis. Images courtsey of Kotaro Maruyama, Chromatograph, and Joseph Chan. Source: unsplash.com.

Library of Congress Cataloging-in-Publication Data available from the Library of Congress.

ASIA
SHORTS

Series Editor: David Kenley
Dakota State University

ASIA SHORTS offers concise, engagingly written titles by highly qualified authors on topics of significance in Asian Studies. Topics are intended to be substantive, generate discussion and debate within the field, and attract interest beyond it.

The Asia Shorts series complements and leverages the success of the pedagogically-oriented AAS book series, Key Issues in Asian Studies, and is designed to engage broad audiences with up-to-date scholarship on important topics in Asian Studies. Rigorously peer-reviewed, Asia Shorts books provide cutting-edge scholarship and provocative analyses. They are jargon free, accessible, and speak to contemporary issues or larger themes. In so doing, Asia Shorts volumes make an impact on students, fellow scholars, and informed readers beyond academia.

For further information, visit the AAS website: www.asianstudies.org.

AAS books are distributed by Columbia University Press.

For orders or purchasing inquiries, please visit

https://cup.columbia.edu

COLUMBIA
UNIVERSITY
PRESS

To the people of Hong Kong, whose passionate defense
of freedom is the inspiration for this book.

ABOUT THE AUTHOR

PROFESSOR MICHAEL C. DAVIS, long a professor at the University of Hong Kong and prior to that at the Chinese University of Hong Kong, where he taught courses on human rights and constitutional development until the fall of 2020, is currently a Global Fellow at the Woodrow Wilson International Center for Scholars, a Senior Research Associate at the Weatherhead East Asia Institute at Columbia University, and a Professor of Law and International Affairs at O.P. Jindal Global University in India. He also enjoys research affiliations at New York University and the University of Notre Dame.

He has held several distinguished visiting professorships, including the J. Landis Martin Visiting Professor of Human Rights Law at Northwestern University (2005–2006), the Robert and Marion Short Visiting Professor of Human Rights at the University of Notre Dame (2004–2005), and the Frederick K. Cox Visiting Professor of Law at Case Western Reserve University (2000).

His scholarship engages a range of issues relating to human rights, the rule of law, and constitutionalism in emerging states, for which he has published several books and numerous articles in leading academic journals. He has also contributed essays and commentary to such widely read public affairs journals as *Foreign Affairs* and the *Journal of Democracy*, as well as such popular media as the *Washington Post*, the *New York Times*, *Nikkei*, *Apple Daily*, and the *South China Morning Post*, the latter for which he was awarded a Human Rights Press Award for commentary in 2015. As a public intellectual he has appeared for interviews on crucial human rights topics in such broadcast media as CNN, the BBC, RTHK, NPR, and NBC News. He brings that same in-depth experience to this book.

Acknowledgments

I offer my appreciation to the editorial team of the AAS series led by Jon Wilson. Their dedication and efficiency, as I experienced it before, was the reason I returned to the AAS team to publish this book, on a topic for which timely analysis is so important. I have much appreciated that support again for the current volume. Among that team were the anonymous referees whose helpful suggestions have surely made this book better than the original manuscript. The contributions of eminent scholars who kindly read the final manuscript and contributed the blurbs you see on the back cover is also greatly appreciated, including professors Jerome Cohen, Minxin Pei, and Ching Kwan Lee.

Further appreciation to my wife and life partner, Victoria Tinbor Hui, who is my constant collaborator on issues relating to Hong Kong and otherwise; likewise, to my brilliant and lovely daughters, Mai'a Keapuolani Davis Cross and Hana Meihan Davis, who contributed daily to my work, both as supportive family and loyal Hongkongers. A special thank you to Hana, whose brilliant cover design confronts you as soon as you pick up the book. I'm also grateful to Koa and Hoku, our furry family members, who provided constant companionship while I put the finishing touches on this manuscript.

Appreciation for supporting contributions to my work on Hong Kong goes out to my current and past faculties and especially to several think tanks who have funded or hosted my Hong Kong research at various times in past years, including the Woodrow Wilson International Center for Scholars in Washington DC, the Weatherhead East Asia Institute at Columbia University, the National Endowment for Democracy, the National Democratic Institute, the East-West Center in Honolulu, and the Center for East Asian Law at Georgetown University.

Finally, I would like to include a special thanks to Professor Bruce Ackerman, whose Yale course on justice started me as a student on my life-long journey of comparative constitutional inquiry.

CONTENTS

ABBREVIATIONS AND ACRONYMS

BNO	British Nationality Overseas
CCP	Chinese Communist Party
CFA	Court of Final Appeal
COI	Commission of Inquiry
ERO	Emergency Regulations Ordinance
EU	European Union
HKBORO	Hong Kong Bill of Rights Ordinance
HKDC	Hong Kong Democracy Council
HKIAD	Hong Kong International Affairs Delegation
HKMAO	Hong Kong and Macao Affairs Office
ICAC	Independent Commission Against Corruption
ICCPR	International Covenant on Civil and Political Rights
IPCC	Independent Police Complaints Council
NCNA	New China News Agency
NPC	National People's Congress
NPCSC	National People's Congress Standing Committee
NSL	National Security Law
OLC	Office of Legal Counsel
PRC	People's Republic of China
SAR	Special Administrative Region

TIMELINE

1842:	Treaty of Nanking ceding Hong Kong Island to Britain in perpetuity
1860:	After Second Opium War, the ceding of Kowloon in perpetuity
1898:	99-year lease for New Territories, raising issue of Hong Kong's return
1949:	CCP came to power in China, establishing the PRC
1984:	Sino-British Joint Declaration on Hong Kong
1989:	Tiananmen protest and massacre in China, with protest in Hong Kong
1990:	Hong Kong Basic Law
1997:	The Handover of Hong Kong to China
2003:	Protest over proposed national security legislation under BL Article 23
2004:	Beijing decision on the allowed path to democratic reform
2007:	Beijing decision on universal suffrage
2009–10:	Hong Kong protest over the proposed high-speed rail
2012:	National Education proposal and associated protests
2013:	Occupy Central with Love and Peace campaign announced
2014:	The Umbrella Movement, combines with Occupy Central
2015:	Democratic reform bill proposed by the government and voted down by the opposition
2015–2019:	Prosecutions and electoral disqualifications of protesters
2019:	Anti-extradition protest
2020:	National Security Law promulgated
2021:	Electoral overhaul imposed

1

INTRODUCING HONG KONG AND WHAT IT REPRESENTS

Imagine you live in one of the world's freest, most open cities, a global center of finance, education, and culture, a place where free speech and the rule of law prevail—think New York or London. Then imagine a hard-line regime takes control, introducing the midnight knock, secret police, warrantless surveillance and searches, media suppression, intimidation of civil society organizations, patriotic education, and aggressive prosecutions. Rather than simply using military force to terrify the population into submission and silence, the regime uses aggressive law enforcement and hollows out those liberal institutions that sustain an open society. All the while, to promote the city's reputation for freewheeling business, the regime denies anything has changed respecting its commitments to Hong Kong. This is what just happened to Hong Kong, though the proverbial midnight knock has tended to come at 6:00 a.m. The people of Hong Kong saw a transition from a government that faced a degree of liberal institutional checks, a free press, and public oversight to one seemingly accountable only to Beijing and its supporters.

This book offers an in-depth account of the constitutional journey that both created and repressed this incredible city. It tells a story of the spirited response of Hong Kong's people to the repressive ongoing scenario they have seen unfolding. It offers a forensic look at what was in place and what has been done since the city was handed over to the People's Republic of China (PRC). This narrative embodies the anatomy of how illiberal methods of repression may transform an open society and close off the exercise of basic freedoms. At the end of this account, if history is the judge, it will be clear who are the heroes and who are the villains of this extraordinary story.

The first book in this series, published just after the imposition of the national security law (NSL), laid out the varied roadmaps Beijing had put in place by the middle of 2020.[1] This second book includes those political roadmaps but offers a comprehensive analysis of the repression that followed, of the hollowing out of basic freedoms, liberal institutions, and the rule of law. It invites us to consider how the spirit of this extraordinary city was nurtured and how it was undone under devastating national security policies. Readers will come to understand what sort of authoritarian model China has imposed on Hong Kong and the spirited response of its people, at least until all efforts at public accountability were aggressively silenced.

The wider potential reach of this so-called China model has raised global concern as Beijing employs what Christopher Walker describes as "sharp power" to penetrate open societies and otherwise influence countries worldwide to embrace illiberal alternatives.[2] As described by Leopold Lopez in a recent Wilson Center report, an alliance of autocracies, including China, Russia and others, tends to promote globally an illiberal vision that often maintains the structures of liberal democracy, while abandoning the values, norms, and freedoms that enable such structures to function.[3] Populist leaders in established democracies have increasingly echoed this authoritarian illiberal vision.[4] In this evolving debate, the Chinese Communist Party (CCP) has long seen the chief security threat to its rule as coming from liberal ideas that may give rise to calls for freedom, democracy, and the end of one-party rule.

In this analysis, "liberal constitutionalism" or "liberal institutions" simply refer to a system with built-in institutions—related to the rule of law—to protect human rights and basic freedoms and hold government officials accountable. This generally includes institutions abiding by the separation of powers, with legislative oversight and constitutional judicial review, which are characterized by checks and balances. A liberal democracy would involve such institutions, along with guaranteed democratic choice through free and fair popular elections.[5] It is important to bear in mind, as long appreciated in constitutional theory, that these liberal institutions do not just operate as constraints; rather they are central to constitutional processes of popular choice and inclusion, both enabling and limiting government, as core institutions and the public speak and respond to other institutional choices.

The illiberal alternative that is offered, as will unfold in the following pages, is a system not based primarily on talent or liberal oversight, but on loyalty to a party or a leader or both. In the case of China, that loyalty is to the CCP and its top leader or leaders, while in populist regimes around the world that expected loyalty may be to the person of the populist leader. In the case of Hong Kong this loyalty, as the crackdown ensued and the NSL and "electoral reform" were imposed, would ultimately be expressed by the regime in the language of "patriotism." Such patriotism is framed not in the traditional sense of love of country, but in the language of loyalty, imposed in the "patriots only" elections, and national security overreach. In this frame, as will be seen in the latter chapters, the non-loyal may not only be excluded from the process but in many cases jailed for their expressions or activities deemed non-loyal to those in power. What is at stake for Hong Kong and any society facing such illiberal imposition is the very public capacity to guard the community's autonomy, core values and public preferences, including fundamental protection of human rights and maintenance of the rule of law.

China's chief struggle with Western democracies has been an ideological one over these liberal values. Larry Diamond, a leading democracy theorist, has emphasized that for liberal democracy, "the greatest threat by far is from the world's most powerful autocracy, China."[6] He notes, "The hard truth is that the world's two major autocracies—China and Russia—are waging sophisticated and well-resourced global campaigns to discredit and subvert democracy. . . . A narrative has been taking hold that democracies are corrupt and worn out, that they lack energy, capacity, and self-confidence."

The PRC has recently authored two white papers, one on its vision of Chinese democracy and a second on the application of such a vision in Hong Kong. In the former, it promotes a so-called "whole process people's democracy,"[7] and in the latter, it advances a narrative of saving Hong Kong from its liberal proclivities.[8] We ignore the application of such a vision in Hong Kong at our peril.

The Hong Kong story is a constitutional story of hope, passion, and deprivation that very much intersects with this debate between liberalism and illiberalism. As a human rights and constitutional law professor who taught in Hong Kong universities from 1985 to late 2020, I had both the privilege and the challenge of traveling with Hong Kong on much of this recent difficult journey. I write this book for the city and people who took such great care of me and my Hong Kong family for over thirty years. I can only hope this analysis can support the recovery of the freedoms and energy that have defined this great city.

In 2019, the world looked on as millions of ordinary Hongkongers took to the streets to protest a proposed extradition law and to demand democratic reform. They were witnessing a piece of this great city's history and feeling every ripe emotion alongside Hong Kong's determined protesters. This was a story that began in its modern iteration with the city's carefully orchestrated handover in 1997.

That handover is where this narrative begins; it's the story of a city whose people, since the 1997 handover, have felt the full catalog of emotions inspired by the onslaught of authoritarianism—anxiety, hope, despair, trepidation, fear, and hopelessness. Anxiety had always been part of Hong Kong's handover story. Hope rose from the promises made in the 1984 Sino-British Joint Declaration[9] and the 1990 Basic Law, despair from the extraordinary challenges of Beijing's increased interference and foot-dragging against popular demands for the promised freedoms and democracy.[10] Trepidation stemmed from the repeated protests on the streets and the gnawing worry that Beijing might respond with heavy-handed repression. With Beijing's imposition of the NSL and so-called "electoral reform," fear and hopelessness have now settled on those people who long cherished the city's freedoms.

Three years after the protests began, and twenty-five years after the handover, 2022 gave way to a level of fear and hopelessness about the future previously unseen in the still-optimistic post-handover years. At the center of it all is a fear of the massive arrests of anyone who might have once dared to speak up. This has been brought on not only by the new NSL but also by an aggressive pattern of arrests and prosecutions that followed the 2019 protest, both under the NSL and under preexisting sedition and public order laws. In the wake of this repression, an uneasy silence settled on the city in 2023. At this writing, the year 2024 promises even greater depths of despair as prosecution verdicts and sentences are imposed on some of Hong Kong's most popular political figures.

Beijing's direct and growing interventions have exposed its profound distrust of Hong Kong's liberal institutions. Its operatives have imposed various direct controls at all levels of both the political and criminal justice processes, including the executive, the police, the Justice Department, the legal profession, the courts, civil society, the education sector, and the media. These interventions have brought a chill to Hong Kong's much-vaunted rule of law, independent courts, dynamic press, world-class universities, and its status as Asia's leading financial center. Lockdowns over COVID-19 had both enhanced and camouflaged this chilling effect.

Such a chilling effect is especially dramatic because of Hong Kong's long-established status as the freest economy in Asia and the world.[11] This freedom, however, was not limited to economics. In the decades after World War II, and extending well beyond the handover, there were many dramatic distinctions between life in Hong Kong and life on the Chinese mainland. These differences breathed a very distinct identity into Hong Kong and drove the passions that have exploded on the streets. It was these very freedoms that China promised to preserve in the "one country, two systems" model, as embodied in the Sino-British Joint Declaration and the Hong Kong Basic Law, enacted to carry out the 1984 treaty.

This is a point that the CCP seems to have forgotten as it proclaims comprehensive jurisdiction over the city and fails to uphold those solemn commitments. In Beijing's vision, the city's high degree of autonomy, democracy, basic freedoms, and rule of law have increasingly become rhetorical phrases hollowed of substance. With Beijing promoting an illiberal model around the world, these developments are of more than local interest.

A World City Undone

To understand what is now lost for Hong Kong and the world, we must acknowledge what this city had and how it differed from the notoriously repressive system on the mainland. The most visible spotlight on this distinction has been Hong Kong's annual June 4 vigil in memory of the 1989 Tiananmen massacre.[12] Hong Kong was long the only place on Chinese soil where such a remembrance was permitted. I was privileged to observe nearly every memorial since that violent day in 1989. They all involved a very peaceful and moving candlelight ceremony, with wide participation of young and old. Official tolerance ended in 2020 when the vigil was first disallowed, allegedly due to the coronavirus pandemic.[13] Such vigils have not been permitted since the 2020 ban, and the organizers are now mostly in jail.

A fate like that of the 1989 Beijing protesters now awaits those who continue to defend Hong Kong's dying freedoms. For Hongkongers, this fate arrived by a slow and growing burn of intimidation and arrests instead of tanks in the street, but the destination has been the same.

The last legally held Tiananmen vigil in 2019 attracted an estimated 180,000 participants, the first mass event in a season of discontent. Two weeks later, on June 16, a march of two million people against the hated extradition bill was the largest public protest in Hong Kong history, or, as Jeffrey Wasserstrom points out, one of the largest in the history of the world.[14] This surely stands as testament to the fighting spirit of this city and its tradition of popular protests, a tradition richly highlighted by Antony Dapiran in a 2017 book.[15]

The distinctive constraints on free expression, added in 2020 with the imposition of the NSL, went well beyond blocking the popular vigil. With the help of call-in lines to report offenders to police, even teachers who say the wrong thing now face dismissal or worse. Over many years of teaching human rights and constitutionalism, I have often lamented wryly to my students that my courses were illegal just thirty miles away on the mainland, that one of the starkest differences between Hong Kong and the mainland could be found in our classroom. The entire syllabus was prohibited on the mainland by China's famous Document Number Nine, which forbids promoting or teaching topics like constitutionalism, the separation of powers, and Western notions of human rights.[16] The NSL now effectively brings Document Number Nine to Hong Kong.[17]

Reprimands and dismissals of Hong Kong primary and secondary teachers for supporting the 2019 protests early on raised concern that only a PRC-friendly syllabus could be taught or that teachers who differ with such directives will soon be exposed.[18] Will such pressures threaten the global preeminence of Hong Kong's universities, several of them having been long ranked among the top fifty in the world? Will professors who speak up—or who freely teach critical topics and encourage or inspire dedication to the same—risk arrest or dismissal in the new order? Investigative reporting by John Power, Jeffie Lam, and Elizabeth Cheung found that such risk is widely seen as real.[19] As discussed in chapter 9, these fears have had a predictable impact on the number of teachers choosing to migrate or leave the profession.

Hong Kong's legal profession has likewise felt the brunt, with changes that undermine independence and strike at the heart of the city's rule of law. Hong Kong had long been home to a very active and progressive bar, which immediately expressed deep concern about the NSL.[20] The Hong Kong Law Society, the membership organization of solicitors under Hong Kong's divided profession, has also had many active human rights defenders. In early 2022, Beijing attacks on both organizations, and its threats that it might eliminate their official roles in judicial selection, led both organizations to elect more Beijing-friendly leaders.[21] These organizations have since largely gone silent on critical issues related to human rights and the rule of law.

Considering mainland experience, the city's more committed lawyers were right to be concerned. On July 7, 2015, in the so-called 709 Incident, Chinese authorities on the mainland rounded up around 250 legal advocates.[22] Most were charged under China's national security laws, either with "subversion of state power," "picking quarrels and provoking trouble," or incitement of the same.[23] Nearly all were found guilty. Their crimes were organizing and providing legal defense for human rights activists and protesters. Chinese officials and courts clearly view the provision of a rigorous legal defense as a national security threat. The fear of lawyers promoting basic rights has persisted to this day, with two prominent legal scholars and lawyers, Xu Zhiyong and Ding Jiaxi, sentenced in April 2023 to fourteen and twelve years, respectively, for subversion for merely organizing a "New Citizen's Movement" to promote the basic rights expressed in the Chinese Constitution.[24] Does a similar fate await outspoken members of the legal profession in Hong Kong?

In early 2022, the most recent former president of the Hong Kong Bar Association, Paul Harris, fled Hong Kong after being called in for an interview with the Hong Kong police.[25] In a similar vein, one of the most prominent law firms doing human rights work, Vidler and Associates, closed its doors as its principal partner, Michael Vidler, left town.[26] The lawyer representing the legal profession in the Legislative Council, Dennis Kwok, had fled the city months earlier, soon after his expulsion from the Legislative Council for his efforts to block government-proposed legislation.[27] In 2023 he was one of eight exiled human rights defenders targeted with a HK$1million bounty for his arrest for his human rights advocacy abroad.[28]

Almost copying the tactic of the 709 crackdowns on the mainland, Hong Kong prosecutors have gone after lawyers and others who organized and participated in the 612 Humanitarian Relief Fund, which had raised funds to provide legal assistance and other support for the protesters arrested in 2019.[29] The founding board members were convicted and fined for failing to register the fund, and the fund was forced to disband. The police then filed complaints against lawyers who participated in the fund by providing legal assistance, and they were then investigated by their respective professional organizations.[30] Beyond this fund, the Progressive Lawyers' Group, which had advocated politically against human rights violations in relation to the 2019 protests, also disbanded under pressure, with its leading organizers now effectively living in exile abroad.[31] The leader of that group, Kevin Yam, is also one of those abroad targeted with the HK$1 million bounty.[32]

The NSL raises a host of due process concerns. Under its provisions, only judges designated by the chief executive are allowed to try national security cases, and those judges can be dismissed from the select list of approved judges if they make statements that are thought to endanger national security. Furthermore, regulations issued under the NSL allow for the surveillance of lawyers' offices. The risk to human rights defenders is of deep and obvious concern. As will be discussed in chapter 8, there are many other concerns related to due process and the rule of law.

In the years following the handover, the differences between Hong Kong and the mainland went well beyond the allowance of street protests and academic freedom, or law and lawyers, touching ordinary people's lives in many ways. A bookstore or bookfair in Hong Kong could have a full selection of books commenting on local or global affairs or even criticizing China's leaders. Such books, including an earlier one of my own, were all effectively banned on the mainland. For Hong Kong, the tendency of mainland companies to own most local bookstores already resulted in limitations on offerings.

The availability of a wider selection of books in independent bookstores in Hong Kong was an attraction for mainland tourists who would then have to figure out how to smuggle them home. Within a week of the passage of the NSL, public libraries in Hong Kong were already removing sensitive books from the shelves, and schools were being told to ban such books. In the schools more widely protest-related speech was to be prohibited.[33]

Targeting publishers and booksellers was not new; it would just now be legal. In 2015, five Hong Kong booksellers who ran a local bookstore that sold salacious books on China's leaders were famously abducted and disappeared to mainland detention. One was picked up in Thailand, one just went missing, two disappeared while traveling on the mainland, and one was directly abducted in Hong Kong. They later reappeared in jail on the mainland and were pressured to offer confessions on mainland TV.[34]

A Chinese-Canadian billionaire, Xiao Jianhua, who displeased mainland authorities, met a similar fate in 2017, being abducted by mainland operatives from a luxurious Hong Kong hotel.[35] After years disappeared in custody, in 2022, he was finally tried and sentenced to thirteen years in prison, with his company fined 55 billion yuan (US$8.1 billion).[36] Such apprehension will no longer be illegal under the national security law since it can now be done secretly, with no local court jurisdiction to provide oversight.

The prior contrast in the two systems was even more dramatic when it came to the press. In 2002, Hong Kong was ranked eighteenth in the world on press freedom by Reporters Sans Frontières (RSF; in English, Reporters Without Borders); it was eightieth in 2021 and 148th out of 180 in 2022.[37] This has largely closed the gap with mainland China, which has long been among the worst in press-freedom rankings and was 175 out of 180 in 2022. RSF defines press freedom as, "The effective possibility of journalists, as individuals and as groups, to produce and disseminate news and information in the public interest, independent from political, economic, legal and social interference, and without threats to their physical and mental safety."[38] RSF considers political context, the legal framework, economic context, sociocultural context, and security, all of which have been implicated in the Hong Kong crackdown. In the 2019 protests, hundreds of journalists were subject to police violence and harassment, while nearly a dozen have since been detained under the NSL.[39]

Except for a couple Chinese state-owned newspapers controlled by the central government's Liaison Office in Hong Kong, the *Ta Kung Pao* and the *Wen Wei Po*, newspapers in Hong Kong have long been privately owned, with the publisher's editorial control protected. Until recently, among the private newspapers and magazines in Hong Kong were several distinctly opposition or pro-democracy papers. While mainland companies generally boycotted these papers in placing advertising, their popularity among subscribers sustained them very well, with the pro-democracy *Apple Daily* having the second-largest readership in Hong Kong. Under CCP rule, there has never been such a vibrant media scene on the mainland, where all media are officially controlled and subject to strict censorship.

Hong Kong press freedom and much more are now at stake under the NSL. In the crackdown that followed, nearly all opposition or pro-democracy oriented newspapers, such as *Apple Daily*, the *Stand News*, and *Citizen News*, have been forced to close, with many members of their production team under arrest.[40] Even the government-controlled broadcaster, RTHK, has been brought under strict censorship under new publishing guidelines.[41] A handful of independent, or at least not aggressively pro-establishment, newspapers survive, such as the *South China Morning Post*, *Ming Pao*, and the *Hong Kong Economic Journal*, as well as online media, including *Inmediahk* and the *Hong Kong Free Press*, but they operate in an environment of increasing risks in relation to national security controls and political pressure.

With such controls, many local newspapers and other media may carefully attempt to provide independent media coverage and not cross the rather ambiguous government red line. For the larger established papers, such as the eminent English-language paper, the *South China Morning Post*, and some prominent Chinese-language newspapers, such as the *Ming Pao*, a debate by media watchers ensues as to how careful they must be as they endeavor to carry on independently. As a rather subtle case in point, a recent media report raised questions—after two reporters resigned—whether the *South China Morning Post* had killed a long-researched story on abuses relating to birth control in Xinjiang, which the paper denied.[42] In addition to political pressure and the risk of arrest, access to advertising revenue controlled by Beijing through control over mainland companies is a factor in media independence. The *Ming Pao* recently found itself the target of official criticism for promoting "biased, misleading and false accusations" for merely publishing a comic strip by Zunzi that implied that a Beijing NSL interpretation on access to foreign lawyers effectively allowed the chief executive and national security committee to "do whatever they want."[43] Clearly feeling the heat, the *Ming Pao* then axed Zunzi's regular comic strip.

In this new environment, independent community organizations and NGOs have especially felt the heat, with many forced to disband. A culture of fear quickly took hold just hours before the NSL went into effect, with several organizations, including the activist group Studentlocalism and the political party Demosisto disbanding.[44] Demosisto had planned to run candidates for the Legislative Council in then planned September 2020 election, an election that would later be postponed, with the rules changed to bar the political opposition. Demosisto's alleged sin was its earlier—later dropped—promotion of self-determination. Compared to those few who advocated independence, this was a moderate position. Four former members of Studentlocalism would later be arrested, allegedly for organizing a new pro-independence group and calling for a "Republic of Hong Kong."[45] Much later five members of Demosisto would likewise be arrested, accused in 2023 of supporting and colluding with Nathan Law, one of the party's founders now in exile, himself among the 8 targeted with the above noted HK$ 1 million bounty.[46] In the first two years after the passage of the national security law, the initial closure of NGOs and independent community organizations turned into a flood, with nearly sixty such organizations being forced to disband, prominently including the abovementioned Progressive Lawyers Group.[47]

Perhaps most heinous among the many arrests under the NSL has been the arrest of fifty-three—with the ultimate prosecution of forty-seven—opposition politicians for conspiracy to commit subversion for simply organizing and participating in an opposition primary election.[48] The primary aimed to afford the opposition an avenue to select the best slate of candidates to contest the Legislative Council election that was then scheduled for September 2020. As will be further discussed in chapter 10, the government later delayed the election for a year and then revised the election law so only "patriots" would be allowed to run. With strict limits on bail imposed under the national security law, up to thirty-three of the defendants lingered in jail, awaiting trial for nearly two years. Eventually, all but sixteen would plead guilty before trial, apparently judging that going to trial would be futile and hoping for a sentence reduction. The conspiracy to subversion charge presumably relates to the opposition's plan to use a majority in the Legislative Council to vote down the government's budget, which, under the Basic Law, when presented twice, could trigger a requirement for the chief executive to resign.

Though not introduced as such, the NSL is effectively an amendment to the Hong Kong Basic Law. As with the Basic Law, it provides for its own superiority over all Hong Kong local laws.[49] In one of its earliest decisions relating to the NSL, the Court of Final Appeal ruled that it has no power to review the national security law for conformity to the Hong Kong Basic Law.[50] Such a finding seemingly follows mainland practice. The Basic Law and the NSL are both national laws of the PRC. Under the PRC Legislation Law, a national law that is enacted later in time and is more specific in content is superior to an earlier, more general national law.[51] A local Hong Kong court is therefore barred from invalidating any provisions of the NSL that conflict with the Basic Law.

Constitutional judicial review, a bedrock of the Hong Kong legal system, has long come under mainland official threat. Earlier, when a Hong Kong court had the temerity to declare invalid a government ban on the wearing of a face mask, which protestors wore during the 2019 demonstrations to hide their identity, officials in Beijing immediately slammed the court. They declared that there was no separation of powers in Hong Kong and thus no basis for judicial review of legislation—a claim long disputed by local judges.[52] In that case, intimidation was clearly intended, and the court of appeals backed off, reversing the trial court and upholding most of the ban.[53] The Court of Final Appeal went even further, upholding the ban in its entirety, fully adopting the government's narrative that the ban was proportionate and necessary in the face of the violence and vandalism on the streets.[54] In an ironic twist, with the pandemic beginning in 2020, masks were required to be worn in public areas.

As discussed in chapter 7 and later, the NSL demonstrated Beijing's distrust of Hong Kong courts by expressly assigning the ultimate power to interpret the new law to the Standing Committee of the National People's Congress (NPC). It also blocked judicial review of national security officials. That only designated judges can hear national security cases further demonstrates such distrust.

With the NSL incorporated into the Basic Law fabric, Hong Kong effectively has a new hard-line national security constitution, which contains multiple limits on basic freedoms and the rule of law. No heed was taken of the deep public concerns with the city's evolving character expressed eloquently by millions of Hongkongers marching through Hong Kong's sweat-drenched streets in the summer of 2019.

The NSL has thoroughly circumvented the firewall designed to secure the city's autonomy. If there was a higher purpose of the "one country, two systems" constitutional framework, it was to enable the city to maintain its autonomy, its cherished rule of law, and its basic freedoms after the resumption of Chinese sovereignty. Both the 1984 Sino-British Joint Declaration and the Basic Law are pregnant with multiple hedges against the intrusion of the mainland authoritarian rule-by-law system into Hong Kong. "Rule by law" is the characterization of the mainland system usually used to reflect Beijing's official tendency to issue laws to control the public while not being effectively bound by such laws itself.

Several Basic Law provisions have been hollowed out under the NSL and its aggressive implementation. The Basic Law's hedges against the intrusion of the PRC's legal system include bars on the application of mainland law in Hong Kong; clearly expressed restrictions preventing intervention by departments under the central government; sole responsibility in the Hong Kong government to maintain public order; provision for the independence and finality of local courts; and the specification that Hong Kong "on its own" enacts laws relating to national security.[55] These restrictions, combined with commitments to democracy, human rights, and the rule of law, sought to equip Hong Kong to maintain its promised "high degree of autonomy" under PRC sovereignty.[56]

Popular protests in Hong Kong have long been driven by fears about the erosion of Hong Kong's autonomy and its implication for the rule of law and basic freedoms. The NSL embodies Hong Kong's worst fears in this regard. That no local officials charged with guarding the city's autonomy have spoken out against the NSL is especially troubling.

Over 2019 and into 2020, the world watched months of protest as hope descended into despair and then outright fear. Before Beijing's interventions, Hong Kong really was an open city much like New York, with wide access to global information and the internet, free travel, a free press, and the rule of law.

Seventy-eight percent of the people expressed support for the police.[57] That figure dropped to 78 percent disapproval in the ensuing months after the repressive police crackdown on the 2019 protests.

For the 2019 protesters, the comparison sometime heard or even acted out on the streets with a three-finger salute was *The Hunger Games*. The story of a totalitarian repressive regime causing total desperation in remote occupied areas resonated with Hongkongers, as captured by the desperate statement, "if we burn, you burn with us," which was heard in both *The Hunger Games* and Hong Kong.[58] Still, the despair on the streets was best captured by Hong Kong's own 2015 dystopian film, *Ten Years*, which envisioned various scenarios ten years in the future if Hong Kong continued down the path of greater Beijing intervention and Hong Kong government complicity.[59] The NSL, followed by a patriots-only election, achieved that premonition in less than the already short decade mark.

The COVID-19 social-distancing restrictions brought the 2019 protests to an end. This did not, however, end the public concern with the loss of autonomy. The NSL and the mainland's insistence on its zero-COVID policies in Hong Kong deepened that concern. While zero-COVID policies are not the subject of this book, their early imposition clearly demonstrated the submission of the city to Beijing control.[60] Though Hong Kong people may lack trust in mainland public health policies and vaccines, local official compliance with mainland guidance and the wide use of mainland vaccines became a test of loyalty. At the same time, these policies were weaponized to excuse the barring of public gathering and protests. These same COVID restrictions are now often used by the Hong Kong government to explain the loss of business and business confidence, ignoring the consequence of the city's deepening repression and loss of autonomy on such confidence.

The strict enforcement of local public order laws further proved that official loyalty. Any hope that the COVID lull in protests would be seized upon by the local government as an opportunity to address popular concerns was dashed by even more arrests and Beijing interventions. Beyond the wider arrests of over ten thousand protesters during the 2019 protests, the early 2020 arrests, under public order laws, of fifteen of the more senior pro-democracy politicians who had long advocated nonviolence—including Martin Lee, the eighty-two-year-old "father of democracy"—revealed a relentless official campaign to stamp out opposition. By mid-2020, the slow drip of Beijing interventions that had become evident since before the handover became a flood, followed by relentless prosecutions.

Despite the popular protest slogan, "Liberate Hong Kong, revolution of our times," and other similar expressions of frustration, the protests clogging Hong Kong's streets in 2019 were not a revolution calling for a totally new order.[61] For most protesters, it was simply a sociopolitical movement pushing back against Beijing's growing encroachment and demanding full compliance with promises already made to Hong Kong. The five demands—discussed later—of the 2019 protesters were essentially demands that the Beijing and Hong Kong governments live up to the commitments in the Basic Law. Even before the passage of the NSL, continued official indifference had surely degraded any confidence in Hong Kong's autonomy. Hope had been replaced with despair and a growing fear that the Hong Kong we knew would be lost. With the passage of the NSL, that fear proved justified.

Why Such a Disastrous Turn?

Scholars struggle to explain Beijing's hard-line behavior with respect to Hong Kong but also more widely. Some argue it is simply insecure about its grip on the country's periphery, while others believe the opposite—that it is supremely confident. As Andrew Nathan explains, some scholars close to the ruling elite believe Beijing's behavior is driven by confidence that it can pretty much do as it pleases and that the business and financial communities will go along, as would presumably the foreign leaders who rely on the economic elite.[62] In a recent review article, Nathan traces the growing official resistance to the sort of liberalizing reforms on the mainland that had earlier been promoted by party General Secretary Zhao Ziyang before his purge in 1989.[63] He notes that current General Secretary Xi Jinping has abandoned reforms that would diminish party control.

Jean-Pierre Cabestan, in another recent assessment, notes that Xi claims to have advanced on the mainland a superior form of "socialist democracy" that is very much at odds with the liberal democracy widely supported around the world.[64] Xi's socialist democracy, by most accounts, is essentially a repressive dictatorship whose survival and public acceptance depends on performance legitimacy. China's rapid economic growth over several decades has supported such legitimacy, but slowing growth and the heavy-handed tactics used in the recent zero-COVID policy may have eroded such support, which seemed evident in the November 2022 protests across the mainland over COVID lockdowns.[65] While the zero-COVID policies have since ended the heavy-handed repression has not, neither on the mainland nor in Hong Kong. Mainland officials like to claim their recent Hong Kong policies are widely supported for bringing a similar order to Hong Kong.

An alternative explanation of China's imposition of the national security law may speak to the supreme insecurity of Xi Jinping and his band of national leaders. As Xi is fond of repeating, his leadership team clearly believes the CCP is essential to China's development, and its survival must be maintained at all costs. In this spirit, instead of carrying forward with reform, including political liberalization, Xi's leadership has seen the restoration of increasingly draconian instruments of control. This wider insecurity has produced a regime that is not just against liberal ideas, but also frankly paranoid about any ideas that challenge or are critical of the regime. Mr. Xi views the promotion of liberal values such as separation of powers, western notions of constitutionalism and free speech as an existential threat.

The regime's passion for control causes it to give high priority to national security, even over economic development. The CCP's version of national security has always emphasized internal over external security, aiming to wipe out internal opposition. As Sheena Chestnut Greitens lays out in a recent *Foreign Affairs* article, China's "national security strategy" emphasizes what Beijing labels a "comprehensive national security concept."[66] According to the CCP Central Committee, this concept broadly includes "political, military, homeland security, economic, cultural, social, technological, cyberspace, ecological, resource nuclear, overseas interest, outer space, deep sea, polar and biological security." Very little of private life escapes national security scrutiny. Nothing could drive this point home more clearly than language in the new draft Public Security Administration Punishment Law that would allow authorities to fine and detain people who wear clothes that "hurt the nation's feelings," further banning garments and symbols "detrimental to the spirit of the Chinese nation."[67]

As Greitens emphasizes, most important is safeguarding party leadership and the socialist system. In this respect, political unrest and ideological contamination are not tolerated. To guard against these twin threats, patriotic education and party penetration of society are viewed as essential. A rash of national security legislation has flowed from these concepts, along with heightened surveillance across the spectrum. Greitens sees the harshest targets of the repressive regime as Hong Kong and Xinjiang.

China's approach to Hong Kong is clearly related to this political DNA, with the noted policies of top-down control applied on the mainland now invoked in Hong Kong. These policies have become more aggressively authoritarian in the Xi era. This same aggressive domestic politics has been manifest in a wolf-warrior-style diplomacy abroad, which has been accompanied by the promotion of Chinese approaches to governance, especially in other Chinese societies.[68] It is noteworthy that Xi, as noted by Greitens, recently added an international component, labeled the "Global Security Initiative," to his national security formula, which aims to push back against US dominance and win over international supporters to the Xi approach.

What we are seeing in the Hong Kong crackdown seemingly represents a Chinese model for achieving top-down control in an ostensibly open society by hollowing out liberal institutions, an approach promoted and taken up under the heading of illiberal democracy. Given the tendency to view foreign liberal ideas that are used to challenge CCP rule at home as international threats, Hong Kong, as a base of such liberal values, will no doubt inform Xi's vision of international security in dealing with open societies more generally. The degradation of liberal democracy worldwide will, in this vision, presumably reduce its threat to China's domestic order. The same would presumably be said about obliterating its attraction in Hong Kong. Furthermore, the police and surveillance training on display in Hong Kong, under the headings of national security or counterterrorism, will no doubt factor in foreign policy outreach.

A new generation of scholars in China, sometimes referred to as "statist," are providing the intellectual arguments for the strong state and the strong national security approach now evident in Hong Kong.[69] We certainly saw this approach tested, first in the crackdown on protesters in 2019 and then in the newly enacted NSL. Have the responses of the business and international community justified the CCP's confidence that it can get away with such overreach, or have sanctions and business exits proven such confidence misplaced?

While fully assessing the underlying reasons for, and the continued viability of, the Beijing model as it has been applied on the mainland and promoted abroad is beyond the scope of this book, the local imposition and reaction in Hong Kong would no doubt inform such an assessment. The implications of such policies on the ground in Hong Kong are the main concern here. Over time, Hong Kong people have shown a willingness to stand up to Beijing. Will they again do so, perhaps triggered by new events, or has the recent repression under the NSL silenced their voice forever?

Will the Hong Kong we have known effectively disappear or become unrecognizable in this new form? With many Hong Kong activists fleeing abroad, the willingness of foreign governments to stand with Hong Kong people has been of growing importance, both in shaping local determination and China's reaction. It is in this vein, as addressed in chapter 11, that foreign support has become relevant. Beijing's ability to hold on to its base of local business elites in Hong Kong and reassure foreign investors will factor into this equation.

The Thesis

The thesis here is that the intrusion of the NSL is not so much a new behavior as it is a progression of a long pattern of increased intervention and distrust that dates to the handover and before. While the current analysis focuses on Beijing interventions since the handover, the system of rewards for and co-optation of local elites to rule Hong Kong on behalf of Beijing dates to the 1980s.[70] This latest, more extreme effort to take direct control of Hong Kong fundamentally changes the constitutional order from a program for Hong Kong people ruling Hong Kong, within historical constraints, to one where Beijing directly rules Hong Kong. As such, from a constitutional perspective, it reflects a shift in Hong Kong's trajectory from the promised liberal constitutional order to a national security constitution.

As a person not given to conspiracy theories, I believe the unwillingness of Beijing to take a hands-off approach is not so much a matter of a long-held secret plan as it is a product of hostility to liberal values encouraged by the culture of control that pervades mainland politics. That penchant has been dramatically enhanced under the Xi regime. When the members of an open society push back, efforts at control will expand, as will the subsequent pushback.

What is new is the tendency of the current Chinese leadership to feel more insecure, and even paranoid, about popular resistance, thus encouraging them to ratchet up efforts to repress and control, both on the mainland and at the periphery. In some sense, this reflects both theses above, a sense of insecurity combined with a degree of confidence that their repressive methods will be accepted.

The hope for the Hong Kong model was that Hong Kong officials and pro-Beijing elites would, in the early years, find their voice to explain Hong Kong's core values and related concerns, compel Beijing officials to show restraint, and allow the liberal model outlined in the Basic Law to be fulfilled. As traced among the several themes in the following chapters, Beijing's economic rewards and political promotions largely silenced any hope for a local establishment voice. For such a voice to emerge on behalf of Hong Kong could have been the first step toward changing course and enabling the promised reforms.

In lieu of restraint, the cycle of heightened Beijing intervention and heightened public response ensued in each post-handover period. This cycle brought us to the current impasse and crackdown. While Beijing officials are fond of arguing that their repressive turn was justified by what they characterize as a violent color revolution in 2019, they fail to appreciate that the mostly peaceful protests, with widely acknowledged violence on the margins, were simply a response to their own policies, to their failure to fulfill their commitments under the Basic Law. Beijing's policies and the people's response are the subject of this book. Rather than more repression, a return to the fundamental commitments outlined in the Basic Law offers the best path forward.

A Roadmap

The following chapters will carefully lay out how the tense conditions in Hong Kong today are a consequence of specific government policies over the first two and a half decades of post-handover Hong Kong. The most recent repressive policies have led to a Hong Kong that many have characterized as a police state. Some fear that continuing the present course will lead to a Hong Kong that not merely resembles other mainland cities but also mirrors the tightly policed Tibet and Xinjiang, where cultural repression and Beijing's hard-line anxieties over national security have festered for decades. It is significant that the "one country, two systems" model applied in Hong Kong was largely modeled after the seventeen-point agreement by which the PRC took control of Tibet in the early 1950s, and that Hong Kong's fate after the implementation of this agreement has largely tracked Tibet's fate.[71] In both cases, CCP instincts for repressive policies of excessive control overwhelmed promises of autonomy.

This book assesses the current state of the "one country, two systems" model that applies in Hong Kong, juxtaposing the people's inspiring cries for freedom and the rule of law against the PRC's increasing efforts at control. The second chapter, with a little historical background, lays out the foundation of China's commitments to Hong Kong contained in the Sino-British Joint Declaration. The following chapters then take us through the long constitutional journey of modern Hong Kong, discussing: in chapter 3, the Basic Law; in chapter 4, growing interventions, along with the responding protests and the umbrella movement; in chapter 5, the increase in Beijing's interference beginning in 2015 and continuing to the lead up to the 2019 protest; in chapter 6, the 2019 mass protests; in chapter 7, the NSL text; in chapter 8, the crackdown under the NSL and its implications for the rule of law; in chapter 9, the NSL's impact on basic freedoms; in chapter 10, the imposition of a patriots-only electoral system; in chapter 11, international support for Hong Kong; and in chapter 12, the challenge ahead.

A Personal Note

In assessing these developments, I have not been strictly a casual observer but rather a constitutional scholar who has been privileged to have a front-row seat over the many years since the handover. I have more than once been given the opportunity to participate in the events unfolding in Hong Kong. At times, that has been professional participation and at others an expression of personal concerns I and my Hong Kong family have had about our city.

While this book begins at the handover, my engagement with Hong Kong began earlier. In 1989, I joined a million Hongkongers who were expressing their support for the protests unfolding on the mainland. The year before, as a visiting professor at Peking University, I had seen signs of student disaffection brewing. In 1989, as a newly minted professor, I also published *Constitutional Confrontation in Hong Kong*, the first English sole-authored book on the "one country, two systems" framework.[72] When the handover occurred, I was at the old Legislative Council building, watching the speeches from the balcony of legislators then expelled from the Legislative Council. The narrative that follows is grounded in those earlier observations.

One of the great world cities of the twentieth and twenty-first centuries, along with the freedoms of its people, has been lost and will remain so unless commitments made to Hong Kong are restored. Some Beijing supporters I occasionally encounter in conversation argue that Beijing could not have intended the liberal model so clearly laid out in the Basic Law, that this was just about economics—maintaining a free market within a socialist country. In their view, since China lacks basic freedoms and the rule of law, it is not realistic to imagine that China intended the liberal model described in this book for Hong Kong.

Such an argument, if taken seriously, makes no sense. What is the point of having "one country, two systems," and multiple promises of the rule of law and international human rights guarantees, if such core commitments were not intended?

THE PROMISE

2

FRAMING HONG KONG'S HANDOVER

COLONIAL RULE AND THE
JOINT DECLARATION

Hong Kong was already an open society and Asia's financial hub in the latter years of British colonial rule, which had lasted from 1842 until the 1997 handover to China. The territory was handed over to Britain in 1842 under the Treaty of Nanking, which China long characterized as one of the colonial era's unequal treaties, signed on the heels of the First Opium War. The Qing Dynasty had already surrendered Hong Kong Island to Britain in 1841. Hong Kong Island then reportedly had around 7,500 residents, several fishing villages, and its own colorful history of sporadic resistance to Qing dynasty rule. Louisa Lim has written about Hong Kong's earlier periods, both before and during colonial rule. She eloquently highlights the roots of the modern city as a local place with its own identity, whose earlier history was largely ignored both in Chinese and British accounts.[1] Ho-fung Hung describes historical Hong Kong as a very economically vibrant and politically contentious area—both in the centuries before and after the start of British colonial rule—and often a point of refuge from politics elsewhere on the Chinese mainland.[2]

Overlaying its distinct and evolving Cantonese roots, British colonial rule over time saw the birth of a great international trading city, built under British administration by Chinese refugees fleeing war and famine across the border. As Hong Kong prospered, it became a sore reminder of China's weakness, which Beijing would grow determined to correct. Britain later acquired the Kowloon Peninsula after the Second Opium War in 1860, and then the much larger New Territories in 1898—the latter under a ninety-nine-year lease.[3]

It was this time-limited lease that would signal the end of colonial rule, making 1997 the year of reckoning. Hong Kong's prosperity complicated the negotiations: it was a very successful place in whose survival both Britain and China were invested. Returning the leased part of Hong Kong without the rest was thought impractical. Due to its colonial status and the time fuse in the last lease agreement, the Hong Kong that emerged during the century and a half of British rule was sometimes described as a "borrowed place on borrowed time."[4] It was wholly different from China across the border, and it had its own distinctive history. A path to end colonialism without destroying the thriving city was needed.

While British rule for the first century was marked by the curses of eighteenth- and nineteenth-century colonialism—of inequality, exploitation, imposed governance by outsiders, heavy censorship, and limited rule of law—colonial rule began to take a more positive turn in the second and third decades after World War II. This more liberal direction was no doubt influenced early on by the postwar global mandate for decolonization and, in the 1980s and beyond, by the need to prepare for Hong Kong's return to China.[5] The amendment of the British colonial Letters Patent and Royal Instruction, along with the enactment of the Bill of Rights Ordinance, designed to fully implement the International Covenant on Civil and Political Rights (ICCPR), would have a dramatic effect on both basic freedoms and the rule of law, elevating popular expectations both before and after the handover.

Colonial Hong Kong was by no means a democracy, and through most of its history Britain only experimented with the inclusion and co-optation of local Chinese elites through their appointment to government advisory bodies. Such appointed bodies included the Legislative Council until well after the signing of the Sino-British Joint Declaration. Functional, and then direct elections (in 1985 and 1991, respectively) were introduced for portions of the legislative seats. The so-called "functional constituencies" were a colonial government invention to allow electoral representation for certain professions and commercial sectors in small circle elections. Unfortunately, as will be discussed in relation to later developments, the use of such functional electoral sectors was carried over into the postcolonial government and has long been criticized for excluding much of the public from electing most legislators.

As a result of these electoral limitations, in the pre-1990s colonial period, local society was not nearly as politically oriented as it is today. There were brief periods of anti-colonial protests, eg. in 1967, when the passions of China's emerging Great Proletarian Cultural Revolution creeped across the border. But otherwise, people would often say the business of Hong Kong was business. That was soon to change.

When I arrived to teach at the Chinese University of Hong Kong in 1985, one year after the signing of the Sino-British Joint Declaration, both the rule of law and basic freedoms were becoming widely admired characteristics of the city. I asked my first class of mostly working-class local students what they would have imagined for the future political arrangement. The students first rejected my question, saying they were not consulted, so why pretend they had a choice? When I persuaded them to humor me and respond, they nearly unanimously favored a line popular at the time of returning Hong Kong to China, with the caveat of contracting the British to run it. As reflected in our discussion, my students felt a mix of cultural affinity for China, anxiety about Chinese rule, and respect for British governance and its associated rule of law. They especially judged the latter to be sorely missing in China under communist rule, especially on the heels of the disastrous Cultural Revolution. The Cultural Revolution, combined with the earlier Great Leap Forward, had been a period when China's estimated deaths from starvation and other unnatural causes reportedly ranged from thirty to forty-five million.[6]

No doubt, the students' weak interest in self-government can be credited to its total lack during colonial rule. This lack of a robust democratic political culture surely inspired the British to concede to a slight degree of democratic reform from the late 1980s onward. With the handover on the horizon, reform was then being demanded by an emerging generation of local reformers, led in part by a small cadre of middle-class intellectuals who called themselves the Hong Kong Observers, and another group of politician intellectuals operating under the name Meeting Point. These nascent reformist groups would become the precursors to the Democratic Party and the pan-democratic camp.[7] Many of these reformers would later work at the core of democratic politics, media coverage, and academic criticism as democratic values began to take hold in Hong Kong. Supporters saw such values as a hedge against CCP overreach, a stand that would later—especially after they mobilized support for the 1989 mainland protests—brand them as the political opposition and the chief Hong Kong targets of Beijing's wrath.

In the last couple decades of British rule, the most valued asset for stability and economic advantage was probably the rule of law, as proven by opinion polls of that era.[8] This was associated with the British common law system, built around case decisions in the courts, where even ruling officials were subject to the law. If Hong Kong people were going to guard their precious autonomy and the associated rule of law, as promised in the Joint Declaration, they would need the political will acquired by belated democratic reforms. Any other approach would simply be replacing one colonial ruler with another. The new one, China, did not share the democratic, rule of law-based culture at home that distinguished the earlier one.[9]

Other important reforms in those later colonial years included the establishment, under Governor Sir Murray MacLehose in 1974, of the Independent Commission Against Corruption (ICAC), which aimed to cure the endemic corruption that plagued the Hong Kong civil service and police, especially in the form of bribes. The ICAC, as a completely independent body admired around the world, moved the needle, turning a notoriously corrupt Hong Kong police force into one of the most respected police forces in Asia. With such oversight the civil service likewise gained popular respect. Recent mainland influence in Hong Kong governance raises concern about a resurgence of corruption in a different form, where Beijing's friends are favored.[10]

Reforms also included the embrace of a human rights culture.[11] This was supported first by the 1976 British ratification of the ICCPR for Hong Kong. In response to the crisis of confidence after the 1989 crackdown in China, that was followed in 1991 with the enactment of the Hong Kong Bill of Rights Ordinance (BORO), a virtual photocopy of the ICCPR. The Joint Declaration had guaranteed that the ICCPR would survive the handover. There was some question whether, given its 1989 British pedigree, the BORO would likewise survive. With some minor amendments, it did. Through judicial review, the BORO would later effectively be incorporated into the Hong Kong Basic Law by reference. With the rule of law and human rights as a foundation, along with a strong civil service, Hong Kong was well placed to thrive after the handover. Human rights were generally protected until the NSL was imposed.

All of this meant that China inherited a healthy, well-developed territory in 1997. The most significant contrast with the mainland in the postwar years, when China was consumed with the communist and cultural revolutions, was Hong Kong's great wealth. Hong Kong's GDP was nearly 20 percent that of China at the time of the handover, and its per capita income was nearly first-world.[12] Though wages for the average worker were low, strong public housing and public health systems somewhat compensated for lower incomes. These features combined to instill a degree of economic caution in arranging the handover to China.

That cause for caution has persisted. While Hong Kong's GDP percentage of China's economy has shrunk as the Chinese economy has expanded, as Professor Ho-Fung Hung notes, Hong Kong's role as an offshore financial center today has maintained or possibly increased its importance to the largely closed-off Chinese economy.[13] As Hung explains, Hong Kong's autonomy in the years after the handover was understood to be of upmost importance to this economic role. International recognition of the city's autonomy even allowed it, as a free trade economy, to hold a separate seat in the WTO, linking China on two paths to the world economy. The separate legal system and rights guarantees recognized in the Joint Declaration were very much core parts of this distinct status. The recent degrading of Hong Kong's autonomy under the NSL could have the opposite effect of diminishing the value of operating through Hong Kong for both Chinese and international companies.

The Sino-British Joint Declaration

Drafted in 1984, the Sino-British Joint Declaration offered a vision that allowed for Hong Kong's return to China, while at the same time preserving the rule of law and human rights protections. These were long considered necessary to Hong Kong's unique status as "Asia's world city."[14] This commitment was no small achievement, given China's then and still persistent ranking as one of the least free countries in the world.[15] However, in the then prevalent spirit of reform, China had included article 31 in its 1982 constitution to allow for the "one country, two systems" model of governance.

While this model initially targeted the absorption of Taiwan, it would first be applied in Hong Kong. Under this formula, Hong Kong was to have a "high degree of autonomy," with "Hong Kong people ruling Hong Kong."[16] The socialist system of the Chinese mainland was not to apply in Hong Kong. Basic freedoms and human rights were to be maintained by incorporating the two human rights covenants and the various other human rights treaties that were then applied in Hong Kong into the Joint Declaration. Most important of all, the high degree of autonomy promised was designed to maintain the rule of law, independent of mainland interference, under the existing British common law system. Finally, and widely considered important to the security of autonomy and local self-rule, there was the promise of democratic reform. The challenge was whether the authoritarian regime in Beijing could stand back and not interfere to enable this model to thrive. Though initially somewhat restrained, time would prove it could not.

The international community became a partner in meeting such a challenge by agreeing to recognize Hong Kong's special status in international trade, immigration, customs, social and cultural relations, and a variety of related areas. In 1979, Deng Xiaoping famously encouraged international investors to "put their hearts at ease,"[17] an expression used widely by Chinese officials to garner public support for the planned return of Hong Kong to China.[18] Confidence in this extraordinary commitment was to be encouraged by the international diplomatic recognition of Hong Kong's special status, achieved in the leading capitals of the world through Beijing's diplomatic solicitations.[19]

This hopeful vision crafted in the Joint Declaration had traveled a difficult journey. In the early 1980s, the outflow of emigrants from Hong Kong had signaled local doubts about Beijing's intentions. The Cultural Revolution had just ended, and even the Chinese leaders, in reaching this wide-ranging agreement, appeared to appreciate that there was cause for doubt. In the negotiations, there was considerable local concern in Hong Kong about British diplomats giving too much ground.[20]

With the signing of the Joint Declaration, such anxiety tapered off. The security of mutual benefit inspired some confidence. The promised society based on the rule of law in Hong Kong would serve as a catalyst for China's own economic growth. The outside world was hopeful that Hong Kong's basic freedoms and level of development, which were to be protected for fifty years, might spark China's liberalization too—though in hindsight, that proved to be a vain hope. The fifty years, "one country, two systems" commitment is still listed by the Chinese leadership as one of the fourteen fundamental national policies of the CCP, even while it has recently appeared largely abandoned in substance.[21]

The entitlement of Hong Kong people to such guarantees should appropriately be viewed as more than unilateral Chinese national policy (as Beijing officials often claim) or even just as a matter of Sino-British mutual agreement. The Sino-British Joint Declaration was agreed to in the context of decolonization. In 1972, Hong Kong was removed from the UN list of colonies entitled to self-determination at China's request, as China wanted to recover territory that had been taken from it.[22] At the same time, the British had a continuing commitment to the local population. While other colonies were to be given a right to determine their future, Hong Kong was not. In this sense, the Joint Declaration should be viewed as a weaker substitute for those UN Charter guarantees. As such, it takes on added importance for the local population, representing a solemn international promise for the integrity of Hong Kong's autonomy.

Seeking to diminish this international obligation, China has gone to great pains to present Hong Kong's "one country, two systems" model as simply a central government policy. As discussed in chapter 6, in a 2014 white paper, though Beijing quoted verbatim the long list of commitments in the Joint Declaration, it appeared to abandon them as solemn international treaty obligations, treating them merely as national policy.[23] To degrade the international obligation even further, recent textbooks on citizenship in Hong Kong seem to deny Hong Kong was ever a colony, instead describing the long colonial period as merely a period of interrupted control.[24] Denials aside, the Sino-British Joint Declaration was registered with the UN as a treaty, which by its language binds both parties for fifty years to carry out all its commitments.

The road to fulfilling the Joint Declaration has not been smooth. Early efforts were made to carry out such commitments, at least in part. While China formally satisfied its treaty obligation to enact a Basic Law for Hong Kong, as discussed in the following chapter, both the content and the implementation of the Basic Law have come up short. Certain provisions in the Basic law have put Hong Kong's autonomy at risk, and with it, Hong Kong's cherished rule of law and freedoms. With the current local government largely reliant on and answerable to Beijing, its capacity to defend Hong Kong's autonomy and rule of law has been lost.

If autonomy is to be maintained, especially under an authoritarian central government, it is critical that the local autonomous government be fully answerable to the people of the autonomous region. With Beijing dragging its heels over democratic reform, this was not the case from the start and remains out of reach now. The 2020 national security law and the subsequent electoral changes, as discussed in later chapters, have effectively undercut any pretense of the high degree of autonomy outlined in the Joint Declaration and ultimately the Basic Law, having hollowed out the liberal and democratic institutions upon which effective autonomy depends.

HOPE

3

THE HONG KONG BASIC LAW

AN ENLIGHTENED COMMITMENT
OR A RUSE?

When I arrived in Hong Kong in 1985, I observed a city that seemed hopeful about the future. An earlier bout of emigration, driven by concern about the handover to Beijing, had receded. The city was encouraged by the signing of the 1984 Sino-British Joint Declaration, with its clearly articulated commitments to a high degree of autonomy, democratic reform, the rule of law, and basic freedoms. The Basic Law would eventually add the ultimate aim of "universal suffrage." A lot of that hope would be crushed during the 1989 crackdown on protesters in Beijing and other mainland cities, but Hong Kong would soon bounce back from that, with the Basic Law roadmap for the future in hand.

The 1990 Basic Law, which was finalized after the 1989 crisis, added a substantial legal narrative to the Hong Kong story. The official Beijing refrain that Hong Kong people and outside investors should put their hearts at ease was reassuring; even more so was the official outreach to foreign capitals for endorsement of the imaginative model. The Basic Law legal guarantees sat rather well with Hong Kong's rule of law tradition. Disputes over compliance with the Basic Law have been at the heart of Hong Kong's development and political debates ever since. This narrative is now severely tested. Sadly, today, protesters who have uttered slogans demanding compliance with Beijing's commitments are accused of subversion or sedition. To understand such popular demands, it is important to understand the commitments made in the Basic Law.

Since treaties are not directly enforceable under Hong Kong's British common law tradition, to be locally enforceable, the commitments in the Joint Declaration had to be transformed into local law. Accordingly, the Joint Declaration expressly requires that a Basic Law be enacted and stipulates its content embody the commitments made in the Joint Declaration.[1] The overriding aim of the Basic Law was to carry out the "one country, two systems" formula specifying a separate system for Hong Kong. Such a separation was to be achieved locally by guaranteeing the city a "high degree of autonomy," with the rule of law, human rights, and ultimate democratic reform. This was backed up by limits on the application of mainland laws and restrictions on mainland interference in local autonomous affairs.

Among the Joint Declaration's stipulated content for the Basic Law is the important proviso on enforcement: executive officials who fail to adhere to Basic Law requirements can be challenged in the courts.[2] This, along with common law principles on the priority of laws, privileges a constitution or basic law over ordinary statutes, and statutes over underlying administrative regulation. Such a priority of laws provides a legal basis for maintaining a liberal system of the separation of powers with constitutional judicial review to secure the rule of law and human rights.[3] To do otherwise, under the common law tradition, would be to fail in the courts' obligation to uphold the Basic Law.

Claims by mainland and local officials that Hong Kong lacks separation of powers—especially as it relates to the judicial review of legislative and executive acts—show a lack of understanding of how the system of legal checks and balances worked in Hong Kong.[4] Worse yet, when local officials parrot Beijing's representations dismissing this role, it reflects yet another example of subordinating themselves to the mainland and failing to guard the city's autonomy. Until recently, the Hong Kong Bar Association had forcefully made clear that such dismissive claims lacked merit.[5]

Accordingly, for the first two decades after the handover, Hong Kong's rule of law and human rights were moderately secured with constitutional judicial review in the Hong Kong courts of both executive and legislative acts, as well as by a more limited capacity of the Legislative Council to serve as a check on the executive. The latter was limited, in that the Legislative Council under the Basic Law could generally just vote up or down on government bills, disapprove budgets, or hold oversight hearings, but it had no power to introduce substantive legislation. An even greater limitation on legislative oversight is the lack of full democracy in choosing the legislature, effectively neutering any opposition.

Without full democracy, and before the recent "reforms" that further limit direct election, the chief executive, under the Basic Law, was selected by a Beijing-friendly Election Committee—as is still the case—and only half of the Legislative Council was directly elected. Under these conditions, the courts exercising constitutional judicial review were the main official avenue for government accountability. This was further supplemented and limited in the Basic Law by mainland interventions through the NPC Standing Committee's overriding power of interpretation.[6] Such mainland oversight was supposedly in areas beyond the scope of autonomy, though with increasing mainland interference, that boundary became blurred. Without full democracy, the popular capacity to constrain such interference was limited or nonexistent. The Basic Law's commitments to democratic reform, the rule of law, and basic rights offered hope that such limitations could be overcome. Until such full democracy was realized, any such public oversight relied on a free press and the public exercise of free speech rights, including the right to protest.

The moderately coherent, if limited, model embodied in this design has now been dramatically degraded by Beijing's introduction of the NSL and the Beijing imposed electoral changes. It is safe to say that Hong Kong's fundamentally liberal constitutional order has now been replaced by a new illiberal model focused on national security. With the police taking such a prominent role, some critics have judged that the city has come to mimic a police state. Its transformation will be discussed in substantial detail in chapters 6 through 9.

The Basic Law Drafting Process

We began chapter 1 trying to imagine what it would be like to have a hard-line authoritarian regime take over a major freewheeling world city, perhaps a city like New York or London. This comparison is not fanciful here, as Hong Kong constantly benchmarks itself against these two cities.[7] We wondered what it would do to the core values and life of the freewheeling city's inhabitants. As we noted, this is the situation Hong Kong people have endured. A lot has now transpired over the intervening twenty-seven years since the handover, especially in the last five years since an aggressive crackdown began. Most troubling, the liberal legal elements in the Basic Law, designed to avoid these dangers, have now largely been hollowed out and undone.

In drafting the Hong Kong Basic Law, as stipulated in the Joint Declaration, the Beijing-appointed drafting committee was assigned to render a legal framework to preserve the essence of modern Hong Kong. Given the huge contrast between the two systems, this required both the capacity for self-rule in Hong Kong and a legal and political firewall between the local autonomous region and the authoritarian regime at the center in Beijing. That mainland officials oversaw this process made achieving the rather liberal goal laid out in the Joint Declaration especially daunting.

The Basic Law Drafting Committee was fully appointed by the central government and made up, with only two exceptions, of mainland officials/academics or local pro-Beijing supporters. There was a consultative committee made totally of local members but with no control over the drafting process. Though drafting the Basic Law was a tall order, with the Joint Declaration's stipulated content as a guide, the drafting committee got most of it right. A couple areas where Beijing sought to maintain control in its hands, however, would eventually prove to be the undoing of the promised freedoms and democratic reform.

The undoing was not immediate, as the central government showed a limited degree of restraint in the first couple years after the handover. I characterize the restraint as limited in that Beijing would avoid open intervention where it deemed it avoidable, though it would heavily manipulate developments behind the scenes. As it had for years leading up to the handover, Beijing went to great pains to identify and reward its supporters while isolating and excluding its opponents, a strategy usually associated, in Beijing parlance, with its "united front" work.[8]

As the drafting effort neared completion in 1989, the Basic Law suffered severe birth pains.[9] China was caught up in a national crisis that would end with the June 4, 1989, crackdown. The final drafting of the Basic Law was briefly suspended through China's 1989 summer of protests. The supporting demonstrations that brought a million protesters to the streets of Hong Kong would later be characterized by Beijing leaders as "turmoil." Being on the street at the time, along with my oldest daughter, who was then twelve, I was amazed at how peaceful the protests were—a million nonviolent marchers without a hint of turmoil.

After the 1989 crisis, the Basic Law drafters brought a certain amount of attitude to the table. In the shadow of the massive Hong Kong protests, Beijing worried that the British might continue to hold a grip on the city. At the same time, they wanted Hong Kong to continue to flourish.

When the drafting resumed, the drafters were sharply focused on national security and heading off any future risk of "turmoil." They added the word "turmoil" to Basic Law, article 18, as providing a basis for mainland intervention. They also beefed up related language of article 23, then in draft form, relating to national security. In other articles, they chose rather flexible language on democratic reform, invoking a very cautious principle of "gradual and orderly progress."[10] Recently declassified documents show that London at the time had expressed its concern about these rollbacks.[11]

A couple of the more liberal drafters, Martin Lee and Szeto Wah, who would later be the founders of the Democratic Party leading the opposition, dropped out of the Drafting Committee during the 1989 protests. Their departure set the stage for the many open political battles between the pan-democratic and pro-Beijing camps to follow. Beyond founding the Democratic Party, which was first named United Democrats of Hong Kong, their pan-democratic supporters were also behind the founding of an advocacy group, the Hong Kong Alliance in Support of the Patriotic Democratic Movements in China.[12]

The alliance, founded on May 21, 1989, during the height of the mainland protests, would go on to lead the annual candlelight memorial vigils to commemorate the June 4, 1989, crackdown. To avoid conflict with his duties as the founding chair of the United Democrats, which later became the Democratic Party, Martin Lee did not take up a leadership role in the alliance. The alliance would later be targeted in the post-2020 crackdown and be forced to disband, with its leading officers charged with violations related to public order and national security.

In spite of their hardened attitude after the 1989 protest, the drafters seemingly still understood the need for a firewall between Hong Kong and the mainland to ensure, as ultimately provided in the final Basic Law, that mainland departments under the central government do not interfere in local matters and that mainland laws generally do not apply directly in Hong Kong.[13] But they also took pains to ensure mainland official control would be maintained in critical respects. It is these levers of central government control, written into the final Basic Law, that would prove to be the source of its ultimate failure.

Hong Kong people would, nevertheless, hope that strict compliance with Basic Law commitments, combined with Beijing restraint, could salvage the situation. In the view of many Hongkongers, that compliance and restraint has ultimately been lacking. While avoiding open confrontation in the early years, Beijing still acted politically to ensure only its supporters held key positions of power and influence. It is important to examine some of the details of the Basic Law text before returning in the next chapter to consider the political narrative that has exploded under it.

The Final Basic Law Text

The Basic Law, on its face, appears to envision the full protection of the promised autonomy and associated liberal values and institutions. It contains nearly all the guarantees stipulated in the Joint Declaration, including commitments to democratic reform, the protection of human rights, and adherence to the rule of law. The liberal character of these guarantees is apparent, with half of the list of approximately sixteen guaranteed human rights relating to freedom expression in one form or another.[14] Article 39 of the Basic Law further includes the Joint Declaration's requirement of adherence to the international human rights covenants. The reference in article 39 to the ICCPR effectively operates to incorporate the Hong Kong Bill of Rights Ordinance—itself a copy of the ICCPR—into the Basic Law, though, as will be discussed later, its protections have been largely vitiated by the 2020 National Security Law.[15]

The rule of law guarantees are contained in the Basic Law requirements that the common law be maintained, the local courts be independent and final, and in the above mentioned requirement that executive acts can be challenged in the courts for adherence to the Basic Law.[16] These explicit guarantees of a superior basic law, human rights, and the rule of law combined to support the widespread exercise of the premier tool used worldwide for enforcing human rights and other constitutional requirements: constitutional judicial review of legislation and executive acts.

Beijing's penchant for control and its capacity to override these guarantees has been sustained by two major deficiencies. These deficiencies laid the foundation for the massive political protests that have occurred over the years in Hong Kong. They relate to the independence and finality of the courts and democratic reform.[17] Combined, they would enable Beijing's frequent interferences that would ultimately cause the system to fail in its higher goals. The lack of judicial independence and finality was paired with Beijing's final power of interpretation, which it did not hesitate to threaten or use at critical junctures.

Beijing's interpretations would sometimes be hidden by labeling them as decisions, a method especially used to withhold democratic reform. The lack of democratic reform, the second weakness, ensured a Hong Kong government totally beholden to and under Beijing's direction, with little capacity to guard the city's autonomy and core institutions. The result was a Hong Kong government, often manipulated by the central government, that would become a lightning rod for public protests. Beijing would in turn use such protests as justification for further interference, a vicious cycle inflaming protests further until the ultimate crackdown.

The Independence and Finality of the Courts

The promise of the rule of law and judicial independence was greatly weakened by Basic Law, article 158, which provides that the ultimate power of interpreting the Basic Law rests with China's National People's Congress Standing Committee (NPCSC), a political body carefully guided by the CCP. Under article 17, the NPCSC also has the power to review local laws upon enactment. Article 158 allows the local courts only a subordinate role in interpreting the Basic Law. This virtual freeway to Beijing interference not only undermined Basic Law commitments but introduced alien elements that served to undermine or hollow out the common law itself.

In convoluted language, Basic Law, article 158, provides that courts of the region—with respect to matters of "central authority" and "local central relations" (essentially beyond autonomy)—are bound "before making their final judgments that are not appealable," if it "will affect the judgments on the cases," to seek an interpretation from the NPCSC through the Court of Final Appeal (CFA). The NPCSC must consult the Basic Law Committee in making its interpretation. The Basic Law Committee is a small separate body made up of mainland officials and local pro-Beijing supporters assigned this advisory role. Consultations with this committee have not been open, driven by an adversarial process, but rather opaque, behind closed doors. The NPCSC presumably guides the committee to the desired advice.

In simple terms, given the great flexibility of mainland interpretations, the NPCSC has had ample room to overturn Hong Kong courts when it does not like, or when it may predict it will not like, the outcome. These provisions simply appear aimed at creating an aura of legality in the exercise of such wide NPCSC discretion.

NPCSC interpretations are binding on the local courts, as was accepted by the CFA in a pair of early cases involving the right of abode in Hong Kong, the *Ng Ka Ling* and *Chong Fung Yuen* cases.[18] The NPCSC first exercised its power to interpret the Basic Law soon after the handover in the 1999 *Ng Ka Ling* "right of abode" case.[19] The CFA had declined to make a referral under Basic Law, article 158, judging the question as to who has the right of abode in Hong Kong to be within local autonomy. Having failed to get the CFA to refer the matter, the Hong Kong government went around the CFA on its own to refer the matter directly to the NPCSC, where the ruling of the CFA as to the right of abode was effectively overturned.[20] The CFA was then required to revisit the matter and accept the NPCSC ruling on the principle of law going forward.

While somewhat more restrained in the early years after the handover, the NPCSC nevertheless made several critical Basic Law interpretations that ensured Beijing's direct control over developments in Hong Kong and degraded local autonomy. These occurred in 1999, 2004, 2005, 2011, and 2016. As noted, the first of these, in 1999, demonstrated the NPCSC's firm oversight over Basic Law interpretations by the Hong Kong CFA. Causing a strain on the common law, the CFA is bound by these nonjudicial NPCSC decisions.

This potential for NPCSC intervention would hang over the heads of CFA justices and degrade judicial independence throughout the post-handover years. Even without direct NPCSC action, over the years, mainland officials have not hesitated to criticize the CFA if they disapproved of its decisions or potential decisions. As previously noted, even the existence of a power of constitutional judicial review in the local courts came under frequent attack.

NPCSC "decisions," as distinguished from interpretations, degraded the city's autonomy further. This was especially evident in a 2004 decision overriding the power of the local government to institute electoral reform for electing the

Legislative Council on its own without NPCSC approval, and in the 2016 dictating of oath-taking requirements that would ultimately be used to expel or disqualify opposition legislators or candidates.[21] Hong Kong people would recognize these interpretations or decisions as a power grab aiming to maintain Beijing's control and to keep its loyalists in control of the levers of power. Such power grabs would drive the lawyers' "silent marches" over the rule of law and the many massive public protests for democracy and against Beijing's interventions. With the direct imposition of the NSL in 2020 and the electoral changes in 2021, Beijing no longer bothers to hide its purpose.

The government's ability to run around the CFA, as was acknowledged in the 1999 NPCSC interpretation, has effectively held the sword of Damocles over the heads of local judges in politically sensitive cases. When one combines this peril with Beijing's frequent interference with respect to democratic reform, Hong Kong was deprived of all institutional capacity to effectively secure the city's autonomy and associated core values. Such guardianship was essentially left to the streets.

Regarding the NSL, where the NPCSC is assigned a similar power of interpretation, every case will be sensitive, and Beijing restraint is unlikely. In November 2022, the Hong Kong government requested Beijing issue a ruling to override the CFA's refusal to block Jimmy Lai from contracting a UK barrister to represent him in his national security trial.[22] When such requests are made, the outcome is predetermined, and the NPCSC quickly issued a ruling giving the local government and the local Committee to Safeguard National Security the power to override the court and ultimately decide if any matter threatens national security—with much broader application than simply hiring a barrister.[23] Throughout the post-handover years, such power grabs and the binding nature of such NPCSC decisions have combined to boost the central government's leverage over Hong Kong and its courts.

As if these constitutional obstacles were not enough, mainland officials have frequently attacked the separation of powers practiced in Hong Kong. Fortunately, until the passage of the NSL, Hong Kong courts had largely stood their ground to guard their role. Under current pressures regarding national security, the courts' ability to guard their independence is much diminished. Without a strong judicial role, basic rights in Hong Kong are at the mercy of the Beijing and Hong Kong governments.

As was evident in the 2003 government proposal for article 23 legislation (which caused the first post-handover massive protests)[24] and again in the 2019 proposal for an extradition law, the Hong Kong government has not been known to guard the city's autonomy.[25] That tendency is even more evident in the current local government's unabashed support for the new national security law and its forceful implementation. The current patriots-only Legislative Council is likewise a weak guardian, leaving the city's capacity to guard its autonomy and rule of law in tatters.

Democratic Reform

The issue where the NPC Standing Committee's influence has been the greatest, and the second area of Basic Law deficiency with respect to Hong Kong's promised autonomy, relates to the pace of democratic reform. The Joint Declaration stipulates that the legislature would be chosen by elections, and the chief executive by elections or consultations held locally. Basic Law, article 45, held out the hope of "universal suffrage" in selecting the chief executive, but just barely:

> Article 45: The method for selecting the Chief Executive shall be specified in the light of the actual situation in the Hong Kong Special Administrative Region and in accordance with the principle of gradual and orderly progress. The ultimate aim is the selection of the Chief Executive by universal suffrage upon nomination by a broadly representative nominating committee in accordance with democratic procedures.

Twenty-seven years on, there has been no gradual and orderly progress when it comes to the election of the chief executive.

Basic Law, article 45 and annex I, combined to create a nondemocratic system for the selection of the chief executive by a Beijing-friendly Election Committee. This system aimed to guarantee China's control over the selection process. The process evolved in two phases. In the first phase, from the handover until the 2021 electoral change imposed by Beijing, the Election Committee made a pretense of being broadly representative but within clear limits that ensured Beijing's control over the selection of the chief executive. The committee was itself chosen by approximately 245,000 Hong Kong resident electors, from four broad functional sectors, who, by design, were mostly in the pro-establishment or pro-Beijing camps. Under this model, about 20 percent of the committee members might come from the pan-democratic camp. The other 80 percent took direction from Beijing, ensuring the selection of its favored candidate.

The 2021 "reforms," as will be discussed in chapter 10, managed to roll this back to fully eliminate opposition participation. In the first exercise under the new model in 2022, only one candidate for chief executive favored by Beijing was nominated to run unopposed in the small-circle committee's selection process.

Under the original pre-2021 model, the only "gradual and orderly progress" was the increase in the four hundred original members of the Election Committee (in the first selection of the chief executive in 1996) to 1,200 (with 1,194 seats actually filled) from the 2012 selection onward. Without an increase in the functional electors and other political figures who elected members to the Election Committee, the "progress" was largely cosmetic. The clever change essentially meant that more committee members from the same political sectors would do as Beijing wished.

Likewise, to maintain Beijing's controlling hand under the original model, Basic Law, article 68 and annex II, combined to eventually provide that half of the Legislative Council was chosen by functional constituencies. Such constituencies mostly represented sectors from the pro-Beijing or establishment camps. Several sectors with corporate electors typically had no contest for legislative seats. The remaining half of the Legislative Council, being thirty-five Legislative Council members, were directly elected by all Hong Kong voters.

Under the new 2021 model, as discussed in chapter 10, the number of legislators has been increased from seventy to ninety, and the directly elected members have been reduced to twenty. This clearly reflects reform in reverse. Forty of the legislative seats are now chosen by the same Election Committee that chooses the chief executive. With many other constraints, opposition candidates were eliminated from the 2021 Legislative Council election.

Beyond the election limitations, the Basic Law further limits public influence and the power of legislators to shape policy by imposing a rule that legislators can only advance legislative proposals that do not relate to public expenditure or government policies.[26] This had left the Legislative Council largely with the role of voting up or down on government bills and investigating government malfeasance through public hearings.

Under the original electoral model, for opposition politicians in the minority, the only effective way to represent their constituents was to oppose government efforts to privilege the establishment. They were then disparagingly accused by top officials as being obstructionists. Over time, dangling democratic reform without delivering it just encouraged more protests, causing greater popular frustration with each denial of the promised democratic reform. Of course, after 2021, that opposition role has been eliminated.

Even before the 2021 overhaul, the government seized every opportunity to reduce opposition influence. This was especially evident in 2019, when the government began to use return officers to vet and exclude candidates for their political beliefs. Such return officers were traditionally used only to ensure candidates met technical requirements like age and residency. With this change, the vetting of candidates for their often spuriously alleged prior advocacy of self-determination or independence was used to block candidates from participation in legislative elections.

The result, even before the 2021 rollback of democracy, was a Legislative Council that did the government's bidding, limited only by the efforts of a minority of elected pan-democrats in opposition. The lack of popular representation that resulted encouraged legislative obstruction and street protests as the only avenue of public influence. Even those avenues have now been closed.

The requirement in article 45, quoted above, that universal suffrage in choosing the chief executive—if it were eventually instituted—be on "nomination by a broadly representative Nominating Committee," was a further obstacle to democratic reform. Beijing long signaled its intention to use this committee to vet the candidates who could be presented to the voters.

In its August 31, 2014, decision responding to the then ongoing electoral reform consultation, Beijing specified that the nominating committee must be formed in the same manner as the existing Election Committee. For Chief Executive this would essentially guarantee only pro-Beijing candidates would be presented to Hong Kong voters.[27] In 2015, this model was ultimately rejected by the pan-democratic members of the Legislative Council, who then had enough seats to block a reform bill where a two-thirds legislative vote was required. Beijing likewise declared that any change in the method of electing the Legislative Council would first require the initiation of universal suffrage for the chief executive, leaving all democratic reform at an impasse.[28]

Even before the 2021 electoral rollback, the result was that Beijing officials exercised ultimate control over both the executive and legislative branches. These officials signaled their preferred candidate for chief executive in the Election Committee and offered support for Beijing-friendly candidates to the Legislative Council. As discussed in later chapters, with the imposition of the new NSL in 2020, the opposition was further closed out by government demands that candidates express support for the NSL and by the disqualification of any candidates who could be accused of ambiguously offending national security as it is broadly understood. The 2021 electoral overhaul, discussed in chapter 10, took such exclusion much further.

Popular demands for democratic reform, in all the years before the recent crackdown, aimed to change the Beijing-dominated system, to put in place a government and legislature that represented Hong Kong people. Oddly, such a government with a popular mandate would likely give rise to less political contention with Beijing, as Hong Kong's autonomy and core values would be more secure.

Constitutional Gridlock

In tandem, these two Basic Law limitations froze in place a Hong Kong government totally beholden to Beijing that was incapable of or unwilling to guard Hong Kong's autonomy. A vocal opposition was allowed to operate, but that has now been silenced. As we will see in chapter 7 and later chapters, the NSL, its enforcement, and the subsequent imposition of the so-called electoral reforms have now hollowed out the liberal democratic institutions promised to Hong Kong.

Hong Kong's high degree of autonomy was initially conceived to protect Hong Kong's rule of law and human rights from intrusion by the mainland system. When it comes to the protection of human rights, the two systems are virtual opposites. Article 51 of the PRC Constitution illustrates this well. Under PRC Constitution, article 51, human rights are guaranteed "subject to the interest of the state."[29] This can be contrasted with the liberal common law system under the Basic Law practiced in Hong Kong until the recent crackdown, where human rights were primarily a limit on the state. The intrusion of the mainland system into Hong Kong has obliterated its liberal core.

Increasing Beijing interference in Hong Kong affairs over the years, leading up to and including the enactment of the NSL, has fundamentally undermined the personal security and way of life of Hong Kong people. This has led to understandable popular resistance and, under the current dire conditions of imposed local silence, to wide international concern. The repressive crackdown has greatly weakened local and global confidence in the Hong Kong model.

For local people, the survival of Hong Kong as they knew it is now deeply at risk. The international community has likewise taken a determined view that Beijing's current policies fail to meet the commitments that international actors relied on in recognizing Hong Kong's special status. As discussed in later chapters, the seriousness of this concern in the US was expressed by the passage and application of the Hong Kong Human Rights and Democracy Act.[30] The US has in fact withdrawn its recognition of Hong Kong's special trade status.[31]

Hope amid Growing Despair

4

POST-HANDOVER INTERVENTIONS, PROTESTS, AND THE UMBRELLA MOVEMENT

With some trepidation, Hong Kong people were hopeful in the early years after the 1997 handover. Beijing had been notoriously repressive in the first decades after the CCP's 1949 takeover, producing a massive influx to Hong Kong as thousands fled the mainland turmoil.[1] Ongoing reform in the 1980s, combined with the Sino-British treaty commitments, had, however, stirred a degree of hope. Sustaining such hope would depend on the Beijing and Hong Kong governments' willingness to deliver on promises of autonomy, the rule of law, human rights, and democratic reform. Would Beijing hold back and not interfere in local affairs? Would sufficient democratic reform be allowed to produce a government capable of representing Hong Kong and defending its autonomy?

A battle between the pan-democratic opposition and their supporters—which generally included around 60 percent of the people—and Beijing over these issues ran through nearly all post-handover political discourse. This conflict was often characterized as a debate between "one country," as emphasized by Beijing, and "two systems," as passionately defended on the street. Much to Hong Kong's disadvantage, from the start, leading local officials and business elites were firmly aligned with Beijing, upon whom they relied for appointments and privileges. Along with the degrading of institutional safeguards, this left civil society popular protests as the primary guardian of Hong Kong's autonomy.[2] As Beijing asserted more control, this put opposition forces increasingly at odds with Beijing officials and their Hong Kong supporters.

In the fifteen years after the handover, there were a series of official initiatives aimed at enhancing Beijing's control in ways that would undermine both autonomy and the rule of law. These initiatives and the political influence peddling that accompanied them allowed a degree of corruption to creep across the border into the city, where official policies and influence increasingly favored Beijing loyalists over critics who spoke out for the people.[3] This form of corruption is like that seen on the mainland, where mainland officials may reward loyalty with prize appointments, influence, or commercial access. Such corruption by official favor for loyalists is distinguished from a model based primarily on the payment of small bribes, which earlier plagued Hong Kong and plagues many developing economies.

In an open society under an authoritarian regime, such widely reported displays of loyalty to an outside power holder may undermine confidence in the local system. In the context of Hong Kong, this took the form of resentment toward mainland officials and sometimes toward mainlanders in general. In the words of a popular Bruce Springsteen album, in the public perception, there was truly "darkness at the edge of town," with only the street to push back. In the first couple decades, as Beijing's interventions increased, protests increased proportionately. Hong Kong's very identity as a free and open society was at stake. These protests profoundly shaped the city's public debate.

The Article 23 Protest and Beyond

After the handover, this debate first came to a head on the same Beijing initiative Hong Kong faced in 2020, the imposition of national security legislation. Both then and in 2020, this occurred inconveniently alongside a pandemic of mainland origin—then SARS, in 2020 COVID-19. In 2003, up to a half million Hong Kong people took to the streets to protest the local government's proposal of a national security bill being advanced under Basic Law, article 23, with Beijing's encouragement. While that bill was ultimately withdrawn, article 23 has returned. Current Chief Executive John Lee has announced plans to put forth new article 23 legislation in early 2024—to supplement the mainland-imposed national security law and expand the national security net. Basic Law, article 23, provides:

> The Hong Kong Special Administrative Region shall enact laws on its own to prohibit any act of treason, secession, sedition, subversion against the Central People's Government, or theft of state secrets, to prohibit foreign political organizations or bodies from conducting political activities in the Region, and to prohibit political organizations or bodies of the Region from establishing ties with foreign political organizations or bodies.

In 1989, as previously noted, Beijing officials were fond of labeling the supporting protests in Hong Kong as "turmoil." As mentioned in chapter 3, the Beijing-appointed drafters took the opportunity to add further constraints to the draft Basic Law. In particular, they added to article 23 language on foreign interference, and to article 18, they added language to impose further mainland control in the event of "turmoil" in the region.

The 2003 protest over the government's proposed legislation was not so much against enacting article 23 legislation as it was against the content of the draft bill. Deficiencies in the proposed legislation included extraordinary police search and seizure power, the proposed banning of organizations that the PRC government might identify as banned on the mainland, and increased liability for the unlawful disclosure of government information.[4] The latter was a matter of special concern for the press, which was also worried about the sanctity of press premises under the bill. Some concessions were made, but the government ultimately refused to issue a white paper with sufficient assurances in its haste to ram the legislation through. As will be seen in chapter 7, the 2003 draft bill was not nearly as offensive as the 2020 NSL, though it was quite objectionable in the much more liberal environment that prevailed at the time.

It is worth noting that most of the areas of regulation required by article 23 are covered by existing legislation passed on from the colonial era and still in force today. These include the Crimes Ordinance's coverage of treason and sedition, the Official Secrets Act, a Public Order Ordinance, a Societies Ordinance, and an antiterrorism law.[5] While such legislation was and still needs substantial reform to comply with human rights requirements, there was no urgent need to pass the 2003 government bill. If the government had made a reform proposal fully consistent with the ICCPR and associated guidance—such as that contained in the Johannesburg Principles—the legislative proposal would have sailed through with little resistance.[6]

On the civil society side, the government's ham-fisted approach gave rise to the first post-handover massive protest. A core group—the Article 23 Concern Group—made up of six publicly spirited lawyers and a two equally dedicated legal academics, of which I was one, inspired the movement by simply supplying a human-rights-sensitive analysis of the proposed legislation.[7] The group's concerns were published in a collection of single-sheet pamphlets—with one side in English and the other in Chinese—distributed like handbills on the streets. When we sat down to write these pamphlets, we started not as activists but as lawyers and legal scholars with an ethical duty to help the community we served understand concerns we had about the proposed article 23 legislation.

I personally remember handing out these handbills to surprised passengers outside the Mong Kok and Causeway Bay mass transit stations. Our distribution was backed up by frequent press conferences. We had no idea our short series of one-page pamphlets—the so-called "rainbow pamphlets," published in nine different colors and reproduced with the group's own personal funds—would strike such a chord. I am obliged to express my admiration for the dedication and hard work of such core members of the Article 23 Concern Group I had the privilege of working closely with as Alan Leong, Audrey Eu, Margaret Ng, Johannes Chan and Mark Daly. They represent the best examples of dedicated and thoughtful community activism.

The resulting public support for the effort was due in no small measure to the logistical efforts of another group that was newly formed at this time, the Hong Kong Civil Human Rights Front. The Civil Human Rights Front was formed by the banding together of various civic groups and NGOs. The Front handled the logistical effort of getting permits and issuing calls to join the protest, ultimately drawing a half million protesters to the street.[8] It cooperated with police requirements to ensure the protesters' nonviolent compliance with legal requirements. This combination of intellectual analysis and organizational capability continued as a driving combination for Hong Kong protests in the years to follow. Unfortunately, as discussed in chapter 9, under police pressure the Civil Human Rights Front disbanded in August 2021.[9]

The government eventually withdrew the bill in the face of insufficient Legislative Council support. At the last moment before the scheduled Legislative Council vote, the pro-government Liberal Party had withdrawn its support for the bill. In a constitutional model, where obstruction is often the only path of influence open to government opponents, this pattern of street protests often repeated itself in response to future unpopular government initiatives—as was well illustrated by the 2019 extradition bill.

The lesson taken from the 2003 protests was that the task of guarding Hong Kong's autonomy and avoiding absorption into the mainland would be left to Hong Kong's civil society. The government could have taken up a commitment to address the public's concerns and advance a bill that was fully compliant with international human rights standards, but it failed to do so. A proper democratic-spirited approach should have required proper public consultation, review by the Law Reform Commission, and a white paper, approaching the problem in the spirit of reform. Refusing this path left Beijing with an excuse to impose its own national security law in 2020.

It is noteworthy that, in addition to the withdrawal of the bill, the article 23 protest resulted in the resignation of Secretary for Security Regina Ip, who had led the government's initiative, and, a year later, the resignation of the first chief executive, C. H. Tung. Some might argue that this reflected a degree of Beijing responsiveness, but my guess is that Beijing was keen to put in place more effective officials to better control such developments in the future. With the increased Beijing interference in the years that followed, that guess appears justified.

The success of the article 23 campaign in blocking the proposed legislation drove a deeper wedge between the two sides of the Hong Kong political divide. On one side was the so-called pan-democratic camp; and on the other side stood Beijing and its supporters. For the former, the success of the article 23 protests inspired a number of subsequent protest actions—unsuccessfully for democratic reform in 2004 led by the Article 45 Concern Group (a new name taken up by the Article 23 Concern Group), which garnered another half million protesters; successfully against Beijing-friendly government proposals for national (patriotic) education in 2012, led by a newly formed youth group called Scholarism; and unsuccessfully again for democratic reform in the "Umbrella Movement" of 2014. Even the 2019 protest saw temporary success—the withdrawal of the extradition bill—but no success with respect to the protesters' four other demands.

The conclusion from this pattern of success and failure is clear: when Beijing was calling the shots, as was especially the case with democratic reform, nonviolent mass protests had not worked. When the matter was left to the local government, sufficient public pressure would sometimes produce results. By 2019, frustration with failed efforts to promote democratic reform would inspire an unfortunate degree of youthful cynicism with respect to nonviolent strategies.

The Pattern of Official Misjudgment

While the protesters learned from their successes and failures, so did the regime, though not the lesson the protesters intended. Popular protests throughout the post-handover years were met with increased official intransigence to resist demands for political reform and contain the influence of the democratic opposition. The more repressive the government's efforts at containment, the more intense the popular resistance became. Moderate government accommodation of public demands for political reform early on would have obviated the cycle of repression and resistance, likely reducing the public anger and protests that followed.

Poorly advised by its local interlocutors, Beijing has consistently misjudged the situation. It has presumably been guided by tactics that work on the mainland but have no hope of winning hearts and minds in an open society. John Burns has written a summary of the various efforts of CCP officials in Hong Kong to control the narrative, efforts that more often than not alienated the local population.[10]

Popular resistance took many forms in the years following the Article 23 protest. In 2004, the Article 23 Concern Group reformed itself into the Article 45 Concern to promote democratic reform. As noted, Basic Law, article 45, specifies, "The ultimate aim is the selection of the Chief Executive by universal suffrage upon nomination by a broadly representative nominating committee in accordance with democratic procedures." This language formed the foundation for the demands for democratic reform.

Article 45 Concern Group leaders such as Alan Leung, Margaret Ng, Audre Eu, and Ronny Tong ran for and were elected to the Legislative Council, while the two members who were academics, Johannes Chan and myself, declined to go down that path, favoring our scholarly role instead. The Article 45 Concern Group eventually became the Civic Party. As a core constituent of the pan-democratic camp, it maintained a slate of legislators until the recent crackdown, only formally deciding to disband in mid-2023. At the same time, the traditional Democratic Party remained active as the core member of that camp. But within a decade, a whole new generation of young activists would join and eventually lead the pro-democracy movement. With such core members as Joshua Wong, Alex Chow, Nathan Law, and Agnes Chow, youthful activism brought sustained passion to the democracy movement until it was crushed.

After a half million people joined the demonstrations over democratic reform in 2004 Beijing issued an interpretation of the Basic Law provisions on democratic reform. It imposed a five-step process for initiating change, with the first step requiring Beijing's approval to launch the official reform procedure.[11] This requirement was directly contrary to the provisions then in annex II of the Basic Law, which essentially provided, with respect to the Legislative Council, that Hong Kong could approve such democratic reform on its own with a two-thirds vote in the Legislative Council and approval of the chief executive. The government needed only to report the change to the NPC Standing Committee "for the record." By moving the approval of political reform out of local reach, this decision was the most damaging act to Hong Kong's autonomy before the passage of the national security law. No doubt a Beijing-appointed chief executive would not have agreed to democratic reform without Beijing's go-ahead, but allowing local initiative and control to launch the reform process may have created room for compromise, a path not taken.

A relentless official campaign to constrict local political space followed. In 2007, the NPCSC issued a decision saying that the promised universal suffrage could be achieved for the chief executive in 2017 and, if that took place, for the Legislative Council in 2020.[12] But in the same seemingly reformist decision, the NPCSC signaled an intention to take away with one hand what it offered with the other. The decision stated that the required nominating committee for Chief Executive "may" be formed in a similar way as the existing (pro-Beijing-dominated) Election Committee.[13] If Hong Kong people were going to be allowed a democratic choice for chief executive, it was going to be a choice vetted by Beijing.

By signaling what "may" be allowed, Beijing signaled its intention to control who could be nominated for presentation to the voters.

The 2007 decision inspired "Occupy Central with Love and Peace" in 2013 and 2014, a civil disobedience campaign that would morph into the Umbrella Movement.[14] Suspicions about Beijing's intentions proved warranted. The eventual August 31, 2014, decision approving a process to generate a potential model for democratic election of the Chief Executive required that "the method of formation and decision of the nominating committee" match that of the existing Beijing-friendly Election Committee.[15] As has been discussed, that Election Committee had long been dominated by Beijing and its supporters.

Before considering other efforts to push democratic reform, a couple other government initiatives clearly illustrate Beijing's consistent efforts to closely control the city. A 2009 proposal for a high-speed rail to connect Hong Kong to the mainland, which attracted a somewhat smaller protest, aimed to draw Hong Kong closer into the mainland's economic orbit,[16] as did a new bridge from Hong Kong to Zhuhai.[17] Both of these projects met public opposition but are now complete.

An agreement in 2018 between the mainland and Hong Kong governments to allow mainland law to be applied in the Kowloon terminus of the high-speed rail fueled further opposition.[18] The risk that Hongkongers might be arrested on Hong Kong soil and subjected to mainland justice came true in August 2019, when an employee of the British consulate, Simon Cheng Man-kit, was apprehended in the West Kowloon high-speed railway station while attempting to enter the city. He was taken to the mainland and subjected to aggressive interrogation before eventually being released.[19] Simon Cheng, now in Britain, is one of the first batch of six overseas individuals reportedly targeted by the national security branch of the Hong Kong police with an arrest warrant under the NSL, presumably for colluding with foreign forces.

Beijing efforts to control Hong Kong have especially targeted youth. CCP officials clearly judge that if they could brainwash local youth to their views, they could better control the city. In 2012, Beijing encouraged a local government national education initiative that sought to address what it perceived to be a lack of patriotism among Hong Kong's protesting youth. The 2012 proposal for national education grew out of a new government-imposed secondary school textbook on Chinese history. The book offered a very filtered and flattering history of the PRC. This backfired, bringing to the fore a new generation of young protesters who refused what they viewed as an attempt at brainwashing.[20] I understood this concern, as I had once been asked to give a lecture on implementing human rights under the Basic Law to staff and faculty of the Education Department. My suggestion that the youth be taught to defend their rights did not seem to go over that well. I was not invited back.

The 2012 protests against patriotic education proved to be a trigger to bring a whole new generation of youth into the pan-democratic camp. Secondary student leaders such as Joshua Wong and Agnes Chow, who formed a youth organization named Scholarism, would later go on in 2014 to lead the much bigger pro-democracy Umbrella Movement. They would also exercise influence in the 2019 anti-extradition and pro-democracy protests, as discussed in the following chapters. Unfortunately, at various times, they have faced arrest and prosecution, with the most prominent youthful leader, Joshua Wong, currently in jail on a guilty plea and awaiting sentencing under the national security law.[21] In those earlier days, more than leadership, they and their youthful colleagues provided inspiration to disenchanted millennials and members of Generation Z. Beijing's passion for patriotism did not die in 2012. As discussed more fully in chapter 9, the NSL has now imposed Beijing's brand of patriotic education on Hong Kong youth.[22]

Occupy Central in Love and Peace

The 2014 Occupy Central campaign would, for the first time post-handover, bring large-scale civil disobedience to Hong Kong. In early 2013, two professors, Benny Tai and Kin-man Chan, and one minister, the Reverend Yu-ming Chu, announced a civil disobedience campaign, under the heading "Occupy Central in Love and Peace." The aim was to promote genuine democracy in the government's official democratic reform consultations planned for 2014. As noted above, the NPCSC had earlier approved the possibility of democratic reform for 2017 in its 2007 decision.[23]

Civil disobedience—purposefully breaking the law, typically by refusing to apply for a permit to demonstrate—in a nonviolent campaign had never been tried on any significant scale as a protest tactic in Hong Kong, where nonviolent and approved marches were the norm. The three Occupy Central campaign leaders were very careful planners. They initiated a yearlong process of civic consultation, where they held training sessions on nonviolent approaches to public protests. By announcing their campaign so early, they inadvertently played into the government's hands, giving the government a whole year to target them as a threat to law and order.

Their planning process also included public meetings to sift through the various democratic reform proposals that had been submitted in the government's first round of official consultations over reform. The government's first-round consultation lasted from December 2013 to May 2014. The official consultation was the planned prelude to a 2015 decision on whether to go forward with the proposed direct election of the Chief Executive in 2017. After sifting through the formal proposals that had been put forth in the official consultations, Occupy

Central's civic deliberations, joined largely by youthful supporters, narrowed down the preferred choices of nomination method to the three most liberal, which they planned to promote in a civil referendum they would use to influence the official deliberations.

The three methods they favored all involved what the movement labeled "civic nomination," where the public would have the final decision as to candidates presented to the voters. All three encountered the government's objection that civic nominations binding on the required Article 45 nominating committee would deprive that committee of its Basic Law duty.[24]

Viewed differently, the government and Beijing did not want to give up official control over electoral outcomes. As it is often said, PRC officials do not mind democratic elections as long as they know the outcome ahead of time. The Legislative Council has long been an example of this, where the pan-democratic camp, usually wining nearly 60 percent of the popular vote, was never able to take a majority of seats. Despite its popularity, it was left in perpetual opposition by Beijing-friendly electoral rules.

In June 2014, the Occupy Central trio, with the assistance of academic polling experts, sponsored a civil referendum to choose one of the three short-listed proposals for promotion in the official consultation process.[25] Participation in the civil referendum gained a huge boost when, just before the vote, the Information Office of the State Council in Beijing issued a highly unpopular "white paper" on the practice of "one country, two systems."[26] The white paper emphasized Beijing's "comprehensive jurisdiction" over Hong Kong, effectively saying Beijing could do pretty much as it pleases.

As a result, nearly eight hundred thousand Hong Kong voters participated in the civil referendum, voting their support for the most conservative of the three civic nomination proposals.[27] Their choice of the most conservative of the three options—presumably choosing the least confrontational option—might suggest that voters would likely have accepted any nomination formula as long as it did not deprive the voters of a genuine choice in the ultimate popular election.

The Beijing White Paper and Official Indifference to Democratic Reform

The June 2014 Beijing white paper, issued by the State Council, was then just the latest in a long series of Beijing interventions. But its extreme views, which undermined nearly all aspects of Hong Kong's autonomy, had an incendiary effect. It sent an unambiguous signal that Beijing intended to exercise more repressive control in any way that it could.[28] It was a lightning rod for the many public protests that would follow in 2014 and 2019, though Beijing has never acknowledged its role as provocateur. The white paper was widely believed to reflect Beijing's true intentions to interfere more and more in Hong Kong affairs and to resist democratic reform, a belief that later proved true.

The white paper took extreme liberties in interpreting both the Joint Declaration and the Basic Law. It abandoned any further commitment to the Joint Declaration by characterizing the twelve articles of the Joint Declaration, written verbatim in the white paper, as merely twelve principles of the Chinese government. It claimed these twelve principles had been announced in 1983, nearly two years before the Joint Declaration.[29] In 1982, China had announced some different principles, but those had been so conservative that they had caused panic and a flood of emigration from Hong Kong.[30]

The white paper sought to go further down the feared road of undermining Hong Kong's autonomy. It proclaimed Beijing as the primary guardian of Hong Kong's rule of law, with "comprehensive jurisdiction" to interpret or amend the Basic Law as it chooses.[31] It characterized Hong Kong judges as administrative officials subservient to Beijing's national security concerns. It likened Beijing's direct control in Hong Kong to the comprehensive jurisdiction it enjoys over local government on the mainland.

The good thing initially about the white paper was that its status was ambiguous. As a State Council report, it was not in any category of law, as listed in the Basic Law, that applies in Hong Kong. So it appeared to be more of a signal of Beijing's intentions rather than a reflection of any applicable rules that would apply. The implementation of those intentions awaited the NSL and electoral changes six and seven years later.

To cause further panic, after issuance of the white paper, some Chinese diplomats in London claimed the Joint Declaration was no longer valid, as it had served its purpose of returning Hong Kong to China.[32] While Beijing later backtracked on this claim, it continued to operate as if it were true, rejecting any right of the UK to criticize its performance under the Joint Declaration or the Basic Law. It frequently accuses foreign governments, who invoke the Joint Declaration, of meddling in China's internal affairs, even though Beijing had used extensive diplomatic outreach to persuade foreign governments to recognize Hong Kong's distinct status under the Joint Declaration.

While the white paper set a bad precedent, a more damning and clearly binding decision on democratic reform came a couple months later in the August 31, 2014, NPCSC decision.[33] The Hong Kong government had issued its first consultation report requesting Beijing's approval to amend the process for selecting the chief executive.[34] The August 31, 2014, decision then gave democratic reform the green light but with the predicted proviso to manipulate the nomination of candidates. It required that "the number of members, composition, and formation method" of the nominating committee be the same as for the existing Beijing-friendly Election Committee.[35]

By further limiting the number of nominees to three, and by requiring that all three receive at least 50 percent support in the nominating committee, Beijing assured itself that a pan-democrat would have no chance at nomination under the approved model and that it could continue to signal its favored candidate.[36] In supporting this Beijing model of "universal suffrage," Regina Ip, the former secretary for security and a current prominent legislator and Executive Council convenor, takes the view that the promise of universal suffrage is not the promise of full democracy and that Beijing will naturally expect to control who can be elected.[37]

The Umbrella Movement

The Occupy Central campaign gained reinforcements in the late summer and early fall of 2014. Beijing's August 31 decision inspired a massive youth movement. Scholarism, from the student campaign against national education of 2012, converged with student leaders from the Hong Kong Federation of Students— then an important organization of university students—to launch class boycotts and various marches to government offices in support of demands for democracy. A trio of youthful leaders—Joshua Wong, Alex Chow, and Nathan Law—would effectively take over the civil disobedience campaign from Occupy Central, which was renamed the Umbrella Movement. Their arrests and jailing later on would brand them worldwide as the youthful leaders, and sometimes political prisoners, of Hong Kong's democracy movement. As previously noted, Joshua Wong is currently in prison for protest-related activities and is facing charges under the NSL that could net him many years in prison. The latter two have continued their activism in exile.

The Umbrella Movement came to life and would acquire its name on September 28 2014, when student protesters who had sought to occupy a civic square by the Legislative Council were blocked by police outside the building.[38] Their social media calls for others to join the protest resulted in a backup outside the nearby Admiralty metro station when police blocked a footbridge over the highway leading to the protest site.

I had come to observe the widely reported confrontation on September 28 when I saw an impasse, as more and more social media-inspired arrivals coming from the Admiralty metro station were held back by the police blockage, creating a tense situation. Eventually, after I had left, the crowd's pressure became too great, and the protesters jumped over barriers and occupied the major highway between them and the protest area outside the Legislative Council. When tear gas was deployed, arriving protesters used the ever-present umbrellas Hongkongers tend to carry in the humid, tropical-rain-prone climate to deflect the gas. The Umbrella Movement was born. A yellow umbrella became the symbol of the movement. Having taken the highway, the protesters would occupy it for seventy-nine days.

The nearby Causeway Bay, and across Victoria Harbor in the Mongkok area of Kowloon, would also be occupied. The Mongkok occupation would prove significant as a source of resistance to protesters from shopkeepers and taxi drivers whose businesses were impacted. But those areas, as well as the main one near the Legislative Council building, were all significant in providing convenient areas to join the protests. Eventually, pro-Beijing labor unions would seek injunctions against the protestors, no doubt influencing the eventual police crackdown.

As an academic whose work focused on Hong Kong's constitutional development, it would not have been possible for me to sit out this protest even if I had wanted to. Since I had taken a prominent role in the 2003 article 23 protests, I had become somewhat of a go-to commentator on Hong Kong's democracy movement, to observe and explain what was going on—often a key aspect of human rights work. The movement was extensively covered by the local and international press. I did my best to visit the protest site every day, sometimes explaining things to various worldwide television audiences on location.

A personal experience highlighted the clash of legal cultures at play in those protests. One day, I was cornered by a BBC radio reporter on the footbridge—the one previously blocked by police—over the highway, asking if I would be willing to debate the situation live with the head of a think tank in Beijing. Surprised by the prospect of a Beijing-based opponent, I agreed and found myself on the footbridge confronted with the disparaging claim on the other side of a phone connection that "those protesters were breaking the rule of law." I responded that civil disobedience meant they were breaking the law, not the rule of law. I urged that a government ignoring constitutional commitments was a bigger threat to the rule of law than a few youngsters illegally occupying a street.

The other BBC speaker, whose name I don't recall, alerted me to something that has stuck with me—the tendency in the mainland view to treat the rule of law and the law as synonymous. This leads to the PRC's official tendency to treat rule by law, including strict party control and law enforcement, as equivalent to the rule of law and leads to the frequent official claim that only the opposition threatens the rule of law, especially when it employs civil disobedience. Throughout the protests, this concern led me to write over twenty commentaries and an open letter addressing the issue in one form or another, always pointing as best I could to reasonable solutions to the impasse.[39]

After the Umbrella Movement's tear-gas-driven start, the original Occupy leaders would then join the street occupation and declare the launch of the Occupy Movement a few days earlier than previously planned and at a different location.

Occupy Central was originally planned to begin on October 1, China's National Day, in Central Hong Kong, instead of the space between the Admiralty station and the Legislative Council.

Effectively anointed the leaders of the movement, at one stage, the youthful Umbrella Movement leaders would engage in a special discussion session on local television, to no avail, with the then chief secretary of Hong Kong, Carrie Lam, who headed the government's electoral reform public consultation exercise.

The takeover of the democracy movement by youthful student leaders would have repercussions in the years ahead, putting at the head of the city's democracy movement a new youthful generation of activists.[40] This generation had become disillusioned by Beijing's neglect of popular concerns. The hard-line attitude of Beijing and its supporters cost both governments the hearts and minds of Hong Kong youth. While a gentler approach that was more consistent with the Basic Law might have eventually won over Hong Kong's youth and the society at large, this path was not taken.

It is worth noting here the usual Beijing tendency to attribute opposition protests to economic motives. C. L. Lim discusses this tendency in a recent book that seeks to highlight divergent Sino-British perceptions of the Joint Declaration.[41] It is true that economic inequality in Hong Kong, with a reported Gini coefficient of 0.539, high housing costs, and youth unemployment, contributes to the passion for protests.[42] But Beijing's attempts over the years to brand youthful protests as inspired by economics offers an insufficient account, given the emerging youthful passion for Hong Kong identity and the freedoms that have long been associated with it. For the youthful protesters, the pride of being Hongkongers appeared to take priority over economic challenges.[43] Labeling the movement as economic-based, and offering government programs to address the economic problems, came across as dismissive of demands for political reform.

The Final Gasp for Democracy

Economics aside, neither the civic referendum nor the emerging youth movement moved the Beijing or Hong Kong governments to meet reform demands. A second round of official consultation to plan reforms in accordance with Beijing's August 31 decision was scheduled for early 2015. After all their proposals were ignored in the first round, the pan-democratic camp and the associated youth movement boycotted the second-round consultation. The government set about coming up with a conservative electoral proposal that would meet Beijing's August 31, 2014, conditions.[44]

Such a proposal was then vetoed by the pan-democratic legislators, who still had enough votes to deny the bill the required two-thirds support in the Legislative Council.[45] Carrie Lam, who as chief secretary (the number two slot in the Hong

Kong government) had chaired the consultation process, was then chosen to be the next chief executive under the Election Committee selection system that remained in place.[46] At the end of her term, she was replaced by the current chief executive, John Lee.

The government subsequently claimed no further interest in reopening the democratic reform process. Instead, it set upon using aggressive law enforcement to suppress opposition protests and further block pan-democratic activists from the political process. As discussed in the following chapter, the frustrated protest movement would simmer, with occasional outbursts, until the next massive protest exploded in 2019.

COMMAND AND CONTROL

5

2015–2019: The Aggresive Official Response

While the successful protests in 2003 against article 23 legislation, and in 2012 against patriotic education, encouraged a degree of hope in Hong Kong, the protests in 2004, and again a decade later in 2014, supporting the promised democratic reform set Hong Kong firmly on the path of despair. The outcome of the Umbrella Movement was clearly less democracy and more Beijing control, along with more and more police investigations and prosecutions of movement leaders. It seems Beijing was only willing to allow Hong Kong people a limited, Beijing-choreographed say in their future. The offer in the August 31, 2014, decision of what was widely seen as "fake democracy" left little hope that Beijing leaders would come around to understand or respond to Hong Kong's core concerns with maintaining the liberal constitutional integrity of their system. Several of Hong Kong's liberal institutions were put under severe official pressure in this interim period between the Umbrella Movement and the 2019 anti-extradition protests. Civil society was clearly waiting for the right moment to launch a pushback against such aggressive policies.

After the 2014 Umbrella Movement, Beijing took a more hands-on approach to guide or encourage the local government to stamp out the opposition and tighten the central government's control. Local tactics included the aggressive prosecutions of protesters, the expulsion of opposition politicians from the Legislative Council, the banning of opposition politicians from elections, more aggressive police tactics, and holding a firm line against political reform.

The August 31, 2014, NPCSC decision, followed in 2015 by the Hong Kong government's proposed political reform legislation, sent a message of indifference toward popular demands for democratic reform.[1] Beijing feared losing control over Hong Kong's political narrative and appeared to take no responsibility for the disaffection it had created. Unpopular Hong Kong officials and their supporters share the blame. They seemingly feared that giving the people an electoral say in the choice of leaders would cost them their jobs. For civil society, under the broad pan-democratic umbrella, the indifference of both governments accentuated resistance and a separate sense of Hong Kong identity, as repression often does.

During this period, popular Hong Kong consciousness about liberal constitutional values can be contrasted with the PRC's domestic policies in these areas. The CCP's infamous 2013 Document Number Nine, more formally entitled the "Communiqué on the Current State of the Ideological Sphere," banned discussion on the mainland of virtually every liberal institution protesters in Hong Kong had sought to achieve or defend.[2] Document Number Nine banned on the mainland discussion of constitutionalism, civil society, so-called nihilistic views of history, universal values, and the promotion of the "West's view of the media."

Mainland universities were prohibited from teaching topics commonly on the syllabus in Hong Kong, such as separation of powers, multiparty systems, the rule of law, and related liberal concepts. After Document Number Nine was issued, I recall wryly telling my students that my courses in Hong Kong on constitutionalism and human rights were effectively illegal just a few miles away across the border.

The clash of political and legal cultures could not have been starker. The CCP's antipathy toward liberal democratic reform is deep-seated. Public pushback against imposing this view in one form or another on Hong Kong has been at the heart of nearly every political protest in the city.[3] Official persistence on the path of increased interference and a refusal to carry out the promised universal suffrage produced a lost generation in Hong Kong. For this generation, affinity for the mainland system was remote at best and hostile at worst. A gentler, less imposing approach that respected local concerns, and that fully adhered to Basic Law commitments to autonomy and reform, would have better bridged this schism and avoided all the vitriol and political conflict that followed.

Yet, in this interim period between the 2014 Umbrella Movement and the 2019 anti-extradition protest, each official Beijing and Hong Kong effort to ratchet up repression and seize control of the political narrative would be met with popular resistance, a resistance that would eventually explode into mass protests in 2019, the largest in the post-handover period. Lurking behind this resistance was protesters' fear that Hong Kong may meet a similar fate as the mainland cities from which their parents or grandparents had fled. The government's efforts at repressing this resistance came to define this period.

Arrest and Prosecution of Protest Leaders

The most daunting policy turn following the 2014 Umbrella Movement was the relentless arrest and prosecution of protest leaders, along with an effort to bar them from political office.[4] Leaders of both the Umbrella Movement and the Occupy Central campaign were targeted.[5] The trial court convicted the Umbrella Movement leaders—Joshua Wong, Nathan Law and Alex Chow—for inciting unlawful assembly, and it initially handed out relatively light sentences of community service.[6]

As is the norm in the common law tradition, Hong Kong judges were traditionally sensitive to protecting free speech rights in cases of public protest or civil disobedience.[7] Such sensitivity might be expressed through higher standards of proof or lighter sentences where conviction is warranted. This sensitivity to basic rights, especially free speech, was an important feature that distinguished Hong Kong from the mainland. It lies at the heart of the justification for "one country, two systems."[8] The community service sentences the three received at trial very much reflected this common law, free speech sensitivity.

In what became a public relations disaster, the Hong Kong government appealed their relatively light sentences to ask for jail time.[9] At the court of appeal, and under new harsher sentencing guidelines announced in court, the government successfully secured revised sentences of six to eight months in prison for the three.[10] The appeals court gave thirteen-month sentences to another group of thirteen defendants who were facing government appeals of community service for the same 2014 protests.[11]

In 2018, the higher Court of Final Appeal reversed the jail terms for the Umbrella Movement leaders. It accepted the appeals court's stiffer sentencing guidelines but refused to apply them retroactively.[12] Regardless of the outcome, the die was cast on the government's effort to aggressively reign in civil society through arrests and prosecutions. This would surely anger the local public who had supported the Umbrella Movement. This period was the calm before the storm that was to be unleashed in 2019. The government likely acquired a false sense of security that its aggressive tactics were working.

After dealing with the youthful umbrella leaders, the government's aggressive prosecutions continued. In early 2019, senior originators and participants in the Occupy Central campaign were prosecuted. Most notorious was the choice to charge the so-called "Hong Kong Nine" with various common law crimes of nuisance and conspiracy to nuisance.[13] Unusual for modern times, these common law crimes were crimes developed in case law as opposed to criminal statutes. Their use was obviously designed to up the sentences for conviction. The three ringleaders of Occupy Central, unlike the youthful Umbrella Movement leaders, did not face the usual charge of unlawful assembly or incitement to the same.

The nuisance charge netted the government a more severe sentence of sixteen months in prison for professors Benny Tai and Kin-man Chan.[14] As a civil disobedient, Benny Tai admits that he would simply have pled guilty if he had been charged more appropriately with unauthorized assembly.[15] Their appeals would later fail.[16] Their colleague, the Reverend Chu Yiu-ming, was given a lighter sentence without prison time due to his age and health. Chan, who now lives in Taiwan, avoided the risk of university dismissal by retiring early before trial. Tai was eventually dismissed from his tenured professorship by the government-friendly University Council of the University of Hong Kong on July 28, 2020, even while his appeal was pending.[17]

The parade of the other aggressive policies that followed only stiffened popular outrage. Hong Kong government officials were clearly not up to the task of defending their city's core values and addressing popular concerns. The government's insistence on expelling six newly elected legislators—who were mostly younger legislators who had been active in the Umbrella Movement, such as Nathan Law—over their somewhat flippant oaths of office further drove a wedge between the government and the people.[18] The polemical oaths were clearly aiming at protest. Officials nevertheless rejected the more moderate path of inviting them to take their oath again.

For the first time, the expulsions left the pan-democrats in the Legislative Council with insufficient votes to block foundational legislation that required two-thirds support to pass. The government was free to push through whatever "reforms" it wanted. It also signaled to democratic activists that they were no longer invited to participate in the political process, setting the stage for the massive protest that would follow in 2019 and the opposition's eventual total exclusion from local politics in 2021.

Worse yet, when these oath-taking cases were brought for judicial review, the NPC Standing Committee intervened directly while the case was still pending in the trial court, issuing a binding official interpretation of the requirements for sincere oath taking.[19] This binding NPCSC ruling would apply retroactively to their prior oaths.

Such expulsions were later followed up by several decisions by election officers that barred so-called pro-independence candidates from running for office.[20] Vetting candidates for their past political statements represented a dramatic expansion of the duties of civil servant electoral officers, who had historically just applied the more technical statutory requirements regarding qualifications like age and residency.

To make the message of political exclusion clear, the government then set about banning the local separatist National Party for advocating independence. It even expelled a longtime reporter for the *Financial Times*, merely for hosting the leader of that party, Andy Ho-tin Chan, as a speaker at the Foreign Correspondents' Club.[21] The minor political party's calls for independence could be viewed historically as more of a polemic, as the level of serious support for such demand was extremely low. Most Hong Kong residence would view calls for independence as futile.

By this time, Hong Kong officials appeared to be playing by the authoritarian playbook, treating talk allegedly related to national security as equivalent to action. While international standards would generally require some evidence of imminent capacity and the intention to act upon secessionist demands, such standards were not required in the government clampdown on local calls for independence or self-determination. There were very few such calls and little interest in action to carry them out.

The new 2020 national security law likewise contains no such requirement of imminent unlawful action for charges related to subversion and succession.[22] For the NSL, merely disrupting official duties or damaging official premises is enough to make out the charge. Indeed, within the first month after the NSL's imposition, four young activists, age sixteen to twenty-one and with virtually no following, were arrested for allegedly advocating a "republic of Hong Kong" and announcing the formation of a political party called the Initiative Independence Party. At trial a year later, the leader of the group, Tony Chung, pled guilty and was sentenced to forty-three months in prison.[23]

"Sai Wan" and the Co-opting of Political Institutions

Heavy-handed prosecutions and expulsions were not the only sign of Beijing's growing impatience with Hong Kong protests. Central government officials and institutions in the region led an effort, often with the support or assistance of the Hong Kong government, to co-opt key local institutions. The exercise of comprehensive control across the board revealed how the city generally enjoyed autonomy in form but not in substance.

The central government was represented in the Hong Kong Special Administrative Region (SAR) by the Liaison Office of the Central People's Government (Liaison Office), located in the Sai Wan area of Hong Kong Island. The name "Sai Wan," or "Western District," has long been synonymous with Beijing encroachment. Such Sai Wan interference in local politics was so substantial that pro-Beijing candidates for the Legislative Council would be informally referred to as "Sai Wan candidates."[24]

The pattern of political intransigence on reform demands, and then Chief Executive Carrie Lam's frequent reticence on sensitive matters in this period, increasingly left the impression Sai Wan was calling the shots on Hong Kong governance long before it would officially do so under the NSL.[25] The 2019 protests and the very unfavorable (for Beijing) results in the 2019 district council elections would put the Liaison Office under critical pressure, with rumors of higher-up efforts to directly manage Beijing's Hong Kong concerns from across the border in Shenzhen.[26]

Under the mainland's opaque authoritarian structure, exactly who exercises oversight in Western District has been rather unclear. For this reason, the degree of mainland interference regarding local autonomy has also been opaque. At the top national level, Hong Kong has come under the direct supervision of the Central Coordination Group for Hong Kong and Macau Affairs, which has been referred to as the "leading group" since 2020—led by a series of top party leaders, most recently Vice-Premier Han Zheng until his retirement in 2023.[27] During the protests in 2019, it was widely believed that Han sometimes issued directives to the SAR through representatives based across the border in Shenzhen. With his retirement in March 2023, Han's position as vice-premier has reportedly been taken up by Ding Xuexiang, the country's executive vice-premier and the sixth-ranking member of the Politburo Standing Committee, who since March 2023 has taken over as the highest leader of the newly revamped Communist Party Central Leading Group on Hong Kong and Macau. The revamp was essentially a move of this leading group from state control to party control, a trend which has been occurring under Xi Jinping in many other areas of mainland governance, as reflected in the newly issued party institutional reform plan.[28]

Below the higher authority of the leading group was the Beijing-based Hong Kong and Macao Affairs Office (HKMAO), which was then under the State Council, a body that answered to the Chinese premier.[29] As part of Beijing's increased interventions in Hong Kong, in early 2020, a noted hard-liner, Xia Baolong, was appointed to take over as head of HKMAO.[30] From the above noted institutional reform plan, it appears that the HKMAO has effectively been abolished, though its name is now seemingly preserved under the CCP's leading group. Xia has reportedly stayed on as the deputy leader of the leading group and head of HKMAO, which is now under the CCP. Interestingly, the CCP, which was to be hands-off at the handover, is now directly in charge of Hong Kong.

At the bottom of this hierarchy, Beijing's Hong Kong Liaison Office is designed to carry out Beijing's united front policies in the city—as it generally comes under the United Front Works Department on the mainland. This representative role was carried out in the colonial period by its predecessor, the Hong Kong branch of the New China News Agency (NCNA, or Xinhua).[31] In 2000, the Liaison Office was established to take over that role. Starting out rather quietly, it has expanded its role ever since, and it now is often seen as Hong Kong's second government.

Just prior to the enactment of the NSL, all restraint was abandoned as Beijing officials claimed that the restriction in article 22 of the Basic Law, which barred mainland departments from interfering in Hong Kong, did not apply to either the

HKMAO or the Liaison Office.[32] As Professor Victoria Tin-bor Hui describes it, "two systems" was effectively subverted into "two administrations."[33]

Beyond the official institutions, the CCP's central leadership in Beijing has increasingly intervened in Hong Kong affairs. On November 1, 2019, the CCP's plenum proclaimed rather menacingly that the central government should "exercise governance" in Hong Kong.[34] Beijing's direct control expanded thereafter. As Xi Jinping entered his third term as CCP general secretary in October 2022, along with a new seven-member Politburo Standing Committee (the top party ruling body), the appointment of new people to top Hong Kong positions at the NPC annual meeting in March 2023 was expected.[35] The new CCP leadership has been keen to ratchet up Xi's direct control over Hong Kong. The party leadership seemingly no longer feels a need to hide its direct interventions.

Beijing's united front tactics have long involved rewarding and co-opting its supporters and isolating its opponents.[36] Before the handover in the 1990s, rewards mostly included appointments to various preparatory committees, favorable treatment in market access, and the offer of business advantages with the mainland. After the handover, the pattern of manipulating rewards and punishments continued and expanded.

As previously noted, this pattern increasingly undermined the level playing field many hoped for, allowing a new form of corruption, in the form of influence, to creep across the border. The opportunities for rewarding support are many, as Hong Kong remains the largest conduit for foreign investments on the mainland. It is also important to China's outbound investments. Many of the mainland's state-controlled companies are listed on the Stock Exchange of Hong Kong.[37]

Official interference from Beijing, usually through Western District, became more open and direct in the lead up to the 2019 protest. This was especially true regarding elections. The Election Committee, which chooses the chief executive, had long been a key target of such efforts, with Western District officials usually signaling their favored candidates and the pro-Beijing electors readily complying. The only vote chief executive candidates needed was Beijing's—or its signaled preference.[38] Once a chief executive was in office, Beijing had further leverage through its power to approve and appoint all the top executive officials.

Beijing's political interference did not stop with the chief executive's office. Prior to the recent electoral overhaul, Beijing's Liaison Office had no official role with respect to electing the Legislative Council, but even so, it was known to coordinate and support electoral campaigns for pro-Beijing candidates to both the Legislative Council and the district councils.[39] It maintained sections in its Western District offices to coordinate its policies in each of the then eighteen district councils in Hong Kong, and to coordinate a network of pro-Beijing organizations to get out the vote for its favored candidates.[40]

The assigned Liaison Office officers were known to spend time in the districts, wining and dining local supporters. The control was so pervasive that critics in Hong Kong compare this Sai Wan or Western District power to the Hunger Games, with an outspoken willingness to step in when things go wrong.[41]

This strong grassroots work had long ensured pro-Beijing control of the eighteen district councils. Therefore, it was a particularly stinging rebuke when the opposition camp took control of all but one of the district councils in the last fair election in late 2019. This stinging defeat no doubt led Beijing officials to the conclusion that such behind-the-scenes manipulation of the electoral process was no longer sufficient to ensure its control. As discussed in chapter 10, after the 2021 electoral overhaul, only patriots, meaning Beijing supporters, would be allowed to run for office. These Beijing formed networks would in the 2021 and after patriots only elections come to form the formal base for selecting a substantial portion of the seats for the legislative and district councils. The 2023 revamp of the district councils' selection process has also dramatically reduced the number of directly elected seats. At all levels, Beijing's influence and control are no longer hidden.

Working to Co-opt Other Sectors

Even before the recent crackdown on civil society, other public sectors of society were long subject to oblique forms of manipulation and censorship. As reported by the Hong Kong Journalists Association, during this interim period between the two massive protests, the media was the target of an increasing mix of direct and self-censorship, with the former presumably aiming to encourage the latter.[42] Direct censorship of free speech and press freedom included, to name a few examples, the previously noted bookseller disappearances, the exclusion of books in a bookstore market that was 80 percent dominated by Chinese-owned companies, the manipulation of advertising revenue by mainland-owned companies, the expulsion of the *Financial Times* journalist, and the oath-taking cases.[43]

Self-censorship has historically been a much bigger problem. The established media has long been known for self-censorship. This has been especially encouraged through the targeting of advertising revenue by mainland companies.[44] Critical media, such as the pro-democracy *Apple Daily*, were especially targeted. Throughout this period, *Apple Daily* could expect no such advertising revenue from mainland companies or other companies seeking mainland approval, and even its reporters were generally blocked from mainland access or covering mainland-sponsored events.[45]

Universities and secondary schools were also targeted. Given the role Professor Benny Tai played in the Occupy Central campaign, the law faculty at the University of Hong Kong, of which I was a member, especially enjoyed Beijing's wrath. Beijing-controlled newspapers attacked the law faculty's former dean, Johannes Chan, after he was selected in a worldwide search for a higher pro-vice-chancellor position. This eventually led to the rejection of his appointment by the school's university council and ultimately to a shorter fuse on his retirement extension.[46]

A precursor to this targeting of universities would certainly include the 2012 national education drive. Perceiving a failure of proper education on their version of Chinese history, Chinese leaders and local supporters pushed forward a government drive for national education.

In the aftermath of the 2012 protests against patriotic education, the effort to impose national education failed but did not die. It came up again and again after each subsequent episode of popular protests. The youthfulness of the Umbrella Movement and the anti-extradition protesters encouraged Beijing's insistence on reeducating Hong Kong youth. Under the NSL, Beijing has now realized its ambition to control the education narrative with strict new national security oversight. This includes the replacement of a previous liberal studies course on critical thinking with a new one on citizenship and social development, where the textbooks present only the CCP's version of Chinese and Hong Kong history and developments—a story that now even denies that Hong Kong was ever a colony.[47] The goal appears to be the erasure of colonial history along with critical liberal values.

Questioning the utility of this, one of the leaders in the pan-democratic camp, the previous Civic Party Chair Alan Leong, noted, "If you brainwash a child at school, they will learn differently at home."[48] He argued in a 2019 interview that the government should be winning people's hearts, not washing their brains.

Because of efforts to tame the academy, academics who speak out have been easy targets of condemnation. During the 2019 protests, Kevin Yeung, who was then secretary for education, suggested secondary principals and teachers who do not handle protest matters correctly could be "disqualified."[49] Earlier, in the 2014 white paper, Beijing accused legal academics and lawyers of a "confused and lopsided" view of "one country, two systems."[50] No doubt I am among those accused. Such accusations have broadly targeted the liberal values long taught in Hong Kong.

Targeting Legal Institutions and the Rule of Law

Sensitive legal institutions and the legal profession were also put under stress in this interim period. The track record of aggressive prosecution detailed above shows that some leading lawyers in the Hong Kong Department of Justice were fully committed to the growing campaign of pressure on the protest movement.

As noted above, this was evident in the serious charges of common law nuisance or rioting advanced against protesters.[51] Things have worsened under the NSL.

There was an especially serious effort to co-opt the Hong Kong police. By turning over to the police a political problem it refuses to address itself, the government placed the police in the middle of political debates that the force could not solve. Heavy-handed enforcement was the only tool at their disposal. That the police received anti-terrorism training on the mainland and were known to frequently interact with mainland security forces further raised public suspicion.[52]

Mainland co-opting of the Hong Kong judiciary or the legal profession would cause much greater concern about the "one country, two systems" framework. It would be difficult for the Hong Kong system to survive such co-optation. The hedge to guard judicial independence has long been embodied in the requirement that judges be recommended for appointment by the Judicial Officers Recommendation Commission, which is made up of the chief justice, the secretary for justice, and seven other members appointed by the chief executive representing diverse sectors of the legal community and the public including those recommended by the bar and the Law Society. The body is supposed to be independent, and during this period, it still appeared to be, with the legal professional organizations fully consulted on judicial appointments. More recently, however, government influence and pressure on the legal profession has degraded this independence.[53]

In this interim period between the two massive protests, the judiciary still appeared moderately resilient and was the most trusted of the three main branches of government. A further safeguard included the established practice provided under the Basic Law of foreign judges being invited to sit on the CFA. The courts, however, with respect to interpreting the Basic Law, have long been at the mercy of the NPC Standing Committee, whose interpretations are binding on the courts. The Standing Committee had, by this point, issued such formal interpretations only four times, but the trend toward central government intervention, through the combination of interpretations, decisions, and official threats, appeared to be growing. This led to concern about the intimidation of the courts in sensitive cases.[54] The 2020 NSL, with its designation of a special list of local judges to handle national security cases, clearly signals Beijing's distrust of the wider Hong Kong judiciary.

At this stage, the legal profession was still pushing back in the face of threats to the rule of law. The Hong Kong Bar Association had long been an outspoken defendant of Hong Kong's rule of law and basic rights.[55] The Law Society, which under the divided bar system of Hong Kong is the association of solicitors, has generally been known to be less outspoken on Basic Law and human rights issues, though some members have been equally vocal, and the group as a whole did speak up from time to time. Some reticence may be attributed to the reality that many solicitors deal directly with mainland clients. Overall, many prominent solicitors and barristers were outspoken.

Many from both professions stepped up in 2019 to represent Hong Kong's growing list of protesters facing public order or rioting charges. On the policy front, a group of lawyers established the Progressive Lawyers Group on the heels of the 2014 Umbrella Movement as an advocacy group to safeguard the city's rule of law and encourage reform and compliance with the Basic Law.[56] After the imposition of the NSL, much of this professional oversight would be silenced, with the Progressive Lawyer's Group itself disbanded. In 2023 its founding member, Kevin Yam, in exile in Australia, is one of the 8 targeted with a warrant and a HK$1 million bounty.[57]

FURY

6

2019 Fury: The Anti-Extradition and Democracy Protest

If there was a little hope, along with a good dollop of despair, at the start of the anti-extradition protests, it surely turned to fury as the 2019 protests wore on. The youthful pro-democracy activists pulled out all the stops. This included some in the front lines of the protest who turned to low-grade violence, including rock throwing and the like. This latter turn was reflected in such popular protest slogans as, "You taught us nonviolence does not work" or, from *The Hunger Games*, "If we burn, you burn with us."[1] Over the previous four years of prosecutions, expulsions, and intimidation, all doubts about the Hong Kong government's commitment to defend the city's autonomy had been confirmed. Now largely ignored in official accounts, despite the public fury, most of the millions of protesters who marched stuck to the nonviolent discipline Hong Kong protests were long noted for. Even youthful hotheads who resorted to throwing bricks or rocks in no way advanced the sort of armed struggle that would justify a violent crackdown on the entire movement. Rather, an official approach that listened to and accommodated the legitimate public concerns shared by most Hongkongers would likely have dissolved the fury or reduced it to a small minority.

With the police resorting to violent methods to contain the protests, the public became increasingly anxious about the evolving situation, especially as it related to the rule of law and free expression. The government's willingness to do Beijing's bidding and adopt its methods for suppressing protests raised concerns about the very survival of Hong Kong as we knew it. In the public mind, how could Hong Kong's fundamental commitment to the rule of law and basic freedoms be secured if autonomy was destroyed? And how could autonomy be secured under a nonresponsive government that was solely beholden to Beijing? Was Hong Kong simply to be absorbed into the mainland, and at what costs?

After months of peaceful marches, comingled with sometimes violent protests on the margins, Hong Kong people made their preferences clear in the November 2019 district council election. The powerless and mostly advisory district councils were the only political bodies where nearly all 479 members were directly elected.[2] With limited resources, the pan-democratic camp had historically not paid much attention to district council elections, but this time around, they turned the election into a popular referendum on the government's recent performance. On the other side, Chinese officials largely did the same. Chinese state media urged voters to "vote to end the violence."[3]

The public view was made clear as the pan-democratic camp and a few supportive independents enjoyed a landslide electoral victory. They took 392 out of the 452 available seats up for election, securing control of seventeen of the eighteen district councils.[4] In the most peaceful form of protest possible, 57 percent of 2.9 million Hong Kong voters who participated in the election spoke clearly on the importance of democracy for maintaining genuine autonomy and their cherished rule of law.

The justification for their concern was evident from the relative 2019 rule of law ranking of the two jurisdictions, with Hong Kong ranking sixteenth and China eighty-second in the world.[5] With the passage of the NSL, by 2022, Hong Kong would drop out of the top twenty to rank twenty-second, a significant drop in a year when the rule of law took a beating worldwide but still significantly above China.[6] In the public mind, democratic reform was the clear answer to the profound risks Hong Kong society faced. As the 2019 protest exploded, Hong Kong's youth took command of this message. Twentysomethings, who had gained experience as middle schoolers in the 2012 protests against patriotic education and then led the Umbrella Movement in 2014, were now the seasoned veterans of the Hong Kong protest movement. 2019 would see a new generation of high schoolers and college students join in what was billed as a leaderless movement. The arrest and prosecution of protest leaders over the previous four years had taught the protesters a lesson about the risks associated with openly proclaiming who were the protest leaders.

The Extradition Bill

The extradition bill put forth by the Hong Kong government certainly justified an impassioned response. Drafted as an amendment to the Fugitive Offenders Ordinance, the bill appeared to give mainland authorities carte blanche in obtaining a rendition of someone charged on the mainland with any of a variety of crimes.[7]

The excuse for putting the bill forward was the claimed need to turn over a Hong Kong resident to Taiwan authorities for allegedly murdering his Hong

Kong girlfriend there. Under the existing ordinance, respecting extradition, Hong Kong could arrange extradition to anywhere in the world except another part of China—effectively, the Chinese mainland, Taiwan, and Macau.[8] The claim that this alleged murder in Taiwan justified opening the door to the mainland system of criminal justice was viewed with wide suspicion. Extradition to other parts of China was long blocked due to the procedural and human rights deficiencies of the mainland legal system. Taiwan was ensnared in this blockage due to Beijing's claim of sovereignty over Taiwan.

Hongkongers distrusted the Hong Kong government's motives. Protesters felt that the Taiwan murder was being used as an excuse to launch an extradition arrangement for the mainland. Beijing officials had long called for such an arrangement but the gap in rights protection had been insurmountable. Though Chief Executive Carrie Lam claimed that she alone had initiated this bill, this claim was not taken seriously. Her team may have drafted the bill, but Beijing officials and their supporters in the Legislative Council were clearly pushing it forward. This bill would offer mainland officials a legal alternative to the earlier bookseller abductions and disappearances.[9]

In the proposed bill, nine crimes were initially taken off the list at the request of local business chambers. The business chambers had worried any alleged breach of contract or falling out with mainland partners could be elevated to a criminal charge. However, the removal of the nine crimes likely achieved very little. China's laws relating to bribery and corruption were not removed from inclusion. Such bribery or corruption laws could easily be used to ensnare a foreign or Hong Kong investor who encountered disfavor from mainland partners.[10] The proposed extradition law could easily be applied to such charges.

It is important to appreciate Hong Kong's key role in China's economy. One in every two companies on the Hong Kong Stock Exchange is affiliated with the mainland.[11] While the relative size of the Hong Kong economy compared to the mainland's has shrunk since the handover, its entrepôt role has expanded. In opposing the proposed legislation, many people in the commercial sector feared that any diminution of Hong Kong's status as an open society based on the rule of law would have grave consequences for such an economic role.

Political activists mobilized on the streets had more personal concerns regarding the extradition bill. Political crimes were ostensibly to be excluded, but again, various mainland laws related to national security would easily fill the gap to reach opposition political actors. This was an especially important consideration given the frequent mainland official accusations that local activists had violated national security.[12]

With these concerns about mainland overreach in mind, there was strong support in both the pan-democratic and establishment camps for withdrawing the extradition bill. After months of protest, the bill was withdrawn, but only after a long fight in the streets. Marches of one million and then two million protesters in successive weeks in June 2019 had no visible impact on the government's determination to ram the extradition bill through.[13] The bill was suspended only after marches gave way to confrontations with police and then vandalism of the Legislative Council chamber. The bill was only formally withdrawn in September 2019 after further months of confrontational protest.

The lack of due process in the mainland criminal justice system was of great public concern. The bill failed to provide protections common to extradition agreements around the world. Such agreements might typically exclude the extradition of local citizens and might generally require the local court to ensure that a procedural standard comparable to that afforded under the local law and bill of rights would be met in the receiving jurisdiction—a standard mainland China fails to meet.[14]

The extradition bill afforded neither restraint, leaving the court to the more limited role of applying the exceptions noted and confirming a proper charge. While the chief executive would be able to refuse to go forward with extradition based on human rights concerns or otherwise, it is generally believed that a Hong Kong chief executive, who is subordinate to officials in Beijing, would be hard-pressed to resist such a request on human rights grounds. Likewise, if the issue were raised in the local courts, would judges be comfortable effectively declaring the entire mainland criminal justice process a human rights violation?

The reality, long inhibiting an extradition agreement between Hong Kong and the mainland, is that the mainland criminal justice system in total does not meet the due process standards applicable under the Hong Kong Basic Law and the local Bill of Rights Ordinance. The latter is a textual copy of the ICCPR to which Hong Kong is bound.[15] The mainland criminal justice system is not subject to the ICCPR and allows considerable interference in judicial proceedings by political or party supervision. It is also greatly deficient in allowing a proper defense and cross-examination of witnesses, to name just a couple issues.

An added feature of the bill, ensuring international opposition, is that any foreigner present in Hong Kong could have been rendered to the mainland under the terms of the bill. Even Hong Kong's then existing extradition agreements with foreign countries would have been put in jeopardy by this bill, as countries would be reluctant to extradite an accused person to Hong Kong if he could in turn be rendered to the mainland. Of course, the later NSL, as discussed in the following chapters, would eventually trigger all these same objections, and several extradition agreements with Hong Kong have, as a result, been suspended by foreign democratic governments.[16]

"The Five Demands, Nothing Less"

Under extreme public pressure, the extradition bill was eventually suspended and then later withdrawn. The government's slow path to doing so, and the aggressive crackdown on public protests along the way, inspired the largest public protests in Hong Kong history. It reeducated the people on the current government's misguided balance of loyalties and its unwillingness to defend Hong Kong. By turning the matter over to the Hong Kong police, who had no power to make political compromises, the government encouraged the heavy-handed police abuse that followed over the summer and fall of 2019. If the protesters had stopped when the bill was withdrawn, they would have left hundreds of their fellow protesters in jail, facing serious charges.

Given the two governments' repeated tendency to use the extraordinary 2019 protests to justify both the aggressive police crackdown and the 2020 rollback of human rights under the NSL, it is important to appreciate the two governments' collective role in causing those protests. Interviews by researchers on the scene of the protests have clearly highlighted the decisive role of police overreach and abuse in motivating protesters.[17] This, along with deep public frustration with Beijing's failure to fully implement its commitments in the Joint Declaration and the Basic Law, offer important public reasons for the protests. This does not justify violence, but for protests of this scale, there is always a risk of violence on the margins. If the police themselves use excessive force, then the likelihood of some protesters turning to violence increases.

The use of such tactics, and the government's failure to address public concerns, very much explains the five demands that were advanced in the protester's slogan "five demands, nothing less."

The five demands included:

1. Full withdrawal of the extradition bill.

2. A commission of inquiry into allegations of police brutality.

3. Amnesty for arrested protesters.

4. Retracting the classification of the protesters as rioters.

5. Dual universal suffrage, meaning for both for the Legislative Council and the chief executive.[18]

None of these demands are calls for independence. The first of these demands was realized when Carrie Lam withdrew the bill on September 4, 2019.[19]

Independent investigation of the police tactics, and the release of those charged, became a minimal moral stance of the protesters. Significant support for a commission of inquiry within the establishment even split that camp to the government's disadvantage.[20] The government attempted damage control by proposing, as a lesser alternative, a non-statutory "committee of review."[21] This proposal by Carrie Lam was later dropped when designated appointees to the committee declined appointment.

Even though there was widespread popular support for an independent investigation of police conduct—measuring as much as 80 percent—the government did not budge on this demand. It claimed that its in-house investigation by the Independent Police Complaints Council (IPCC) was sufficient.[22] To the government's dismay, that body's panel of foreign experts resigned, objecting to its methods and lack of independence.[23] Despite such resignations, the IPCC eventually issued the expected report clearing the police of all wrongdoing.[24]

In a 2019 interview, Umbrella Movement leader Joshua Wong expressed hope Beijing would eventually relent on the demand for an independent investigation.[25] He expected the Legislative Council election, then planned for September 2020, would motivate them to do so, worrying that their candidates would take the same beating they had in the district council elections. But that presumed motivation was taken off the table when Beijing later postponed the election to September 2021 and then revised the electoral system to eliminate the opposition.

By the time the extradition bill was suspended, it became clear that Beijing was directly overseeing the official response to the protest.[26] The Hong Kong government's intransigence was clearly due to Beijing's seizure of control over the government narrative. The demands, relating to amnesty, the characterization of protester conduct, and democratic reform, were ignored.

Beijing's hard line, even before the national security law, would crush any hope that public concerns would be taken seriously. The last demand, to reopen the debate over democratic reform, would be met with reform in reverse in the electoral overhaul of 2021. The demand for democracy had always been at the heart of Hong Kong protests, with the public long appreciating the risk the undemocratic system posed to Hong Kong's autonomy. Beijing and locally complicit government officials consistently proved incapable of governing an open society while guarding the necessary autonomy. The demand for democracy had been rejected in 2004, 2014, and 2020, with democracy effectively obliterated in 2021.

The public order cost of refusing these demands is surely much greater than would have been the case if Beijing allowed the promised democratic reform. An elected government in Hong Kong would have little to gain from constantly confronting Beijing, but we would hope it would better find its voice to explain Hong Kong concerns.

The 2019 Protests

When a million, and then two million, peaceful marchers took to the streets respectively on June 9 and 16, then Chief Executive Carrie Lam should have quickly grasped the level of public objection and made a course correction.[27] Instead, the Hong Kong government, presumably guided by Beijing, dug in its heels. The government's failure to respond constructively to concerns peacefully advanced by millions of Hongkongers, along with aggressive policing, led to increasingly aggressive protest tactics by a few, including vandalism, rock throwing, and similar activities. This was first evident in the storming of the Legislative Council on July 1,[28] and then the airport in mid-August and again in early September.[29] In *City on Fire: The Fight for Hong Kong*, Antony Dapiran describes how government indifference and police efforts at repression at each stage of the protest led to yet further efforts to be heard.[30]

By 2019, there had developed an unfortunate view among some of the more active frontline protesters that nonviolent protests had failed. Popular protest rhetoric highlighted the failure of nonviolence and invoked a slogan from *The Hunger Games*, "If we burn, you burn with us."[31] These were efforts to move the needle when nonviolence, the mantra for years, had failed. Vandalism and rock throwing sadly did appear to move the needle more effectively—bringing the eventual withdrawal of the extradition bill—than the huge nonviolent marches on June 9 and 16.[32] In spite of some skepticism over the efficacy of the nonviolent approach, the more aggressive tactics remained marginal, with most protesters still committed to nonviolence.

With more and more violent clashes with police, the September withdrawal of the extradition bill proved too little, too late. Trying to thwart the police crackdown, protests spread to previously untouched districts in what the protesters likened to the movement of water.[33] As the summer of protests wore on, comparisons to dystopian fiction began to appear.[34] Police efforts at containment became more aggressive, and the frontline response of a few core protesters grew increasingly violent, with bricks and improvised explosives hurled at the police. The death of college student Chow Tsz-lok, who fell from a parking garage, sparked further outrage and protester occupation of campuses.[35]

This escalated further when the police launched a siege on two campuses in November 2019, alleging that protesters were throwing things on nearby highways and using the campuses for the preparation of bombs and other devices. With the campuses surrounded, a war mentality ensued among Hong Kong's young frontliners, first at the Chinese University of Hong Kong and then at the Hong Kong Polytechnic University.[36] Some frontline protesters added bows and arrows and petrol bombs to the protest arsenal.[37] The campus siege represented a turning point in the protests, with violence increasing on both sides.

Protest violence was a contentious issue. Fellow democracy supporters, long committed to nonviolent strategies but concerned about opposition solidarity, were reluctant to criticize the violent acts like rock throwing. Professor Benny Tai, who launched the nonviolent civil disobedience campaign that became the Umbrella Movement in 2014, questioned the need to condemn those who were violent.[38] He appeared to view this as a personal matter, noting that "the nonviolent protester can condemn or not condemn those who are violent based on their personal choice." He no doubt recognized, as did many in the pan-democratic camp, that condemnation would likely create division among democracy supporters. While a late 2019 poll of Hong Kong voters found that only 20 percent supported the use of some violence, public discontent over police and government actions generally outweighed the urge to condemn violence.[39] Tai has long supported nonviolence and conducted training on nonviolent methods of protests in his Occupy Central campaign. Tai offers a nuanced view of protest violence, noting that "violence is sometimes justified in self-defense in the face of enforcement of an unjust law." Perhaps many supporters of the protest shared this view and put their qualms aside in the face of abusive police practices.

Nevertheless, there was a limit to such tolerance as protest violence sometimes got out of hand. Local people and the world looked on in horror when a man confronting protesters was doused in gasoline and set on fire just hours after a police shooting of another protester.[40] A few days earlier, a seventy-year-old street cleaner died when he was hit with a brick reportedly thrown by a masked protester.[41]

The siege on the airport in mid-August resulted in further protester violence that was widely condemned, even moving a protest spokesperson to issue an apology the next day. In the airport incident, passengers were harassed, and two mainlanders—thought by some protesters to be undercover security officers, though one later proved to be a reporter for a mainland publication—were set upon and beaten by protesters.[42] Though examples of violence resulting in grave personal injury of protest opponents were relatively rare, given the scale of the protests, they clearly deserved condemnation, as the protester apology after the airport violence acknowledged.

Nonviolence had long been the dominant protest mantra in Hong Kong. Martin Lee, the barrister and Democratic Party founder, is widely viewed as the father of Hong Kong's democracy movement. In the Gandhian tradition, Lee has long been an advocate of nonviolence in public protests and often spoke out against violence.

Despite this nonviolent tradition, in 2019, there was widespread suspicion that the government was trying to provoke violence to reduce protest support. There was speculation that the government wanted the violent acts to continue until the November district council election so people would associate violence with the democracy movement.[43] In this view, young protesters might be more easily trapped into committing violent acts, as the police seek to "tempt the snake to come out of the hole." It seems that provocative police brutality had the opposite effect from what the police may have intended. It attracted wider public disapproval of the government, as seen by the landslide results for democrats of the 2019 district council elections.

Pan-democrats, at least early on, hoped to capitalize on such disapproval in the planned Legislative Council election, which was originally scheduled for September 2020.[44] After a year of protest, the Legislative Council election was widely expected to favor opposition candidates. Unfortunately, in July 2020, the government moved to head off such a risk, disqualifying a dozen prominent opposition candidates, including four sitting legislators.[45] It then put off the Legislative Council election for a year and would later, in 2021, revise the electoral system to effectively bar opposition participation.[46]

Pro-government politicians had sought to justify postponing the election due to the rise in COVID-19 cases, but nobody doubts that Hong Kong could manage safe elections—as Singapore, South Korea, and others had done—without taking such drastic measures.[47] The prospect of the establishment camp losing the election probably weighed heavily on the delay decision, as no doubt did Beijing's plan to overhaul the system.

The question of violence or nonviolence in the Hong Kong protest cannot be assessed without reference to police enforcement tactics. The Hong Kong Civil Human Rights Front, a long-established consortium of forty-nine civic groups, had been at the core of Hong Kong protests since 2003, when it helped organize the article 23 demonstrations. As the organization that often submitted the formal permit applications for a public procession, it stood firmly by nonviolent discipline. The previous international spokesperson and vice convener, Bonnie Leung, emphasized in an interview in December 2019 that they continued to adhere to such a principle.[48] Like Professor Tai, they were reluctant to condemn those "front-liners" who resorted to a more aggressive response to police brutality.[49] Rather, their approach was to affirmatively promote nonviolent protest.

A December 8, 2019, march from Victoria Park to Chater Garden in Central Hong Kong was the first march on Hong Kong Island the police had approved since mid-August. Eight hundred thousand protesters successfully conducted a nonviolent march. In an interview on the morning of the protest, Ms. Leung noted that they had conveyed the view to the police that if the police did not use violent tactics, the protesters would not either. Her prediction proved to be correct, with the protest march I observed that day ending peacefully.

Remaining united is not only a challenge for politicians planning an election strategy but for protesters as well. New student groups often find themselves in competition with older, more established groups. The Hong Kong International Affairs Delegation (HKIAD) was a case in point. An umbrella organization formed to represent student unions at all twelve universities in Hong Kong, it shared the common reluctance to condemn protester violence. This was presumably to maintain unity among the largely youthful frontline activists and the many moderate nonviolent protesters. Formed in July 2019, the group—which later folded—was set up to articulate an international voice on behalf of the student unions.

Several members of HKIAD that I spoke to in late 2019 claimed to be mostly "localist."[50] This placed them ideologically on the more radical end of the opposition movement. One member of the group explained the organization's position on violence in comparison to the US experience: "It was sensible to have Malcolm X and Martin Luther King cooperate together."[51]

The student activists I spoke to, however, expressed pessimism about the potential for sustained unity going forward in ordinary politics within the democracy movement. They worried that the proportional representation electoral system in the Legislative Council elections, then scheduled for 2020, would tend to divide the camp over the allocation of seats. Of course, that would later become a moot question when the election was postponed and the electoral rules revised to effectively bar all opposition candidates. Furthermore, they expected the police, under Chris Tang, the new police chief, to attempt to split the radicals from the moderates with targeted arrests.[52]

With youthful inexperience, such groups usually found it difficult to overcome obstacles related to unity and international outreach. In any democracy movement, the challenge for movement leaders is to channel such youthful exuberance toward a common purpose. In many respects, the pan-democratic camp's primary election held in July 2020 was an attempt to do just that, to avoid the problems of unity that the students raised. With the imposition of the national security law, and later the electoral changes, that path to unity was closed. The primary instead offered the police an excuse for the mass arrests under the NSL of fifty-three opposition politicians, forty-seven of whom—with 33 denied bail—would be tried over two years later, as will be discussed in later chapters.

Despite wide popular demand[53] that the police behavior be independently investigated under a statutory commission of inquiry, the government refused this along with all the remaining four protest demands.[54] Firmly taking up and agreeing to these demands would have eliminated the reason for continued protest. At a minimum, it would have caused reduced public support for carrying the protest forward and allowed a path to bring the crisis to an end without the repressive policies that followed.

With such striking misjudgment, it seems certain, as previously noted, that Beijing was calling the shots. Earlier experience had taught Hong Kong people that when the local government was in charge, it was sometimes capable of a course correction in the face of massive public resistance—as was also seen with the article 23 protests and the protests against national education. Beijing, on the other hand, being inexperienced with an open society, has generally remained inflexible and typically becomes more rigid in the face of public opposition. It presumably worries that any sign of weakness will invite more resistance—a rigidity consistently chosen over political reform. It commonly uses repressive tactics against opposition on the mainland.

In spite of Beijing's intransigence, throughout 2019 and into early 2020, many Hong Kong democrats remained optimistic. They judged that the cost of a major crackdown, using mainland troops or security personnel, would be too high. This judgment is now in question with the enactment of the national security law, an aggressive alternative to sending in the army.

Protesters believed they could sustain the democracy campaign for the long haul.[55] This view was echoed by several pan-democratic legislators I had a chance to meet in December 2019. One legislator, who wished to remain anonymous due to fear of retribution, emphasized the importance of combining local and international support. The public did not share this optimism. Eighty percent of voters in a December 2019 poll expressed a pessimistic view, expecting an eventual crackdown.[56]

With the long-term future in mind, other, more enduring strategies beyond street protests, such as strikes and boycotts, emerged. Most noteworthy in this regard was the "yellow economic circle," which emerged as one of the more innovative long-term strategies. Under this strategy, local businesses that supported the protest efforts were entered on a yellow list, offering a moderate avenue of support for the movement among businesses and consumers. This strategy amounted to a boycott of "blue" businesses that supported Beijing's hardline stance.[57] Popular targeting of blue businesses took on more fury when the daughter of the founder of the Maxim's restaurant chain offered critical testimony against the protesters at a UN hearing.[58] Maxim's franchises, including Starbucks Coffee in Hong Kong, were all targets of a boycott. With the entry of Beijing state security officers into Hong Kong under the NSL, the former yellow businesses have ceased displaying their open support for the protest cause.[59]

We cannot fully appreciate the inspiration protesters took from the protests without appreciating the ways in which protesters and their supporters were positively encouraged in their Hong Kong identity. The invention of what became a Hong Kong anthem, "Glory to Hong Kong," epitomized the new, stronger sense of Hong Kong identity.[60] The fact that the Education Department would ban the singing of this song and other slogans in 2020 under the NSL, as discussed below, demonstrates that officials understood this power of identity as well.[61] The song would later in 2023 be effectively banned and become the target of an open injunction sought by the government—which the trial court refused--as well as a basis for prosecution under under the national anthem law.[62] In 2022, a man was arrested for sedition for merely playing the tune, along with the UK national anthem, on his harmonica at a memorial vigil for Queen Elizabeth.[63] In late 2022, a forty-two-year-old woman was convicted under the national anthem law and sentenced to three months in jail for simply waving a colonial-era flag in a shopping mall while a Hong Kong athlete received a gold medal at the Tokyo Olympics—as observed on a shopping mall television screen.[64] Beyond local use and prosecution, the government found itself in a constant battle against numerous overseas hosts of sporting events playing this seeming Hong Kong anthem off the internet instead of the Chinese national anthem.

Even the slogan "Liberate Hong Kong, revolution of our times," which did not seem to take hold when pro-independence activist Edward Leung coined it, became a slogan that conveyed local identity—now also banned.[65] Leung was later convicted of rioting and sentenced to six years in prison for his participation in the so-called "Fishball Revolution" in Mong Kok in 2016.[66] But most Hongkongers were not so much advocating revolution as they were arguing for compliance with Beijing's earlier commitments, as captured by the protest slogan "five key demands, not one less."[67]

Not everyone was imbued with this new sense of identity. With the economic impact in mind, the pro-establishment camp was severely divided in 2019 by protest developments. While there were Beijing-friendly calls for a harsher crackdown, the mainstream, more moderate wing of the pro-establishment camp hoped for some moderate concessions to bring the crisis to an end.

A prominent businessman, who had long been active in establishment politics, expressed a skepticism one might hear in quiet discussions in the establishment camp.[68] In an interview in his office, he argued that moderate concessions early on could have satisfied the mainstream of the protest movement, leaving the radical fringe protesters with little support. He attributes the poor response to Carrie Lam, who he then thought might step down sooner rather than later. If she did not step down soon, then he felt she would remain in place and step down at the end of her term—which later proved to be the case. Under such a scenario, he expected a continued decline in business activities as international companies moved away from Hong Kong.

With mainland businesses in Hong Kong also suffering, the flight of international companies would entangle Hong Kong further in the trade war, which was then being waged in the US by then President Trump. Of course, with the US's withdrawal of Hong Kong's special trade status in 2020, in response to the NSL and the emergence of the pandemic, the prediction of business decline proved correct.[69]

The moderate pro-establishment businessman I interviewed urged the opposition democrats to reconsider the August 31, 2014, proposal for democratic reform offered by Beijing. He worried that a "commission of inquiry could drag on for two or three years" and that, "if you start an investigation, the police could go on strike." Regina Ip, a pro-establishment legislator, echoed this skepticism, though their views had no support on the street.[70]

The Police and Law Enforcement

29-01   Use of Force

Police officers shall display self-discipline and exercise a high degree of restraint when dealing with the public and shall not resort to the use of force unless such action is strictly necessary and he is otherwise unable to effect the lawful purpose.

2.   Police officers shall identify themselves as such and, when circumstances permit, a warning shall be given of the intention to use force and of the nature and degree of force which it is intended to use. Persons shall be given every opportunity, wherever practicable, to obey police orders before force is used.

3.   The principle governing the use of force is that only the minimum force necessary to achieve the purpose may be used and once that purpose has been achieved, the use of such force shall cease. The force used must be reasonable in the circumstances.

Figure 1. An excerpt of chapter 29 of the Hong Kong
Police Department's Force Procedures Manual.

Public outrage at the repressive tactics of the Hong Kong police was a major driving force sustaining the Hong Kong protests throughout 2019. Daily press and social media images, as well as videos of police abuse, angered the public in Hong Kong and drove the international response.[71]

To be fair, from the start of the protest, the Hong Kong and Beijing governments had placed the police and prosecutorial officials in an impossible position by criminalizing popular protests. Both governments failed to address the legitimate concerns of a public that had experienced years of official disregard of international and constitutional commitments to autonomy and democratic reform. Rather, the government left it to police to repress the expression of such concerns. The dramatic 2019 shift of the burden to the police left the reputation of the police in tatters. Starting with a 78 percent approval rating at the start of the Carrie Lam administration, by the end of 2019, the police faced a similar level of disapproval.[72]

At the same time, the police handled this role with a level of force that clearly warranted the independent investigation that became the number one protest demand.[73] Through an investigative report, the *Washington Post* uncovered the reportedly secret Hong Kong police internal guideline on the use of force (see figure 1).[74] This general guideline was relaxed by the force just before the massive October 1, 2019, national day protest. They replaced the line, "officers will be accountable for their own actions," with the provision, "officers on the ground should exercise their own discretion to determine what level of force is justified."[75] This suggests less oversight and more discretion. The original guidelines on the use of force, and several others regarding the indiscriminate use of tear gas and water cannons, appear to have been violated.

How this might affect the public attitude toward more violent means of protest was easy to predict. The former Hong Kong chief secretary, Mrs. Anson Chan, emphasized, "When the discipline force is empowered to have considerable powers, you must convince the public that you are exercising those powers judiciously."[76] Or simply put, the police should not be just another gang on the street.

In their defense, the Hong Kong police issued a response to the *Washington Post* inquiry before the publication of the report. They argued that only a necessary degree of force had been used in the face of widely perpetrated extreme acts of violence and vandalism, and they complained about the general level of media reportage.[77] An independent investigation would have helped to fairly resolve the discrepancy between these competing accounts. Instead, with massive arrests and the passage of the NSL, the two governments have chosen the opposite course of increased repression.

The local government claimed the public concern for accountability was sufficiently addressed by the police internal investigation, noted above, that was completed by the IPCC. As previously discussed, however, that internal police body was criticized by its own panel of experts—who later resigned, claiming a lack of sufficiently independent investigation capacity.[78] The IPCC's lengthy final report, as widely predicted, largely cleared the police of any significant wrongdoing.[79]

These issues later came up in a judicial review in the High Court, where Judge Anderson Chow ruled that the Complaints Against Police Office (CAPO), which operated within the police department, did not provide an independent oversight of the police.[80] The failure to adequately display officer IDs was wrapped up in the same case, with both instances being found in violation of article 3 of the Bill of Rights, which prohibits "torture and cruel, inhuman or degrading punishment."

The officers were hiding their names out of a concern of being doxed. The court ruled that the current two-tier system involving CAPO, monitored by the IPCC, did not effectively provide independent oversight. Judge Chow cited the lack of "segregation of personnel of CAPO from the rest of the force." Furthermore, he noted that while the "IPCC is institutionally and practically independent . . . it lacks the necessary investigative powers of its own." On appeal, the police were invited, in a September 2022 High Court ruling, to introduce further evidence on the issue regarding the police's display of identity.[81]

In a December 2019 interview, Regina Ip worried that a statutory Commission of Inquiry (COI), as demanded by the protesters, would similarly lack sufficient investigative tools for this type of complex inquiry.[82] Ms. Ip's comment may not appreciate that a COI has the power of a court to compel witness testimony and document presentation. It would further have the right to enlist law enforcement officials to assist in gathering evidence.[83] In making this demand, the protesters are most interested in the independence of the COI.

The list of allegations against the police that should be investigated in an independent inquiry was long and complex. A summary here will suffice. The police were accused of being too generous in their use of tear gas, rubber bullets, and water cannons. They were often seen in various reportage videos chasing after fleeing protesters while shooting these devices in a seemingly indiscriminate manner toward the fleeing crowd. From early in the protest, both protester statements and media coverage alleged that these devices were being aimed in a way that intentionally risked damage to the eyes and face.[84] In circulated videos, the police appeared aggressive and unwilling to offer a more measured response. Such indiscriminate shooting of riot-control weapons reportedly often targeted frontline medical workers, passing pedestrians, and media workers in the vicinity of demonstrations.[85] The use of tear gas—over sixteen thousand cannisters were fired—was so excessive that very toxic gases were alleged to have seeped into nearby residential apartments and businesses.[86] Some critics have complained that the tear gas purchased from China was more toxic than usual.

The police were also openly filmed using excessive force to apprehend protesters who were already held down, ramming their heads into the pavement.[87] There were reports that the police, using water cannons with blue dye, followed and arrested protesters who sought treatment at hospitals, raising concerns that injured protesters would be discouraged from seeking medical help.[88] In the intense urban setting of Hong Kong, these tactics can easily undermine public safety as well as confidence in the police.

Additional alleged abuses included the police's use of live ammunition and face targeting with nonlethal rubber bullets. Some police tactics, such as surrounding and laying siege to universities, raised further concern about overreach in police strategy. Numerous videos purporting to show police abuse were available online.[89] These were all topics that could have been independently investigated.

There were also notorious cases where triad gangsters attacked protesters with limited or no police intervention. In the most notorious case in Yuen Long, where white-shirted gangsters were seen indiscriminately attacking bystanders and train passengers, a senior officer was seen speaking with white-shirted thugs before the attacks. That only a small number of such thugs were arrested immediately afterward raised public suspicion that the police were in cahoots with the attackers.[90]

In a stunning development thirteen months later in August 2020, legislator Lam Cheuk-ting, who attempted to intervene to mediate and stop the Yuen Long attacks, was himself arrested for rioting and damaging property regarding the event.[91] Lam believed the Yuen Long attacks and the associated suspicions of police complicity turned public opinion against the police. He believed, with respect to alleged police complicity, a formal investigation by the Independent Commission Against Corruption (ICAC) would be most appropriate. Lam would later be acquitted under similar circumstances in another prosecution relating to a protest in Tuen Mun, where he had likewise tried to calm things down; as the judge said, "Lam was like a man putting out fires here and there."[92]

As Lam's former university teacher, I can say that the judge's characterization of his efforts is very consistent with his exemplary character. I had many opportunities, in attending protests over the years, to meet up with him and see this exemplary young man, and later a leading legislator, work to protect his community. At one point, he even worked in a law enforcement role himself as a staff member of the ICAC. He also later worked as a staff member of the Democratic Party before he ran for the Legislative Council. "Putting out fires" is just a small part of his contributions.

Lam would later be convicted and sentenced to four months in prison for revealing the name of a police superintendent who was under investigation in relation to the attacks.[93] He would also be charged with rioting over the Yuen Long arrest, but with major delays he was only in pre-trial where he plead not guilty on October 23, 2023.[94] That Lam and his party colleague were arrested looked to many observers as if the victims of these horrendous attacks were being blamed. Lam suffered a bone fracture.[95] He is currently in jail and denied bail, along with forty-seven others who are facing NSL charges for the primary election, which I discuss below.

The final IPCC report noted above claimed a lack of evidence of such police collusion. Of course, an independent commission with the power to compel testimony might uncover such evidence or the contrary. Two years later, seven of the white-shirted attackers were convicted and sentenced to jail time of between three-and-a-half to seven years.[96] Radio Television Hong Kong (RTHK) reporter, Choy Yuk-ling (aka Bao Choy), who checked on car registrations to trace possible police misconduct, was also convicted for improperly accessing such registration information-- though this was later overturned in the CFA.[97]

Beyond the allegations of police violence, the overall posture of the protest containment effort raised deep concern. With massive arrests in 2019 and in the years following, 10,496 protesters had reportedly been arrested as of January 2022, with 2,909 prosecuted.[98] The largest numbers of arrests occurred during the protests and into early 2020, before and immediately after the imposition of the national security law.

Of the nearly three thousand persons charged with protest-related offenses, about 750 have been charged with the very serious charge of rioting, an offense that carries a maximum sentence of ten years.[99] In late 2019, pan-democratic legislators tried to push back against this with a bill in the Legislative Council that would redefine the offense of rioting, but they lacked the numbers to push through the bill.[100] Such rioting charges and trials for the 2019 protesters continue well into 2023.[101]

There was a widespread belief, encouraged by cross-training and frequent interactions between the two forces, that the Hong Kong police had been penetrated by the mainland Public Security Bureau. Such interpenetration is now likely to increase, with the NSL expressly authorizing police recruitment from the mainland and the Office for Safeguarding National Security operating directly in Hong Kong. The only way to objectively verify the truth of the many reports and allegations of abuse, only a few of which are discussed here, would have been for the government to have ordered an independent investigation.

Criminal Justice System

The massive arrests during the 2019 protest jeopardized the administration of criminal justice in Hong Kong. The widely observed police behavior at the ground level already left the system in tatters, but the prosecutions that followed raised wider concern about prosecutorial discretion, judicial independence, the rule of law, and the protection of basic freedoms in the city.

The earlier prosecution appeals and promotion and acceptance of stiff sentencing guidelines for offences against public order, signaled a change in law enforcement attitudes away from the purposive, rights-sensitive approach that had long prevailed in Hong Kong. Protester criminal defendants have confronted an unrelenting brick wall of prosecutorial aggression against speech-related crimes. Severe pressure on the judiciary points to high probability of both conviction and stiff sentences. Efforts to push back against this trend would soon be hamstrung with imposition of the NSL.

During the protests, progressive sectors of the legal community took a decisive stand against this growing pressure. Interviews I conducted in Hong Kong in December 2019 unearthed at least three new organizations committed to mobilizing criminal defense work and other services for the approximately six thousand protesters who were then already under arrest.[102] A separate fund, the 612 Humanitarian Relief Fund, was established to provide financial assistance to protesters by paying their legal fees, medical expenses, and fees for psychological counseling.[103] On the policy front, an earlier established group of lawyers, the Progressive Lawyers Group, worked to encourage reform and compliance with the Basic Law.[104] As will be discussed in later chapters, all of these civic legal defense organizations have now been forced to disband. Organizers have been arrested and accused of crimes or have fled into exile.

Lawyers I interviewed in late 2019 about their criminal defense experiences described difficult challenges in providing criminal defense services for protesters. A leading senior barrister who helped coordinate a hotline on legal services for the Civil Human Rights Front noted that about 75 to 80 percent of arrested protester clients, when first met by volunteer lawyers, showed signs of physical abuse.[105] This barrister noted that there were also problems with police abuse of bystanders, journalists, and medical professionals in the protest areas. The impression was that this abuse included both heavy-handed police tactics in the field during arrests and abuse while in custody, noting, "We are not talking about the degree of force necessary to effect arrest but rather hostile punitive behavior."

Another problem several of the volunteer lawyers I interviewed in Hong Kong highlighted was a shell game in getting access to clients. Arrestees were encouraged to call the abovementioned hotlines for assistance. Lawyers complained that after receiving such calls, they frequently had difficulty locating their clients. They suspected that police were obstructing such access in the hope arrestees would voluntarily offer compromising statements before a lawyer arrived. There were also widely reported instances of arrestees being removed to a remote police station near the border. There is no reliable police data on these complaints.

As anecdotal evidence, one lawyer from a prominent law firm oriented around civil rights reported a case where a client called from the North Point Police Station. He knew the call was from that station because he recognized the phone number, but when he went there, the officer at the front desk said he could not locate the client there. He then tried a second time, calling by phone from outside the station, and again was told the arrestee could not be located. Only when he entered the station to file a missing persons' report was his client suddenly located in the station.

By far, the most troubling problem facing defense lawyers was the soaring number of arrests and the severity of charges that their clients faced. Philip Dykes, who was then chairperson of the Hong Kong Bar Association, noted that the numbers were not just a problem for defense lawyers but also for the courts, which he described as then being about 20 percent understaffed.[106] He worried further about the number of prosecutions. He emphasized that prosecutorial discretion should be guided by the public interest and that "prosecuting numerous arrestees for unauthorized assembly or even for some of the more serious offenses would not necessarily be in the public interest." He worried, as he noted, "A flood of civil cases for damages could also hit the courts if charges were found to be unsubstantiated."

Concerning cases then pending, Dykes said, "The severity of charges laid so far has been a big problem. The data is poor, but it seems many clients who would be expected to be charged merely with unauthorized assembly were facing more severe charges. The worst of these is rioting, which carries a possible ten-year sentence. In the emerging enforcement climate, a mere breach of peace could too readily be turned into a rioting charge." In the subsequent two years, many of the cases that went to trial over the 2019 protests included rioting charges.

In the face of such massive protests and arrests, the police often have a very weak factual record. For this reason, historically, such charges following a protest would often be dropped in the magistrate's court. In this new repressive climate, defense lawyers I met expressed concern that the magistrates had begun to show less of the sensitivity that was traditionally expected in public order cases. They noted that defendants in this harsher environment would expect to be more readily held over for trial, in many cases without interim release on bail. Being held over without bail can result in months or even years in prison, awaiting trial under adverse conditions. Under NSL charges, a now established presumption against granting bail in most cases nearly guarantees such a fate.

Without the widely demanded independent commission of inquiry, these problems were all left to fester, angering the public even more. Public trust was badly damaged, and the protests the government hoped to end were only agitated further. This left the criminal justice system in tatters. The NSL and its enforcement would practically obliterate trust in the criminal justice system.

Beijing's Growing Interference

With the 2019 protests and the subsequent imposition of the NSL, direct Beijing intervention in local Hong Kong affairs increased dramatically. In the midst of the protests, the CCP ended its fourth party plenum in November 2019 by signaling its increased attention to national security with respect to Hong Kong.[107] China's National People's Congress (NPC) took this up in May 2020, directing the NPC Standing Committee to draft a new national security law for Hong Kong, which was promulgated on June 30, 2020. These moves signaled more of the same failed policies of overreach that got Hong Kong into the current crisis. Beijing offered no indication of its intention to meet any of the remaining four public demands raised in the 2019 protests.

Beijing already had a long-standing track record of behind-the-scenes manipulation of Hong Kong governance and the local political narrative through united front tactics. Nearly all core institutions—from the business and legal sectors to elections, the media, and educational institutions—were targets of this sort of manipulation and coercive pressure. This was sometimes done through direct decisions or comments and other times done through a system of rewarding local officials or supporters for handling or supporting Beijing concerns. Little regard was shown for the corrupting impact of such favoritism on Hong Kong's political and economic environment.

In an obvious contradiction, such influence peddling was combined with official rhetoric claiming a moral high ground as the guardian of the Basic Law and the rule of law. Such rhetoric was first most comprehensively articulated in the 2014 white paper but has been pervasive in official and supportive statements since the handover.[108] While there was a degree of restraint in the initial years after the handover, by late 2019, such restraint had completely evaporated. In the post-NSL era, no effort is even made to camouflage the contradiction between such influence peddling and the rule of law.

Former Chief Secretary Anson Chan, who served in the number two position in the Hong Kong government both before and after the handover, notes that she had no contact with Beijing's Liaison Office, which was established in 2000, during the last year of her three-year post-handover tenure.[109] That initial hands-off approach changed radically in subsequent years, with regular interactions and public criticisms leading to the Liaison Office effectively becoming the second government, in ways previously discussed. By the time of the Carrie Lam administration, there was little effort to hide this interference in Hong Kong affairs. Regarding Carrie Lam, Anson Chan noted, "The problem is that in the eyes of the Hong Kong people, she is not seen to serve two masters but to only serve Beijing."[110]

The November 2019 closing report of the fourth CCP plenum, the subsequent NPC resolution on national security, and the Standing Committee's national security law all proclaim a commitment to uphold the Basic Law. Unfortunately, Beijing officials appear to have little understanding of what the Basic Law says and what it realistically aims to achieve. An interpretation of the Basic Law that ignores the text makes little sense. The CCP version of the Basic Law generally takes scant account of the underlying commitment to guard Hong Kong's autonomy to avoid intrusion of the mainland system. That system is very much at odds with Hong

Kong's liberal rule of law tradition. That Deng Xiaoping long ago asked Hong Kong people and investors to put their hearts at ease based on this fundamental commitment appears to have gotten lost in translation.

Such a disconnect was especially evident in a related 2019 Beijing intervention, which began with the Hong Kong government using the Emergency Regulations Ordinance (ERO) to issue a regulation banning the use of face masks. Protesters had been using such masks to conceal their identities during demonstrations.[111] The ERO is a rarely used 1922 draconian ordinance, which allows the government nearly unfettered power to issue regulations during periods of emergency or public danger.[112] Upon challenge in the High Court, a lengthy opinion issued by a special two-judge panel found the ERO unconstitutional insofar as it authorized the chief executive to make regulations relating to public dangers where no emergency had been declared.[113] The special regulation issued under the ERO was also found to be too broad and not proportional to the intended purpose.

Controversy arose when the NPC's Office of Legal Council (OLC) in Beijing issued a statement attacking the court's judgment and challenging the power of Hong Kong courts to even review the constitutionality of ordinances under the Basic Law.[114] It was not clear whether this statement would predict a formal interpretation challenging the court's ruling or whether the statement was designed to intimidate the court of appeals with a threat to issue a binding interpretation if the court failed to overturn the High Court ruling and accept Beijing's view.

In either case, the statement was seen as Beijing interference in a matter fully under local autonomy. Critics worried that any NPCSC interpretation along the lines of the OLC statement would pose a grave danger both to judicial independence and the rule of law.[115] The OLC statement appeared to have been influential. In April 2020, the court of appeals reversed the carefully crafted two-judge decision regarding the use of the ERO and the ban on masks in protests,[116] and the Court of Final Appeal ultimately agreed, upholding the government's use of the ERO and its imposition of the mask ban.[117]

The ERO later seemingly become a favored tool for the government to get around legal restrictions. It was notoriously used to postpone the September 2020 Legislative Council election for a year.[118] The government claimed this was due to the pandemic, but more likely, this was done to put off an election they expected to lose. The government backed up the move by requesting an NPCSC ruling on how to maintain an interim Legislative Council, which it did with Beijing's blessing while awaiting Beijing's radical electoral overhaul.

A steady flow of Beijing rhetoric branding the protesters as terrorists and rioters, or even accusing them of a color revolution, has served to signal to Hong Kong officials Beijing's wrath and expectations not only for the government but also for police and prosecutorial authorities.[119] During the 2019 protest, this was backed up by statements and videos hinting at an intention to assert direct mainland control over the situation if needed.[120] A widely circulated documentary showing mainland security forces practicing riot control using Cantonese in an urban environment clearly sent this message.[121] There have even been unproven rumors that mainland public security officers heard speaking Mandarin have infiltrated the Hong Kong police.[122]

A steady drumbeat of mainland official praise for the aggressive tactics of the Hong Kong police, very much out of the police's historical character, reinforced the impression of mainland control or encouragement of these forceful operations. It was rumored that a senior mainland public security official, who was based across the border in Shenzhen, monitored, and to some extent oversaw, Hong Kong police operations during the 2019 protest.[123] These sorts of interventions are usually defended as a matter of national security. The fourth plenum statement had, in hindsight, signaled future moves of mainland direct intervention by pledging a greater effort to guard national security.

At the same time, all three branches of the Hong Kong government are frequently lectured by mainland officials on their national security responsibilities. This theme, which was originally expressed in the 2014 white paper, included judges among administrative officials with such responsibilities. Such Beijing messaging has long projected beyond Hong Kong to shape the global narrative by branding protests in Hong Kong as a separatist movement promoted by foreign interference.[124] The NSL represents Beijing's response to the protests and alleged foreign interference.

FEAR

7

2020: The National Security Law (NSL)

By the end of 2019, the government's indifference to protester concerns and the aggressive police crackdown had already put Hong Kong's autonomy, rule of law, and basic freedoms in severe jeopardy. A much bigger threat was on the horizon. At 11:00 p.m. on June 30, 2020, Beijing imposed a new national security law (NSL) on Hong Kong. Though officials claimed it would be narrowly applied the NSL quickly became Beijing's chief tool for silencing political opposition in the city. The most common defense of this imposition offered by Beijing and Hong Kong officials is that western democracies also have national security laws. It is likely that most countries in the world have laws to protect national security. What these officials fail to appreciate is that it is not the mere existence of a national security law that is of concern, but rather its content and application. On that score the NSL fails in many respects.

During the first couple months after its promulgation, official claims that it would be narrowly applied were quickly dispelled. Hope of central government restraint went out the window as Beijing officials imposed hands-on enforcement through their Office for Safeguarding National Security and Hong Kong's special NSL police unit. A textbook authoritarian crackdown, of the type Asian people have too often seen elsewhere in the region, quickly ensued. In July alone, fifty-three organizers of, or participants in, a people's political primary—in which 610,000 voters participated—were arrested for violating the NSL; forty-seven would later be charged.[1] Other actions that promptly followed the imposition signaled the NSL's primary role in the continuing crackdown: twelve opposition candidates for the then September 2020 Legislative Council election were disqualified from running, in some cases merely for not supporting the NSL;[2] ten protesters in the annual July 1 protest were arrested under the NSL, along with 360 protesters for other public order offenses;[3] one protester was charged with terrorism under the new law; four youngsters, ages sixteen to twenty-one, were arrested for allegedly supporting a new pro-independence organization; and there were reports of warrants against six Hong Kong supporters overseas.[4] As discussed in the next chapters, the policy of aggressive enforcement under the NSL is still ongoing three years later, with for example, Hongkongers arrested and even charged and convicted for such quirky things as publishing or circulating a children's book about sheep and wolves. The government seems to know who the wolves are.

The ensuing crackdown was not limited to arrests and criminal prosecutions. It quickly included other actions beyond the NSL to silence or intimidate the opposition, including the firing of Professor Benny Tai by the governing university council at the University of Hong Kong, and Chief Executive Carrie Lam declaring that the September Legislative Council election was to be delayed for a year.[5] The latter move was allegedly due to the pandemic, though the opposition generally believed the election was put off due to the prospect of government-supported candidates losing.[6] The delay gave Beijing the time needed to revamp the election rules to ensure only "patriots"—meaning supporters of the regime's policies— could run or be elected, a revamp completed in 2021.

Then, with August came the first salvo of the media crackdown. Jimmy Lai, the publisher of *Apple Daily*, was arrested, along with his two sons and four executives at his company, as well as the leading student activist in the youth movement, Agnes Chow.[7] Lai and six executives (no longer including his sons) were later charged with two counts under the NSL of conspiracy to collude with foreign forces, and one count of collusion with foreign forces (left on file but not being pursued), while Lai separately was later charged with one count under the colonial sedition ordinance of conspiracy to print, publish, sell or distribute seditious publications between April 2019 and June 2024.[8] Three of Lai's companies share in these various charges, though this may not matter much, as they have been largely wound up and are under an appointed receiver.. Lai was separately charged with fraud in relation to his office lease. The initial allegations against *Apple Daily* defendants were vague but appear to involve nothing more than newspaper articles and speeches attacking the government's overreach and seeking foreign solicitude, as well as actions supporting a group advocating people stand with Hong Kong—a form of human rights promotion entirely legal in every country where it was advanced. Of course, Lai, who had met the previous year with then US Vice President Mike Pence and Secretary of State Mike Pompeo, was already a target of Beijing's wrath.

The Hong Kong police did not stop at simply arresting Lai and his colleagues. They sent two hundred officers into the *Apple Daily*'s newsroom and management offices, searched through reporter and management desks alike, and carted away over thirty crates of documents—all of this captured live on Facebook by *Apple Daily* reporters.[9] The trove was no doubt a fishing expedition to justify more charges, including the sedition charges that later followed.

Hong Kong people signaled their contempt for this brazen display of power the next morning by buying 550,000 copies of the *Apple Daily* newspaper, an eightfold increase in normal circulation. Supporters were even buying piles of the paper to leave on the streets in little stacks for others to freely take away. A surge in investment in Next Digital, the holding company of *Apple Daily*, led to a 1,100 percent increase in stock value—all of which would later presumably be lost when the company was forced to close.[10]

After Jimmy Lai's arrest, the concern that judges would be put under mainland official pressure to convict in NSL cases was immediately confirmed. While Hong Kong officials identified Mr. Lai as a "suspect," the Chinese Foreign Ministry spokesman in Hong Kong identified him as an "anti-China troublemaker" who put "the long-term stability of Hong Kong in jeopardy."[11] Lai languishes in jail over three years later, denied bail and awaiting trial, a trial that finally began on December 18, 2023.[12]

The above-noted arrest of Agnes Chow oddly took on dramatic life three years later, clearly demonstrating Hong Kong's shift to mainland law enforcement tactics. Chow's alleged involvement in the claimed collusion is not clear. She was given police bail and had not been prosecuted over three years later when she was allowed to go abroad to study in Canada with a requirement that she return to Hong Kong and report to police periodically. This became headlines when she later declared she would not return, that she had been put under severe mental pressure, being forced to go on an escorted mainland propaganda trip to visit patriotic exhibitions, subject to constant photo-taking presumably for planned propaganda purposes, and to later write a letter of gratitude to the police as a condition for receiving back her passport.[13] She expressed concern that if she returned to Hong Kong she would be placed under great stress and forced to play a continuing propaganda roll against her personal beliefs. After her announcement of her intention not to return to Hong Kong, Chief Executive John Lee declared in a press conference that she would be aggressively pursued for life, as one might expect if the target had committed some heinous crime.[14] These threats were extraordinary when it appeared her only alleged "foreign collusion" was human rights advocacy.

These arrests spread fear and loathing well beyond the narrow application of the NSL officials had promised. As discussed in chapters 8 and 9, the NSL has now been applied in a whole-society approach that reaches nearly every sector, aiming to convert Hong Kong from a liberal open society to, effectively, a national security state.

The Status of the NSL

The NSL effectively amends the Basic Law. Both the Basic Law and the NSL are PRC national laws of otherwise equal status; but under the PRC Legislation Law, articles 83 and 85, conflicting provisions in a national law that are more specific and later in time are superior to a more general earlier national law—a principle widely familiar in most legal systems.[15] If this rule is applied, then the NSL would presumably have a higher status than even the Hong Kong Basic Law, prevailing over the Basic Law in any clause where conflict exists.[16] This status is reinforced by article 62 of the NSL, which provides it with priority similar to the Basic Law over all locally enacted laws.

My colleague at the University of Hong Kong, Professor Hualing Fu, has argued that "basic laws" in China have a special status such that the Basic Law should take priority over conflicting provisions of the NSL, or at least shape interpretation of the NSL.[17] But it is hard to see how this would be achieved in practice given the presumed lack of power in the local courts to review the NSL for compliance with the Basic Law. Local courts offering interpretations of NSL requirements that are friendly to human rights also face the risk of being overruled by the NPC Standing Committee. With the pressure the courts have faced, this avenue has also not been promising.

Despite these daunting challenges, any defense lawyer would be bound to argue that the NSL cannot override Basic Law guarantees, as the Basic Law embodies the stipulated requirements of two international treaties, including the Sino-British Joint Declaration and the International Covenant on Civil and Political Rights (ICCPR). Furthermore, Basic Law, article 159, provides a specific requirement as to the amendment of the Basic Law. The enactment of the NSL was not in compliance with those procedures. Basic Law, article 11, further provides that the systems applied in Hong Kong, including the protection of human rights and legislative and executive processes, shall be based on the Basic Law. Under Basic Law, article 18, as previously noted, national laws are not to be applied in areas governed by autonomy.

Such argument could be further bolstered by the NSL's own requirement, in NSL, article 4, that the Basic Law and the ICCPR continue to apply.[18] Sadly, there has been little evidence that judges or prosecutorial officials will have the courage to push back against Basic Law violations in the face of conflicting NSL requirements given the constraints of NPCSC interpretive override and the other pressures put on the courts and law enforcement officials in the name of national security.

In other words, while the NSL is stand-alone national legislation, various constraints beef up its status to equality with and—sometimes, where conflicts exist—superiority over the Basic Law in providing the effective constitution of Hong Kong—now a national security constitution. Areas where conflicts might arise especially include the Basic Law guarantees of human rights and due process, which are undermined by the vague language and procedural limitations of the NSL.

The text of the NSL left little doubt as to what was in store. It seeks to "prevent, stop and punish" any "act or activity" related to "secession," "subversion," "terrorist activities," and "collusion with foreign and overseas forces." While article 4 of the law promises to uphold the human rights guarantees in the Basic Law, including the international human rights covenants, it provides no effective mechanism to achieve that purpose.

On the contrary, the law is profoundly distrustful of Hong Kong institutions and puts Beijing officials on the ground locally to oversee or override nearly all local mechanisms of official constraint. There is mainland oversight or direct supervision in one form or another over executive officials, the police, prosecutorial authorities, and the courts. Such direct mainland control undercuts both autonomy and the rule of law, posing a severe risk to basic freedoms.

The NSL reflects a textbook case of how overreaching national security laws can undermine the very foundations of an open society. Conflicts with the original commitments in the Basic Law are numerous and profound, effectively transforming the Hong Kong SAR from a territory with a promised "high degree of autonomy" and a liberal constitutional order into an insular part of a police state. The following analysis breaks down prominent areas of concern regarding the text of the NSL. Serious problems in application will then be addressed in the chapters that follow.

The Path to Enactment Ignored Important Legal Restraints

The NSL was passed in a furtive arrangement by the NPCSC in a month-long drafting process, under the cover of total secrecy and without public consultation. This process even ignored the requirements in the PRC's national legislation law for wide consultation with "all concerned parties."[19] Strikingly, the Standing Committee represents the very highest leadership in China, meaning this must have been at the direction of China's top leaders, including General Secretary and President Xi Jinping.[20] The Chinese text went into immediate effect, despite being revealed for the first time and promulgated at 11:00 p.m. on June 30, 2020.[21] Even then Hong Kong's chief executive, Carrie Lam, claimed to have seen it for the first time on that day of release.[22]

Beyond ignoring public consultation, the NSL's imposition also ignored the firewall provision contained in Basic Law, article 18. This firewall provision aimed to better secure local autonomy by blocking, with limited exception, the application of mainland laws. Basic Law, article 18, provides that national laws do not apply in Hong Kong unless added to annex III of the Basic Law. In this respect, article 18 states that, "Laws listed in Annex III . . . shall be confined to those relating to defense and foreign affairs as well as other matters outside the autonomy of the Region as specified by this law." Many of Beijing's concerns addressed in the new law relate more to public order than to national security; but Basic Law, article 14, makes clear the "Hong Kong Special Administrative Region (SAR) shall be responsible for the maintenance of public order in the region."

The NSL, furthermore, directly undercuts the required local enactment of legislation relating to national security, as provided by Basic Law, article 23.[23] Official claims that national enactment was justified due to the local government's failure to act are not convincing. As discussed in chapter 4, the government attempted in 2003 to enact article 23 legislation that did not conform to ICCPR requirements applicable under the Basic Law. While this effort was blocked by public protests, nothing would have obstructed putting forth proper reform legislation under article 23. Instead, the NSL was imposed on Hong Kong.

Undermining Local Autonomy

In April 2020, the Hong Kong and Macau Affairs Office in Beijing and Beijing's Liaison Office in Hong Kong proclaimed themselves not bound by Basic Law, article 22, which bars departments of the central government from interfering in Hong Kong's internal affairs.[24] This signaled what was to come. Inflicting great harm on the promised local autonomy, the NSL now creates and empowers multiple bodies of direct control over Hong Kong governance. The sheer pervasiveness of the institutional arrangements defies any claim that it is only of marginal effect. The subsequent pattern of aggressive enforcement by these institutions, as further discussed in chapters 8 and 9, has demonstrated their expansive reach.

At the local level, article 12 of the NSL creates a Hong Kong Committee for Safeguarding National Security, which is chaired by the chief executive and composed of several cabinet-level ministers along with top local law enforcement officers. The committee is said to answer directly to the Central People's Government and includes a mainland-appointed national security adviser.[25] Beijing immediately appointed the then head of the local Beijing Liaison Office, Luo Huining, as the first national security adviser, thereby inviting that office to intrude directly into Hong Kong local affairs. Luo is the first mainland official to function openly inside a local Hong Kong government body.[26]

The local Committee for Safeguarding National Security is required to coordinate all aspects of national security operations under the local government, including the analysis of developments, oversight of enforcement mechanisms, and coordination of all major work relating to national security.[27] How this works may never become clear, as the committee's deliberations are to be held in secret and are not subject to judicial review.[28] Its budget is hived off and not bound by current legal restrictions.[29] The only apparent oversight over the committee itself is that directed by mainland officials. Given the subordinate position of this committee to the central government, it would presumably ignore the advice of its mainland national security adviser at its peril.

Mainland officials tasked with such oversight are close at hand. The NSL establishes in Hong Kong a powerful central government Office for Safeguarding National Security, whose officials are assigned from the PRC's state and public security bureaus. As a sign of things to come, Beijing quickly appointed as the head of this office a powerful Guangdong official known for his hard-line stance, Zheng Yanxiong.[30]

The Office for Safeguarding National Security completely overrides Hong Kong's promised autonomy, as its officials are to guide, oversee, and supervise local officials in national security matters.[31] With the mainland's whole society approach to national security, there is little local governance beyond their reach. Locating this office within Hong Kong and assigning it extensive oversight authority over local public order completely wipes out the autonomy firewall between Beijing and the SAR—in direct conflict with article 22 of the Basic Law.[32]

As with the local Committee for Safeguarding National Security, the Office for Safeguarding National Security completely escapes legal oversight, except presumably from officials in Beijing. While mainland security officials based in Hong Kong are ostensibly required to obey local laws, article 60 of the NSL explicitly states that these officials exercise their duties outside of the purview of local jurisdiction. In other words, the only check to compel obedience with local laws is the oversight of their mainland superiors.

Without local oversight, they have the prerogative to refer "complex" and "serious" cases to mainland jurisdiction upon a request from the chief executive, a request that will surely be made if the mainland officials who are overseeing security operations so desire.[33] Once that determination is made, the entire prosecution can be transferred to the mainland, where the Supreme People's Court will decide which mainland court will try the case. The earlier proposed extradition law pales in comparison.

On the mainland, the National Criminal Procedure Law and related procedural laws will apply.[34] This move erases the protections of the ICCPR that apply in Hong Kong, as the PRC has not ratified the treaty and has never complied with it.

Moreover, both the local police force and the Department of Justice are to maintain special branches related to national security enforcement, each of which is headed by an official approved by the above central government controlled Office for Safeguarding National Security.[35] The most threatening aspect of the special branch of the police department is its almost unchecked power in conducting investigations and surveillance under newly issued regulations.

On July 6, at its first meeting, the local Committee on the Safeguarding of National Security issued regulations respecting police investigations.[36] Mirroring the NSL's release, these regulations were issued in Chinese, with the English translation being "for reference only"—even though both English and Chinese are official languages in Hong Kong. English has offered a necessary component for the continued application of the common law system.[37] As a likely sign of mainland intervention, the lengthy, 116-page regulation was very likely drafted in advance (presumably with the aid of mainland public security officials) and handed to the committee.

Police and Security Office Investigations Lack Legal Oversight

The same provisions that undermine local autonomy with respect to the Committee for Safeguarding National Security and the Office for Safeguarding National Security also undermine the rule of law. Article 14 of the NSL commands that no institutions, organizations, or individuals in the region can interfere with the work of the committee and that its decisions are "not amenable to judicial review." In effect, this means that neither the courts nor other bodies like the Equal Opportunities Commission or the Legislative Council, can hold the committee accountable.

For the central government's Office for Safeguarding National Security, the situation is even worse, as mainland officials who work there are, as previously noted, beyond local jurisdiction entirely. That this lack of legal accountability implicates human rights protections under the ICCPR, as well as due process requirements, is apparent.

Under various related UN mandates, a collective group of human rights special procedures rapporteurs have written a scathing letter to the Chinese government laying out in detail, with appropriate references, the NSL's total failure to comply with international human rights requirements.[38] This scathing report notes that not only does transfer to the mainland circumvent ICCPR requirements, but the definitions of the four NSL crimes also fail for vagueness.

In line with these criticisms, a team of UK lawyers purportedly representing the publisher Jimmy Lai have appealed to UN experts to investigate the comprehensive set of charges against Mr. Lai, arguing that they "constitute prosecutorial, judicial, and legal harassment of Mr. Lai, because of his advocacy of democracy and the rights to protest and freedom of expression in the Hong Kong

SAR, and his work as founder and editor of Apple Daily."[39] A strong suggestion of the intent to harass is borne out not only by the numerous charges against Jimmy Lai related to national security but also by his conviction for fraud, allegedly for using his leased newspaper office for a side-consulting business he maintained for years—for which he was convicted and sentenced to five years and nine months in prison.[40] As far I can discover, such landlord-tenant cases were never historically treated as criminal cases, being typically civil matters.

Presumably, even the implementation rules issued by the committee are not subject to judicial review. These rules, as noted above, regulate police investigations. They offer a lack of police accountability that profoundly offends the oversight of official behavior expected in open societies based on the rule of law, as promised by the original Basic Law.

The risks to human rights, and due process expectations further downstream in the criminal justice process, are apparent. Most of these national security investigations are to be conducted in secret, though a judge will be designated to issue search warrants. However, under the implementation rules noted above, if "for any reason it would not be reasonably practicable to obtain a warrant," assigned police officers may proceed without a search warrant.[41]

Under the same rules, an officer or official conducting such an investigation can conduct surveillance, confiscate travel documents, and freeze the assets of the person or entity under investigation. Property can be seized, communications intercepted, and interrogations conducted, all without a warrant or judicial order.[42] Because the local police department has been encouraged to recruit personnel from the mainland, mainland methods of interrogation and surveillance risk being imported to Hong Kong.[43] It seems likely that such presumably secret activities will not be subject to judicial oversight during criminal proceedings under circumstances where improperly seized evidence might otherwise be objected to and excluded at trial. With such an aggressive operation of secret police units, in the authoritarian mode, the frequent accusation that Hong Kong has become a police state appears increasingly credible.

With the first arrests under the new law, the problems with such secrecy were already apparent, with several people being apprehended with no initial indication of what illegal activities they were alleged to have engaged in. The alleged crimes were reported but with insufficient factual predicate. At the same time, the media were barred from reporting all except the most mundane outcomes of preliminary hearings in the courts.

How will others know which activities to avoid with respect to such vague crimes? In the Jimmy Lai case, only after the defendants were briefly released was it possible to guess that some allegations might relate to a foreign campaign to stand with Hong Kong, though beyond some newspaper clippings, the full extent of the factual basis for the charges is still not clear three years after the arrests; meanwhile, the defendants linger in jail, denied bail.

Such lawlessness may be fortified even more regarding mainland officers under the Office for Safeguarding National Security, an office as noted not subject to local jurisdiction. Mainland police are notoriously known for secret surveillance and abusive practices to obtain confessions.[44] Human Rights Watch (HRW) has reported that former detainees on the mainland describe physical and psychological torture, including "being hung by the wrists, being beaten with police batons or other objects, and prolonged sleep deprivation."[45] The risk of forced confessions is fortified by express language in NSL, article 59, that provides that when mainland officials take jurisdiction, any person with information pertaining to an offense is "obliged to testify truthfully." What are the consequences for a failure to speak up? Is there a right to remain silent?

With numerous national security defendants recently pleading guilty after many months in jail while denied bail, it appears such long incarceration without trial is proving another way to wear defendants down and obtain confessions for alleged criminal activities most observers clearly would not view as criminal. This pressure for confession is enhanced by provisions in NSL article 33 that provide for lighter sentences for those who confess and turn in their comrades.

While confession is widely encouraged in criminal justice, the offense to human rights is a matter of whether improper coercion is applied. Without effective local jurisdiction over law enforcement behavior, there will be no effective judicial oversight to evaluate claims of coercion. That the NSL takes priority over all local laws would further limit a court's ability to maneuver in its evaluation of the appropriateness of law enforcement investigatory behavior.[46]

Judicial Independence and the Rule of Law Degraded

The courts, as already noted, surely do not have the power to find parts of the NSL unconstitutional or in violation of the Basic Law or human rights guarantees. This has been blocked by the claimed superior status of the NSL. In a letter to the Chinese government UN Special Rapporteur Margaret Satterthwaite outlined further the restrictions on judicial review of security operations that promise to undermine judicial independence.[47]

Most prominent among these is the provisions for a special list of judges to hear national security cases. Because the chief executive is required to choose a limited list of judges to try national security cases, there has been enormous pressure on judges to conform with Beijing's expectations.[48] Such pressure is backed up by a further requirement that such selected judges will be removed if they "make any statement or behave in any manner endangering national security."[49] Since Hong

Kong judges are bound by ethical constraints not to be active in local politics and are quite careful to avoid bias in court, offending statements or behavior would presumably arise out of judgments or rulings in court that did not meet mainland official expectations. The inclusion of such a provision in the law signals Beijing's distrust of local judges.

What leeway the local courts have is not stated, but clearly a local judge will not be able to review the validity of the NSL itself and will have no jurisdiction over mainland national security officials. With the prospect of dismissal from the national security judicial list hanging over their heads, it would appear their capacity to oversee the enforcement behavior of the police units discussed previously will be extremely limited.

Further limitations include the vesting of the power to interpret the NSL in the NPC Standing Committee.[50] Judges will surely be looking over their shoulders in judging what the NPCSC might accept in this sensitive area. Given the stellar historical reputation of the judiciary, Hong Kong people will surely expect and hope that local judges will interpret the NSL in ways that best conform to the rule of law and protection of basic freedoms in Hong Kong. But with the many constraints noted here, such expectation is in peril. As we will see in the next chapter, these concerns have proven fully justified. Some earlier national security cases went through to conviction with little or no mention of human rights.

Criminal Defense Rights Lost

Defendants under the NSL text also face multiple procedural hurdles that offend basic rights under common law practice and human rights standards. The NSL expressly presumes a denial of bail "unless the judge has sufficient grounds for believing that the criminal suspect or defendant will not continue to commit acts endangering national security."[51] A so-called "police bail" was granted for all defendants in the case involving Jimmy Lai and his associates. But once charges were pressed, this bail was withdrawn. On Lai's special appeal, the Court of Final Appeal (CFA) upheld the presumption against bail as an exception to the common law rule.[52] With this ruling will all the human rights failings embodied in the NSL text be treated as exceptions? Notions of exceptional justice surely have a checkered human rights history around the world.

The prosecution also has the discretion to deny a jury trial, as was done in the very first NSL prosecution and has been done in every case since. Such denial now appears to be the default norm for national security cases.[53] While trials can be conducted in open court, the law allows for closed trials to protect state secrets and to "safeguard public order."[54] Secrecy requirements could further limit a judge's capacity to forcefully uphold the ICCPR.[55] One way to protect rights under such a law would be for the courts to exercise some discretion in interpreting statutory language. Still, it remains unlikely the courts will exercise much discretion in this regard given the NPC Standing Committee's power to overturn any interpretation and the likely official criticisms that would follow.

The defendant's right to defend against the government's many questionable national security claims is further obstructed by a power of the chief executive, under NSL, article 47, to issue a binding certificate that an act or piece of evidence "involves national security." As discussed later, this power of the chief executive was shored up by the first NPCSC interpretation of the NSL directing a binding power in the Chief Executive or the Committee in this regard.[56] This has meant that many acts under prosecution, which have essentially been public order matters involving free expression, have been officially branded as threats to national security.

These procedural limitations might be tolerable if all that was at risk was a slap on the wrist, but these NSL crimes risk punishments that involve long years of incarceration, in most instances ranging from three years to life imprisonment. Even for those who plead guilty in order to gain a mitigating reduction in sentence, the CFA has already ruled that any mitigation cannot go below the minimum sentence provided.[57] Given the breadth of activity covered by the four crimes, the risk of enduring excessive or unusual punishment is high.[58] One can imagine young protesters spending years in prison for excessive zeal during a protest march of the sort widely allowed in Hong Kong before passage of the NSL. As we will see in chapter 8, these same procedural limitations of the NSL have been extended by the CFA to apply to Hong Kong's old colonial sedition statute, which has been resurrected after having not been used for decades. The basis for such extension is the court's conclusion that sedition inevitably involves national security.

On the first day the new NSL went into effect, a young protester was arrested for riding his motorcycle into a police cordon, causing injury to three officers, while displaying a flag bearing the words, "Liberate Hong Kong, revolution of our times."[59] Twenty-three-year-old Tong Ying-kit was charged under the NSL both with secession and terrorism.[60] Tong was the first person in Hong Kong to challenge the bail provision under a petition for a writ of *habeas corpus* (a common law order to be released from jail), arguing that NSL, article 42, was an unconstitutional no-bail provision. The High Court rejected the challenge, a result which would later receive the blessing of the CFA in the Jimmy Lai case. As discussed in chapter 8, Tong would later be convicted of both secession and terrorism and sentenced to nine years in prison.

Added to these legal defense limitations are concerns over the full capacity of lawyers to secure communications with their clients. Lawyers have expressed fear that the new law gives police the power to conduct surveillance against lawyers doing defense work, putting attorney-client privilege at risk. Under the implementation rules for article 43, police in "exceptional circumstances" may get authorization from the chief executive to intercept communications and conduct surveillance at a lawyer's office or residence when authorities have grounds to suspect their involvement in seditious activities.[61] Such secret surveillance would of course not be known to the targeted lawyer. Given the frequent arrest of human rights defender lawyers on the mainland, this should not be taken lightly. These various procedural irregularities have caused several countries to suspend extradition agreements with Hong Kong.[62]

Vague Crimes Cause High Risk to Free Speech Protections

Still, the substance of the four crimes themselves is the most damning blow to life in Hong Kong.[63] Around the world and historically, basic freedoms have been at their greatest peril under vague prohibitions respecting national security. Although NSL, article 4, promises protection for "the freedoms of speech, of the press, of publication, of association, of assembly, of procession and of demonstration" in accordance with the international human rights covenants, the vague statutory language and limited oversight puts such guarantees in serious jeopardy.

The vague statutory language defining these crimes draws no protective boundary between free expression and a criminal offense. All individuals are said to be responsible for national security, raising the specter that even an academic or journalist reporting critical facts from their research risks being prosecuted.[64] Mainland academics critical of the government are commonly charged with revealing state secrets even though they likely would not possess such secrets.[65]

Upon the NSL's imposition, Beijing and Hong Kong officials claimed that the new law targets only a tiny minority of extreme offenders. The vague language of the NSL suggest otherwise. Under the NSL "subversion" covers not only "acts by force or the threat of force" but also "other unlawful means,"[66] which could include acts similar to the unauthorized peaceful protest—viewed as civil disobedience— that occurred in Hong Kong before the NSL was imposed; "terrorism" includes violence against property and the disruption of transport, as well as more serious activities;[67] and "collusion" involves disrupting government policies, undermining elections, calling for sanctions, provoking hatred, and "other hostile activities."[68]

The collusion prohibition clearly arises out of Beijing's fear of foreign criticism, and it especially targets human rights advocacy to foreign governments and other international bodies. Such advocacy has reached out in particular to the leading common law jurisdictions, the United Kingdom and the United States, and those governments have been among the most vocal critics of the NSL. Consequently, they have likewise been the frequent targets of Beijing's ire. As previously noted, the arrest of Jimmy Lai and others was rumored to relate to their support of an international human rights campaign respecting Hong Kong involving the lobbying of foreign governments in regard to human rights violations.

As will be discussed in chapter 9 in relation to human rights advocacy, the effort to silence activists and others who have lobbied foreign governments has not stopped with the allegations against Jimmy Lai. So far well over a dozen activists in exile abroad have been the targets of warrants, and in some cases bounties—not including the rumored targeting of many others not publicly announced –for lobbying and public advocacy activities that are perfectly legal in their current overseas locations.[69] While the Hong Kong government cannot reach these targeted activists, targeting their activities effectively bars them from ever returning to Hong Kong.

Such vague and broad definitions of potential speech crimes clearly fail to match the free speech standards for national security laws provided under the ICCPR, as outlined in international resolutions such as the Johannesburg Principles.[70] These standards have also been addressed in the special procedures letter to the Chinese government regarding the NSL.[71] These four NSL crimes encompass not only concrete "acts" but also loosely defined "activities" of "incitement," "assistance," and "abetment," as well as the "provision" of financial and other forms of support.[72] Even inciting hatred toward authorities is a crime.[73]

When completely under the control of mainland public security officials, these crimes conceivably have no limits. In the face of such severe constraints, would any local human rights NGOs, of which there were numerous before the recent crackdown, feel free to submit shadow reports before various international human rights bodies overseeing the human rights covenants and treaties? Worse yet, would testimony before a local legislative hearing or a foreign parliamentary body be a crime? Is writing or publishing this book a crime? It would seem the only certain way to avoid prosecution is to avoid commenting on public affairs. As more fully developed in the next chapters, the answer to all these questions appears to be yes, as would soon be borne out by attacks and arrests leading to over sixty critical local NGOs disbanding.

A Growing Culture of Intimidation and Enforcement Prevails

Uncertainty especially creates a chilling effect on free speech. Indeed, that is what is intended, as was evident in the first weeks after the imposition of the NSL. A comprehensive investigative report by Mary Hui in *Quartz* likened this chilling effect to "Cultural Revolution 2.0."[74] Hui describes a culture of intimidation that arose even before the imposition of the new law, born from the heavy-handed enforcement during the 2019 protests: civil servants had to hide their political views, teachers were rebuked and fired, and hospital workers were harassed for missing work because of citywide strikes.

The first full day of the newly promulgated NSL, July 1, 2020, was the twenty-third anniversary of Hong Kong's handover on July 1, 1997. The police wasted no time in deploying the new legislation. For the first time since the handover, the annual handover anniversary protest was banned, ostensibly due to COVID's social distancing requirements, thereby rendering all protest that day as an "unauthorized assembly."

As protesters nevertheless gathered, riot police immediately posted this warning: "If you are displaying flags or banners/chanting slogans or conducting yourself with an intent, such as secession or subversion, which may constitute offences under the HKSAR national security law, you may be arrested and prosecuted."[75] The police arrested 370 protesters that day, ten of them under the new NSL for holding or possessing prohibited materials, mostly flags or signs calling for "independence" or to "liberate Hong Kong."[76] The remainder were arrested for various public order offences.

Statements and slogans routinely used in the 2019 protest, mostly as polemical language to demand compliance with China's commitments, were now officially banned, including the popular slogan, "Liberate Hong Kong, revolution of our times." In response to such heavy-handed prohibitions, Hong Kong protesters became more creative, holding blank posters or using patriotic slogans such as "Arise, ye who refuse to be slaves," taken from China's national anthem.[77] It is interesting that protests in December 2022 across the mainland against the zero-COVID policy used the same blank-paper tactics, as a testament to protester ingenuity in the face of free speech repression.[78] Pro-democracy "yellow businesses" were warned by the police to take down "Lennon Walls" of sticky notes with political messages, though some left blank ones up in retaliation.[79]

Media, the Internet, Education, and the Corporate World

On its face, the new law poses a special risk to social media, NGOs, educational institutions, and news media organizations. As an indication of the perceived overreach of the internet surveillance provisions, Facebook announced that it would no longer process routine Hong Kong government requests for user data. Still, questions remain as to what Facebook would do if faced with a broad court order under the new law to do so.[80]

NSL, article 9, goes further than regulating data collection, providing that the Hong Kong SAR, "shall take necessary measures to strengthen public communication, guidance, supervision and regulation over matters concerning national security, including those relating to schools, universities, social organizations, the media, and the internet." Under NSL, article 54, The Office for Safeguarding National Security is called upon to provide assistance to "strengthen the management of services for" NGOs and media agencies of foreign countries.[81] Many observers fear Beijing may soon aim to extend the mainland's great internet firewall to encompass Hong Kong.

The dual-pronged supervision and management of NGOs and media organizations causes grave concern for assembly, press, and academic freedoms. A June 2020 annual survey by the Hong Kong Journalists Association demonstrated that Hong Kong press freedom had already reached an all-time low.[82] The survey showed that 98 percent of the members of the Hong Kong Journalists Association opposed the new law due to fears for their own safety.[83]

As a friend of many journalists, among both my former students and reporters that frequently call with questions, I have received inquiries about what to do in response to the risks they face. Certainly, many media organizations will be careful in their reportage, further encouraging self-censorship.[84]

Nervous about these various provisions on both data access and oversight of foreign media, in July 2020, the *New York Times* moved portions of its operations out of Hong Kong. With such vague crimes and an arsenal of enforcement tools, there is concern about the broader consequences of the legislation: Is Hong Kong facing a future where media organizations leave, academics leave or refuse to come, and corporations shift their headquarters?[85]

Declining school enrollments, university faculty exits and reluctance to come, falling housing prices, and investment flight, among other things, suggest that future has already arrived. As will be seen in chapter 9, the national security law has hit the education sector especially hard due to Beijing's concerns about training youth on the correct patriotic view. Under the new law, the government is required to "promote national security education in the schools and universities and through social organizations, the media, the internet and other means."[86] The breadth of planned application to educational institutions became immediately apparent when Hong Kong Education Minister Kevin Yeung, armed with the new law, proclaimed schools must stamp out political activity.[87] For universities, the fear will increasingly relate to the recruitment and retention of scholars and a possible culture of self-censorship that would be damaging to the reputation of Hong Kong's world-class higher education institutions.[88]

After university heads were pressured to throw their support behind the new NSL, the presidents of five universities issued a joint statement expressing their support.[89] Did this about-face from the 2019 outspoken defense by university heads concerning students' right to protest clearly signal a tightening of basic freedoms on campus?

Businesses have also felt the pressure. The level playing field that historically characterized Hong Kong is under stress, as Beijing and Hong Kong officials put pressure on corporate leaders to support the NSL and repressive government policies. Cathay Pacific Airlines, HSBC, and Standard Chartered all succumbed to such pressures. Cathay did this by blocking staff who participated in the 2019 protests from flights to China, while all three companies publicly proclaimed their support for the new NSL—as did Hong Kong's richest man, Li Ka-shing.[90] It appears, just like on campus, the tide has shifted from an earlier tolerance of employees joining protests to a wholehearted support for the NSL.

Of course, Hong Kong is famously an international city. It is not just local businesses that feel the pressure, and Hong Kong people do not just depend on local businesses for their livelihood. The likelihood of international businesses leaving Hong Kong is real. After the NSL's imposition, 83 percent of the members of the US Chamber of Commerce in Hong Kong indicated their concern about the new law.[91] Hong Kong's greatest asset for attracting international investment and business location has always been its strong rule of law and associated freedoms, which enabled a safe working environment and other perks such as world-class liberal education for children. Without these guarantees and perks will businesses stay? The Hong Kong government has now been put to the tactics of aggressively selling the merits of Hong Kong much like mainland cities. Will it prove a hard sell?

Repressing Democratic Politics

Problems with the new law do not end with the reach of criminal law and political intimidation. The requirement in NSL, article 6, which restates the Basic Law requirement that legislators swear loyalty to the Basic Law, has clearly taken on an expanded meaning. There were early signals of the changes to come. Of the twelve Legislative Council candidates barred from running in the then planned 2020 election, three from the more moderate Civic Party were reportedly blocked because of their expressed disapproval of the NSL.[92] Swearing loyalty to the Basic Law already presumably meant supporting the NSL. Since nobody outside the government and pro-establishment politicians supported the new law, such requirement was clearly aimed at blocking nearly all leaders of the opposition camp from running for office. As will be discussed in Chapter 10, this happened long before the 2021 "electoral reforms" did so expressly.

As noted in chapter 3, the only power the opposition has had under the Basic Law was the power to say no. Political reform would offer a way to change this sorry condition and create a healthy political environment. The NSL is clearly a move in the opposite direction.

At the same time, with the growing culture of political influence and pressures, the level playing field for local and international businesses is equally under threat. Under this new national security constitution, "one country" has largely gobbled up "two systems." As the previous chapters highlight, these conditions are largely a creation of official overreach over many years in both Beijing and Hong Kong. The next two chapters will highlight how this new national security order has been weaponized.

Rule by Law

8

THE NSL, THE RULE OF LAW, AND THE CONSTITUTIONAL ORDER

What is written in the law is only half the story; how it is applied is the more important half. As highlighted in the previous chapter, while the NSL, on its face, puts numerous rights and freedoms at grave risk, its overall impact in practice offers an even more profound and comprehensive challenge to Hong Kong's constitutional order, including the rule of law and human rights.

CCP officials in the PRC have long expressed hostility to the liberal constitutional model employed in most modern democracies, including such features as separation of powers and electoral and judicial checks on public officials. Domestically, this has meant that suggestions by Chinese constitutional scholars that the PRC liberalize its political system or establish an independent constitutional court have been consistently slapped down.[1] As noted in the introductory chapter, this hostility was most clearly evident in the 2013 Document Number Nine issued by the Central Committee of the CCP, which banned the promotion or teaching of constitutionalism, including such prohibited concepts as individual rights, constitutional democracy, the separation of powers, a multiparty system, general elections, independent courts, and a free press. The CCP clearly sees liberal ideas as an existential threat to continuing CCP rule. In some respects, the NSL effectively represents a somewhat modified and weaponized Document Number Nine for Hong Kong, even more so when it is combined with Beijing's later electoral overhaul.

Beijing's top-down illiberal model of control especially challenges the long-standing liberal order in Hong Kong. With frequent attacks on the city's liberal institutions by officials, their local surrogates, and the Beijing-controlled media, as well as the occasional official report or ruling, Beijing's expressed policies consistently offended the city's liberal core values. These values include genuine democratic choice, separation of powers, the rule of law, independent courts, a free press, and basic freedoms. The previously noted 2014 Beijing white paper on Hong Kong predominately emphasized control and submission.[2] With the promulgation of the NSL and Beijing's decision on "improving the electoral system," the substance of the mainland Chinese system has now deeply penetrated Hong Kong.[3]

Regarding the new electoral system, the late Suzanne Pepper aptly described the new Hong Kong model as "a variation on the mainland People's Congress system, which is itself a mix of direct elections, indirect selection, and consultative appointments—all with strict CCP vetting."[4] The liberal democratic order promised to Hong Kong in the Sino-British Joint Declaration[5] and the Hong Kong Basic Law has been completely hollowed out, leaving Hong Kong with an illiberal undemocratic system.[6]

If, as long speculated, China plans to offer an alternative model to liberal democracy globally, then this new repressive illiberal Hong Kong model is likely it, reflecting a repressive adaptation within the institutional architecture of an open society. Countries across Asia and Africa that have often been the target of Beijing's largesse would be well advised to guard against the importation of this constitutional model.

As previously discussed, the Basic Law promises Hong Kong a slate of liberal institutions, including a "high degree of autonomy," a liberal human rights regime in accordance with the ICCPR, and the rule of law guarded by independent and final common law courts. The Basic Law further promises the "ultimate aim" of "universal suffrage."[7] In this context, the guarantee of independent common law courts only makes sense if it aims to afford the liberal foundation for legal checks on official power, along with human rights enforcement.

The repressive policies now being executed under the NSL and related laws are discussed in this and the following chapter. This chapter emphasizes the impact in areas related to the legal processes. It considers the legal institutions important to a liberal constitutional order under the following headings: degrading criminal justice under the national security law, aggressive prosecutions under related laws, undercutting judicial independence, and targeting lawyers. The following chapter will then take up the ways basic freedoms are implicated. The comprehensiveness of this affront to Hong Kong's historically liberal constitutional order cannot be overemphasized. The hollowing out of electoral institutions under new electoral amendments to the Basic Law will then be discussed in chapter 10.

Degrading Criminal Justice under the National Security Law

Without question, what has shocked Hong Kong people and horrified the global community since the crackdown began in 2019 has been the aggressive criminal prosecutions that have targeted freedom of expression in all its forms. With approximately 260 reported national security arrests and over 160 prosecutions so far—for which the government disturbingly claims a 100 percent conviction rate—the chilling effect on free expression has been breathtaking.[8] Nearly 3,000 prosecutions under other public order laws have greatly added to the chill. In the face of this onslaught one of the most politically vibrant cities in the world has largely gone silent. The four NSL crimes, a variety of public order laws, and the colonial-era Sedition Ordinance have all been used to silence opposition voices. In this section we focus more specifically on several prominent NSL prosecutions and their impact on the criminal justice process.[9] Other cases will come up under other headings below.

Failings in the judicial process quickly emerged from the NSL's textual limitations discussed in the previous chapter. This was apparent in several cases either in trial or pre-trial following the imposition of the NSL. The government's enforcement effort began immediately the next day after the NSL's imposition during the traditional July 1 protests—conducted annually on the anniversary of Hong Kong's handover. With such vague statutory language and no advanced consultation over the text of the new law, ordinary people could not have understood its comprehensive nature. There were ten NSL arrests of protesters that first day, along with several hundred other arrests under preexisting laws regulating public order.

The most prominent NSL arrest that day, and the first NSL prosecution to go to trial, was the arrest of Tong Ying-kit. As mentioned previously, Tong, a young protester, was arrested after running his motorcycle into police cordons near a protest site while carrying a flag containing a slogan widely used during the 2019 protests, "Liberate Hong Kong, revolution of our times." The three-judge panel, allowed under the NSL in lieu of and after denial of a jury, convicted him under NSL article 21 of inciting subversion, and article 24 of terrorism. He was sentenced to nine years in jail.[10] There was no evidence that he intended or in fact incited anyone, nor that he inspired terror.[11]

The lengthy Tong judgment made no mention of human rights, nor of the applicable international human rights standard for incitement in national security cases.[12] The international standard, best articulated in the Johannesburg Principles, principle 6, requires that the speaker "intended to incite imminent violence (and was) likely to incite such violence."[13] Comparative case law in other common law jurisdictions imposes a similar standard of intended imminent unlawful action and its likelihood of occurrence.[14] Adding insult to injury, the trial court later assessed costs of HK$1.38 million against Tong for two pretrial legal bids, one to be released pretrial under a petition for *habeas corpus*, and the second challenging the denial of a jury under an NSL provision providing a three-judge panel as an alternative; he lost.[15] Sadly, Tong later chose not to appeal, leaving this damaging judgment untested. Of further concern, Tong in custody would later be paraded on a police-produced mainland style TV show where he would blame his behavior on his having been swayed by society's atmosphere.[16]

Other prosecutions under the NSL have generally involved political speech alone, with no allegations of violence.[17] Several of the pending cases have targeted the media. Most notorious among these was the previously mentioned August 2020 arrest and prosecution under the NSL of Jimmy Lai, the publisher of *Apple Daily*, along with several top members of the paper's management and editorial staffs and three related companies.[18]

Lai's case quickly found its way to the Court of Final Appeal (CFA) on an appeal of his bail application. Denying him bail, the CFA upheld the presumption against bail in NSL, article 42, ruling that it had no power to review the constitutionality of the NSL as a national law.[19] The judgment treated the NSL presumption against bail as an "exception" to the normal common law presumption in favor of bail. The common law presumption is based on the principle that a criminal defendant is innocent until proven guilty. Presumably, other human rights offended in the NSL text are likely to also be deemed exceptions beyond judicial challenge. As an addendum to this bail limitation, due to new legislation allowing the government to appeal acquittals by an NSL three-judge panel, defendants may even find themselves denied bail after already being found not guilty pending the government's appeal.[20]

As previously noted, prosecutors eventually charged Jimmy Lai and the others under the NSL with two counts of conspiracy to collude with foreign forces and one count of colluding with foreign forces; a sedition charge under the colonial sedition law was added later.[21] The cases for all defendants were moved for trial to the Court of First Instance, commonly referred to as the High Court, to be heard by a three-judge panel, the secretary for justice having taken the liberty under the NSL to remove the right to a jury, a cherished right in Hong Kong.[22] With Lai's six colleagues all pleading guilty to the collusion charges, Lai and the three companies finally went on trial on December 18, 2023, by which time Lai had languished in prison denied bail for over three years awaiting trial.[23] The companies face the same conspiracy and sedition charges, with Lai obviously the main target.

Raising further questions about the government's commitment to justice, the Department of Justice sought to bar Lai from being represented by UK barrister Timothy Owen but lost its challenge on pretrial appeal to the Court of Final

Appeal (CFA).[24] Senior common law lawyers from other jurisdictions are routinely admitted in Hong Kong on a case bases to represent clients or the government where their expertise is desired. The government, apparently uncomfortable with the attention a prominent UK barrister would bring to the case, requested the NPC Standing Committee to overturn the CFA and bar foreign lawyers from such NSL cases.[25]

In its first interpretation of the NSL in December 2022, the NPC Standing Committee overruled the CFA, ruling that the Hong Kong chief executive and the city's national security committee had the final say on any right of a foreign defense lawyer to appear in any matter involving national security.[26] The NPCSC interpretation appeared to suggest that the Chief Executive and the NSL Committee would have the final say on whether any matter involves national security, suggesting implications beyond simply the hiring of counsel. On the issue of foreign counsel, the government subsequently put forth, and the Legislative Council unanimously passed amendments to the Practitioners Ordinance to impose such rule.[27] Lai then asked the High Court to nevertheless allow his foreign counsel, which the court promptly rejected, noting that under the NSL, the court lacks jurisdiction to review the NSL committee's decision refusing his request.[28]

All the defendants in the *Apple Daily* case, as further discussed below, also face one count of conspiracy to print, publish, sell, offer for sale, distribute, display, or reproduce seditious publications, a charge added in December 2021.[29] The sedition charge is presumably being used to reach activities that occurred before the enactment of the NSL. Its use may have been encouraged as well by presuming some greater ease in prosecuting this traditional common law crime. The NSL collusion charge can net up to life in prison while the maximum sentence under the colonial sedition law is two years. While not yet clear, these charges presumably relate to publications in the newspaper that were critical of the NSL and that encouraged foreign solicitude.

Another set of lawyers representing Lai in London, in a petition to the UN special rapporteur on freedom of opinion and expression, noted that, overall, he risks "spending the rest of his life in prison for making speeches seeking to defend press freedom, democracy and the rule of law in Hong Kong."[30] While Lai has languished in jail awaiting trial the freezing of his newspaper's assets has resulted in its closure. Since being denied bail, Lai has been sentenced to twenty months in jail over various protest-related cases, including a 2020 banned Tiananmen vigil. As previously noted, he has further been sentenced to five years and nine months for alleged fraud in a landlord-tenant case.

Equally notorious has been the ongoing prosecution of forty-seven opposition politicians for conducting an unofficial primary election in 2020 to select the best candidates for the then planned Legislative Council election, along with a plan to then use their hoped-for majority to force the chief executive to step down. The targeted election was later officially postponed pending Beijing's electoral overhaul.

The prosecution seemingly alleges that merely taking part in this primary election constitutes the conspiracy element, and that forcing the chief executive's resignation under the Basic Law requirement relating to budget approval would amount to subversion.[31] The latter involved the organizers plan to use a Legislative Council majority to repeatedly vote down the government's budget, which, under Basic Law, article 52, can lead to a requirement that the chief executive resign.

Among the defendants, Professor Benny Tai has seemingly been the target of the most serious charges. In the trial that began in February 2022, the prosecution appears fixated on private statements made by Tai to his primary colleagues characterizing majority control of the Legislative Council as a "lethal constitutional weapon" that could cause "mass destruction," accompanied by government witness testimony that Tai tried to "politicize" the district councils and radicalize the movement.[32] That such polemical language may just be the ordinary hyperbole of politics protected as free expression is dismissed. The prosecution goes further, claiming Hong Kong's stability and livelihood could have been "gravely affected."[33]

The primary aimed to overcome the bias against the opposition built into the then existing electoral model by strategically consolidating electoral support. Though the pan-democratic opposition had consistently won nearly 60 percent of the popular vote, due to the system's design, they had never been able to hold sufficient seats to block most government initiatives, except for matters requiring a two-thirds vote.

Following the lifting of a media ban on court reporting on August 18, it was reported that five of the 47 defendants were to be prosecuted as major organizers, suggesting that they would be in the category of "principal offender," subject under NSL, article 22, to sentencing of ten years to life if convicted. "Active participants" face three to ten years, while "other participants" face less than three years. The five facing the most serious charge includes Tai, who had conceived the idea of a primary, and Au Nok-hin, a former legislator and chair of the Democratic Party. Seemingly hoping to knock time off any sentence, Au later plead guilty and agreed to testify for the prosecution.[34]

As stated by Maya Wang in a Human Rights Watch report, these prosecutions of the 47 appear to be "part of the Chinese government's relentless efforts to smother Hong Kong's democracy movement," showing "Beijing's utter contempt for both democratic political processes and the rule of law."[35] It seems only in Hong Kong that the opposition simply seeking to defeat the government in accordance with provisions in the Basic Law results in criminal prosecutions. Not only are these tactics provided for in the Basic Law, but the universal suffrage the candidates ultimately sought is also provided for in the Basic Law. With thirty-three of the defendants having remained in jail and denied bail for nearly three years after their initial arrests and charge,[36] it seems the Department of Justice found a way to lock up the government's opponents without trial.[37]

Another case highlights the youth of many being prosecuted in Hong Kong. In late 2022 five children—one only fifteen years old—were convicted under the NSL and sentenced to three years' detention for abetting "armed revolution."[38] They were accused of being part of a twenty-strong group called Returning Valiant that organized street booths and press briefings, labeling themselves "embers of revolution." The UN OHCHR expressed outrage at the conviction, noting the violation of fundamental rights and freedoms guaranteed both by the ICCPR and the Convention on the Rights of the Child, both to which Hong Kong is a party.[39] One can certainly doubt if any audience to their youthful statements would in fact have been incited to imminent action in accordance with human rights standards.

The list of NSL arrests and prosecutions is long, with room for only these three examples here.

With long periods in jail and virtually no chance of prevailing at trial, there has been a rash of guilty pleas in national security cases by defendants presumably hoping for sentence reductions. The near certainty of conviction, and prolonged pretrial detentions, appear to have worn down the will of many of those being held. Twenty-nine of the above noted forty-seven are now reportedly among those pleading guilty, including Tai and Au.[40] With guilty pleas opening the possibility under Hong Kong law of a one-third reduction in sentence, a defendant who sees little chance of winning may judge it better to avoid the ordeal of a trial and plead guilty.

Aggressive Prosecutions under Related Laws

The NSL and the previous 2019 crackdown have seemingly encouraged an aggressive approach to prosecutions under a variety of preexisting colonial laws related to public order and rioting, and even under the long-neglected colonial-era sedition law. This was all presumably done with the same objective of intimidating and silencing political opposition. A recent excellent forensic report by the Georgetown University Center for Asian Law focuses on the first two years of the current crackdown from mid-2019 to mid-2021, highlighting the government's new aggressive posture toward enforcing the Public Order Ordinance, including mass arrest (over 10,000) and mass prosecutions (nearly 3,000 up to 2023); more aggressive use of the more severe crimes under the Public Order Ordinance, including unlawful assembly and rioting charges; the aggressive targeting of anyone on the streets in the vicinity of protests; aggressive demands for incarceration with lengthy prison terms; and aggressive appeals when the prosecution falls short of achieving its demands.[41] This contrasts with the historical Hong Kong tradition of solicitude toward free speech rights. The report highlights how the courts have abandoned those traditions with much higher conviction rates and harsher prison sentences.

A concerning trend has related to a pattern of delayed prosecutions, sometimes waiting until a young person, who had been arrested during the 2019 protests, attempts to leave Hong Kong. They may be stopped at the airport and then belatedly charged and prosecuted. Of the 182 convictions for the November 2019 protests at Polytechnic University, for example, seventeen were convicted in 2021, seventy-two in 2022, and ninety-three in 2023.[42]

Given process delays, reports of convictions for prior protest activities continue unabated. Some of these prosecutions have appeared to be score-settling against some of the older democratic politicians, including many who long advocated for nonviolence both prior to and during the 2019 protests. In my interviews of pandemocrats and activists in December 2019, I found that nearly all the old-guard democrats were then advocating nonviolence and, in fact, were not that active in the 2019 protests. Nevertheless, many of the most prominent older democratic leaders have since been prosecuted and convicted under the public order or related charges, including such prominent, internationally known leaders like Martin Lee (the father of Hong Kong's democracy movement), Margaret Ng, Lee Chuek-yan, Albert Ho, Yeung Sum, and many others. Martin Lee and Margaret Ng were effectively under house arrest—having received eleven-month sentences, suspended for two years—while the others were simply sent to prison. The Hong Kong Democracy Council currently list over 1,600 political prisoners in its Hong Kong political prisoner's database.[43]

Such aggressive public order prosecutions have caused many activists and politicians to flee abroad. A notorious case involved twelve Hongkongers who had set off to Taiwan by boat to avoid prosecution on public order charges, and who were then apprehended in mainland waters and imprisoned on the mainland. Eventually, when they were released and upon their return they were arrested and sentenced in Hong Kong to an additional ten months in jail for perverting the course of justice.[44] For some, such a sentence would be in addition to sentencing for any other charges for which they had fled.

Two of the twelve, activist Andy Li and paralegal Chan Tsz-wah, have pled guilty to a charge of conspiring to collude with Jimmy Lai to call for foreign sanctions on Hong Kong. With their sentencing held off until after the Jimmy Lai trial, Li is expected to eventually testify against Lai in his planned 80-day trial which began on December 18, 2023.[45] A recent *Washington Post* report has drawn attention to the mistreatment Andy Li experienced during his incarceration both on the mainland and in Hong Kong, raising question about the reliability of his planned testimony.[46] Their earlier confessions implicated Jimmy Lai and his former colleague Mark Simon, though their confessions alone cannot be used in Lai's trial.

The sedition charge, which was added to the Jimmy Lai prosecutions, has also been used frequently in other national security prosecutions—reportedly over sixty cases so far.[47] It was, for example, used to target five members of the General Union of Speech Therapists, who published three children's picture books showing wolves attacking sheep in a village; the government judged itself to be the wolves. In a pretrial appeal, the CFA upheld applying the same NSL bail standard to deny bail under the Sedition Ordinance, citing national security as the basis.[48] The long pretrial detentions sedition defendants face when they are denied bail are especially anomalous when you consider that the maximum sentence for sedition is two years. Defendants denied bail will have practically served the maximum sentence before trial!

In the trial court's late 2022 final judgment in the sheep case, the court essentially adopted the government's three main justifications for vigorously employing the sedition law.[49] First, instead of applying the international human rights standard requiring that the speaker intend violence and that it be likely to occur, as articulated in the Johannesburg Principles and previously employed by the Indian Supreme Court, the court claimed common law sedition did not require violence. Second, the court, while citing a similar set of principles, the Siracusa Principles, to justify its defense of sovereignty, ignored in this government rebranding of the 2019 protests similar human rights limits those principles impose. The position of the prosecution, and ultimately the court, was that such limitations are not appropriate for Hong Kong, as an exceptional case. It appears after the CFA judgment in the Jimmy Lai bail case Hong Kong human rights exceptionalism has taken root.

Finally, the judgment in the sheep case articulated a factual premise that clearly underlies the current vigorous official crackdown, essentially crediting tens of thousands of of 2019 protesters with seditious intent to overthrow the government and gain independence. With such a premise, it then applies guilt by association to the authors of the sheep books for supporting the 2019 protests through the explanations in the books. That most protesters, in promoting the five demands, merely demanded compliance with the Basic Law and the rule of law is ignored. Under this logic, the government takes no responsibility for provoking the protests, and a simple children's fairy tale explaining the protests results in a stiff prison sentence.

The prospect of reigning in the Hong Kong government's repressive zeal in this area presumably awaits a future human rights challenge in the CFA. Whether the NSL will be judged to have created an exceptional human rights standard with regard to sedition can only be surmised. As evident in a recent *Washington Post* editorial on the sheep case, the world will be watching to see if this absurd conviction is upheld.[50] The speech therapists were each ultimately sentenced to nineteen months in prison. Two speech therapists, Lorie Lai and Samuel Chan, have applied to appeal their conviction.[51] As if jailing the publishers of the sheep book were not enough, the police struck again in March 2023 by arresting two middle-aged men for merely for possessing these "seditious" children's books, which had apparently been mailed from the UK.[52]

It appears that any prosecution related to alleged national security claims, including sedition, will also encounter the previously mentioned NSL procedural limitations as matters involving national security. Similar colonial-era sedition laws in other jurisdictions, including before India's top court, have been suspended as outdated, "not in tune with the current social milieu."[53] Sixty years earlier, the Indian Supreme Court had required that any sedition charge be linked to calls for violence. In its latest ruling, the Indian Supreme Court reportedly did not overturn the law but suggested that the parliament suspend it.

Though it has considered procedural requirements, the CFA has not considered the boundaries of sedition with regard to the human rights guarantees in the Basic Law. As pointed out by Hong Kong civil rights lawyer Angeline Chan in an important commentary, the first reasoned judgment regarding the sedition conviction of activist radio host Tam Tak-chi, also known as "Fast Beat," did not even consider the core human rights issues under the Basic Law.[54] Tam had shouted common protest slogans and attacked the national security law, the police, and the Chinese Communist Party. His conviction is under appeal.

In finding Tam guilty of eleven charges, District Court Judge Stanley Chan Kwong-chi simply ruled that insulting or verbally abusing the Hong Kong government amounts to a challenge against Beijing's authority, and thus sedition, and that the sedition offense under the Crimes Ordinance is constitutional.[55] This judgment is surprising in that it is widely believed that the sedition law had not been used in decades because of doubts about its compliance with Basic Law and ICCPR human rights guarantees. That the government now claims a 100 percent conviction rate in its renewed use of the sedition law, is a sad testimonial to the shrinking space for free expression in Hong Kong.[56]

As Angeline Chan points out, the previously established Hong Kong constitutional principle requires that restrictions on fundamental human rights (a) must be prescribed by law and (b) must pass a proportionality test. To be prescribed by law, it must be adequately accessible and sufficiently precise for a person to know what is prohibited. Proportionality goes to a proper purpose, with no more restriction than is necessary. As Chan notes, the district court in the Tam case seemed unconcerned that language in the sedition law, such as "bring into hatred or contempt," "to raise discontent or disaffection," or "to promote feelings of ill-will and enmity," lacked sufficient precision. Judge Chan seemed content that the court could assign ordinary meaning to these vague words.

The NSL appears to be only the first step in the downward spiral respecting speech-related freedoms in Hong Kong. In this regard the government has set upon a plan to enact article 23 legislation, "on its own" as specified in the Basic Law, to regulate treason, secession, theft of state secrets, and activities by foreign political groups. While the government's draft proposal at this writing is still awaited, based on some government statements and what we have seen so far under the NSL, we can predict several problems likely in the new legislation. On the process front, Secretary for Justice Paul Lam has already declared that the stricter bail rules under the NSL will also apply to the planned local legislation.[57] As we have seen in relation to enforcement of the colonial sedition law, we might expect, not just bail rules but all the NSL process limitation discussed here will equally apply to the new legislation, simply on the basis of it likewise being categorized as national security legislation. Beyond legal procedures, other risks are apparent. The secretary for security has announced that such a law will especially target espionage as well as some vague notion of "soft resistance and internet loopholes."[58] This surely signals that the language of the new legislation will likely suffer the same vagueness concerns evident in the NSL. I personally worry that the language on official secrets will take a very broad approach, much like the mainland, thereby putting academic and media research at risk. Without evidence, Beijing has long blamed foreign interference for Hong Kong protests. If mainland influence prevails in the law's content, will Hong Kong NGOs and universities face increased scrutiny over any foreign contacts or support? Will university faculty collaborations with foreign institutes suddenly be branded as prohibited foreign political activities? The track record so far offers little evidence to justify an expectation of official restraint.

Further Undercutting Judicial Independence

As discussed in the previous chapter, on its face, the NSL reflects Beijing's profound distrust of Hong Kong's historically independent judiciary and legal profession. What has unfolded in practice demonstrates that distrust even more. This has been evident in the many attacks on judges handling NSL and other protest-related cases. As previously noted, NSL, article 44, provides that only judges designated by the chief executive can hear NSL cases, and, further, that a judge who makes any statement officials believe offends national security can be removed from designated status.

In a recent statement, the mainland director of the newly established Office for Safeguarding National Security in Hong Kong left little doubt that the intention was in fact to compromise judicial independence. He noted that Hong Kong's "independent judiciary's power is authorized by the National People's Congress." In his view, the judiciary must "highly manifest the national will and national interest, or else it will lose the legal premise of the authorization."[59] This statement does not appear to exclude nonpolitical or business-related cases from such national will—and presumed mainland oversight. An investor will certainly want to take such risks into account, especially in cases involving intellectual property, or where the opponent is a mainland state-owned enterprise (SOE).[60] These have tended be sensitive areas in Hong Kong mainland relations.

Long before the imposition of the NSL, mainland officials had expressed reservations about Hong Kong courts carrying out constitutional judicial review, insisting there was no separation of powers in Hong Kong. The 2014 white paper on "one country, two systems" referred to judges as administrative officials and admonished them to actively guard national security.[61] In spite of such criticisms and admonitions, the Hong Kong courts then continued a rich tradition of judicial review and ignored such attacks, producing the many cases that have shaped Hong Kong's constitutional landscape.

Since the imposition of the NSL, Beijing has become more assertive, openly attacking judges for dismissing public order charges or granting bail in national security cases. Most famously, in the above noted Jimmy Lai bail decision, the *People's Daily* branded Lai a dangerous criminal and appeared to threaten to transfer the Lai case to a mainland court if the CFA granted bail.[62] This was no idle threat, as NSL, article 55, opens the door to such transfers to the mainland by the Office for Safeguarding National Security if mainland officials judge the case sufficiently complex.

A key path under the Basic Law to underpin judicial independence has been a practice of inviting prominent foreign judges to serve on the Hong Kong CFA as nonpermanent judges. Even before this arrangement, Hong Kong long had a tradition of employing qualified lawyers from other common law jurisdictions to sit as regular judges in the ordinary courts. This was further backed up by appeal to the Privy Council (then the UK's highest court) during the colonial period. Many such ordinary judges remained in their tenure after the handover.

With the post-handover creation of the local CFA to replace the Privy Council as the highest court, the Basic Law sought to sustain confidence in the rule of law by including nonpermanent appointments of eminent foreign judges to the CFA, often including the leading judges of the highest common law courts. With the perceived degrading effect of the NSL on judicial independence, questions arose whether such foreign judges should continue to serve in this role. The initial answer appeared to be yes. While an Australian judge withdrew, all the others initially remained, apparently in the hope that their presence would push back against the feared diminution of judicial independence.

As the situation further degraded, however, the verdict started to shift when two judges of Britain's Supreme Court, Robert Reed and Patrick Hodge, with the encouragement of the British government, resigned in March 2022. They cited Hong Kong's departure under the NSL "from values of political freedom, and freedom of expression."[63] This put pressure on the remaining foreign judges from Canada, Australia, and Britain to resign, but nine announced their intention to continue, in a perhaps vain hope they can sustain their restraining role.[64]

An eminent group of international jurists, including former UK Attorney General Robert Buckland, have challenged this in an international legal opinion, warning that these nonpermanent foreign judges are being used by the Hong Kong government as an undeserved vote of confidence. The opinion warns further that they are operating in an environment where judicial independence has been wholly compromised and where the CCP can dictate the outcome of cases.[65] They argue the degradation will intensify. Given that nonpermanent judges will likely be excluded from national security cases, the hoped-for restraining influence of such judges may be sparse.

Criticisms regarding the degradation of judicial independence and the rule of law are being met by the government with a public relations campaign encouraged by John Lee, the new chief executive. Tasked with such promotion, Paul Lam, the new secretary for justice, has proclaimed his intention to "speak up about the city's claimed high degree of rule of law."[66] He shared his plan to enlist retired judges, business leaders, and expatriates to help convince overseas audiences that the rule of law remains robust. This public relations campaign extends beyond lawyers to international businesses, with a planned annual conference engaging international corporate leaders to project the officially desired image that Hong Kong is open for business, a message that also emphasizes the city's acclaimed rule of law, a message that has earned NGO pushback against corporate participants.[67]

The government's hard sell is falling on increasingly deaf ears, with Moody's recently switching Hong Kong to a negative credit rating, commenting as follows: "Following signs of reduced autonomy of Hong Kong's political and judiciary institutions, notably with the imposition of a National Security Law in 2020 and changes to Hong Kong's electoral system, Moody's expects further erosion of the (city's) autonomy of political, institutional and economic decisions to continue incrementally."[68]

Lam appeared in part to be reacting to recommendations made by the US Congressional-Executive Commission on China (CECC), calling on the White House to impose sanctions on him and sixteen other prosecutors over their role in bringing excessive prosecutions under the NSL.[69] Later, in 2023, the CECC called for similar sanctions on the prosecutors in the Hong Kong Forty-Seven case. In May 2023, the CECC escalated its objections to call for sanctions on all NSL-designated judges, arguing that the NSL had created a parallel legal system overseen by such designated judges.[70] Lam's response to the CECC calls was to accuse the commission of "cheap, bullying behavior" and "trampling on legal justice."[71] In the face of the current crackdown, it seems unlikely a public relations response to foreign criticism will be sufficient to restore confidence in Hong Kong's rule of law.

Targeting Lawyers

Hong Kong's historically independent legal profession has likewise come under withering attack, with mainland officials objecting to the professions' alleged political statements. What Beijing considers political, the profession has seen, until recent leadership changes, as part of its historical duty to stand up for the rule of law and Basic Law guarantees. Under Hong Kong's divided bar, the Bar Association has historically been especially outspoken in comparison to the Law Society. The Law Society, which represents solicitors and may rely more on mainland clients, has generally been less outspoken. Beijing's tolerance of such a guardian role greatly diminished after the passage of the NSL. The *People's Daily* has referred to the Bar Association as a "street rat," and ahead of the 2021 leadership elections, it admonished both branches to stay out of politics, a view echoed by Hong Kong's then secretary for justice.[72]

The Bar Association had historically elected outspoken leaders. The most recent, the human rights lawyer Paul Harris, was a frequent target of Beijing's wrath, especially when he had the temerity to suggest revisions of the NSL to bring it into compliance with the Basic Law. Harris would eventually be called in to meet with police, which he viewed as an implied threat. He left Hong Kong for the UK the same day.[73]

The pressure targeting the 2021 Law Society and Bar Association leadership elections implied that their official roles in the Judicial Officers Recommendation Commission might be lost if they did not toe the line. The seriousness of this threat was evident in the refusal over the previous five months of the chief executive to confirm the appointment of the bar's nominee to that seat.[74] Taking such threats to heart, both organizations elected more moderate leaders from the pro-establishment camp, who avowed that they would stay out of politics, though they would speak up regarding the rule of law.[75] The boundary between politics and the rule of law remains unclear. It now appears that the new Beijing-friendly Bar Association leaders have enjoyed consultations with Beijing officials and "ice-breaking" trips to Beijing that had long been denied.[76]

The Law Society is traveling on a similar path. The August 2022 vote ousting Mark Daly, a leading human rights lawyer, from the Law Society's governing council certainly portended less attention to human rights.[77] Daly, who had previously gotten the most votes in the council election, got the least votes this time. He had long been a leading light on human rights issues in the governing council.

Official hostility toward outspokenness in the profession was earlier evident when the legislator who was elected to represent the legal professions in the Legislative Council, Dennis Kwok, was disqualified and expelled from the body on November 11, 2020, under Beijing pressure—along with three other Legislative Council members.[78] This especially related to his use of a filibuster to block proposed legislation that would make it a crime to disrespect the national anthem. All opposition members then resigned in protest at the expulsions, and the legislation was eventually enacted.

Public oriented lawyers' organizations that have defended the protesters also felt the heat. The Progressive Lawyers Group and the 612 Humanitarian Relief Fund, an organization set up to provide legal support for arrested protesters, were both placed under investigation in 2021 and effectively forced to disband.[79] The five board members of the 612 Humanitarian Relief Fund were later arrested for their legal relief efforts. The five included Hong Kong's ninety-year-old, highly respected senior Catholic cardinal and former head of the Hong Kong Catholic Church, Cardinal Joseph Zen, as well as prominent barrister Margaret Ng, who had long served as the legal professions representative in the Legislative Council.[80] The five were accused of conspiring to collude with foreign forces in violation of the NSL, though they have yet to be charged under the NSL. Instead, in a September 2022 trial, they faced the rather spurious charge of failing to register the 612 Fund under the Societies Ordinance.[81]

Amnesty International condemned the "callous disregard for basic rights" as a "shocking escalation" of repression.[82] The national security police have even targeted the lawyers who worked with the 612 Fund to provide legal services to arrested protesters, filing complaints with the professional organizations for both solicitors and barristers, claiming they took funds while claiming to provide these services pro bono.[83] As a result, the Bar Association then probed thirty-five barristers who were accused of receiving such funds directly, not through solicitors, as generally required under the code of conduct.[84] These attacks on lawyers doing human rights work smack of similar attacks on human rights defenders mentioned earlier on the mainland.

Criminal defense has also felt the heat, as government-funded legal aid services have been revised under new guidelines that appear to impinge on a defendant's right to choose their preferred counsel.[85] Clearly, one of the most vibrant legal professions in the world has been tamed, and along with it, important guardians of Hong Kong's liberal constitutional order and basic freedoms have been taken off the field.

Silenced

9

THE NSL, POLITICAL CONTROL, AND THE ASSAULT ON FREEDOM

The 2020 Beijing imposed Hong Kong National Security Law (NSL) poses a threat to basic freedoms that extends well beyond the criminal justice and rule of law concerns discussed in the previous chapter. With nearly all NSL prosecutions relating to freedom of expression, in one form or another, the NSL represents a substantive threat to nearly all the core freedoms cherished in an open society. It represents the ultimate result for ordinary people of Beijing's imposition of its favored illiberal model on Hong Kong, and at the same time a textbook on the wider risks of such illiberal trend. In the face of the prosecutions highlighted in the previous chapter, open public protests and human rights advocacy against these draconian policies have largely gone silent. A tactic of targeting a few prominent speakers to silence the many so far appears to be working. Public speakers and protesters are typically prepared to endure arrest and a few weeks in jail as a price of speaking truth to power. But with convictions in national security cases and even public order cases routinely involving years in prison, and for the former possibly life in prison, the official message encouraging silence is coming through loud and clear.

Free expression in general, and academic and media freedoms in particular, are clearly among Beijing's primary targets under the NSL. Beyond the dramatic media intimidation inherent in prosecutions under the four vaguely defined crimes of secession, subversion, terrorist activities and collusion, NSL, article 9, requires the Hong Kong government "to strengthen public communication, guidance, supervision and regulation over matters concerning national security, including those relating to schools, universities, social organizations, the media, and the internet." NSL, article 10, requires the government "to promote national security education in the schools and universities . . . the media," and otherwise in society at large. NSL, article 54, directs the Office for Safeguarding National Security to "take necessary measures to strengthen the management of and services for," among other entities, "news agencies of foreign countries." So far, the official effort has shown no sensitivity for preserving Hong Kong's historically vibrant public advocacy and media culture.

The maintenance of Hong Kong's liberal constitutional order, in the absence of democracy, historically depended largely on a free press, academic freedom, and an informed and engaged civil society. All have been severely damaged by the NSL and the resurrected colonial-era sedition law. This chapter addresses this substantive and comprehensive assault on basic freedoms under the following headings: news media in Beijing's crosshairs, books and film censorship, social media and cybersecurity, academic freedom under stress, hollowing out freedom of association, freedom to protest, civil society silenced, and freedom lost. Populist and authoritarian leaders around the world will surely find inspiration in this evolving Beijing model for silencing and controlling critics in erstwhile open societies.

News Media in Beijing's Crosshairs

Hong Kong, once the bastion of press freedom in Asia, slipped from eighteenth in the Reporters Without Borders world press freedom ranking in 2002 to 148th in 2022.[1] While it had begun to slip after the crackdown on the 2014 and 2019 protests, the most dramatic plunge—seventy places in a single year—unambiguously followed the 2020 imposition of the NSL and the subsequent revival of the colonial-era anti-sedition law, which has been used to target journalists with arrests and intimidation. Local satisfaction with press freedom has tracked these international assessments, dropping to a record low in 2022.[2] In a 2022 Hong Kong Journalists Association (HKJA) survey of press freedom, 97 percent of Hong Kong media workers found that press freedom had gotten worse, with 53 percent of the public feeling the same.[3]

Supplemented by the colonial-era Sedition Ordinance, the government wasted no time taking up Beijing's NSL agenda. The most prominent opposition newspaper, the *Apple Daily*, was quickly targeted with arrests, prosecutions, asset freezing, and closure. *Stand News* soon followed. Two senior editors and others at the online newspaper were charged with "conspiring to publish seditious publications," and the company's assets were frozen.[4] A subsequent arrest of Allan Au, a contributing columnist at *Stand News*, followed under the same sedition charge.[5] In a trial that stretched on for months, the *Stand News* editors would be grilled in court about the credibility of reported police brutality reports and opinion articles published by the paper.[6]

The sedition charge has become a convenient substitute for charges under the NSL, targeting both the news media and ordinary speakers. After the special NSL police unit abusively charged six defendants with sedition for clapping in court, Amnesty International proclaimed, "There is no context in which the act of clapping should be considered a crime."[7] Adding to the seriousness of such a turn, the sedition charge has already been brought under the umbrella of the NSL, with courts applying the NSL's presumption against bail and other NSL procedural rules to all cases involving charges related to national security.[8] This effectively gives the NSL procedures a retroactive effect, even if the statute itself is not supposed to be retroactive.

In a media crackdown that has put over one thousand journalists out of work, other online outlets closed in 2021. The online *Citizen's News* closed down rather than risk the fate of *Stand News*.[9] Smaller outfits soon followed, including *Rice Post*, *Mad Dog Daily*, and *White Night*,[10] with *Factwire* following in 2022.[11] Another online publication, *Passion Times*, originally founded by the now defunct political organization Civic Passion, was warned to remove allegedly sensitive postings left from 2016 on its website.[12] As with NSL procedural rules, treating such earlier statements that remain in the public space as ongoing NSL violations is another way of giving the NSL a retroactive effect.

The *Hong Kong Free Press* has assembled a long list of the many press freedom incidents since the enactment of the NSL.[13] Among the many problems faced is an unexplained practice of excluding many registered digital media outlets, including wire services and the *Hong Kong Free Press*, from official events.[14] Another practice is simply to intimidate publishers by publicly attacking output that criticizes government policy. Most notorious in this regard was the attack on Hong Kong's most eminent cartoonist, Wong Kei-kwan, aka Zunzi, who had for decades published political cartoons in the *Ming Pao* and *Apple Daily*. This official attack quickly resulted in his firing and, soon after, the removal of his many books from Hong Kong public libraries.[15]

In spite of such threats to media freedom, a number of small Chinese-language online media, some started by former *Apple Daily* reporters, have sprung up largely under the radar and continue to resist the government's narrative.[16] These typically focus on narrow areas, ranging from community culture to feature writing or photojournalism, and they may publish through traditional online services such as Facebook, YouTube, or Instagram, though some still distribute directly to subscribers. Whether these publications based on social media will survive the ongoing crackdown being applied to social media more generally is yet to be determined. They do, however, represent an underlying continuing struggle by civil society voices to be heard, as was recently featured in a US congressional hearing and report that assembled interviews across the grassroots sector.[17]

Even RTHK, the government's highly respected public broadcaster that was built on the model of the BBC, has been targeted for containment. Pro-Beijing forces in Hong Kong have long had RTHK in their crosshairs, arguing that a public broadcaster funded with tax dollars should merely be the government's mouthpiece. Efforts to reign in its critical news coverage had resulted in the dismissal of prominent freelancers, no doubt including myself, who brought a critical edge to news and opinion. With the introduction of the NSL, the public broadcaster's media space closed dramatically. Public trust in RTHK likewise went down dramatically, as reflected in a Reuters Institute survey.[18]

In early 2021, a government administrative officer without media experience was appointed to the top RTHK position, as the director of broadcasting, followed in late 2022 with another administrative officer taking up the post.[19] The first appointment was followed by the issuance of lengthy new editorial guidelines imposing strict adherence to NSL requirements and direct top-down editorial control.[20]

Critical public broadcasting coverage of government behavior, especially relating to the national security crackdown, has now been severely muted, with a number of RTHK talk shows on sensitive topics being axed and prominent journalists being fired.[21] Carrie Lam, who was then Hong Kong chief executive, even proudly announced that RTHK will be partnered with the PRC's state-run CCTV so that programming will "nurture a stronger sense of patriotism."[22] With a large portion of the population depending on the public broadcaster for news and information, a major liberal check on official behavior has been taken off the field.[23] Critical outside contributors are no longer invited for comment on these controversial issues. Personally, after years as a regular contributor under contract with RTHK, I am no longer called in for my periodic commentary on the RTHK morning news program, *Hong Kong Today*, nor invited, outside such contract, to join *Back Chat*, as I was frequently in the past.

The HKJA has also been targeted. Some of Hong Kong's most respected journalists have led the organization, long the chief watchdog on media freedom. Its current head, Ronson Chan Ron-sing, has spoken out against the abuses described above. Yet, both the HKJA and the Foreign Correspondents' Club (FCC)—the organization representing the many international reporters based in Hong Kong—have felt the sting of official condemnation threatening the same sort of investigations and financial oversight that targeted *Apple Daily* and other media organizations.[24]

Under pressure from Secretary for Security Chris Tang to disclose its membership and financial records, the HKJA is reportedly considering whether it should disband.[25] Tang also accused the organization of infiltrating local schools to lure student journalists. The Beijing-controlled newspaper *Wen Wei Po* has attacked the HKJA as an "anti-government political organization," accusing it of "wantonly smearing the Hong Kong government, the police and the national security law."[26] As a consequence, the HKJA has reportedly passed amendments to its constitution that would allow it to disband more easily.[27]

As if the official attacks on the HKJA were not enough, Ronson Chan, the organization's chair, was arrested in September 2022 at a community event he was reporting on. He was charged with obstructing police for allegedly refusing to provide his ID to a police officer.[28] In Chan's account, his alleged obstruction related to him asking the police officer "which unit he comes from and to show his warrant card." He was eventually given a five day jail sentence.

An earlier ban in national security court cases on reporting statements made in pretrial committal proceedings represented one of the most severe legal restrictions on the press. As a preliminary matter, such pretrial committal proceedings consider whether the case is sufficient to justify transfer to the High Court, where a higher sentencing ceiling applies and where a jury right may arise. Such a reporting rule, available under an ordinance, is designed to allow defendants to request limits on reporting in such proceedings to avoid prejudice at trial. It was instead imposed by magistrates in all national security cases, limiting reporting to the names of defendants, magistrates, and lawyers, the alleged offense, the court's decision, whether legal aid was granted, and future court dates.

With national security prosecutions hovering over the city, this reporting ban not only deprived defendants of full public proceedings where their arguments could be reported, but it also, for over two years, deprived the public at large of a needed understanding of the national security law and its impact on the system of justice. With vague legislation, judicial proceedings might improve clarity. Thankfully, the High Court overturned this reporting ban on an appeal challenging it by human rights lawyer and national security defendant Ms. Chow Hang-tung.[29] The High Court noted that this statutorily allowed media restriction was primarily there to protect the defendant, leaving slight room for a magistrate to impose such a ban only when "strictly necessary" in the interest of justice.[30] In a display of political censorship, in a later hearing on matters relating to her national security trial, Chow Hang-tung was barred by the court from using the phrase "Tiananmen Massacre," a matter that would not have been reported under the restrictions that were lifted.[31]

If you factor in the added national security oversight to be provided by the Beijing-controlled Office for Safeguarding National Security, the silencing of news media in Hong Kong does not stop at the city's borders. The international press and its membership organization, the FCC, have also felt the heat. Sensing the danger, when the NSL was imposed, the *New York Times* quickly moved part of its operation out of town reportedly to South Korea.[32]

The pressure on the international media was most clearly on display in early 2022, when the FCC canceled its very prominent annual Human Rights Press Awards. A selection committee had already chosen the winners for the 2022 awards. Fearing awardees or the FCC itself might be targeted, FCC officers moved to head off such a risk by canceling the awards.[33] It was a telling story about the rule of law when the FCC president, Keith Richberg, justified the action, explaining that anyone targeted could not count on a fair trial.[34] It is noteworthy that the other two sponsoring organizations of the awards, the HKJA and Amnesty International, had already withdrawn. As one of the winners of such a press award for commentary in 2015, I found this cancelation personally disturbing. Many fear the voice of the FCC on media freedom has been silenced. Hong Kong's status as a base for international media is clearly under threat. Several international reporters have been denied visas to remain in the city.[35] In this environment, expats are departing at a faster pace than ever before.[36]

Books and Film Censorship

Aggressive media censorship now stretches well beyond news organizations to films, bookstores, bookfairs, libraries, and the internet. These all face strict censorship relating to national security. In an environment where major bookstores have been generally owned by mainland-controlled companies, sensitive books have long been harder to find, but now that problem goes beyond the store's own self-censorship to market-wide exclusion. There is some pushback. Start-up independent bookstores, sometimes created by former reporters who lost their jobs, have become part of Hong Kong's silent landscape, offering selections they hope to sustain under the radar.[37]

Publishers who carry sensitive books are also denied registration at popular bookfairs.[38] In 2022 an attempt by independent publishers and authors to organize an independent bookfair was nixed when the organizers were accused of breaching their property lease.[39] In 2023 they managed to pull off an independent bookfair but worried about arrest throughout.[40] Such pressures have effectively pushed publishers to avoid sensitive topics or shut down altogether, considerably narrowing the breadth of readings locally available in Hong Kong.[41]

Under pressure from the Hong Kong government, libraries have likewise stepped up efforts to root out books "manifestly contrary" to national security, even inviting public suggestions of books to be removed.[42] When many prominent titles were removed from libraries, Hong Kong Chief Executive John Lee made the rather facetious claim that this should be no problem since an interested reader could simply find the removed books in bookstores—seemingly ignoring the unlikelihood of that.[43]

Film has also felt the heat. Under the newly amended film censorship law, anyone who exhibits an unauthorized film judged to be against national security can be fined up to HK$1 million and imprisoned for up to three years. Furthermore, the Film Censorship Ordinance affords no appeal when a film is banned on national security grounds.[44] A recent film about a young gay man's struggles, *Losing Sight of a Longed Place*, was blocked because the filmmakers refused to remove a short scene depicting the 2014 umbrella movement.[45]

While they are shut down and blocked at home, Hong Kong protest films are enormously popular with the diaspora overseas. While the film *Revolution of Our Times* is presumably illegal to download or watch in the city, it sold out overseas.[46] The revolution film was screened at the Cannes Film Festival and won the prize for best documentary at Taiwan's Golden Horse Awards.

Social Media and Cybersecurity

A recent *China Digital* report highlights how social media have come under increasing pressure.[47] This has been especially true for transparency-oriented chat groups that target government accountability. This risk was apparent following the arrest for sedition of two civil servants who administered a Facebook group that shared anonymous comments about conditions in the city's civil service. Two other civil servants were then arrested for posting seditious messages on the group chat.

After these arrests, several other media transparency groups either shut down as a precaution in the face of implicit or expressed warnings or were forcefully shuttered.[48] What led to the closures is not always clear, as a message simply comes up at the link saying the site is no longer available. This has reportedly occurred for several such groups, including a Facebook page called Civil Servant Secrets, a page for sharing information about health care workers, and pages from various universities, including a page labeled "CUHK Secrets." Historically, such groups have been venues not only to share personal experiences but also to bring important issues to the public's attention through media follow-up.

A new angle on internet suppression came up over 2022–2023, when the Hong Kong government set about trying to ban a protest song, Glory to Hong Kong, which had become a defacto city anthem sang by protesters during the 2019 protest.[49] The authorities accuse singers or users of this song of subversion based inclusion in its lyrics of such phrases as "liberate Hong Kong." The government was especially incensed that foreign hosts of sporting events were finding and playing this song during medal awards as the Hong Kong national anthem instead of China's national anthem. This spawned a crackdown where some locals were arrested and sentenced to 3 months in jail for playing or circulating the song. The government specifically became concerned to stamp out the song on the internet, with various platforms, such as Google, Facebook and Youtube reportedly declining to remove it without a court order.[50]

So the government sought an open injunction against any performance or use of the song. The High Court in July 2023 surprisingly refused the injunction, citing the government's already available access to criminal sanctions under national security laws and the chilling effect on free expression.[51] That the government chose such a heavy-handed path is regrettable. Though somewhat surprising as a rare government loss in a national security case, the judgement simply tells the government to rely on the criminal sanctions already available. We might also wonder, if this judgment reflects even a small degree of judicial independence, how long it will be tolerated.

Similar closures and charges are also applied widely toward those who disseminate allegedly seditious messages online "that promote feelings of ill-will and enmity toward the government or between different classes of the population," as expressed in the previously discussed colonial-era sedition law. This is a vague standard that can be applied arbitrarily toward almost any public criticism. If such laws are combined with China's well known technical capacity for surveillance in the emerging official cooperation over national security very little online activity will escape scrutiny.

Various lawmaking efforts have sought to expand control over the internet. In 2021, the government passed an anti-doxing law, with violators facing fines of up to HK$1 million and five years in jail. The government has also begun discussing the enactment of a law on "fake news." These are both areas where internet surveillance risks overreach.[52] Eight months into the doxing law, the privacy watchdog reported it had already told fourteen social media sites to remove 3,900 doxing items from social media.[53] The proposed law on fake news especially raises legal risks for social media platforms and even independent news outlets that are trying to provide factual content.[54] Small online platforms will certainly find it difficult to police all postings and relying on judicial protection of free speech rights may be risky. Officials are especially concerned with reports on their activities and may be overzealous in attempting to silence critical platforms or reportage.

These forms of censorship especially target social media outlets such as Telegram, a popular protest site that the government may be looking to ban. As noted in the *China Digital* report cited previously, the Hong Kong police have now established an online tracker that will monitor online discussions that smear the police. Connected to this, the police have set up a special public relations wing to monitor social media, which will also put out positive propaganda to tell good stories about the police. This effort at censorship has even included blocking overseas NGO websites, including efforts to block the Hong Kong Democracy Council and Hong Kong Watch whose leaders have also been police targets.[55]

To add to this oversight and censorship, the Law Reform Commission has proposed new laws to attack cybercrime in relation to the NSL.[56] These proposed laws will cover areas of existing laws, though they may include updated language and stiffer sentences. The government had already tried to use an existing law prohibiting "access to a computer with criminal or dishonest intent" to reach such crimes, but in a pre-NSL decision in 2019, the CFA held that the existing section 161 of the Crimes Ordinance did not reach a person using their own tech devices. Before this decision, section 161 had been widely used to criminalize various computer-related speech.

The Law Reform Commission, chaired by the secretary for justice, has proposed five new cybercrime offenses: unauthorized access to program data, illegal interception of computer data, illegal interference of computer data, illegal interference of computer systems, and making available or possessing a device or data for committing a crime.[57] The patriots-only Legislative Council quickly started hearings and will likely embrace the Law Reform Commission's recommendation as an avenue to contain alleged national security threats.[58] The proposed prison sentences range from two years to life. The commission recommends worldwide jurisdiction, which has also been emphasized by legislators. The breadth of these charges certainly opens the door to abusive prosecutions relating to national security.

Charles Mok, the former Hong Kong legislator representing the information technology sector and who is now in exile, describes an environment of ever-growing internet surveillance.[59] He notes that, previously, Hong Kong had among the freest internet environments in the region. The NSL has enabled virtually unchecked internet surveillance by national security police in ways that profoundly offend principles of privacy and free speech outlined in the UN Charter of Human Rights and Principles for the Internet.[60] Citing increasing surveillance and the new laws and proposals noted above, Mok is concerned that China's great firewall may eventually grab the city, though this has still not occurred.

Academic Freedom under Stress

Academic freedom in universities and secondary schools has been among the highest impact areas targeted under the NSL. Beijing's hostility to liberal education was earlier evident in the Hong Kong government's 2012 failed attempt to impose patriotic national education through textbook revisions.[61] That effort backfired badly when protests, led mostly by secondary students, pushed back against perceived efforts at brainwashing. The fallout of government overreach would prove to be even more challenging when many of the same students went on to lead the massive protests for democracy in 2014 and for the five demands in 2019.[62] Sadly, many of these youthful protesters, often among Hong Kong's best and brightest youth, have recently been jailed or have fled the city.

Under the abovementioned NSL directives regarding the oversight of schools, the Hong Kong government has issued comprehensive new regulations that impose a tight rein on the education sector. These regulations require schools at all levels to teach national security, and they are accompanied with warnings that any violations of the NSL will be dealt with severely.[63]

Under the strict oversight of the education sector provided for in the NSL, schools have been pressed to address national security across the board in their curricula, to promote patriotism with government-prepared music videos, and to add on frequent flag-raising ceremonies and related events.[64] These coerced "patriotic" activities may remind readers of similar requirements reported about reeducation camps in Xinjiang and monasteries in Tibet, as well as across the mainland following the 1989 Tiananmen crackdown. Such efforts fail to appreciate what Hong Kong's youthful protesters understood early on: When schools no longer teach opposition political views, or when libraries cease to carry books critical of government policy, then that is no longer education; it is just indoctrination, or what is colloquially called brainwashing.

At the university level, this has meant that the faculty members who have long vigorously engaged in the public debate over human rights and democracy have largely gone silent, as have their students. The Beijing-controlled press had long characterized the universities as hotbeds of foreign intervention under such article titles (in translation) as "Exposé of Criminal Evidence of the US Employing a Thousand University Students in Hong Kong to Participate in Demonstrations as Riot 'White Rats,'" and "American Research Incites Protests, Brainwashes University Students."[65]

There really has never been any evidence to support these claims of foreign interference, which appear to be simply based on a competition of ideas. C. Y. Leung, the former Hong Kong chief executive who is now a vice-chairman of the Chinese People's Political Consultative Conference, has argued that there is no need to reveal evidence of such alleged foreign interference.[66] Despite the lack of evidence, the well-tested official mainland narrative that has long blamed foreign interference for mainland problems is now playing out in Hong Kong. This has been raised through multiple channels, including white papers, fact sheets, and even public accusations that foreigners have orchestrated a color revolution.[67] None of these official explanations consider what the protesters themselves clearly demand, which is generally some version of compliance with Beijing's prior commitments.

The foreign targets include organizations that openly provide funding for human rights promotion, such as the US National Endowment for Democracy (NED) and various international human rights NGOs such as Amnesty International or Human Rights Watch. The local NGOs that receive such funding or advocate for freedom and the rule of law are branded as being under Western influence. That these ideas promoted by students and others are core global values widely shared in Hong Kong appears particularly galling to Beijing officials.

The crackdown has vigorously gone after professors and students from the 2014 and 2019 protests. Professors Benny Tai and Kin-man Chan, who had been leaders in the 2014 "Occupy Central" democracy campaign that morphed into the Umbrella Movement, had already been convicted in early 2019 and jailed for sixteen months under a rarely used common law nuisance charge.[68] As previously discussed, Chan served his sentence immediately, but Tai would eventually lose his appeal and be sent back to jail to serve out his sentence. His conviction would result in the University of Hong Kong (HKU) firing him from his faculty position. He would later be among the forty-seven defendants prosecuted for organizing a primary election, which suggests he would be in jail and denied bail concurrent with and beyond the sentence, if he were not already serving a sentence.

Beijing-controlled media have attacked several other academics. Tai's former boss, the former HKU law faculty dean, Johannes Chan, was earlier criticized for allegedly supporting Tai.[69] Hong Kong's Public Opinion Research Institute (PORI), a private organization that has long provided surveys on public opinion, has also felt the heat. Its deputy executive director, Chung Kim-wah, months after being questioned by police about the group's involvement in the primary election, fled the city, citing "threats from powerful bodies."[70] Professor Brian Fong at the Education University likewise departed Hong Kong after being attacked in the Beijing-controlled press.[71] Justin Wong, a professor at Baptist University, though not targeted in the Beijing press, felt similar threats and left Hong Kong after his article in an academic journal on the use of visual arts in the 2019 protest attracted similar national security scrutiny.[72] Baptist University had reported him to the police. The strategy of targeting the few has likely had the intended effect on campus of silencing the many.

Most surprising was the criticism of Professor Hualing Fu, the law dean at HKU, for simply being present, along with many other highly respected academics, years earlier at a conference where a staff member of the Open Society Foundation was present.[73] Professor Fu's other seeming sins included writing two academic articles funded by the UGC, one on police power and the other on the suppression of human rights defenders in China.

Visa denials have been used to block the hiring or continuance of foreign faculty with human rights backgrounds, including the prominently reported cases of Dr. Ryan Thoreson and Dr. Rewena He.[74] A highly-qualified scholar with advanced degrees from Yale and Oxford, Dr. Ryan Thoreson, was denied a visa in February 2022 to take up an appointment at HKU to teach human rights, including one of the courses I taught for years there in the human rights program.

Dr. Thoreson's scholarship focuses on LGBTQ rights and appears to include nothing that should be politically sensitive in Hong Kong. That he worked for Human Rights Watch, which Beijing has long targeted, appears to be the only explanation. Dr. Rewena He was fired from her existing appointment in the history department at CUHK after being denied a visa to return after leave abroad. The Immigration Department's presumed objection was her earlier publication of a book about the 1989 Tiananmen crackdown, even though this had not obstructed her initial hiring in 2019. It is not clear whether other cases of this nature have gone unreported. There appears to be a clear message for existing faculty: Sensitive topics and controversial hires should be avoided.

Related to these restrictions on hiring and firing there is a knock-on effect I have observed that young Hong Kong scholars now encounter. Historically, my brightest students who aspired to become professors might go abroad to study for a doctorate and then return to take up an appointment in Hong Kong. This return to Hong Kong was either a personal preference or compelled due to the shortage of jobs in the country of their studies. Either way, their presence in the academy worked to the great advantage of Hong Kong and China studies. In the face of the NSL, for those who have engaged in social or political issues relating to Hong Kong or China this path may now be closed. Pursuing their academic career in Hong Kong may now be too risky. With the continuing shortage of such prestigious jobs abroad, they may justifiably question whether they should pursue such advanced studies at all, certainly another form of talent-drain for Hong Kong.

The most fundamental attack at the tertiary level was contained in the Beijing-controlled *Ta Kung Pao* in early 2022 with a series of articles targeting Hong Kong's body for allotting research grants, the Research Grants Council (RGC) under the University Grants Council (UGC). The articles attacked the presence of too many foreign scholars engaged in evaluating research grant proposals. It further describes the UGC as a "cash machine for anti-China scholars who have disrupted Hong Kong."[75] The attacks on Brian Fong and Johannes Chan noted previously were included in these media reports. I should acknowledge that I served personally on the RGC for two three-year terms and frequently continue to evaluate research grants passed on to me for review.

Critical academic scholarship on developments in China, which was long Hong Kong's academic bread and butter, are clearly now a target of Beijing's concern. The Beijing-controlled media reports imply that RGC/UGC grant applications must now be evaluated on national security grounds. These attacks on Hong Kong's most prominent academic bodies and scholars clearly aim to send an intimidating message to constrain Hong Kong's highly respected tradition of critical scholarship and academic freedom.

Top university leaders in Hong Kong have offered little resistance to the stringent national security regulations and guidelines.[76] At the same time, there appears to be an exodus of both university heads and regular faculty, with three university heads already electing not to renew their contracts. At the faculty level, for the first time, the local exodus has led to academics from the mainland outnumbering local faculty across Hong Kong universities.[77] Some have attributed this exodus to the pressures they have experienced under the current crackdown.[78] University governing councils, largely appointed by the government, have generally been stacked with pro-government figures. Ongoing efforts in the "patriots only" Legislative Council are seeking to increase government control over appointments to such councils by providing for more outside members, in this case targeting the one at Chinese University of Hong Kong (CUHK).[79] Student unions that were historically supported and provided with campus space have now mostly been disavowed and purged from campuses.[80]

In what appears to be an indirect consequence of all these political pressures, both CUHK and City University have announced plans to restructure their departments that teach politics, allegedly due to low enrollment.[81] Under proposals at CUHK, political science would reportedly be merged with other disciplines in a new school. The fifty-one-year-old Department of Government and Public Administration (GPA) at the Chinese University of Hong Kong (CUHK), in which I taught for many years, was long one of the most popular and influential academic departments in Hong Kong. Several prominent graduates are now among those facing national security charges, while many others hold prominent positions in the government, the media, the professions, and the business sectors. That GPA was reportedly under-enrolled speaks volumes about the fraught political environment students now face.

This purge has been especially evident with respect to student organizations. When the student union at HKU in 2019 passed a resolution expressing sympathy for a man who had attacked a police officer and then later committed suicide, the student leaders were first barred from campus by the university, and then four of them were later arrested and charged under the NSL with inciting terrorism, which carries a maximum sentence of ten years.[82] Theirs is the first NSL case related to university affairs and the first where all the defendants were granted bail.[83] The four students were later sentenced to two years in prison under a revised charge of incitement to wound."[84] The university soon disavowed the student union and expelled it from the campus. These measures were taken despite the student union quickly reversing its position and apologizing for its resolution.

Even human rights memorials, such as HKU's "pillar of shame" sculpture commemorating the 1989 Tiananmen massacre, have been removed from campuses.[85] I fondly remember passing that memorial every day for years on my way to work at HKU and feeling assured of Hong Kong's commitment to free expression. Seemingly stung by criticism of its national security policies, the governing body of the University of Hong Kong recently proposed a change to the University Ordinance that aims to block criticism of such measures as it has taken by imposing penalties on students who "bring disrepute" to the university.[86]

All universities now require that graduates complete a course on national security in which mainland China's history and cultural values are to be emphasized. The HKU version requires that all undergraduates complete an online interactive "self-directed" course as a condition of graduation.[87] Students are required to complete a multiple-choice test on what they have learned in a course entitled Introduction to the Constitution, the Basic Law, and the National Security Law.[88] Students who have watched the HKU online course have noted the course explains the law but fails to answer where the red lines are drawn, rendering it rather boring.[89] Perhaps adding to this concern, the course reportedly uses lots of hypotheticals but no real-life examples.

As with lawyers and the media, the government has also targeted secondary and primary teachers. Even before the NSL, several secondary teachers were disqualified or reprimanded for their activities relating to the 2019 protest or for allegedly using one-sided or biased teaching materials.[90] A primary teacher was deregistered for allegedly giving pupils a factually incorrect account of the Sino-British Opium War.[91] Leaving little to chance, Hong Kong police have reportedly suggested that schools install CCTV cameras on campus, including in the classrooms—the latter presumably to monitor teaching content.[92]

Under the NSL, the monitoring and regulation of teachers at government schools is more comprehensive. Like all government employees, they are now required to swear an oath of allegiance to Hong Kong or risk their jobs. This seemingly innocuous requirement has huge implications, as subsequent behavior judged inconsistent with such oath—under the comprehensive national security constraints now being applied—could result in dismissal and loss of pension, not to mention possible prosecution. It must be remembered that such oath taking is no longer just a matter of swearing dedicated service but has been weaponized to limit critical or disapproved statements in the teaching process. In an extraordinary move, the government has extended this requirement to foreign native English teachers in government schools, who are typically brought in under two-year contracts from abroad.[93] Even teachers teaching part-time continuing education courses, while not required to take an oath, have been brought under national security guidelines and admonished to "acquire a correct understanding" and not engage in activities "contrary to the interest of national security.[94]

The Professional Teachers' Union (PTU) has likewise come under attack. In the middle of 2021, after Beijing accused the PTU of being too political and accused secondary teachers of brainwashing their students against China, the Hong Kong government ended its decades-long relationship with the hundred-thousand member PTU, and the police announced a criminal investigation. China's Xinhua News Agency and the *People's Daily* had branded the PTU a "malignant tumor."[95] This was yet another example of the Hong Kong government and police following Beijing's lead, with shadowy messengers reportedly in the background urging closure. Worried about the police investigation, the PTU disbanded in August 2021.

In its evolving mainland style, the Hong Kong government in November 2021 announced nine moral and civic values for all primary and secondary courses.[96] Law-abidingness and PRC national identity were to be stressed, while the more traditional liberal education values of human rights and critical thinking were dropped. The Education Bureau has even created a special picture book, *Our Country, Our Safety*, to be gifted to all kindergartens and primary schools.

As if these nudges to conform to the new national security environment were not enough, and lest any commitment to critical thinking slip through the growing net, the Education Bureau in 2022 produced new strict Guidelines on Teachers' Professional Conduct.[97] These new official guidelines, which replaced the profession's previous self-regulation, come with a bite, with noncompliance risking banishment for life from the profession, in addition to the already evident risk of criminal prosecution. While the guidelines contain the usual platitudes on professionalism, the operative guidance at this critical junction aims to tame the academic freedom long respected in Hong Kong in favor of national security.

The new guidelines require teachers to nurture "affection for the country," acquire a "correct understanding" of the PRC Constitution and the NSL, "consciously safeguard national security," and "support and promote national education actively." Teachers are to "guard against risks and incidents, prevent and stop activities in breach of law and regulations from infiltration into the schools." Similar restrictions apply to course materials. Repetitive language on these aspects also requires teachers report anyone seen to violate these guidelines. The traditional emphasis on critical thinking is missing. In the current Hong Kong environment, these words and requirements are loaded with the national security meanings and associated risks that have overwhelmed society. A teacher would presumably offer critical views of such policies at his or her own risk. Since students are encouraged to report teacher deviation, the risks could be considerable. When combined with the previously noted oath-taking requirements imposed on all public school teachers, the career risks are evident.

The effort to revise Hong Kong's traditional historical narrative and promote national values has especially targeted school textbooks. A new required textbook on citizen values, which is to be used in the new course on "citizenship and social development" that has replaced "liberal studies," now denies that Hong Kong was ever a colony, claiming that it was simply "occupied."[98] New Chinese history textbooks being prepared for the revised syllabus for junior secondary students only briefly mention the 1989 Tiananmen Square crackdown and make no mention of the annual commemorative vigils that were held annually for over two decades in Hong Kong.[99] As Ian Johnson highlights in a recent book, this airbrushing of Chinese history is very much a part of Xi Jinping's campaign against what he labels historical nihilism—referring to efforts to challenge official history.[100]

At the lower secondary level—forms one, two, and three—a similar move has been made with the introduction of a new required course on "citizenship, economics, and society" that has the same patriotism-inducing goals.[101] To make matters worse, a recent directive from the education minister directed that a quarter of the teaching time in kindergarten and primary school be given over to national patriotic education, seemingly brainwashing on speed.[102] This airbrushing of Chinese history gives rise to wider concerns over disinformation, as the government seeks to convey a rosy image of its policies. As previously noted, censorship has long been combined with disinformation on the mainland.

These changes, along with the banning of books that endanger national security, have put teachers and school librarians under great stress, with many choosing to leave. A 2021 PTU survey found that four in ten teachers want or plan to quit.[103] As reported in 2022, the turnover rate in the 2021–2022 academic year was 7.8 percent, nearly double the initial estimate, with 5,720 teachers, as reported by the Education Bureau, leaving their jobs during that time.[104]

A 2023 survey conducted by the Hong Kong Association for Academic and Teaching Exchange revealed that up to 70 percent of Hongkongers want to emigrate for students to study overseas, with half of adults wanting to work overseas.[105] Most associate this with life pressures and the political environment. The choice of immigration, whether by teachers or parents is not an easy one. Teachers qualified in Hong Kong may find they do not meet licensing or other requirements in their target country; while parents who emigrate for their children's sake may likewise face severe burdens to meet job qualifications required for their professions abroad. In both cases they may face unemployment or the need to take jobs for which they are overqualified, certainly a problem that needs to be addressed in diaspora communities.

In Hong Kong this level of displeasure surely signals downward pressure on school enrollment. A recent report noted that over 27,000 students left Hong Kong's secondary schools in 2022.[106] The same pressures have hit international schools as well, with expat students in Hong Kong schools declining by 12 percent.[107] The Education Bureau still claims schools are functioning normally. Such normality is reportedly achieved by teachers doubling up and by less qualified outsiders being brought in on short-term contracts to cover courses. The reality of the student and teacher exodus belies the claim that all is well. The high rate of teacher attrition is not just about the more extreme risks of arrest or dismissal but also more generally about the straitjacket of censorship and dishonesty that lingers over their work.[108] When teachers are required to promote ideas they question, and that clash with what students hear at home, trust will be lost.

The efforts at reeducating the society have seemingly not stopped at the campus boundary, as prisons are reported to have launched a course program to "deradicalize" the many young protesters now in prison—an initiative seemingly taken from the mainland playbook as seen in Xinjiang.[109] The government has tried to beat back accusations of brainwashing with no success.

In the face of this growing onslaught, the Global Public Policy Institute's global academic freedom index now gives Hong Kong a D rating. Hongkongers seemingly agree, with large numbers migrating or sending their children abroad.[110] This concern has diminished applications to local universities, resulting in higher acceptance rates.[111]

In comparing critical liberal education and Beijing's preferred patriotic education, a personal story captures the essence. Several years ago at the University of Hong Kong, one of my visiting university students from Beijing University had to go back to Beijing to do an interview for continued funding. When asked why she thought continuing her studies in Hong Kong was important, she emphasized critical thinking. She relayed to me that the committee interviewing her seemed perplexed as to why that mattered. It appears that same skepticism is now being applied to the city at large as national education more and more replaces Hong Kong's traditional liberal education.

Hollowing Out Freedom of Association

One of the mandates of article 9 of the NSL, "to strengthen . . . supervision and regulation over . . . social organizations," civil society, and labor organizations, has inspired a particularly hard hit on community organizations that have offered a critical check on the government. Over sixty local NGOs, under direct or indirect pressure, have so far disbanded.[112] This often begins with a condemnation in the Beijing-controlled media from which local law enforcement agencies appear to take their cue. This might be combined or followed up with shadowy middlemen calling or meeting with members of the organization and suggesting the wisdom of disbanding.[113]

Prominent organizations, such as the Labor Party, the Confederation of Trade Unions, the Social Workers General Union, the League of Social Democrats, the Hospital Authority Employees Alliance, the Civil Human Rights Front (CHRF), and the Alliance in Support of the Patriotic Democratic Movement in China, notably disbanded after direct official condemnation.[114] The experience of the CHRF and the Alliance in Support of the Patriotic Democratic Movement in China best illustrate the form of such direct targeting.

The Alliance in Support of the Patriotic Democratic Movement in China has been subject to investigation over accusations of foreign collusion and funding. Albert Ho Chun-yan and Chow Hang-Tung, both prominent lawyers and alliance leaders, as well as labor and alliance leader Lee Cheuk-yan, had already been jailed for encouraging illegal assemblies relating to the now banned June 4 commemoration. They face further prosecution under the NSL for "inciting subversion of state power" and for "inciting others to subvert state power," a crime that carries a potential sentence of five to ten years.[115] This charge allegedly relates to continuing as officers of the Alliance after the NSL was imposed. In this regard, the charges presumably relate to the Alliance's previous calls for "ending one party dictatorship" and encouraging memorialization of the June 4, 1989, Tiananmen massacre.[116] A candlelight vigil for this memorial had been officially permitted every year from 1989 to 2019 without incident (as I personally observed). The Alliance's assets were then frozen, effectively forcing it to disband.[117] In March 2023, national security officers took the further extraordinary step of arresting unionist Elizabeth Tang, the wife of Lee Cheuk-yan, outside the prison after she had returned from exile in the UK to visit her husband. Though her continuing overseas work appears to be labor-related, she was arrested under the NSL on suspicion of colluding with foreign forces.[118]

For years, the Tiananmen vigil was famously the only memorial on Chinese soil of the 1989 crackdown. Yet it was banned from 2020 forward, allegedly for reasons related to COVID, though that argument became increasingly suspect. In 2020, twenty-six pro-democracy activists, including, famously, Joshua Wong and Jimmy Lai, were arrested for participating or inciting others to attend the banned 2020 vigil, with many ultimately receiving suspended sentences or prison terms ranging from four to fifteen months.[119]

Chow Hang-tung had been given a twelve-month prison sentence for the 2020 vigil and then was arrested again for allegedly inciting others to participate in a 2021 vigil, for which she was given fifteen months. In a surprise ruling, the High Court overturned the latter conviction, noting that the police did not follow the Public Order Ordinance requirement that they consider imposing conditions rather than ban the requested public assembly.[120] The noted NSL prosecutions of Chow, Lee, and Ho represent even more severe charges. Chow's attempts in September 2022 to get the case dismissed and block its transfer to the High Court, where a more serious punishment of five to ten years is permitted, failed.[121] The court rejected her argument that such nonviolent advocacy was protected speech.

The NSL arrest of Chow Hang-tung and colleagues over the June 4 vigil drew a swift reaction from a group of UN experts, who noted, "Terrorism and sedition charges are being improperly used to stifle the exercise of fundamental human rights, which are protected under international law, including freedom of expression and opinion, freedom of peaceful assembly, and the right to participate in public affairs."[122] The UN experts noted further concern with accusing such organizations of foreign collusion merely for receiving foreign funding. Chow and two other colleagues in the alliance were convicted and sentenced to four and a half months merely for refusing a police request to turn over data regarding their donors, for which they have filed an appeal.[123] The only bright spot in these prosecutions was the decision in August 2022 to grant bail to Albert Ho Chun-yan after he had completed his public order sentence in a protest-related case, though in March 2023, he was rearrested, allegedly for speaking to witnesses.[124] Banning the vigil and the various prosecutions has huge symbolic implications for freedom of assembly in Hong Kong.

For nearly two decades, the CHRF, since its founding in the 2003 article 23 protests, had been an umbrella body that united pro-democracy organizations. It had typically handled the logistics of applying for the required clearance for a public protest. It was known to work with the police to ensure adherence to any protest requirements and to insist on the principle of nonviolence. Personally, as one of the founders of the Article 23 Concern Group, which was associated with the CHRF's founding, I had seen the results of its principled efforts many times.

I last had an opportunity to interview CHRF leaders on December 10, 2019, in relation to a planned protest on Hong Kong Island that day. The CHRF leaders had persuaded the police that if they avoided aggressive enforcement tactics— the kind frequently used in 2019—there would be no violence. This was done, and no violence occurred. Such cooperation was abandoned in 2021. In May 2021 the CHRF convenor, Figo Chan, was jailed for eighteen months for unauthorized assembly. Beijing's Hong Kong and Macau Affairs Office then accused the CHRF of colluding with foreign forces and promoting a color revolution. When the police took the cue and signaled an intention to investigate, the CHRF disbanded.[125]

Trade unions, many of which have aligned with the pro-democracy camp and, in some cases, put forth political candidates, have also felt the sting of official pressure. Beyond the couple mentioned above, including the umbrella Confederation of Trade Unions, over sixty employee unions disbanded over 2021 and 2022.[126] To ratchet up the pressure further, a new directive requires trade unions to declare they will not "endanger national security" in order to legally register.[127] In the current climate, this is essentially a mandate to stay away from politics. The exception would presumably be the pro-Beijing unions that routinely support the government.

Religious organizations likewise feel the heat. Though Hong Kong has firm guarantees on religious freedom, this may no longer be secure. The biggest threat appears to come in the form of Sinicization, with increasing cross border visits and official encouragement or pressure to track the patterns of the mainland's official churches.[128] The outgoing representative of the Vatican in Hong Kong has warned local church members that the freedoms they enjoyed for decades are over.[129] They were told to protect their property, files, and funds. Monsignor Javier Herrera-Corona warned, "Change is coming, and you'd better be prepared." Religious associations have long been important, especially in running a large proportion of schools in Hong Kong. Even before the national security crackdown, the church had begun moving cases of archives overseas for safekeeping. Beijing's Liaison Office in Hong Kong has reportedly arranged for mainland bishops to brief city clerics on the mainland system of religious control.[130]

Such pressures threaten the commercial sector as well. In August 2022, the pro-democracy retail chain Chickeeduck announced its intention to close its remaining lifestyle stores.[131] The chain had been popular in the pro-democracy camp for displaying artwork and pro-democracy products. This reportedly led to the termination of its leases, supply chain problems, and visits by national security police. Mainland suppliers had reportedly received state media reports about the store. While companies have received pressure to support Beijing policies, Chickeeduck presumably paid for its failure to do so. Government-controlled land leases are an especially easy target, with the government now adding a national security clause to all land leases, burdening property values.[132] International businesses have felt the heat as well. As has long been the case in the Chinese mainland, international companies, anxious about surveillance and censorship, are now in some cases directing their staff to use burner phones when they visit Hong Kong.[133]

International human rights organizations have also felt the pinch. Beijing has proclaimed its intention to "improve" the system for exercising "comprehensive jurisdiction" over Hong Kong and devise "legal weapons" to counter foreign forces.[134] As previously mentioned, the most aggressive foreign target has been the US National Endowment for Democracy and its affiliates. The PRC Foreign Ministry issued a special fact sheet in May 2022, accusing the NED, among a long list of alleged sins, of spying, undermining elections, and supporting the 2019 protests.[135] The NED is known to openly provide funding and training to organizations around the world to promote democracy and human rights. Its funding for Hong Kong NGOs, which was openly listed on the NED website, was highlighted in the Beijing fact sheet. The NED-affiliated organizations, the National Democratic Institute (NDI) and the International Republican Institute (IRI), are included in Beijing's criticisms, both in the fact sheet and more generally.

It is noteworthy that NED has openly provided electoral training in Hong Kong for both pan-democratic and pro-Beijing political parties, with IRI previously openly operating on the Chinese mainland.. In the fact sheet, Beijing more broadly accuses NED of inciting "division and confrontation" to meddle in other countries' internal affairs, "causing catastrophic consequences." It accuses NED of "instigating color revolutions," colluding with local political organizations to meddle in local affairs, funding separatist forces, engaging in disinformation campaigns, and participating in academic activities to infiltrate universities, all of which the report raised in the context of Hong Kong. These accusations presumably represent the front line of Beijing's war on liberal ideas. Local pro-Beijing commentators emphasize that this report serves as a warning to local NGOs not to accept NED funding or to interact in any way with the organization.[136] This effectively renders human rights advocacy regarding basic political rights illegal.

Beijing's attacks extend beyond such foreign government-funded human rights NGOs. With similar attacks, both Human Rights Watch and Amnesty International have closed their long-established offices in Hong Kong.[137] The activist lawyer Chow Hang-tung wrote a moving tribute from jail to Amnesty International upon its departure, noting its capacity to "transcend cultures and borders" and bring "together the power of ordinary people into a force that no country can ignore."[138] She notes, "The departure of Amnesty is an unmistakable warning sign to the outside world about just how dire the state of human rights is in Hong Kong." She notes that the loss of Hong Kong's status both as a base for international media and international human rights monitoring is a great loss for the entire Asian region and the world.

No Freedom to Protest

While the aggressive prosecutions of thousands of protesters engaged in civil disobedience or other protests activities tells the story of severe restraints on freedom to protest, it is now important to consider the continuing legal limits on protest authorization in the NSL post-Covid environment. Basic Law article 27, in protecting free expression in its many forms, expressly protects freedom of "assembly, of procession, and of demonstration." Public protest authorization has long been granted under the local public order law by the police issuance of a "notice of no objection."[139] Before 2019 such notices of no objection were routinely given. During the Covid pandemic that stopped, and public protests were largely banned under official claims relating to public health. Since the NSL was imposed, with the intimidating environment and the disbanding of many key groups that would typically organize political protests, the police see fewer requests.

After Covid the NSL has become the main obstacle, with the police largely blocking political protests. Even when requested political demonstrations are on non-sensitive topics, such as land reclamation or to honor Labor Day or International Women's Day, obstacles have been imposed. In March 2023, the police put on a show of liberalizing protest approvals by allowing a community group to protest a harbor reclamation project.[140] The authorization included demonstrators being corralled into enclosed areas surrounded by police, required to wear numbered tags, banned from wearing black clothes, and required to submit any banners for approval in advance.[141] More recently two labor organizers who planned a march on Labor Day withdrew the application after being pressured by police.[142]

More threatening than an army of police watching over a small group of corralled protesters or intimidation to withdraw are the conditions police have imposed. In March 2023 when the Hong Kong Women Workers Association sought permission to march on International Women's Day, they were duly issued the required notice of no objection, but with a hitch that presumably resulted in them calling off the march.[143] Women's rights have not been among the political topics that might typically be viewed by officials as a national security concern. Nevertheless, the letter of no objection reportedly stated that the organizers were required to ensure that the rally "would not be contrary to the interest of national security," an added requirement after the NSL. In a media interview Chief Executive John Lee reportedly said, "Anyone who is not confident, is incompetent, or is worried about whether they can do this should not organize public activities, because they have to bear the legal responsibility." On top of these statements, four members of a pan-democratic political party, the League of Social Democrats, were reportedly told that if they showed up at this event they would be arrested. The bottom line appears to be that an organizer of any protest or assembly will be responsible for anything that occurs at the event. The organizers of the women's march might easily have decided not to take the risk.

These various obstacles and the ongoing intimidation of opposition groups surely seem calculated to insure there will be very few protests applications. The message appears to be don't organize protests, or if you do avoid a political message, but if your proposed content is political then proceed at your own risk that fellow protesters may say something forbidden for which you will be accountable. In such environment it seems silence is golden. All of this has been accompanied by reports of increased surveillance and intimidation, employing the mainland playbook, by "preemptively discouraging rallies before applications are filed, paying home visits in the lead-up to days seen as politically sensitive and summoning organizers for warning chats."[144]

Civil Society Silenced

An October 2022 Congressional-Executive Commission on China (CECC) report on the state of civil society in Hong Kong offers the most comprehensive analysis of the impact on people's lives from the suppression under the NSL of the city's civil society.[145] Through interviews with forty-two civil society leaders and prominent actors, the report offers an oral history of the severe and comprehensive challenges civil society has faced.

The claims in these oral history accounts were further verified in the July 2022 UN Human Rights Committee's (HRC) fourth concluding observations on Hong Kong's lack of compliance with the ICCPR.[146] In that report, the HRC highlighted many of the pressures civil society organizations have faced. As discussed previously in this and the preceding chapters, these have included the forced closure and deregistration of media and civil society organizations, the arrest of media and civil society leaders, the undermining of due process in criminal prosecutions, and pressures on NGOs to cease participating in international human rights reporting or to leave Hong Kong entirely. The CECC report gives voice to the practical consequence of these failings for civil society members on the ground. The Hong Kong government promptly dismissed both reports as inaccurate, claiming they failed to understand the national security threat.[147]

In the face of such a comprehensive onslaught, a city with one of the most vigorous traditions of critical public debate through multiple venues has now largely been silenced, though hidden resistance still filters through. Lending further credence to the above reports, both Human Rights Watch and Amnesty International have complained that the diminution of civil society in Hong Kong has undermined UN human rights mechanisms, in that local NGOs were the most prominent contributors to such review processes in the past.[148] They note that of the fifteen groups who filed Hong Kong reports to the HRC in 2020 for the review hearing that took place in late 2022, nearly half have closed, left Hong Kong, or stopped all activities. With more than sixty community groups disbanding overall, several of their leaders are now detained and awaiting trial on national security charges. Such groups especially worry that submitting to the HRC review comes with the risk of being charged with collusion with foreign powers or, in many cases, accusations of sedition—another obvious constrain on human rights advocacy.

The Free Expression of What Cannot Freely Be Expressed versus Government Speak

While public voices have largely gone into hiding, the silence is not total. Jerrine Tan, a Hong Kong English professor who grew up in Singapore, notes that the surveillance states of Hong Kong and Singapore have become mirror images of each other, with similar controls on public debate.[149] One familiar item she notes is a new Hong Kong hotline for people to report on each other on matters related to national security. She sees familiar behavior developing among Hong Kong people, where they speak in hushed tones about sensitive issues.

At the same time, she notes how Hong Kong people, like Singaporeans before them, have found inventive hidden ways to protest, with somewhat obtuse slogans written on city walls or along hiking trails. Blank Post-its now appear where colorful Lennon Walls used to flourish, what she calls "the free expression of what cannot freely be expressed." Even numbers written in various locations reflect a memorial to a protest date.[150]

Tan contrasts these hidden voices with the Hong Kong government's efforts to impose its own truths over what is or is not democracy or freedom. She highlights the government's specious claims that Hong Kong is now more democratic and even that it was never a colony, an official view now promoted to schoolchildren.

Perhaps the most notorious examples of the government's effort to silence such obtuse statements are the bail denials and sedition convictions, described previously, against five speech therapists—including Lai Man-ling, Melody Yeung, and three other members of their General Union of Speech Therapists—for publishing a children's picture book about a sheep village that comes under attack by wolves.[151] The UN HRC has featured this case in its attack on the overly broad application of the sedition charge.

In relation to the current crackdown, it is important to note that there has long been a dark side to Hong Kong social organizations. This dark side includes outspoken organizations officially orchestrated or controlled by Beijing and complicit Hong Kong officials—which is what I call "government speak." Government bodies, or government-orchestrated or government-controlled bodies, are not civil society in the true sense. As referenced in the CECC report, the UN high commissioner for human rights has defined "civil society" as including autonomous society-based actors such as "human rights defenders, human rights NGOs, bar associations, student clubs, trade unions, university institutes, bloggers, environmental rights activists, or charities working with discriminated groups."[152] Hong Kong had famously supported a very vibrant civil society in this regard, as was especially evident in the years before the recent crackdown.

While this definition does not necessarily exclude all organizations that support Beijing policies, it does exclude organizations whose existence and decisions are orchestrated or controlled by officials in Beijing or Hong Kong. Many such organizations, which are essentially proxies for Beijing, have emerged and remain active; as we will see in chapter 10, some are even given a special role in elections. These conditions track similar conditions on the mainland, where remnants of civil society that may have developed during reformist periods have largely been obliterated in recent years.[153]

In the early years, well before the handover, Beijing had made a concerted effort across all sectors to infiltrate the city with Beijing-friendly people.[154] In her book, *Underground Front*, Christine Loh estimates that eighty-three thousand mainland officials entered Hong Kong between 1983 and 1997.[155] These officials created a channel for China's United Front Works Department to exercise influence and co-opt and organize Hong Kong officials, business elites, and grassroots organizations with PRC loyalists. The civil society components of such efforts often aimed to match and create a rival to existing community organizations. A liberal labor union would be matched with a leftist one, a democratic political party with a pro-Beijing one. This included leftist schools, newspapers, and other civic organizations, and it also involved co-opting business organizations and elites who might be motivated to gain Beijing's favor or largesse. This nurturing process especially targeted key areas of the civil service and the police.

Given the central government's official manipulation and management, such orchestrated organizations do not reflect civil society in the true sense. They merely reflect an appearance of civil society out of which officials aim to construct Beijing's version of civil society, one made up of patriots designated to rule Hong Kong. As opposition calls for the promised democracy grew louder, Beijing had an army of business and other loyalists with a vested interest in Beijing's growing control who were ready to push back. After the crackdown, those same loyalists supply the patriots who are designated to rule Hong Kong.

At the same time, some Hong Kong pro-Beijing local business elites, who have been hedging their investment bets in the West, and have been cynically characterized as "loyal rubbish," are slowly being replaced for local appointments and influence by newly arrived mainland business elites.[156] Professor Ho-fung Hung offers a comprehensive account of the evolving dominant role of mainland companies in Hong Kong's financial, banking, construction, and property markets and the consequent diminution in influence and status of local business elites.[157] As Hung highlights, this growing influence of mainlanders has concurrently degraded the political influence of local business elites. The evolving world of patriots-only domination may see more mainlander political influence, along with the exit of more international and local businesses.

The NSL Long Arm and Human Rights Advocacy

The long arm of the NSL has deeply challenged basic freedoms on a global scale, with warrants targeting activists engaged in free expression abroad. Early on, six warrants were reportedly issued targeting foreign human rights advocacy by Hong Kong activists in the US and the UK. The warrants especially appeared to target people active with NGOs that had lobbied governments concerning developments in Hong Kong. More recently the Hong Kong police issued warrants with a HK$1 million bounty on 8 Hong Kong human rights advocates active abroad. This has included detaining and questioning their families in Hong Kong.[158] In December 2023 the Hong Kong government added the HK$1 million bounty to five other overseas activists, including Simon Cheng, Francis Hui, Joey Siu, Johnny Fok and Tony Choi.[159] These warrants and bounties clearly signal that such human rights advocacy abroad is now illegal under the NSL in Hong Kong.

These warrants appear to especially target activists active with the most effective human rights NGOs. Early on, Samuel Chu, a US citizen, and the founder of the Hong Kong Democracy Council (HKDC), was reportedly targeted with a warrant for his lobbying efforts that resulted in the US passage of the Hong Kong Human Rights and Democracy Act.[160] Anna Kwok and Nathan Law, the current director and board chair respectively of HKDC are among the 8 overseas activists recently targeted with a HK$ 1 million bounty. The British-based Hong Kong Watch has also been targeted with emails from the Hong Kong Police and the National Security Bureau, ordering it to take down its website, saying that its activities amounted to collusion and posed a threat to China's national security.[161] Its CEO, Ben Rogers, was warned he could face life in prison and a fine of $100,000 for his activities.[162] Rodgers wrote publicly, rejecting such an order.

Three Hongkongers in exile, including ex-legislator Baggio Leung Chung-hang, have been targeted by national security police under NSL, article 22, for subversion of state power for their efforts in Canada and the US to create a Hong Kong parliament in exile, modeled on the Tibetan one based in India.[163] As Mr. Leung noted, concerns have been raised about whether Hong Kong police might target not only the organizers but voters in such a parliament, which would raise further concerns about the security of the group's possible online voting system. The parliament proposal appears motivated by a desire to unite an otherwise somewhat fractured diaspora.

The above noted 2023 placing of a HK$1 million bounty on eight Hongkongers living abroad, along with the harassment of their family members in Hong Kong, signals a stepped-up effort to undercut their support and silence human rights criticism abroad.[164] Chief Executive John Lee promoted an extreme view, labeling these popular human rights advocates "street rats" who are to be "avoided at all costs."[165] The Justice Secretary then filed professional misconduct complaints against two lawyers in the group, claiming their conduct brought the profession into "disrepute" and "undermined public confidence in the judicial system and rule of law."[166] These extraordinary bounties attracted condemnation across the international bodies representing the legal profession and the usual dismissal of such criticism by the Hong Kong government.[167]

Beyond the openly reported warrants and bounties, media reports indicate dozens of unknown Hong Kong residents are also on the police national security wanted list.[168] Whether publicly verified or not, such reports signal the risk in returning to Hong Kong for anyone abroad who has been outspoken on human rights in the city. Furthermore, many might worry about being placed on the Interpol red list, raising travel risk, though such alleged political crimes should be barred from the list. Even though Hong Kong has no way of reaching these exiled activists the branding exercise clearly signals an effort to degrade support for their human rights advocacy and to intimidate would-be supporters to avoid the targeted activists. The policy has included arresting several Hongkongers who are accused of providing funds to overseas activists.[169]

The sad reality is that these dedicated young Hong Kong activists now face a life of permanent exile, as returning to Hong Kong after lobbying for the city's human rights abroad risks arrest or even being secretly picked up and transported across the border to face charges. Some targeted individuals have cut off communications with their families in Hong Kong out of fear of putting them in danger. This is a long way from the open society based on the rule of law that was promised Hong Kong.

As human rights defenders well know, when local legal protections are inadequate, speaking to the international press and petitioning international human rights bodies or foreign governments are the only avenues to draw attention to human rights violations. Before the NSL was passed, Washington and London saw a parade of petitioners—as did Germany, France, and the European Union headquarters in Brussels—in response to the 2019 crackdown on protesters in Hong Kong. The testimony that was given was consistently aboveboard and openly circulated in the country, where it was unquestionably protected speech. Such advocacy is the essential work of human rights NGOs. By branding such activities as foreign collusion or subversion, the NSL has effectively made human rights advocacy a crime.

In general, such foreign campaigns have merely called for China to fulfill its existing commitments to Hong Kong, as foreign governments are usually reluctant to support separatist activities in other countries. A more detailed discussion of international engagement and how support for Hong Kong is mobilized abroad is addressed in the penultimate chapter, where these issues are addressed separately from the local policies and controls that are the primary focus of this book.

POWERLESSNESS

10

DEMOCRATIC REFORM IN REVERSE

Hong Kong's electoral system has never been fully democratic, and Chinese officials have continually dragged their feet on the Basic Law promise of "universal suffrage." But under the previous Basic Law model, as it had developed up to the recent electoral overhaul, there were direct geographical elections for half of the then seventy seats in the Legislative Council and nearly all the district council seats. This prior model still ensured that pro-government forces would dominate the Legislative Council, combining most of the functional seats, which were made up of constituencies heavily stacked in the government's favor, and a minority of directly elected seats the pro-establishment politicians might win under the proportional representation system. The 2020 opposition primary election, for which participants would be prosecuted, aimed to strategically encourage cooperation in the opposition camp to attempt against great odds to break that hold.

Historically, the opposition did not take the district council elections that seriously due to a lack of resources and the limited advisory role of the eighteen district councils. But when the opposition did take it seriously in the 2019 district council elections, which were cast as a referendum on the protest demands, they won control of seventeen of the eighteen districts in a landslide, though most new counsellors would later effectively be ousted by loyalty tests.

Despite these limitations, Hong Kong people have always enthusiastically engaged the democratic process with regard to the directly elected seats. Because Hong Kong is a dense city, somewhat like New York and London, most people get around on mass transit or on foot. This means elections under the prior system have been very visceral affairs with very competitive campaigning out in the open, with lots of candidate posters and in-person appearances on the streets.

I have fond memories during campaign season of coming and going from exits of the mass transit railway, seeing legislative and district council candidates in person. Their presence reminded me of elections I had worked on in my youth in Hawaii, where politicians also have a tradition of standing out on the streets with signs and shaking hands. In Hong Kong, the enthusiasm on the streets for such elections was always palpable, as was the enthusiastic support for more democracy that was seen in the mass protests. As a core member of the Article 23 Concern Group in 2003, in this campaigning tradition, I recall standing outside stations in Mangok and Causeway Bay, distributing the pamphlets regarding the article 23 proposals. As a foreigner, I would get some strange looks along with curiosity as to what I was handing out. This very much had the feel of the open campaigning seen in the electoral season. This open, street-based participation defined and developed the sense of community in Hong Kong, as it did my own.

Attacking Western-style democracy as a "doom" for Hong Kong, mainland officials have imported the mainland system of elections, which offers top-down control and no genuine electoral choice.[1] Beijing now claims the new electoral model is more democratic. It appears that a form of "universal suffrage," where everyone can choose from candidates handpicked by Beijing, is the version Beijing has in mind. Before the recent crackdown, there was freedom without full democracy, but now there is neither freedom nor democracy.

Elections under the new model, with no genuine political contest of opposing camps and a lack of freewheeling engagement, have surely deprived the city of election enthusiasm and the sense of community it inspired. This diminution of enthusiasm was very much evident in the approximately 30 percent turnout under the new system for the 2021 Legislative Council election and 27.5 percent turnout for the 2023 District Council election.[2] The vote in both cases was clearly a vote against the Beijing model, expressed in not voting.

The same disdain that is evident in the CCP's approach to the liberal elements of constitutionalism has also been evident in its approach to democratic elections. On a wider scale, this hostility has spawned a global debate that pits liberal democracies against a somewhat vaguely articulated illiberal PRC model. In a recent PRC white paper on what the CCP labels its "whole-process people's democracy," it becomes painfully evident that Beijing's preferred model is neither liberal nor democratic.[3]

Both the recent white paper on the mainland system and a separate PRC white paper on Hong Kong issued around the same time go on at great length about China's allegedly representative institutions.[4] Both documents say almost nothing about what the people themselves expect or are allowed to openly defend regarding public policies and values, much less genuine democratic choice, and the independent protection of human rights. Instead, China is ruled by a small cadre of powerful men who view CCP rule as imperative to China's interest and are prepared to guard it at all costs. They have imported the same spirit as to their approved "patriots" chosen to rule Hong Kong, and they are prepared to lock out and lock up anyone who openly opposes this arrangement.

The Prior Electoral Model

Under the prior Basic Law model employed from the 1997 handover until 2021, the chief executive of Hong Kong was chosen by a 1,200-member Election Committee, selected by a small circle (around 246,000 voters in total) of mostly functional electoral constituencies that were heavily weighted toward the pro-Beijing camp. The occasional pan-democratic opposition candidate, seeking to expose the limitations of the system by running in the selection process, would not garner more than about 20 percent of the committee's votes. With the committee's heavily pro-Beijing slant, PRC officials in Beijing's Hong Kong Liaison Office could generally signal their favored candidate, and most electors for the committee would go along with it.

The Legislative Council was likewise slanted toward the government, with half of its seats filled by similar functional constituencies, mostly from the pro-Beijing camp. While the opposition would typically win about 60 percent of the popular vote in the directly elected geographical constituencies, they would be left in a permanent minority position in the Legislative Council. This was due to the limited number of directly elected seats, with only a handful of functional sectors where the opposition held sway. The only level of government where most of the candidates were directly elected was the rather powerless, largely advisory district councils, to which the opposition, with little to gain, had historically committed few resources.

This all changed in the November 2019 district council elections. As previously noted, with the crackdown on the 2019 protests in full swing, both the opposition and pro-government camps turned the district council election into a referendum on the protests' reform demands. With a record turnout of over 70 percent of registered voters, the pro-government side was badly defeated, with the opposition taking 90 percent of the seats and fully controlling seventeen of the eighteen district councils.

Outraged at the shellacking it had received, the government then weaponized the oath-taking requirements to push out the victors under a threat of dismissal or even prosecution for violating their oath. It appeared that the required oath was much more than simply pledging to faithfully execute their office but rather an oath of allegiance to the Hong Kong government as constituted—effectively targeting loyalty to the central government and the CCP—that further signals agreement with its Hong Kong policies. This is not stated in the oaths, but the various disqualifications from running for office and rhetoric surrounding some dismissals from office seem to suggest this wider intention. Consequently, previously expressed disagreements with such policies could put the person taking the oath at risk of disqualification. Of those candidates who were elected, 260 resigned, leaving 196 who chose to stay and take the oath. Of those 196, forty-nine were disqualified, as were six who did not show up to take the oath.

In late July 2020, the government used the excuse of the COVID pandemic to postpone the planned September 2020 Legislative Council election. It was clearly anticipating another shellacking. The election would only be rescheduled for December 2021, after Beijing unilaterally amended the Basic Law to provide a "patriots only" election.

Electoral Reform in Reverse

For Beijing, the campaign of intimidation orchestrated under the NSL was clearly not enough. In 2021, it imposed "electoral reforms" that now ensure the complete exclusion of the pan-democratic opposition from running for political office. As characterized by the European Union in its Twenty-Fourth Annual Report on Hong Kong, with these reforms, Hong Kong has taken an "authoritarian turn," which has "weakened the already modest democratic elements of the electoral system and ensured that pro-establishment voices could control all levels of government."[5] Only "patriots," as Beijing understands that term, are allowed to compete for electoral office. The old quip—that Beijing does not mind elections if it knows the outcome ahead of time—is now fully implemented.

The Election Committee, now expanded to 1,500 from the previous 1,200 members, has become the new center of power, with the power to vet all candidates for electoral office and elect the chief executive and forty members of the expanded Legislative Council. Under the new model, the number of constituents to choose the 1,500 Election Committee members dropped by 97 percent, from a select, mostly pro-Beijing group of 246,440 voters in 2016 to only 7,891 select voters in 2021.

The committee was always chosen mostly by a variety of functional sectors. The newly established functional constituencies now favor the pro-Beijing camp even more. The few constituencies that formerly might have chosen an opposition candidate have now been neutralized by the limitation to only pro-Beijing electors. Sectors where the pan-democrats had traditionally performed well, such as education, higher education, social welfare, and medical and health services, have been merged with their seats effectively halved, while other professional sectors were neutralized in other ways by giving pro-Beijing associations the power to nominate or elect members. The 117 seats formerly representing the district councils were eliminated with the replacement seats to be filled largely by government-appointed area committees. The three hundred additional seats are now filled by Hongkongers appointed by Beijing to represent Hong Kong in mainland bodies.

Previously, the Election Committee only selected the chief executive through a majority committee vote. It now also selects nearly half of the Legislative Council. While the number of Legislative Council members has increased from seventy to ninety, the number directly elected has been reduced from thirty-five to twenty. All Legislative Council candidates are now required to be nominated by the heavily pro-Beijing Election Committee. Beijing is taking no chances. Opposition candidates are effectively barred under the vetting process. Beijing and the Hong Kong government are guaranteed a clean slate of support by appointing the voters who determine the outcome.

To achieve reliable vetting, the Election Committee is advised in its nominating role by a newly created and rather small (under ten members) Candidate Eligibility Review Committee, made up primarily of senior pro-Beijing politicians. This vetting committee is advised by the Office for Safeguarding National Security. To assist these bodies, each prospective candidate will be investigated by the special police unit on national security, with the aim of ensuring only "patriots"— understood as excluding all pan-democratic opposition—are allowed to run. The investigations associated with these vetting processes are all done in secret, and the candidates will not be told the grounds for any disqualification, nor allowed to appeal.

The Human Rights Committee under the ICCPR has made it clear that the ICCPR's criteria for the promised universal suffrage includes not only that every citizen can vote but also that there be in place a system that enables genuine choice.[6] The new Beijing-imposed electoral model meets none of these requirements. In the Hong Kong white paper on democracy issued after the 2021 Legislative Council election, Beijing characterized this model it had imposed as more democratic, and it even suggested the promised "universal suffrage" may be achievable under such a model—where every Hong Kong voter would be allowed to vote for the Beijing-approved candidates.[7]

The Patriots-Only Election to the Legislative and District Councils

Hong Kong set about carrying out these patriots-only elections with gusto in 2021, 2022 and 2023. As described above, on September 19, 2021, first came the election for the newly empowered Election Committee.[8] Only about a quarter of the 1,500 seats were contested, while three-quarters of the seats were either ex officio or were filled by select groups where the seats were uncontested. Under the vetting processes, Beijing forces were in control, with no opposition participation in the election. This election clearly met Beijing's electoral standard, where the outcome was clear in advance.

The December 2021 Legislative Council election, the first under the new law, was equally a one-sided, fully managed affair. Of the three "elections" in this initial two-year period under the new electoral regime, the Legislative Council election was the only one providing some electoral role for a wide spectrum of voters, being the voters for the twenty seats filled by direct election in geographical constituencies. Of course, those ordinary voters were given no genuine choice of candidates under the vetting process and therefore had little incentive to participate—thus explaining the 30 percent turnout.

The intrusive vetting process left no remaining incentive for people from the old pan-democratic camp to run for office, and none did. There was controversy in the opposition Democratic Party, leading to the expulsion of two of its members who had sought to ignore the party's earlier decision to sit out the election.[9] The two members reportedly were concerned that officials had threatened the party with prosecution under the NSL for the seeming boycott. Other than such controversy, the Democratic Party, formerly the leading pro-democracy party in the Legislative Council, has largely gone silent, with limited exception.

With many Democratic Party members now under arrest, including several among the forty-seven being prosecuted in relation to the election primary, the risks of speaking out are presumably judged to be high. The party has encouraged the new government to clarify national security boundaries and pardon the 2019 protesters.[10] Its September 2023 annual policy proposal confined its advocacy to maintenance of an open society, for the first time omitting its usual mention of voting rights.[11] As early as October 2022, it appeared likely the number two pan-democratic party, the Civic Party, would simply disband, which it did in May 2023.[12] The problem had been that no members were willing to take up the party leadership roles. Being in the spotlight as an opposition party leader is now risky, with a high prospect of being investigated or even jailed.

With only twenty directly elected seats, the remaining seventy Legislative Council seats were filled either by the Election Committee (forty seats) or narrow functional sectors (thirty seats). In most constituencies, it proved difficult to get more than one candidate, and there were rumors that Beijing pressured candidates to find or encourage someone to run against them. The membership of the newly elected Legislative Council is made up entirely of pro-Beijing supporters, though one member, previously from the opposition camp, claims he is independent.

The "patriots-only" election left most Hong Kong people on the sidelines with no path to public advocacy. It especially slammed the door in the face of ethnic minorities and marginalized groups that had long viewed the pan-democratic legislators as the most fruitful avenue to address grassroots concerns and that now find the new legislative class of patriots largely unapproachable.[13] Even public hearings on matters of concern to minorities have been cut back. Asylum seekers have especially been the target of new legislation on immigration and removal that degrades their already dire conditions. Foreign domestic workers have likewise been left out and face new legislator calls to further restrict their employment conditions.

The Hong Kong government, aware that few voters will want to vote in such a managed election, imposed a new law, making it a crime to advocate for a voter boycott. This would only be relevant to the Legislative and District Council elections since there is little likelihood of a voter boycott in the other two elections, where the narrow circle of voters was all selected by Beijing's managed processes. The new law aims to block all such advocacy of voter boycott. The law was later upheld as constitutional by a lower court, and two people locally would later plead guilty of violating this law; others were charged for sharing the Facebook posting by former opposition lawmaker Ted Hui, who had fled overseas, calling for a boycott.[14] Up to a dozen people were reportedly arrested for passing on Hui's call to boycott or cast blank votes.[15] Unrelated to this matter, Mr. Hui has been sentenced in absentia for obstruction of justice for fleeing town on a number of other cases related to public order that were pending against him.[16]

The law bans advocacy of voter boycott but does not bar individual voters from boycotting the election. Even without such open advocacy, only 30 percent of voters voted in the December 2021 Legislative Council election.[17] The cynical view of this election was especially pronounced among young voters, with only a 6.69 percent turnout among registered voters in the eighteen-to-twenty-year age range.[18] The dim popular view of this rigged electoral system is obviously shared by many governments around the world, including the US, who issued condemnations.[19] Of course, with all its members from the pro-establishment camp, the Legislative Council is now mostly a talk shop of pro-government supporters, where no opposition is assured in areas of fundamental constitutional importance.

Presumably to encourage the government to retain direct elections for district councils, in late 2022, the Democratic Party had indicated that it would participate if direct elections to the district council were maintained.[20] If the aim was to preserve the largely democratic character of the district councils, this proved to be largely a vain wish. In May 2023, the government announced its revamp of the district councils with only 19 percent, or eighty-eight of the 470 seats, to be directly elected.[21] Of the remaining seats, 179 are to be filled directly by the government and 176 by government-appointed neighborhood committees. The government is taking no chance on losing future elections. All candidates in this "patriots-only" district council election are required to both be vetted for patriotism and gain nine nominations from members of three heavily pro-Beijing municipal level committees. As was expected, in the first district council election under the new rules only pro-government candidates cleared these two hurdles. Local municipal level committees refused to even nominate opposition candidates, while shamelessly nominating many of their own members. This meant the few opposition candidates that joined the process did not even reach the patriotism vetting stage, while all the pro-government candidates passed the test."[22]

To diminish public influence even further, under the new scheme each local district council will be chaired by a government official. The Democratic Party initially decided to put forward eight candidates for directly elected seats, a move that surely tested the vetting and nomination processes. The result, as with the legislative and chief executive elections, was that no Democratic Party or opposition candidates cleared the hurdles, leaving the voters with no genuine electoral choice.[23] The party's concern was justified when none of their proposed candidates were able to gain the required nominations from the pro-government committees, whose members notoriously mostly nominated their own members. The Hong Kong public effectively voted against this fake version of democracy by not voting, with only a 27.5 percent voter turnout for the directly elected portion, the lowest turnout in any election since the handover.[24]

This district council model had caused a dilemma for the Democratic Party. Should they run candidates for the few directly elected seats, facing the risk of disqualification in the vetting process, or effectively become irrelevant and lose all sources of funding as a political party not participating in politics?[25] When combined with the oath-taking requirements, there is little chance of significant pan-democratic participation more generally, much less a pan-democratic candidate winning a seat. Most potential pan-democratic candidates might judge there is no incentive to participate in a seemingly hopeless election, especially given the limited role district councils play.

Selection of the Chief Executive

The May 2022 "election" by the Election Committee to choose the chief executive proved to be even more of a farce. In April 2022, then Chief Executive Carrie Lam, with Beijing's approval, announced she would not seek a second term. Speculation became rife as to who would follow.[26] As in the past, signals from Beijing would be determinative. In this tradition, Carrie Lam was presumably told whether she should seek a new term.

It had long been the case that Beijing would signal its preferred candidate and that most electors on the committee would happily go along. The old model had required that a maximum of three candidates could be nominated. It also required a sufficient base of support that only a pro-Beijing candidate could win in the heavily pro-Beijing Election Committee.

Under the new Election Committee for the chief executive election in May 2022, a candidate for chief executive was—as discussed above for the Legislative Council—required to undergo the same comprehensive vetting as a patriot. At the same time, they were required to have at least 188 nominations from Election Committee members, with at least fifteen from each of the five sectors of the Election Committee.[27] Given that one of the sectors is made up entirely of Beijing appointees to national bodies and all the sectors are dominated by pro-Beijing forces, there was no chance a candidate from the opposition camp could be nominated.

As it turned out, in the first selection of the current chief executive under this new model, Beijing-anointed John Lee received 786 nominations and ran unopposed as the only approved candidate for chief executive. His supporters included all but three of the city's ninety legislators and nearly all the commercial elites.[28] He eventually received 1,416 votes out of the 1,428 electors who showed up to vote in the Election Committee—with eight nonsupport votes.[29]

It seems Beijing has largely abandoned even the pretense that this was a genuine election or that the chief executive enjoys genuine support in the community. The unambiguous message is that the chief executive serves and owes his position to Beijing. In this selection, Beijing has effectively mimicked the earlier British colonial model where London chose the colonial governor and all or most representatives in the Legislative Council.

John Lee's resume has been of particular concern to those committed to civil liberties in Hong Kong. A career police officer, Lee has only known police and security work, signaling Beijing's primary interest in pushing him forward.[30] He notoriously oversaw the 2019 police crackdown and the 2020 rollout of the national security law.[31] On his watch as security chief, and briefly as chief secretary, the primary emphasis was on clamping down on supposed national security risks, with then over two hundred opposition figures arrested under the new NSL.

Lee has vowed to put through a local national security law in 2024 to cover treason, espionage, and theft of state secrets, as specified in Basic Law, article 23. The government has stated this is under current review. His most appreciated quality in Beijing's eyes is the expectation that he will "faithfully implement the directives of the Central Government."[32] At the same time, his appointment signals the decay and Beijing's profound distrust of the systems of local accountability in Hong Kong.[33]

Instead of democracy, what has emerged is a system where top officials in Hong Kong seek to mimic mainland official behavior. They are expected to hang carefully on every word or directive from mainland officials, especially Xi Jinping.[34] On his first full day in office, John Lee shared a picture of himself with Xi's Hong Kong speech featured prominently on his desk.[35] Even more jarringly, and harkening back to mainland study sessions about Xi Jinping's thought, the patriots-only Hong Kong legislature quickly held a six-hour study session on Xi's speech on Hong Kong; even the civil service held a study session for hundreds of top officials entitled "Spirit of the President's Important Speech."[36]

Weaponizing Loyalty

Beyond a rigged election process, the Beijing and Hong Kong governments have taken no chances in their efforts to ensure only Beijing loyalists serve in government. The government has weaponized the oath-taking process for both elected officials and for all civil servants. Those who don't take the oath or take it and are later found to be in violation of the government's version of loyalty are barred from holding office. Civil servants who fail to take the oath or who are found to have violated it can be fired for cause and are at the risk of losing their pensions. The same requirement has been extended to teachers at government schools and seems likely to be extended further going forward.

This coercive and somewhat hostile environment may explain why the number of civil servants and teachers resigning over the past year has reportedly doubled.[37] The number of applicants for administrative and executive officer positions in government, previously among the most sought-after jobs for fresh university graduates, has likewise fallen dramatically. To address the problem for what used to be highly treasured positions, in May 2023, the government announced it would open up such civil service applications to university students in their penultimate year, whereas before, they could only apply in their year of graduation.[38]

GLOBAL SUPPORT

11

INTERNATIONAL SUPPORT
FOR HONG KONG

"By saving Hong Kong, you save the values of the free world."
— Jimmy Lai, *The Hongkonger*, a 2021 documentary

I put this account of international foundations and support for Hong Kong here near the end so as not to depreciate the core analysis driven by local experience, mainland policies, local governance, and the Hong Kong people's response. The international presence has largely been on the sidelines except for the deep impact of internationally shared ideas and values embodied in international human rights treaties to which Hong Kong is bound and notions of liberal constitutionalism shared by democracies around the world, as promised in the Basic Law. This international support shows up not as the claimed outside intervention that Beijing and Hong Kong officials are fond of alleging but in open expressions of support for the city's human rights and rule of law values. Member nations of the UN and signatories of UN human rights treaties are obligated to monitor and support such human rights values around the world. This chapter considers briefly how these shared values took root in Hong Kong and how supporters and the diaspora abroad can work with locals to address and publicize their concerns.

The modern city of Hong Kong is very much a mix of British colonialism and Chinese refugee settlement, with the bulk of its pre-handover population being of the first or second generation who fled the communist revolution on the mainland.[1] As noted in chapter 2, a combination of local inhabitants and mainland settlers escaping poverty and repression built the megacity we see today from an earlier collection of fishing and farming villages on Hong Kong Island, in the Kowloon area, and across the New Territories.[2]

From the start, this essentially Cantonese city was an amalgamation of local culture and the global interaction brought on by British colonialism. Settlers often imagined they might move on to other destinations within a generation. This expectation led to the characterization of the city, as described by Richard Hughes, as "a borrowed place on borrowed time."[3] But in time, the generations born in the city came to call it home.

As generations passed, the combination of local Cantonese culture and entrepreneurship, and the international engagement encouraged by the colonial power, allowed Hong Kong to develop its own local identity distinct from other parts of China. During the closing years of British colonial rule, with various reforms, the city would acquire a deep and enduring connection to the free-world values of human rights and the rule of law. It became a safe harbor during the long years of political turmoil following the 1949 establishment of the PRC on the Chinese mainland, a time when the bulk of the current population or their ancestors arrived.

International engagement gave rise to the city's development as a global financial center with mutual ties and an identification with other similar global cities such as London and New York. In the decades after World War II, the decolonization mandate and these developments, as well as the anticipated handover, favored the consolidation of core human rights and rule of law values both in education and in the society at large. In the view of many Hongkongers, to snuff out the city's freewheeling nature and its rule of law is to snuff out Hong Kong itself. These qualities created both local and global attachments to the city that are both legal and cultural.

In the colonial era, the legal identity was based on policies or responsibilities associated with colonial rule; in the early years, these were largely European principles of colonial acquisition. This became bound up by broader responsibilities in the era after World War II, when colonialism was in disfavor and its abolition was required by the UN Charter. The postwar UN Charter provided guidelines on self-determination and decolonization. Such guidelines included local human rights and democracy as instruments to enable local choice concerning the path forward for a colonized community. These seeming protections were taken from Hong Kong with the 1972 removal of the city, at China's request, from the UN list of colonies.

Some Hongkongers who have supported self-determination have been concerned that Hong Kong got shortchanged by the 1972 removal. In effect, whether it was intended or not, Hong Kong was given a lesser substitute in the Sino-British Joint Declaration. The Joint Declaration expressly incorporates many of the international requirements expected for former colonies exercising the right of self-determination, though it does not afford such right, nor does it fully guarantee the democratic conditions to enable such exercise. Tracking many of the core values rooted in the UN Charter and the Universal Declaration of Human Rights (UDHR), those requirements include the rule of law, human rights, and basic freedoms, plus democracy. After three decades living under the ICCPR, which was eventually transformed locally in the Bill of Rights Ordinance, these values were and are widely shared by Hong Kong people.

Under such UN mandates, and under international law more generally, it should not have been open for China and Britain to completely ignore the preferences of Hong Kong people. Under the UN Charter, the UDHR, and the ICCPR, it is not now appropriate for international human rights institutions and foreign governments to ignore violations of the core commitments made to Hong Kong in the Joint Declaration and the Basic Law.

With respect to both the Joint Declaration and the Basic Law, the PRC government approached the capitals of the world to solicit international recognition of Hong Kong's special status as a separate system under Chinese sovereignty. This recognition was akin to a partnership where China would adhere to the Joint Declaration and the Basic Law, and the international community would respect Hong Kong's special status. China has both a legal and moral responsibility, both in the text and in spirit, to fulfill these commitments that it has asked both Hong Kong people and the international community to accept.

While PRC officials are fond of calling Hong Kong China's "internal affair," this arrangement says otherwise. Until these commitments were breached, Hong Kong was widely recognized as a free and open society distinct from China. Most critical to such recognition is the maintenance of the rule of law, which is still lacking in China. When China degraded Hong Kong's "high degree of autonomy," rule of law, and basic freedoms, the basis for special recognition failed, and a foreign response withdrawing such special recognition was justified. But such withdrawal does not relieve the parties or the international community of their obligations to Hong Kong people.

The NSL is not an ordinary national security law operating within constitutional and human rights restraints. Instead, it is an overwhelming imposition that displaces those restraints and the associated checks on official behavior. With the agreement and the Basic Law in tatters, the aim of international oversight and foreign policy must be to restore both the substance and the spirit of those assurances and guarantees that both Hong Kong people and the global community relied on. Monitoring and publicly reporting on compliance is minimal. For countries and international bodies directly involved in Hong Kong, relief measures are morally compelling.

In granting most Hongkongers access only to the British Nationality Overseas (BNO) passport at the handover, Britain unilaterally deprived the city's people of basic nationality rights. BNO passports afforded a travel document with diplomatic protection but only a right to visit—but not live permanently—in the UK. This degraded status was presumably accepted as long as the Hong Kong commitments remained secure. With the breakdown of those commitments, Britain was expected to step up and address Hong Kong's concerns. By offering the possibility of achieving permanent status in Britain, it has taken an important step in that direction. Over three million holders or potential holders of BNO passports, along with their families, are eligible to apply for such status and should remain so. Even with improved policies, it should be born in mind that emigration is no panacea. Those who out of desperation choose such path will often face severe livelihood challenges adapting to their new environment, challenges to which both the diaspora communities and host countries should be attentive. At the same time both Britain and the international community remain obligated to monitor developments in Hong Kong and prevail on Beijing to adhere to its treaty commitments.

Human Rights Monitoring and Oversight

Countries party to the UN human rights regime in general, and democracies in particular, share the burden of monitoring and responding effectively to degradations of human rights in Hong Kong. When the degradations are extreme, as they have been under the NSL and the ongoing crackdown in Hong Kong, then that duty is acute. Both UN treaty bodies and foreign governments, especially the US and the UK, have been vocal in condemning the current crackdown, the imposition of the NSL, and the subsequent rollback of democratic rights.

The US Department of State (DOS) has annually reported on compliance with China's treaty commitments under the US Hong Kong Policy Act. In its March 2022 DOS report, armed further with the Hong Kong Human Rights and Democracy Act, a traditionally gentle and encouraging approach was completely abandoned in favor of severe criticism of Beijing's failure to meet core obligations under the Basic Law and the Joint Declaration.[4] The same US report notes that, under such pressures, fifteen thousand US citizens were estimated to have left Hong Kong in 2021, both due to COVID measures and "other factors." It notes that Americans publicly critical of Chinese policy were at "heightened risk of arrest, detention, expulsion or prosecution. This same level of criticism of the many failures to uphold Hong Kong commitments were again expressed in the March 2023 DOS report, and again met with the disapproval from the Hong Kong government.[5]

In its July 2022 concluding observations under the ICCPR, the UN Human Rights Committee (HRC) joined such criticism, severely condemning the failure of the Chinese and Hong Kong governments to meet their obligations to the city under the ICCPR.[6] The HRC pointed out that both the national security law and the electoral reforms failed to comply with multiple requirements of the human rights covenant. The committee was "deeply concerned" that the national security law "prevails over other local laws in case of conflicts and consequently overrides fundamental rights and freedoms protected by the covenant." Given that the CFA has felt compelled to extend this override to even the Basic Law, this concern is of fundamental importance. During the hearing before the concluding observations were issued, Hong Kong officials took a defensive posture and failed to satisfy the HRC on any of the concerns raised.[7]

The HRC noted that the imposition of the NSL produced numerous violations resulting from the NSL's passage without public consultation, the vagueness of the four NSL crimes, the allowed transfer of cases to the mainland beyond the covenant's reach, the allowance of criminal investigations by mainland authorities without judicial oversight, a presumption against bail, and the allowance of unrestricted surveillance—to name just a few of the condemned violations.[8] The overly broad application of the law troubled the committee greatly, as did the aggressive targeting of civil society organizations and the media. The committee was equally concerned that the electoral overhaul effectively blocked political opposition. The committee emphasized that it was not the mere enactment of a national security law but the Hong Kong version that was the problem.

Instead of offering a constructive response, Beijing simply accused the HRC of arrogance and encouraged it to "face the fact that the national security law had restored stability in Hong Kong."[9] This response offered no acknowledgment of Beijing's failure to meet its commitments as a primary cause of that instability. During the hearings, Hong Kong government officials brazenly denied that any of their behavior constituted human rights violations and claimed that Hong Kong was now more democratic.[10] Paradoxically, even the defensive claim that the crackdown brought more stability and order is up against the government's reported spike in crime.[11]

Hong Kong people, to their credit, have historically taken responsibility for their own conditions, as was demonstrated in the several and sustained massive protests that have occurred. The local government has not taken such responsibility. The suppression of protests, pressures on civic organizations, censorship of the press, and arrest of speakers who offer or support critical views mean that local people are now largely blocked from pushing back against such human rights violations. There lies the problem. It is on this basis that international concern has been expressed and sanctions on responsible officials have been imposed.

Foreign governments have expressed further concern about the global reach of the NSL. The collusion charge under the NSL aims to cut off global support for Hong Kong.[12] It applies to individuals and corporations and residents and nonresidents alike who commit the prohibited activities both inside and outside China.[13] Foreign nationals and local residents are subject to the same punishment, though nonresidents are further "subject to deportation as the sole or an additional punishment."[14] Human rights defenders abroad have been targeted with warrants and even bounties on their heads for simply doing human rights work. Such long-arm reach of this excessive national security law demands a strong response. International human rights advocacy should be protected and never treated as a crime.

The Hong Kong prohibitions are so extreme that a member of the HRC, in the July 2022 dialogue, raised the question of whether a submission to the HRC amounted to such collusion with foreign forces. Will submitting a critical report during the HRC consultation violate the NSL? Interestingly, most of the NGO reports submitted in 2020 for the 2022 hearing were submitted before the NSL, and many of those organizations have since been disbanded. The Hong Kong officials giving testimony were noncommittal about this specific concern. Testifying before a foreign parliament attempting responsible oversight, as I and many others have done, may prove even more damning under NSL requirements.

Human Rights Advocacy

Hongkongers, both in Hong Kong and scattered in the diaspora overseas—like those targeted with arrest warrants and bounties under the NSL—have lobbied for governmental and parliamentary support around the world. Though such individuals and groups are sometimes accused by Beijing of promoting independence, such accusations miss the mark. Advocacy of independence, as it came up only in the last decade before the imposition of the NSL, was always a minority, somewhat marginal position, mostly among the young, with little hope of succeeding.

Though public surveys in 2019 had shown that up to 55 percent of those surveyed identified as "Hongkongers," as opposed to Chinese, support for independence lingered at 17 percent.[15] This was likely a pragmatic view, as very few people judged independence was possible. Beyond skepticism, calling for independence was a double-edged sword. While promoting the passionately held Hong Kong identity, at the same time, it offered Beijing an excuse to crack down.

Activists seeking international support for their cause had to recognize that foreign governments that maintain relations with China are not likely to engage with separatist movements. As a result, activists both in Hong Kong and in exile have, for the most part, remained focused on the promised democracy, rule of law, and human rights contained in China's existing commitments, as articulated in the Basic Law. China's sovereignty and national security have not been at risk from such demands, nor from foreign support.

What is generally demanded, both by foreign governments and by most Hong Kong supporters, is compliance with China's commitments to Hong Kong. With no meaningful direct access to Beijing, Hong Kong protesters and their supporters have historically traveled to capitals of the world to push for policies that will encourage China's compliance with its treaty and Basic Law obligations.

Under the current crackdown, those activists and supporters in exile or abroad have simply continued this tradition of peacefully raising these concerns. Promoting human rights is itself a basic right and not a threat to national security. With the NSL, Beijing has condemned such human rights appeals as criminal collusion, rendering simple human rights advocacy a crime. This has sent a chill through those who stand with Hong Kong abroad. Such condemnation is an affront not only to those who speak for Hong Kong but also to those parliamentarians and others who are determined to listen and add their voice, as they are bound to do in compliance with their own human rights commitments.

Hearings in parliamentary or congressional bodies have been the primary targets of such public appeals. The US House Foreign Affairs Committee held a hearing on July 1, the first day of the new national security law.[16] Lee Cheuk-yan, the Hong Kong labor leader and former legislator, testified from Hong Kong online in that hearing. He is now in prison serving two eighteen-month sentences for participating in pro-democracy protests in Hong Kong, and he faces further charges under the NSL.[17]

Lee well represents the courageous effort to draw attention to public concerns in Hong Kong. Despite the NSL's serious global reach and the potential punishment of life in prison under the collusion charge, Lee was not deterred. At the time, he already faced the noted prior charges for joining local unauthorized protests, for which he has since been jailed. As previously noted, as one of the organizers of the annual June 4 vigil, he has been charged under the NSL with inciting subversion along with fellow prominent activists Albert Ho, Chow Hang-Tung, and the Alliance in Support of the Patriotic Democratic Movement in China, which they headed.[18] The now disbanded alliance was accused of working as a foreign agent.

Lee Cheuk-yan has been a friend of my family for many years, and I cannot help but note that he is one of the most dedicated and responsible people I know. Yet, Beijing and local officials have branded him a common criminal for calling out human rights violations at home and sharing his concerns with foreign parliamentary bodies. Adding insult to injury, when his wife, the prominent labor leader Elizabeth Tang, out of compassion for her husband returned to Hong Kong to visit him in Stanley Prison, she was likewise arrested and accused under the NSL of collusion. This net even reached Elizabeth Tang's sister, who received a six-month jail sentence for merely removing her sister's computer and electronic devices from her sister's apartment as the arrests ensued, devices that proved to have no suspicious content. Looking at the sum of these charges, the real alleged crime is presumably human rights advocacy.

Are China and the Hong Kong government prepared to fill Hong Kong jails with dedicated members of the community like Lee Cheuk-yan? This is a question I asked in a book three years ago. Three years on, the answer is clearly yes. Can the international community afford to stand by and say nothing as this unfolds? Human rights advocates are driven by these concerns in their efforts to form NGOs, organize public protests, and lobby for international support.

Mobilizing Human Rights Advocacy Abroad

It is worth taking a close look at how such international advocacy is mobilized. In the summer of 2019, and for the first time through this long trajectory, I found myself in the regular company of extraordinary members of the Hong Kong diaspora working for Hong Kong in Washington, DC. Like many of them, most of my earlier human rights advocacy had been on the ground in Hong Kong. I had met some Hongkongers abroad in the past when I had testified in a congressional hearing on Hong Kong before the Congressional-Executive Commission on China. But this time, with the drastic repression of protests in Hong Kong, I was seeing a whole new level of determination among Hongkongers abroad. Like me, they worried what would happen to family and friends then protesting on the streets of Hong Kong in the face of the extraordinary show of police force. Those meeting in Washington were Americans, but they felt a strong loyalty to their place of origin where many of their families still lived.

To address the problem, they were exploring ways to dislodge the Hong Kong Human Rights and Democracy Act, which had languished in the US Congress for five years. Their path to doing this—and what has since been branded by Beijing as criminal collusion—was through open and totally legal organizing to appeal to their representatives in Congress.

Their efforts reflect a textbook case of human rights advocacy. As a human rights scholar and lawyer, I was asked to write a letter explaining the situation in Hong Kong to Congress, which I agreed to do. This letter would then be circulated to academics, former diplomats, and Hong Kong supporters around the world for their signature before being submitted to congressional leaders. Other letters were being circulated for signature at the grassroots level in congressional districts across the country.

The combination of front-page coverage of the ongoing Hong Kong protests, popular grassroots organizing in the US, and testimony from leading protesters visiting from Hong Kong would dislodge the bill in Congress. As with the original Hong Kong Policy Act, which had been passed nearly three decades earlier, the goal was to provide Chinese officials, who may want to maintain the special arrangement for Hong Kong, with the political guidance, political cover, and political pressure needed for Beijing to return fully to its prior commitments. If human rights are to prevail in the world, such advocacy, and the protests it seeks to support, needs to be protected and maintained as a central plank of foreign policy.

The US Hong Kong Human Rights and Democracy Act was advanced as amendments to the Hong Kong Policy Act. The amendments would provide additional tools to encourage compliance short of terminating Hong Kong's special treatment, though termination was also an option. The strong United States commitment to Hong Kong had survived through the 2008 financial crisis and even the trade war during the Trump administration. It was China's continued commitment to "one country, two systems" that was in doubt.

It soon became clear to Hong Kong supporters in Washington that letters to Congress would not be enough, and a move was made to form an NGO called the Hong Kong Democracy Council (HKDC) to promote the bill and to serve more generally as a resource on Hong Kong affairs. An extraordinary team was assembled. The core board members included Anna Cheung, a New York-based professor, as president; Victoria Tinbor Hui, an associate professor at the University of Notre Dame, as secretary; Joseph Ng, a successful software engineer, as treasurer; and Samuel Chu, an experienced social activist and lobbyist, as the director. An assortment of mostly American academics formed the advisory board. Their efforts paid off as the bill quickly moved through both houses of Congress and landed on the president's desk.[19]

With protests raging in Hong Kong, the Hong Kong Human Rights and Democracy Act had passed unanimously in the US Congress and was signed by then President Trump in late November 2019. Beijing called it improper interference in China's internal affairs, while Hong Kong activists viewed it as critical international support for their cause.[20]

As a reward for his efforts, Samuel Chu, the dedicated Hong Kong American social activist, reportedly became the target of a Hong Kong arrest warrant, facing NSL charges of collusion. When China reacted badly to the legislation, a subsequent Hong Kong Autonomy Act was also passed and signed into law. In getting these two bills through, the valuable contributions of Samuel Chu and the HKDC were then recognized on the floor of the House by the vice-chair of the Foreign Affairs Committee.[21] Can this deeply democratic path to law passage and human rights protection possibly be worthy of the criminal treatment it is being given under the NSL?

The 1992 Hong Kong Policy Act had long provided for a degree of oversight respecting Hong Kong's autonomy, but US officials had generally not been that forceful in the face of Beijing's growing encroachment. State Department reports had generally taken a somewhat gentle approach, mentioning China's overreach without imposing any sanctions for shortcomings or formally declaring that Hong Kong's autonomy had been lost.[22]

International Oversight

International oversight takes many forms. The Hong Kong Human Rights and Democracy Act reflects several possible strategies. It requires the US Secretary of State to assess whether China has continued to afford Hong Kong the high degree of autonomy, democratic reform, basic freedoms, and the rule of law it has promised. It aims to put pressure on Beijing to make good on these promises through several specific measures. These include an annual report certifying compliance, recommending whether Hong Kong's special treatment should be continued, offering measures for sanctioning individuals and entities found to have violated these requirements, issuing special visa waivers regarding criminal records with respect to protesters who have been arrested during demonstrations, and creating directives limiting technology transfers.

The new US act was deployed to impose the ultimate sanction much sooner than anticipated. In the wake of the announcement of the NSL, in his first report under the act, Secretary of State Mike Pompeo declared that Hong Kong's autonomy was no longer intact. Such a declaration provided justification for the US withdrawal of recognition of Hong Kong's special trade status, as well as the imposition of several targeted sanctions.[23]

In the July 2020 executive order that followed, the US president declared a national emergency and elaborated a long list of measures to be taken in direct response to China's promulgation of the NSL in Hong Kong. These included the elimination of policy exemptions in US law that apply to Hong Kong, the suspension of differential treatment for Hong Kong, the specific elimination of differential treatment with regard to immigration controls, the revoking of export license exemptions for Hong Kong, the planned suspension of the extradition agreement with Hong Kong (which, in fact, was later suspended), the elimination of assistance in training Hong Kong police, the termination of Fulbright exchanges in Hong Kong and China, the provision of refugee allocation for Hong Kong, and the provision for sanctions or asset seizures in respect of actors supporting China's new Hong Kong NSL.[24]

Sanctions against a specific list of senior officials in the Hong Kong government and the mainland's Hong Kong offices were subsequently announced by the US Treasury Department on August 7, 2020.[25] The sanctions, which targeted then Chief Executive Carrie Lam and ten other senior officials, involved asset seizures and a prohibition on travel to the US. Beijing and Hong Kong officials were quick to condemn these actions and followed up by targeting several congresspersons and human rights NGO heads in the US.[26]

Efforts have also been made to protect Hong Kong activists who have fled or plan to flee persecution or who are active abroad. Because of the long reach of the NSL, ten countries have opted to suspend their extradition agreements with Hong Kong, including the United States, Australia, Canada, France, Finland, Germany, the Netherlands, Ireland, the United Kingdom, and New Zealand.[27]

The NGO Safeguard Defenders has reported that China and Hong Kong have a much longer list of activists that they may target through Interpol.[28] Hong Kong exiles traveling abroad could find themselves at risk of arrest in countries that still maintain extradition arrangements with Hong Kong. Given China's aggressive record of pursuing fugitives abroad—under its global anti-corruption campaign called Sky Net—these are not idle concerns.[29] Safeguard Defenders has asked Interpol to remove any such names, should they be submitted, in compliance with the Interpol Charter, which bars Interpol from intervention in alleged political crimes.[30] A Taiwanese sought by China in Poland recently obtained a ruling from the European Court of Human Rights that may effectively bar extradition from Europe to China—by eliminating the need to make an individual showing of a fear of torture.[31] With Hong Kong increasingly coming under Beijing's shadow, a similar rule may soon arguably apply to Hong Kong.

In the US, the use of targeted sanctions against top Chinese and Hong Kong government officials has given rise to wider questions about the effectiveness of sanctions and the merits of extending them to wider targets, including national security judges and prosecutors engaged in prosecuting cases related to public order and the NSL. Several congresspersons had earlier advocated such targeted sanctions be extended to judges and prosecutors whose actions infringe basic rights.[32] This recommendation took on substance in a July 2022 Congressional-Executive Commission on China report naming several midlevel prosecutors as possible targets of such sanctions.[33] While such wider sanctions targeting judges and midlevel officials sends a clear message and may encourage their colleagues to avoid similar behavior, the impact on actual government policy may be minimal. With this limitation in mind, targeted sanctions may be viewed as an important partial response and an expression of concern.

With or without such sanctions, a more comprehensive approach to upholding human rights in foreign policy is indicated. A regulatory approach that targets inappropriate business practices respecting human rights, much in the same way that business engagement in corrupt practices is regulated, would likely be more effective. Companies that have faced pressure from Beijing to support its national security law and the related crackdown should be subject to comprehensive US regulations that prohibit human rights violations or support for violations. Human rights and the rule of law are core US values that US laws should uphold, with or without short-term sanctions.

Davis, Polk, and Wardwell, a US law firm, was recently about to participate in a conference sponsored by the Hong Kong government to uphold and assess the NSL. Under public pressure, the firm's senior partner withdrew.[34] Laws could be enacted to discourage such support. In such cases, sanctions would then target companies that ignored such requirements. In practice, such a regulatory regime would discourage such behavior in the first place, thereby imposing costs related to attracting international investment on regimes that seek to require such support, and giving companies avenues to resist such pressures.

In further response to Beijing's passage of the NSL, the US Congress passed, and the president signed into law, the Hong Kong Autonomy Act, which in many respects duplicates the Hong Kong Human Rights and Democracy Act, though it gives some special attention to financial institutions.[35] This is significant because, as previously discussed, Beijing was putting pressure on corporations to line up behind its Hong Kong policies. US laws discouraging such support may enable those targeted companies to better resist such Beijing pressures. Other proposed laws relating to refugee status and immigration have languished in Congress in various forms.

Condemnations of the NSL also flowed from a number of other countries, with the UK, as noted, opening its doors to potentially over three million Hongkongers and their families who are holding or entitled to the British National Overseas passport for possible permanent residence in the UK.[36] The European Union has also drafted legislation to ban the export of products that could be used for "internal repression, the interception of internal communications or cyber-surveillance."[37] A draft 2020 EU plan described the NSL as a "matter of grave concern" and "not in conformity with China's international commitments under the Sino-British Joint Declaration of 1984 or the Hong Kong Basic Law."[38] It describes planned actions relating to asylum, migration, visas, residency, student reception and universities. This list tracks with actions planned by other leading democracies around the world.

As a matter of desperation, Hong Kong protesters and opinion leaders had encouraged international support for the 2019 protests, with a parade of visits to Washington and other capitals to promote similar legislation.[39] When we consider the original efforts of Beijing to enlist foreign support and recognition of Hong

Kong's special status during the initiation of both the Joint Declaration and the Basic Law, it is difficult to make the case that such legislation and the determinations thereunder are an improper interference in China's internal affairs.[40] But this is what Beijing officials have long argued.

Those same foreign governments are simply taking measures to ensure compliance with the commitments that justified their special treatment of Hong Kong. None of these goals offend China's sovereignty. Quite the contrary, they could be viewed as encouraging and assisting China's original efforts to maintain Hong Kong as a distinct capitalist free-market territory, with protections of basic freedoms and the rule of law, as promised in the Joint Declaration and the Basic Law.

IS HOPE LOST?

12

THE ROAD TRAVELED AND
THE CHALLENGE AHEAD

"What happened in Hong Kong is not an anomaly but a warning."
— Quoting Hong Kong human rights defender Chow Hang Tung's
speech written from prison upon receiving a human rights award.

We began this journey by imagining a major global city being taken over by a hard-line regime that aggressively threatened its basic institutions and freedoms. In the chapters that followed, we traced that process, which has sometimes been slow and sometimes dramatic, for just such a city, Hong Kong. We watched the slow burn of early anxiety turn into the hope offered both in a treaty and the Basic Law. We saw this hope give way to despair as new laws, directives, and policies were imposed to hollow out liberal institutions and erode commitments to democratic reform. We then felt the explosion of despair, and eventually fear, on the streets in the 2003 article 23 protests, the 2012 protest against patriotic education, the 2014 Umbrella Movement, and the 2019 anti-extradition protests, as well as continuing protests over democracy along the way.

At the end, under the NSL, Beijing imposed an illiberal version of top-down control, much like the mainland, as an alternative to the promised liberal democratic model. Under this top-down model, driven by national security concerns, nothing is left to chance. Liberal institutions to check those in power are hollowed out to ensure that critical opposition is silenced. To achieve the desired control, government opponents who have gained public attention are removed from the playing field of public opinion through the strict regulation of national security. Law enforcement bodies, the courts, and the legal profession are guided or intimidated to conform to the expected behavior. In mainland China, this is achieved with little pretense of protecting basic freedoms under a top-down notion of the rule by law.

In quasi-open societies not fully subject to communist party discipline, such control is largely achieved through a system of threats and rewards combined with the hollowing out of liberal institutions. Under the heading of "autocratisation," Eric Yan-ho Lai traces this tendency in Hong Kong, first in the earlier colonial period, when officials faced few checks on their power, then later in the late colonial period, along with liberal reforms, human rights guarantees, and moderate democratization, and then eventually in the post-handover era, with a sharp turn toward autocratic rule.[1]

The newly imposed Hong Kong model is illustrative of Beijing's version of so-called "whole process people's democracy" applied in a quasi-open society. Under this model, as it has been applied in Hong Kong, vague criminal laws afford wide official discretion to target and incarcerate critical opponents, local law enforcement is brought under Beijing's guidance through the Committee and Office for Safeguarding National Security, and liberal legal institutions are degraded to ensure compliance with official aims.

A premium is placed on loyalty, party loyalty on the mainland and a similar loyalty under the label patriotism in Hong Kong. Compliant senior police officials are rewarded with promotions. The current chief executive of Hong Kong and his secretary for security are among police officers who have been richly rewarded for their passionate adherence to Beijing's national security policies. Judicial independence is diminished and guided by allowing only select judges to hear national security cases. Such judges likewise have better prospects at promotion. Judges who stray face official wrath, which is often expressed in the Beijing-controlled and compliant media. All of these expectations are backed up by official oaths where compliance is measured by political loyalty to the regime.

The opposition is excluded and further silenced by investigations and intimidation targeting both opposition press and social organizations. While the three most prominent opposition media outlets faced closure and prosecutions, the city's historically respected public broadcaster was brought under disciplined guidance. The disbandment of over sixty community organizations clearly demonstrates that wider society has gotten the message. This combination of aggressive enforcement, managed top-down control, and the hollowing out of established liberal institutions eliminates popular voices and ensures government control over political outcomes.

Beijing has taken to labeling its illiberal authoritarian model at home as "whole process people's democracy." This clearly offers neither an effective process of oversight and accountability nor genuine democratic choice. Most of all, it deprives the citizens of a previously open society of the world-class freedoms and rule of law they long enjoyed. The promised aim of universal suffrage has been denied. The so-called gradual and orderly progress has become progress in reverse. With all these changes and denials, freedom has been undone, and the hoped for vision of accountable government has been lost.

As highlighted in the preceding chapters, over the course of this evolving process, Hong Kong descended into ever-increasing repression. The Umbrella Movement, faced with official indifference, gave way to simmering confrontations followed by prosecutions and disqualifications in the interim period between 2015 and 2019. This was followed by a tangle of police abuse, bursts of responsive violence, and finally with the mass arrests in the 2019 protests. Following that, instead of mitigation and compromise, the sharp edge of an authoritarian national security state was brought down upon the freewheeling city and its people. The NSL and its related laws on public order, rioting, and sedition were aggressively enforced. In the aftermath of this repression, Hong Kong's respected advocates for democracy, human rights, and the rule of law were jailed, pushed into exile, or silenced in an unrelenting crackdown.

When it appeared nothing more repressive could be done to this previously freewheeling city, Beijing then imposed its new patriots-only electoral reforms, which added political powerlessness to the already fearful conditions. In this process, Hong Kong was transformed from one of the world's freest, most open societies, based on the rule of law, into a city where government opponents are now mostly political prisoners or in exile, where democratic institutions have been degraded, where critical civil society organizations have been shut down and silenced, where liberal legal institutions have been hollowed out, where critical liberal education has been transformed to memorized patriotic education, and where those who dare to speak out await the 6:00 a.m. knock.

The people of Hong Kong and supporters around the world have been left to search for a path forward. Whether in the face of mass exodus or more unrest, will responsible officials be persuaded to change course, to step back from this repressive national security model, and renew the "one country, two systems" commitments to Hong Kong? With Beijing having invested so much of its social capital and the CCP's legitimacy in this narrative, such a reverse of course seems unlikely. Without carrying out these agreed commitments both in text and spirit, the decolonization of Hong Kong—so richly guaranteed first in the UN Charter and then in the Sino-British Joint Declaration and Basic Law—remains unfulfilled.

Unfortunately, Beijing's approach to Hong Kong, which is very much consistent with its approach to governance on the mainland, emphasizes control over accommodation. The complicit Hong Kong government, with little popular support, has been poorly equipped to perform its primary role as the guardian of autonomy and liberal governance in the city. For both governments, the repression of political opposition has taken precedence over adjusting to public demands. Beijing and its supporters have claimed that this repressive approach was well intended and necessary to bring stability and order to Hong Kong. But, as this narrative shows, it has been the consistent thread of interference and the associated repressive policies that are the primary source of pushback, instability, and disorder. Every action begets a reaction, as escalating protests follow escalating repression.

One can only imagine the consequences of all this for Hong Kong's continuing status as a financial and commercial center. It seems clear that business investors, whether they be local or international, can no longer significantly distinguish Hong Kong from mainland cities when it comes to doing business. From a business point of view, Hong Kong's key assets were always its rule of law and basic freedoms. Local Hongkongers and international corporations centered their business base and related investment activities in Hong Kong because it was the gateway to China, with the rule of law and corruption-free opportunities that were not available on the mainland. They stayed or came because they knew their children could have world-class educations, that they could live in relatively safe environments where buildings were built to code, where they could travel in and out freely, where information access was unencumbered, where needed products for their daily lives were available, and where they were free to speak their mind. When you change such a system to one favoring loyalty over performance, and control over freedom, much of these advantages the city offered are lost.

This seemingly predicts a future where some people will stay and international businesses will still arrive to gain access to the Chinese market but where confidence in the above qualities will be lost. No doubt mainland investors will come to Hong Kong for slight advantages offered by whatever may remain of Hong Kong traditions, to list on its stock market, and to take advantage of its outside connections, but with much fewer of the above advantages. What seems likely, given the incentives for the mainland government to show Hong Kong still thrives, is much less the open and bright city Hong Kong was famous for and much more a somewhat shadowed version of its former self.

What will this mean for the average worker in Hong Kong who faces the question "to go or not to go"? Long ago, I wrote an article with this title in the *Far Eastern Economic Review*, before the handover and after the 1989 crisis.[2] It seems this question has returned. As we have seen recently, more talent will leave, seeking opportunities in democratic societies abroad. This will surely have an impact on the schools and quality of life in the city. No doubt the two governments will then encourage mainlanders to come and fill the void, which is also already evident in recent policies. At the end of it all, the glowing light of this world city will be missed. Both the people and the government need to seriously reflect if they want to bet on the new model now on offer, a model of repressive control with freedom undone.

NOTES

Chapter 1

[1] The Law of the People's Republic of China on Safeguarding National Security in the Hong Kong Special Administrative Region (hereinafter, national security law, or NSL), G.N. (E.) 72 of 2020, http://www.xinhuanet.com/english/2020-07/01/c_139178753. htm. Subsequent references will be to this official English version, with appropriate articles indicated, also available at https://www.gld.gov.hk/egazette/pdf/20202448e/egn2020244872.pdf; Michael C. Davis, *Making Hong Kong China: The Rollback of Human Rights and the Rule of Law*, New York: Columbia University Press, Asia Society Series, 2020.

[2] Christopher Walker, "Rising to the Sharp Power Challenge," *Journal of Democracy* 33, no. 4 (October 2022): 119–132, https://www.journalofdemocracy.org/articles/rising-to-the-sharp-power-challenge/.

[3] Leopoldo Lopez, Challenging Autocracy From The Front Lines, Wilson Center Report, July 2023, https://www.wilsoncenter.org/publication/challenging-autocracy-front-lines

[4] Marc Fisher, "Leaders of Democracies Increasingly Echo Putin in Authoritarian Tilt," *Washington Post*, October 16, 2022, https://www.washingtonpost.com/national-security/2022/10/16/authoritarian-world-leaders-putin/.

[5] Tom Ginsburg, *Judicial Review in New Democracies, Constitutional Courts in Asian Cases*. Cambridge: Cambridge University Press, 2003; Alexander Bickel, *The Least Dangerous Branch: The Supreme Court at the Bar of Politics*, 2nd Edition. New Haven: Yale University Press, 1986; Mauro Cappelletti, *Judicial Review in the Contemporary World*. Indianapolis: The Bobbs–Merrill Company, 1971.

[6] Larry Diamond, "All Democracy is Global: Why America Can't Shrink from the Fight for Freedom," *Foreign Affairs* (September/October 2022), https://www.foreignaffairs.com/united-states/all-democracy-global-america-cant-shrink-fight-freedom-larry-diamond.

[7] "China: Democracy That Works," The State Council Information Office of the PRC, December 2021, https://english.www.gov.cn/archive/whitepaper/202112/04/content_WS61aae34fc6d0df57f98e6098.html.

[8] "Hong Kong: Democratic Progress under the Framework of One Country Two Systems," The State Council Information Office, December 2022, http://www.news.cn/english/2021-12/20/c_1310383195.htm.

[9] Joint Declaration of the Government of the United Kingdom of Great Britain and Northern Ireland and the Government of the People's Republic of China on the Question of Hong Kong (hereinafter "Joint Declaration"), December 19, 1984.

[10] Basic Law of the Hong Kong Special Administrative Region of the People's Republic of China (hereinafter "Basic Law"), https://www.basiclaw.gov.hk/en/basiclawtext/index.html.

[11] Hong Kong has dropped to the second position on the list behind Singapore. Terry Miller, Anthony B. Kim, and James M. Roberts, with Patrick Tyrrel, *2020 Index of Economic Freedom*. Washington, DC: The Heritage Foundation, https://www.heritage.org/index/pdf/2020/book/index_2020.pdf.

[12] "World Marks 30 years since Tiananmen Massacre as China Censors All Mention," CNN, June 4, 2019, https://www.cnn.com/2019/06/03/asia/tiananmen-june-4-china-censorship-intl/index.html.

[13] Still thousands jumped over barriers to attend. "Defying Beijing, Thousands in Hong Kong Hold Tiananmen Vigil," *New York Times*, June 4, 2020, https://www.nytimes.com/2020/06/04/world/asia/tiananmen-hong-kong-china.html.

[14] Jeffrey Wasserstrom, *Vigil: Hong Kong on the Brink*. New York: Columbia Global Reports, 2020, 24.

[15] Antony Dapiran, *City of Protest: A Recent History of Dissent in Hong Kong*. New York: Penguin Books, 2017. For another view, Daniel Vukovich usefully examines the violent trend and roots of some frontline protesters during the 2019 protests, though I worry he credits too much to this violent minority without sufficiently accounting for the much deeper nonviolent movement core and its more traditionally liberal goals. Daniel Vukovich, "A City and a SAR on Fire: As If Everything and Nothing Changes," *Critical Asian Studies* (December 20, 2019): 1–17, https://doi.org/10.1080/14672715.2020.170 3296. See also Ho-Fung Hung, "Three Views of Local Consciousness in Hong Kong," *ChinaFile*, November 26, 2014, https://www.chinafile.com/reporting-opinion/viewpoint/three-views-local-consciousness-hong-kong. For an audio account by the same author about factors behind the Hong Kong protests, see Yasmin Yoon, "Hong Kong Protest with Ho-Fung Hung," *Asia in Washington,* by the Edwin O. Reischauer Center for East Asian Studies, June 17, 2020, https://www.reischauercenter.org/podcasts/the-hong-kong-protests-with-ho-fung-hung/.

[16] "Document 9: A ChinaFile Translation," *ChinaFile*, November 8, 2013, https://www.chinafile.com/document-9-chinafile-translation.

[17] Lest there was any doubt about the arrival of such standards, the *Global Times*, a famously nationalistic mainland newspaper, heaped praise on Hong Kong education book publishers for removing the traditional Hong Kong praise for its strong tradition of the separation of powers from newly prepared textbooks. "Revised HK Textbooks Correct Political Misconceptions, Stress Chinese Identity," *Global Times*, August 18, 2020, https://www.globaltimes.cn/content/1198164.shtml.

[18] "Hong Kong Teachers Fired and Afraid as China Targets Liberal Thinkers," *Wall Street Journal*, July 19, 2020, https://www.wsj.com/articles/hong-kong-teachers-fired-and-afraid-as-china-targets-liberal-thinkers-11595175839?mod=searchresults&page=1&p

os=1; "6 Hong Kong Teachers Disqualified over Complaints Related to the 2019 Protests," *Hong Kong Free Press*, April 13, 2022, https://hongkongfp.com/2022/04/13/6-hong-kong-teachers-disqualified-over-complaints-linked-to-2019-protests/.

[19] John Power, Jeffie Lam, and Elizabeth Cheung, "National Security Law: For Hong Kong Scholars a Fear of the Unknown," *South China Morning Post*, August 8, 2020, https://scmp.com/week-asia/politics/article/3096370/national-security-law-hong-kong-scholars-fear-unknown. It should be noted that this academic concern was widely shared among scholars abroad, as echoed in the statement of "deep concern" offered by the Association of Asian Studies. "Statement on the 2020 Hong Kong National Security Law," Association of Asian Studies, July 17, 2020, https://www.asianstudies.org/statement-on-the-2020-hong-kong-national-security-law/. During COVID, elite foreign universities were coming up with strategies to protect their students taking online courses from the risk of prosecution at home for openly discussing sensitive topics. "China's National-Security Law Reaches into Harvard, Princeton Classrooms," *Wall Street Journal*, August 19, 2020, https://www.wsj.com/articles/chinas-national-security-law-reaches-into-harvard-princeton-classrooms-11597829402.

[20] "The Law of the People's Republic of China ("PRC") on Safeguarding National Security in the Hong Kong Special Administrative Region ("HKSAR") Statement of the Hong Kong Bar Association," Hong Kong Bar Association, July 1, 2020, https://www.hkba.org/sites/default/files/20200701%20HKBA%20statement%20on%20Safeguarding%20National%20%20Security%20in%20HKSAR.pdf. The New York City Bar Association had earlier expressed similar sentiments when an outline of the new law was first published. "New York City Bar Association Statement on China's Proposed National Security Law," New York City Bar Association, May 27, 2020, https://s3.amazonaws.com/documents.nycbar.org/files/HK_National_Security_Law_Statement_200527.pdf.

[21] Chris Lau, "Hong Kong Bar Association's new chief walks a tightrope and mends ties with Beijing while speaking up on issues," *South China Morning Post*, May 16, 2022. https://www.scmp.com/news/hong-kong/politics/article/3177813/can-hong-kong-bar-associations-new-chief-walk-tightrope-and

[22] "Fifth Anniversary of 709 Crackdown: Updated Chart of Persecution of Lawyers and Legal and Rights Advocates," Human Rights in China, HRIC Resource, July 9, 2020, https://www.hrichina.org/en/fifth-anniversary-709-crackdown-updated-chart-persecution-lawyers-and-legal-and-rights-advocates.

[23] Ibid.

[24] Vivian Wang, "China Sentences Leading Rights Activists to 14 and 12 Years in Prison," *New York Times*, April 10, 2023, https://www.nytimes.com/2023/04/10/world/asia/china-activists-prison.html?fbclid=IwAR39fg-HptPcgTTcSgOFEi4_NMB2S096_NPvzpuA9EQMWwVrONVu0U9-yXU. It is important to appreciate the context of these attacks on human rights defenders—as highlighted in numerous UN human rights reports—has been a mainland environment of nearly total disregard for, and breach of, human rights. Willian Nee, "A UN Review Shows the Limits of China's Loud Microphone Communications Strategy," *OpenGlobalRights*, April 17, 2023, https://www.openglobalrights.org/un-review-shows-limits-chinas-communications-strategy/.

[25] Greg Torode and James Pomfret, "Ex-Chief of Hong Kong Barristers Says He Left City after Police Interview," *Reuters*, March 2, 2022, https://www.reuters.com/world/china/ex-chief-hong-kong-barristers-says-he-left-city-after-police-interview-2022-03-02/.

[26] Peter Lee, "Hong Kong Law Firm Vidler & Co, Which Handled Protest-Related Cases, to Close after 19 Years," *Hong Kong Free Press*, April 21, 2022, https://hongkongfp.com/2022/04/21/hong-kong-law-firm-vidler-co-which-handled-protest-related-cases-to-close-after-19-years/.

[27] "Disqualified lawmaker Dennis Kwok fled to Canada," *The Standard*, April 6, 2021. https://www.thestandard.com.hk/breaking-news/section/4/168915/Disqualified-lawmaker-Dennis-Kwok-fled-to-Canada

[28] Clifford Lo, "Hong Kong national security law: police offer HK$1 million rewards for arrests of 8 people, including 3 ex-lawmakers," *South China Morning Post*, July 3, 2023. https://scmp.com/news/hong-kong/law-and-crime/article/3226372/hong-kong-national-security-law-police-offer-hk1-million-rewards-arrest-8-people

[29] James Lee, "Hong Kong national security arrest 10 linked to 2019 protester relief fund," *Hong Kong Free Press*, August 10, 2023, https://hongkongfp.com/2023/08/10/breaking-national-security-police-arrest-6-linked-to-2019-protester-relief-fund-reports/

[30] Christy Leung and Chris Lau, "Hong Kong national security police lodge complaint against lawyer who allegedly took fees from legal defence fund despite claims of pro bono services," *South China Morning Post*, May 12, 2022, https://www.scmp.com/news/hong-kong/law-and-crime/article/3177540/hong-kong-national-security-police-lodge-complaint

[31] Candice Chau, "Security law: At least 8 Hong Kong pro-democracy groups disband in the past 2 weeks, including lawyers' group," *Hong Kong Free Press*, July 6, 2021, https://hongkongfp.com/2021/07/06/security-law-at-least-8-hong-kong-pro-democracy-groups-disband-in-past-2-weeks-including-lawyers-group/

[32] Clifford Lo, "Hong Kong national security law: police offer HK$1 million rewards for arrests of 8 people, including 3 ex-lawmakers," *South China Morning Post*, July 3, 2023.

[33] "National Security Law: Hong Kong Libraries Pull Books by Some Localist and Democracy Activists for Review," *South China Morning Post*, July 4, 2020, https://www.scmp.com/news/hong-kong/politics/article/3091842/national-security-law-hong-libraries-pull-books-some.

[34] "Missing Hong Kong Booksellers Paraded on Chinese TV," BBC News, February 29, 2016, https://www.bbc.com/news/world-asia-china-35685999.

[35] "Billionaire Is Reported Seized from Hong Kong Hotel and Taken into China," *New York Times*, January 31, 2017, https://www.nytimes.com/2017/01/31/world/asia/xiao-jianhua-china-hong-kong-billionaire.html.

[36] "Chinese Canadian Billionaire Sentenced to 13 Years for Financial Crimes," *New York Times*, August 19, 2022, https://www.nytimes.com/2022/08/19/business/chinese-canadian-billionaire-xiao-jianhua-sentenced.html.

[37] "World Press Freedom Day: Hong Kong Nosedives in Press Freedom Ranking—below Cambodia, Somalia, Sri Lanka," *Hong Kong Free Press*, May 2, 2022, https://hongkongfp. com/2022/05/03/world-press-freedom-day-hong-kong-nosedives-in-press-freedom-ranking-below-cambodia-somalia-sri-lanka/?utm_medium=email.

[38] Ibid.

[39] Oiwan Lam, "Hong Kong's Press Freedom Plunged from Satisfactory to a 'Difficult Situation' in a Matter of Years," *Global Voices*, May 4, 2022, https://globalvoices. org/2022/05/04/hong-kongs-press-freedom-plunged-from-satisfactory-to-problematic-and-then-to-difficult/.

[40] Jessie Pang and Edmond Ng, "Hong Kong Citizen's News says closure triggered by Stand News collapse," *Reuters*, January 3, 2022. https://www.reuters.com/world/china/hong-kongs-citizen-news-says-closure-triggered-by-stand-news-collapse-2022-01-03/

[41] Arthur Kaufman, "New Editorial Guidelines leash RTHK to National Security Law," *China Digital Times*, September 30, 2021, https://chinadigitaltimes.net/2021/09/new-editorial-guidelines-leash-rthk-to-national-security-law/

[42] Tom Grundy, "Team of Journalists Resigned after SCMP Axed 3-part Series on Xinjiang Abuses, Ex-Editor Says," *Hong Kong Free Press*, October 25, 2022, https://hongkongfp. com/2022/10/25/team-of-journalists-resigned-after-scmp-axed-3-part-series-on-xinjiang-abuses-ex-editor-says/.

[43] Candice Chau, "Hong Kong Newspaper Ming Pao Criticised by No. 2 Official over Comic Strip about Beijing Ruling on Security Law," *Hong Kong Free Press*, January 6, 2023, https://hongkongfp.com/2023/01/06/hong-kong-newspaper-ming-pao-criticised-by-no-2-official-over-comic-strip-about-beijing-ruling-on-security-law/.

[44] "Leaders of Hong Kong Pro-Democracy Group Demosisto Step Down as Security Law Passes," *Hong Kong Free Press*, June 30, 2020, https://hongkongfp.com/2020/06/30/breaking-hong-kong-activists-joshua-wong-nathan-law-and-agnes-chow-withdraw-from-pro-democracy-demosisto-group-as-security-law-passes/.

[45] "Four Members of Hong Kong Pro-Independence Group Arrested by Police Officers from National Security Unit," *South China Morning Post*, July 29, 2020, https://www.scmp. com/news/hong-kong/law-and-crime/article/3095240/least-three-core-members-hong-kong-pro-independence.

[46] Kelley Ho, "Hong Kong national security police arrest one more man over alleged conspiracy to fund self-exiled activists," Hong Kong Free Press, July 6, 2023. https://hongkongfp.com/2023/07/06/hong-kong-national-security-police-arrest-one-more-man-over-alleged-conspiracy-to-fund-self-exiled-activists/

[47] "Timeline: 58 Hong Kong Civil Society Groups Disband Following the Onset of the Security Law," *Hong Kong Free Press*, June 30, 2022, https://hongkongfp.com/2022/06/30/explainer-over-50-groups-gone-in-11-months-how-hong-kongs-pro-democracy-forces-crumbled/.

[48] Natalie Wong, "National Security Law: 47 Hong Kong Opposition Figures Charged with Conspiring to Subvert State Power, after Arrests over Roles in Bloc's Primary," *South

China Morning Post, February 28, 2021, https://www.scmp.com/news/hong-kong/politics/article/3123475/national-security-law-47-hong-kong-opposition-figures.

[49] NSL, Article 62.

[50] *HKSAR v. Lai Chee Ying*, Final Appeal No. 1 of 2021, Hong Kong Court of Final Appeal, February 9, 2021, https://legalref.judiciary.hk/lrs/common/ju/ju_frame.jsp.

[51] People's Republic of China (PRC), Legislative Law, March 15, 2000, Amended 2015, articles 83 and 85, http://eng.mod.gov.cn/publications/2017-03/02/content_4774201.htm.

[52] "Beijing Condemns Hong Kong Court for Overturning Mask Ban, Says It Alone Has Constitutional Authority," *Hong Kong Free Press*, November 19, 2019, https://hongkongfp.com/2019/11/19/beijing-condemns-hong-kong-court-overturning-mask-ban-says-alone-constitutional-authority/.

[53] "Hong Kong Mask Ban Legal When Aimed at Unauthorized Protests, Court of Appeal Rule in Partially Overturning Lower Court Verdict," *South China Morning Post*, April 9, 2020, https://www.scmp.com/news/hong-kong/law-and-crime/article/3079197/hong-kong-mask-ban-legal-when-aimed-unauthorised.

[54] *Kwok Wing Hang et al. v. HKSAR Chief Executive in Council*, Court of Final Appeal, Final Appeals 6 and 7 of 2020, from CACV Nos. 542 and 583 of 2019, December 21, 2020; Shibani Mahtani, "Hong Kong's Highest Court Upholds Ban on Masks at Protests," *Washington Post*, December 21, 2022, https://www.washingtonpost.com/world/hongkong-mask-ban-ruling/2020/12/20/f2722af0-4340-11eb-a277-49a6d1f9dff1_story.html.

[55] Basic Law, articles 14, 18, 22, and 23.

[56] The Basic Law provides for an ultimate aim of universal suffrage. Basic Law, articles 45 and 68.

[57] "Police Reputation in Tatters across the Political Divide According to Online Survey of Hong Kong Voters," *South China Morning Post*, December 21, 2019, https://www.scmp.com/news/hong-kong/politics/article/3043030/police-reputation-tatters-across-political-divide-according; also discussed in interview with Professor Puja Kapai, December 5, 2019.

[58] Hana Meihan Davis and Jeffrey Wasserstrom, "Hong Kong and 'The Hunger Games,'" *The Millions*, January 24, 2020, https://themillions.com/2020/01/hong-kong-and-the-hunger-games.html. See also, Jeffrey Wasserstrom, *Vigil: Hong Kong on the Brink*: 20–21.

[59] Theodora Yu, "'Ten Years' portrayed a dark vision of Hong Kong. Life imitated art in barely half that time," *Washington Post*, April 2, 2021, https://www.washingtonpost.com/world/2021/04/02/hong-kong-china-ten-years-movie/

[60] William Nee, "China's Insistence on 'Zero Covid' in Hong Kong Has a Deeper Meaning," *The Diplomat*, February 18, 2022, https://thediplomat.com/2022/02/chinas-insistence-on-zero-covid-in-hong-kong-has-a-deeper-meaning/.

[61] Professor Wilson Wong of the Chinese University of Hong Kong lays out how the 2019 protest, what many called the "water revolution," was not a revolution but mainly a movement demanding China's compliance with its commitments to Hong Kong.

Wilson Wong, "The Water Movement Represents the Best of Times for Hong Kong," *Asia Dialogue*, September 27, 2019, https://theasiadialogue.com/2019/09/27/the-water-movement-represents-the-best-of-times-for-hong-kong/.

[62] Nathan was writing in 2019 amid the protest but well before the national security law. Andrew J. Nathan, "How China Sees the Hong Kong Crisis, The Real Reason Behind Beijing's Restraint," *Foreign Affairs*, September 30, 2019, https://www.foreignaffairs.com/articles/china/2019-09-30/how-china-sees-hong-kong-crisis

[63] Andrew J. Nathan, "The Alternate History of China," *Foreign Affairs* (September/October 2022), https://foreignaffairs.com/reviews/alternate-history-china-beijing-different-path

[64] Jean-Pierre Cabestan, "Xi Jingping and Democracy Storytelling in China," *Asia Trends* (Summer 2022): 13–21, https://asiacentre.eu/2022/09/05/asia-trends-8-automne-2022-a-year-in-indo-pacific/.

[65] Lily Kuo, "Rare Protests against China's 'Zero Covid' Policy Erupt across Country," *Washington Post*, November 27, 2022, https://www.washingtonpost.com/world/2022/11/27/china-covid-lockdown-protest-xinjiang/.

[66] Sheena Chestnut Greitens, "Xi Jinping's Quest for Order, Security at Home, Influence Abroad," *Foreign Affairs*, October 3, 2022, https://www.foreignaffairs.com/china/xi-jinping-quest-order. In another recent *Foreign Affairs* article, Taisu Zhang offers a somewhat complementary analysis, law being the controlling instrument to advance national security, noting Xi's increased emphasis on legality. Taisu Zhang, "Xi's Law-and-Order Strategy," *Foreign Affairs*, February 27, 2023, https://www.foreignaffairs.com/china/xis-law-and-order-strategy.

[67] Yuanyue Dang, "Abuse fears sparked by China's proposed 'hurt feelings' legal change," *South China Morning Post*, September 9, 2023, https://amp-scmp-com.cdn.ampproject.org/c/s/amp.scmp.com/news/china/politics/article/3233901/abuse-fears-sparked-chinas-proposed-hurt-feelings-legal-change. The NPC Observer has published and English translation of the draft legislation, https://npcobserver.com/2023/09/01/china-npc-consultation-public-security-administration-company-vat-education-law/

[68] Michael Beckley and Hal Brands, "China's Threat to Global Democracy, " *Journal of Democracy*, Vol. 34/1, January 2023, https://www.journalofdemocracy.org/articles/chinas-threat-to-global-democracy. A recent *Washington Post* article notes the perceived threat this poses in Singapore. Shibani Mahtani and Amrita Chandradas, "In Singapore loud echoes of Beijing's positions generate anxiety," *Washington Post*, July 24, 2023. https://www.washingtonpost.com/world/interactive/2023/singapore-china-news-influence-lianhe-zaobao. Evans Osnos has described the current repressive turn as producing an "age of malaise." Evans Osnos, "China's Age of Malaise," *The New Yorker*, October 23, 2023. https://www.newyorker.com/magazine/2023/10/30/chinas-age-of-malaise

[69] Chris Buckley, "'Clean Up This Mess': The Chinese Thinkers Behind Xi's Hard Line," *New York Times*, August 2, 2020, https://www.nytimes.com/2020/08/02/world/asia/china-hong-kong-national-security-law.html. It is important to appreciate that China has long had rich competing traditions. Professor Qianfan Zhang's work on the Chinese

Constitution incorporates a rich appreciation of the liberal constitutional tradition. Qianfan Zhang, *The Constitution of China: A Contextual Analysis*. Oxford: Hart Publishing, 2012.

[70] Didi Kirsten Tatlow offers a nice summary of China's United Front tactics of early intervention in Hong Kong well before the handover. Didi Kirsten Tatlow, "How Hong Kong Was Lost," *Sinopsis*, August 12, 2020, https://sinopsis.cz/en/how-hong-kong-was-lost/.

[71] Professor Ho-fung Hung develops this comparison at length. Ho-fung Hung, *City on the Edge: Hong Kong Under Chinese Rule*. Cambridge: Cambridge University Press, 2022, chapter 5, https://www.cambridge.org/core/books/city-on-the-edge/0127C29BEA800F011A320F9BB338FF9E. Regarding the consequences, see Victoria Tinbor Hui, "Hong Kong's New Police State," *The Diplomat*, June 1, 2021, https://thediplomat.com/2021/05/hong-kongs-new-police-state/.

[72] Michael C. Davis, *Constitutional Confrontation in Hong Kong*. New York: Macmillan Press, 1989.

Chapter 2

[1] Louisa Lim, *Indelible City: Dispossession and Defiance in Hong Kong*. New York: Riverhead Books, 2022.

[2] Ho-fung Hung, *City on the Edge: Hong Kong under Chinese Rule*.

[3] Ibid.

[4] This common colonial-era saying eventually found its way into the title of a book. Richard Hughes, *Hong Kong: Borrowed Place, Borrowed Time*. New York: F. A. Praeger, 1968.

[5] For a thorough account of issues regarding rule of law and heavy media censorship in the colonial era, see Michael Ng, *Political Censorship in British Hong Kong: Freedom of Expression and the Law (1842–1997)*. Cambridge: Cambridge University Press, 2022.

[6] Frank Dikotter, *Mao's Great Famine: The History of China's Most Devasting Catastrophe, 1958–1962*. New York: Bloomsbury USA, 2011.

[7] See Ian Scott, *Political Change and the Crisis of Legitimacy in Hong Kong*. Honolulu: University of Hawaii Press, 1989, 209; Ho-fung Hung, *City on the Edge: Hong Kong under Chinese Rule*, 122–129.

[8] "Public Perception towards the Rule of Law in Hong Kong—An Opinion Survey," Research Public administration and legal system, 2019–2020, http://www.bauhinia.org/index.php/english/research/106.

[9] See Stephen Vines, *Hong Kong: China's New Colony*. Knutsford: Texere Publishing, 2000. Ching Kwan Lee mentions this new colonization that largely became a reality in the years after the handover. Ching Kwan Lee and Sing Ming, editors, *Take Back Our Future: An Eventful Sociology of the Hong Kong Umbrella Movement*. Ithaca: Cornell University Press, 2019, 4. See also Ching Kwan Lee, *Hong Kong: Global China's Restive Frontier*. Cambridge:

Cambridge University Press, July 2022, https://www.cambridge.org/core/elements/hong-kong/52262049437D84C544F8C1B04BCE7C94.

[10] See "Why Hong Kong's Culture of Corruption is Alive and Well, and Extremely Difficult to Prove," *South China Morning Post*, May 10, 2019, https://www.scmp.com/magazines/post-magazine/short-reads/article/3009519/why-hong-kongs-culture-corruption-alive-and; "Hong Kong Loses a Corruption Watchdog: The Politization of the ICAC Shows Beijing's Growing Political Control," *Wall Street Journal*, July 14, 2016, https://www.wsj.com/articles/hong-kong-loses-a-corruption-watchdog-1468495979.

[11] See generally, Michael C. Davis, "The Basic Law, Universal Suffrage and the Rule of Law in Hong Kong," *Hastings International and Comparative Law Review* 38, no. 2 (2015): 275–298.

[12] "Hong Kong Used to Be 18 Percent of China's GDP. Now It's 3 Percent," *Vox*, September 28, 2014, https://www.vox.com/2014/9/28/6857567/hong-kong-used-to-be-18-percent-of-chinas-gdp-now-its-3-percent.

[13] Ho-Fung Hung, *City on the Edge: Hong Kong under Chinese Rule*, chapters 3 and 4.

[14] Long rated at the top of the Heritage Foundation's Index of Economic Freedom, Hong Kong was dropped and merged with China in 2021. Edwin J. Fuelner, "Hong Kong is No Longer What It Was," *The Heritage Foundation*, April 5, 2021, https://www.heritage.org/asia/commentary/hong-kong-no-longer-what-it-was. In a world of increasing authoritarianism and declining freedom, Hong Kong achieved a ranking of 42/100 in late 2022. *Freedom in the World*, 2022, https://freedomhouse.org/country/hong-kong/freedom-world/2023.

[15] China is rated "not free" in *Freedom in the World*, 2023, Freedom House's annual study of political rights and civil liberties, https://freedomhouse.org/country/china/freedom-world/2023.

[16] Joint Declaration, paragraph 3, section 2. The provided "one country, two systems" model was to last for fifty years until 2047, though Deng Xiaoping suggested it could eventually be extended further.

[17] Steve Tsang, *A Modern History of Hong Kong*. London: I. B. Tauris, 2007, 215. At the same time, Deng made it clear that Hong Kong would be handed back to China.

[18] See, generally, Michael C. Davis, *Constitutional Confrontation in Hong Kong*.

[19] Michael C. Davis, "The Basic Law, Universal Suffrage and the Rule of Law in Hong Kong," 275–298.

[20] Much of the backstory was contained in contemporary interviews conducted by Professor Steve Tsang, eventually released under the British Official Secrets Act. Louisa Lim, *Indelible City: Dispossession and Defiance in Hong Kong*. See also an excerpt in Louisa Lim, "The Unofficial Story of the Handover of Hong Kong," *Wall Street Journal*, April 22, 2022, https://www.wsj.com/articles/the-unofficial-story-of-the-handover-of-hong-kong-11650633610.

[21] Its erosion would go against China's internal guidelines elaborated in "Xi Jinping Thought on Socialism with Chinese Characteristics for a New Era," added to the China's Communist Party's Constitution in October 2017, where one of fourteen principles focused specifically on continuing the "one country, two systems" framework for Hong Kong under the heading "Reaffirming National Unity." Thanks to Professor Brian Fong for alerting me to this in an interview on December 4, 2019. See "His Own Words, the 14 Principles of 'Xi Jinping Thought,'" BBC Monitoring, October 14, 2017, https://monitoring.bbc.co.uk/product/c1dmwn4r.

[22] John M. Carroll, *A Concise History of Hong Kong*. Lanham: Rowman and Littlefield, 176. The notion of self-determination for colonies was grounded in the UN Charter provisions on decolonization and the 1960 UN General Assembly Declaration on Decolonization.

[23] The practice of the "One Country, Two Systems" Policy in the Hong Kong Special Administrative Region, Information Office of the State Council, June 2014, Region (hereinafter "2014 white paper"), https://www.scmp.com/news/hong-kong/article/1529167/full-text-practice-one-country-two-systems-policy-hong-kong-special.

[24] "In These New Textbooks Hong Kong was Never a British Colony," *New York Times*, June 16, 2022, https://www.nytimes.com/2022/06/16/world/asia/hong-kong-textbooks-british-colony.html.

Chapter 3

[1] Joint Declaration, paragraph 3, section 12.

[2] Ibid., annex I, paragraph XIII. The right to exercise such legal proceedings is carried forward in Basic Law, article 35.

[3] For efficient access to the then evolving case law under this tradition, Danny Gittings developed and maintained a leading materials book. Danny Gittings, *Introduction to the Hong Kong Basic Law*, 2nd edition. Hong Kong: Hong Kong University Press, 2018.

[4] "Hong Kong Leader Carrie Lam Sides with Education Chief on No Separation of Powers in the City, Defends Move to Delete Phrase from Textbooks," *South China Morning Post*, September 1, 2020, https://scmp.com/news/hong-kong/education/article/3099729/hong-kong-leader-carrie-lam-insists-there-no-separation.

[5] Statement of the Hong Kong Bar Association (HKBA) about the Separation of Powers Principle, September 2, 2020, http://www.document-hkba.org/ccc59c4ee62a1003fd94e0bf4241aff8fff24c72.pdf.

[6] See *Ng Ka Ling v. Director of Immigration*, [1999] 1 HKCFA. 72 (CFA), (1999) 1 HKCFA 315, 318, https://www.hklii.hk/eng/hk/cases/hkcfa/1999/72.html.

[7] Chris Lau, "Hong Kong to Constantly Benchmark Itself against London and New York, Finance Chief Vows," *South China Morning Post*, February 27, 2023, https://scmp.com/news/hong-kong/hong-kong-economy/article/3211680/revitalised-hong-kong-investor-immigration-scheme-unlike-singapore-policy-aims-entice-worlds.

[8] China's united front under the United Front Works Department has taken on new life in the Xi Jinping era. The policy essentially rewards friends and isolates people or countries

deemed enemies, both at home and abroad. Takashi Suzuki, "China's United Front Work in the Xi Jinping Era—Institutional Development and Activities," *Journal of Contemporary East Asia Studies* 8, no. 1 (2019): 83–98, https://www.tandfonline.com/doi/full/10.1080 /24761028.2019.1627714. See also Jessica Batke, "Holding Sway," *ChinaFile*, September 28, 2023: https://www.chinafile.com/reporting-opinion/features/united-front-work-department-domestic

[9] Victoria Tin-bor Hui, "Crackdown: Hong Kong Faces Tiananmen 2.0," *Journal of Democracy*, 31, no. 4 (October 2020): 122–137, https://www.journalofdemocracy.org/articles/crackdown-hong-kong-faces-tiananmen-2-0/.

[10] Ibid.

[11] "UK Knew Early about Holes with Political Reforms and Interpretation in the Basic Law, Raised Amendments with Beijing but Rejected," *Apple Daily*, January 5, 2020. Held by author. Online access to the Apple Daily has been closed under forced closure.

[12] Hong Kong Alliance in Support of the Patriotic Democratic Movement of China, About Hong Kong Alliance, updated 2015, https://hka8964.wordpress.com/hkaeng/.

[13] These two constraints were expressly provided in Basic Law, articles 18 and 22.

[14] Basic Law, chapter III, Fundamental Rights and Duties of Residents.

[15] Cap 383, Hong Kong Bill of Rights Ordinance, https://www.elegislation.gov.hk/hk/cap383

[16] Basic Law, articles 8, 11 and 35.

[17] Ibid., articles 85, 45, and 68, and annexes I and II.

[18] *Ng Ka Ling & Ors v. Director of Immigration (No 2)* (1999) 2 HKCFAR 141, http://legalref.judiciary.gov.hk/lrs/common/ju/ju_frame.jsp?DIS=34248; *Director of Immigration v Chong Fung Yuen* (2001) 4 HKCFAR 211, http://legalref.judiciary.gov.hk/lrs/common/ju/ju_frame.jsp?DIS=22558).

[19] *Ng Ka-ling & Ors v. Director of Immigration.*

[20] Interpretation by the Standing Committee of the National People's Congress Regarding Paragraph 4 in Article 22 and Category (3) of Paragraph 2 in Article 24 of the Basic Law of the Hong Kong Special Administrative Region of the PRC, http://www.npc.gov.cn/zgrdw/englishnpc/Law/2007-12/12/content_1383897.htm The CFA would subsequently make a referral under article 158 in only one case since the handover, which was a very clear case of foreign sovereign immunity. *Democratic Republic of the Congo v. FG Hemisphere Associates LLC,* FACV 5 of 2010, 2011 14 HKCFAR 95 and 395.

[21] Zheping Huang and Echo Huang, "A Brief History: Beijing's Interpretations of Hong Kong's Basic Law, from 1999 to the Present Day," *Quartz*, November 7, 2016, https://qz.com/828713/a-brief-history-beijings-interpretations-of-hong-kongs-basic-law-from-1999-to-the-present-day/.

[22] Jeffie Lam, "What You Need to Know about Hong Kong's Request for Beijing to Interpret the National Security Law amid Jimmy Lai Trial," *South China Morning Post*, November 29, 2022, https://scmp.com/news/hong-kong/politics/article/3201429/what-

you-need-know-about-hong-kongs-request-beijing-interpret-national-security-law-amid-jimmy-lai.

[23] "Explainer: NPCSC's Interpretation of Hong Kong National Security Law over Jimmy Lai's Foreign Defense Council," *NPC Observer*, December 30, 2022, https://npcobserver.com/2022/12/30/explainer-npcscs-interpretation-of-hong-kong-national-security-law-over-jimmy-lais-foreign-defense-counsel/.

[24] See Research on Article 23, University of Hong Kong, Human Rights Portal, http://www.law.hku.hk/hrportal/basic-law/research-article-23.

[25] See Mike Ives, "What Is Hong Kong Extradition Bill?" *New York Times*, June 10, 2019, https://www.nytimes.com/2019/06/10/world/asia/hong-kong-extradition-bill.html.

[26] Basic Law, article 74.

[27] Decision of the Standing Committee of the National People's Congress on Issues Relating to the Selection of the Chief Executive of the Hong Kong Special Administrative Region by Universal Suffrage and on the Method for Forming the Legislative Council of the Hong Kong Special Administrative Region in the Year 2016 (hereinafter "2014 NPC Standing Committee Decision"), August 31, 2014, http://www.china.org.cn/china/2014-08/31/content_33390388.htm

[28] Decision Relating to the Method for Selecting the Chief Executive of the Hong Kong Special Administrative Region and for Forming the Legislative Council of the Hong Kong Special Administrative Region in the Year 2012 and on Issues Relating to Universal Suffrage (promulgated by STANDING COMM. NAT'L PEOPLE'S CONG., 2007) (hereinafter "2007 NPC Standing Committee Decision") (2007) (China), paragraph 9. For analysis of Beijing's long-standing obstruction of democratic reform in Hong Kong, see Stephan Ortmann, "Political Development in Hong Kong: The Failure of Democratization," *Asian International Studies Review* 17, no. 2 (2016): 199–219.

[29] Constitution of the People's Republic of China, article 51, http://www.npc.gov.cn/zgrdw/englishnpc/Constitution/node_2825.htm.

[30] Hong Kong Human Rights and Democracy Act, passage in the House, https://www.congress.gov/bill/116th-congress/house-bill/3289/text; "US Senators Try to Fast-Track Hong Kong Democracy Bill as Violence in City Rises," *South China Morning Post*, November 15, 2019, https://www.scmp.com/news/china/politics/article/3037826/us-senators-urge-passage-hong-kong-democracy-bill-violence-city; "Trump Signs Hong Kong Democracy Legislation, Angering China," *New York Times*, November 27, 2019, https://www.nytimes.com/2019/11/27/us/politics/trump-hong-kong.html.

[31] "The President's Executive Order on Hong Kong Normalization," July 14, 2020, https://hk.usconsulate.gov/2020071403/.

Chapter 4

[1] Ronald Skeldon, "Migration from China," *Journal of International Affairs* 49, no.2 (1996): 434–456, https://www.jstor.org/stable/24357566; John P. Burns, "Immigration from China and the Future of Hong Kong," *Asian Survey* 27, no. 6 (1987): 661–682, https://online.

ucpress.edu/as/article-abstract/27/6/661/22385/Immigration-from-China-and-the-Future-of-Hong-Kong.

2 Michael C. Davis, "Popular Civil Society Resistance and the Survival of Hong Kong: A Clash of Civilizations," in *China's National Security: Endangering Hong Kong's Rule of Law?* edited by Fiona de Londras and Cora Chan. London: Hart/Bloomsbury, 2020.

3 "Hong Kong Loses a Corruption Watchdog: The Politization of the ICAC Shows Beijing's Growing Political Control," *Wall Street Journal*, July 14, 2016, https://www.wsj.com/articles/hong-kong-loses-a-corruption-watchdog-1468495979.

4 Carole J. Petersen, *Balancing National Security and the Rule of Law: Article 23 of the Hong Kong Basic Law*, Hong Kong Watch, November 1, 2018, 11, https://static1.squarespace.com/static/58ecfa82e3df284d3a13dd41/t/5bdad90e0e2e72d167262728/1541069085674/article+23+report_hkw_v1.2_online.pdf.

5 For a brief analysis of existing laws on these topics see Ibid., 8–10.

6 The Johannesburg Principles generally offer guidance on how to regulate national security in a way that is consistent with the free speech guarantees contained in article 19 of the ICCPR. The Johannesburg Principles on National Security, Freedom of Expression and Access to Information, Article 19, October 1, 1995, https://www.article19.org/wp-content/uploads/2018/02/joburg-principles.pdf. See also UN Human Rights Committee, general comment 34, article 19: Freedom of Opinion and Expression (proposing a necessity and proportionality test for such legislation), July 11, 2011, https://www2.ohchr.org/english/bodies/hrc/docs/gc34.pdf.

7 The Article 23 Concerned Group, after defeating the bill, transformed into the Article 45 Concern Group to push for democracy, as summarized in the group's Wikipedia entry, https://en.wikipedia.org/wiki/Article_45_Concern_Group.

8 The Hong Kong Civil Human Rights Front was formed in conjunction with the article 23 protests and remained active in organizing nonviolent protest in Hong Kong up until the NSL caused it to disband, https://www.facebook.com/CivilHumanRightsFront/. The granting of permission was not technically a permit, but in fact a police "statement of no objection" under the Public Order Ordinance, Cap 245.

9 Candice Chau, "Organizers of Mass Hong Kong Demos Civil Human Rights Front Disbands Citing 'Unprecedented Challenges,'" *Hong Kong Free Press*, August 15, 2021, https://hongkongfp.com/2021/08/15/breaking-organiser-of-mass-hong-kong-demos-civil-human-rights-front-disbands-citing-unprecedented-challenges/.

10 John P. Burns, "The Chinese Communist Party in Hong Kong," Special Report, the King Faisal Center for Research and Islamic Studies, June 2022.

11 The Interpretation of Article 7 of Annex I and Article III of Annex II to the Basic Law of the Hong Kong Special Administrative Region of the People's Republic of China (promulgated by STANDING COMMITTEE NAT'L PEOPLE'S CONG., Apr. 6, 2004), §3 (2004) (China), https://www.elegislation.gov.hk/hk/A107%21en.assist.pdf.

12 2007 NPC Standing Committee Decision.

13 Ibid.

[14] See Michael C. Davis, "Hongkong Umbrella Movement and Beijing's Failure to Honor the Basic Law," E-International Relations, October 29, 2014, available at http://www.e-ir. info/2014/10/29/the-umbrella-movement-and-beijings-failure-torespect-the-hong-kong-basic-law/.

[15] 2014 NPC Standing Committee Decision.

[16] "'This is part of the plan': A New Train Blurs Line between China and Hong Kong," Guardian, October 4, 2018, https://www.theguardian.com/cities/2018/oct/04/high-speed-train-brings-chinese-border-into-heart-of-hong-kong.

[17] "China Opens Giant Seabridge Linking Hong Kong, Macau, and Mainland," New York Times, October 23, 2018, https://www.nytimes.com/2018/10/23/world/asia/china-bridge-hong-kong-macau-zhuhai.html.

[18] "National Law Enforced in Hong Kong's High-Speed Rail Terminus from Midnight, as 800 Mainland Officers Set to Be Stationed in Port Area," South China Morning Post, September 3, 2018, https://www.scmp.com/news/hong-kong/transport/article/2162573/national-law-be-enforced-hong-kongs-high-speed-rail.

[19] Simon Cheng Man-kit, personal narrative on Facebook entitled "An Enemy of the State," November 19, 2019, https://www.facebook.com/notes/cheng-man-kit/for-the-record-an-enemy-of-the-state/2490959950941845. As discussed later, Simon Cheng, now in Britain, later became the target of a HK$1 million bounty and arrest warrant. "Hong Kong puts arrest bounties on five overseas activists including US citizen," The Guardian, December 14, 2023. https://www.theguardian.com/world/2023/dec/14/hong-kong-puts-arrest-bounties-on-five-overseas-activists-including-us-citizen.

[20] "Protest against National Education to End after Government Climbdown," South China Morning Post, September 9, 2012. https://www.scmp.com/news/hong-kong/article/1032535/protest-against-national-education-end-after-government-climbdown.

[21] "Hong Kong Activist Joshua Wong Says He Will Be 'Prime Target' of New Security Law," Reuters, June 25, 2020, https://www.reuters.com/article/us-hongkong-protests-legislation-joshua/hong-kong-activist-joshua-wong-says-he-will-be-prime-target-of-new-security-law-idUSKBN23X04L.

[22] National security law, article 9.

[23] See NPCSC 2007 decision.

[24] Rimsky Yuen, "Civic Nomination for 2017 Is Plainly Inconsistent with the Basic Law," South China Morning Post, January 28, 2014, https://www.scmp.com/comment/insight-opinion/article/1415804/civic-nomination-2017-plainly-inconsistent-basic-law.

[25] "Hong Kong's Referendum: Voting to Vote," Economist, June 21, 2014, https://www.economist.com/analects/2014/06/21/voting-to-vote.

[26] 2014 white paper.

[27] "Hong Kong Democracy 'Referendum' Draws Nearly 800,000," BBC, June 30, 2014, https://www.bbc.com/news/world-asia-china-28076566.

[28] See, generally, Michael C. Davis, "The Basic Law, Universal Suffrage and the Rule of Law in Hong Kong," 289–294.

[29] 2014 white paper, part 1, paragraph 2.

[30] See Tsang, *A Modern History of Hong Kong*, 219–224.

[31] 2014 white paper, part V, section 1, paragraph 1.

[32] "Beijing Abrogates 1984 Treaty It Signed with Britain to Guarantee the City's Autonomy," *Wall Street Journal*, December 14, 2014, https://www.wsj.com/articles/gordon-crovitz-china-voids-hong-kong-rights-1418601004.

[33] 2014 NPC Standing Committee Decision.

[34] See, generally, Hong Kong Government, Report on the Public Consultation on the Methods of Selecting the Chief Executive in 2017 and for Forming the Legislative Council in 2016, July 2014, available at http://www.2017.gov.hk/filemanager/template/en/doc/report/consultation_report.pdf. See also Hong Kong Government, Report by the Chief Executive of the Hong Kong Special Administrative Region to the Standing Committee of the National People's Congress on Whether There Is a Need to Amend the Methods for Selecting the Chief Executive of the Hong Kong Special Administrative Region in 2017 and for Forming the Legislative Council of the Hong Kong Special Administrative Region in 2016, July 2014, available at http://www.2017.gov.hk/en/liberal/related.html.

[35] 2014 NPC Standing Committee Decision, paragraph II, section 1.

[36] 2014 NPC Standing Committee Decision, paragraph II, section 2.

[37] Interview with legislator, executive council convenor, and former secretary for security, Regina Ip, December 6, 2019.

[38] "'We Are Back': Hong Kong Protesters Mark Anniversary of the Umbrella Movement in Face of Police Water Cannons," *Washington Post*, September 28, 2019, https://www.washingtonpost.com/world/asia_pacific/hong-kong-protesters-mark-5th-anniversary-of-umbrella-movement-protesting-beijings-influence/2019/09/28/4e07c6b4-e11c-11e9-be7f-4cc85017c36f_story.html.

[39] As a measure of wide interest in the protests that year, most of the Human Rights Press Awards were related to the Umbrella Movement. These awards were sponsored by Amnesty International, the Hong Kong Foreign Correspondence Club, and the Hong Kong Journalists Association to encourage reportage on human rights, https://humanrightspressawards.org/winners-2014.

[40] For an overview of the causes and shape of contentious politics that interrogates underlying data in the Umbrella Movement see, Ngok Ma and Edmund W. Cheng, editors, *The Umbrella Movement: Civil Resistance and Contentious Space in Hong Kong*. Amsterdam: Amsterdam University Press, 2019. For an account of the movement by a keen Hong Kong observer and social activists, see also Jason Y. Ng, *Umbrellas in Bloom: Hong Kong Occupy Movement Uncovered*. Hong Kong: Blacksmith Books, 2016.

[41] C. L. Lim, *Treaty for a Lost City: The Sino-British Joint Declaration*. Cambridge: Cambridge University Press, 2022, https://www.cambridge.org/core/books/treaty-for-a-lost-city/F27FF3683EFEFD1EBD89E2A4964756E1.

[42] "Why the Wealth Gap? Hong Kong's Disparity between the Rich and Poor is Greatest in 45 Years, So What Can Be Done?" *South China Morning Post*, September 27, 2018, https://www.scmp.com/news/hong-kong/society/article/2165872/why-wealth-gap-hong-kongs-disparity-between-rich-and-poor.

[43] See Ching Kwan Lee and Ming Sing, editors, *Take Back Our Future: An Eventful Sociology of Hong Kong's Umbrella Movement*. Ithaca: Cornell University Press, 2019, 4–12.

[44] "2017 Seize the Opportunity: Method for Selecting the Chief Executive by Universal Suffrage Consultation Report," January 2015, http://www.2017.gov.hk/en/second/document.html.

[45] "Hong Kong Vetoes China-Backed Electoral Reform Proposal," *Reuters*, June 17, 2015, https://www.reuters.com/article/us-hongkong-politics/hong-kong-vetoes-china-backed-electoral-reform-proposal-idUSKBN0OY06320150618.

[46] "Newly Elected Hong Kong Leader Carrie Lam Vows to Unite Sharply Divided City," *South China Morning Post*, March 27, 2017, https://www.scmp.com/news/hong-kong/politics/article/2082304/newly-elected-hong-kong-leader-carrie-lam-vows-unite-sharply.

Chapter 5

[1] Richard C. Bush, "Hong Kong Government Announces Electoral Reform Details," *Brookings*, April 23, 2015, https://www.brookings.edu/blog/up-front/2015/04/23/hong-kong-government-announces-electoral-reform-details/.

[2] See Document 9: ChinaFile Translation, ChinaFile, November 3, 2013, https://www.chinafile.com/document-9-chinafile-translation.

[3] For historical background, see Suzanne Pepper, *Keeping Democracy at Bay: Hong Kong and the Challenge of Chinese Political Reform*. Washington, DC: Rowman and Littlefield Publishers, 2008.

[4] See Michael C. Davis, "Promises to Keep: The Basic Law, the 'Umbrella Movement,' and Democratic Reform in Hong Kong," in *Information Politics, Protests, and Human Rights in the Digital Age*, edited by Mahmood Monshipouri. Cambridge: Cambridge University Press, 2016, 239–266.

[5] "Hong Kong Umbrella Movement Leaders Are Sentenced to Prison," *New York Times*, April 23, 2019, https://www.nytimes.com/2019/04/23/world/asia/hong-kong-umbrella-movement.html?login=email&auth=login-email.

[6] "Hong Kong Protest Leaders Sentenced to Community Service," *New York Times*, August 15, 2016, https://www.nytimes.com/2016/08/15/world/asia/hong-kong-occupy-sentences-joshua-wong.html.

[7] Judges may be inclined to consider the purpose of their act of civil disobedience. David A Graham, "What's the Right Punishment for Tearing Down a Confederate Monument?" *Atlantic*, September 17, 2017, https://www.theatlantic.com/politics/archive/2017/09/durham-confederate-monument-judicial-system-civil-disobedience/539004/.

[8] "'Lenient' Hong Kong Court Sentences Come with a Warning: Patience for Violent Protests Has Run Out," *South China Morning Post*, October 10, 2018, https://www.scmp.

com/comment/insight-opinion/hong-kong/article/2167666/lenient-hong-kong-court-sentences-come-warning.

[9] The Hong Kong secretary for justice, Rimsky Yuen, explains the government stance. Rimsky Yuen, "Joshua Wong, Nathan Law and Alex Chow Are in Jail Because Hong Kong Law Demands It," *South China Morning Post*, August 23, 2017, https://www.scmp.com/comment/insight-opinion/article/2107959/joshua-wong-nathan-law-and-alex-chow-are-jail-because-hong.

[10] Ibid.

[11] "13 Activists Who Stormed Hong Kong Legislature Jailed Following Successful Appeal by Justice Dept," *Hong Kong Free Press*, August 15, 2017, https://www.hongkongfp.com/2017/08/15/13-activists-stormed-hong-kong-legislature-jailed-following-successful-appeal-justice-dept/.

[12] "Hong Kong Court Throws Out Protest Leaders' Prison Sentences," *New York Times*, February 6, 2018, https://www.nytimes.com/2018/02/06/world/asia/hong-kong-joshua-wong-appeal.html.

[13] "Hong Kong: Drop Case against 'Umbrella Nine,'" Human Rights Watch, November 14, 2018, https://www.hrw.org/news/2018/11/14/hong-kong-drop-case-against-umbrella-9.

[14] "Hong Kong Court Convicts Nine Activists behind Pro-Democracy 'Umbrella Movement,'" *Washington Post*, April 9, 2019, https://www.washingtonpost.com/world/hong-kong-court-convicts-nine-activists-behind-pro-democracy-umbrella-movement/2019/04/08/a16e524c-5a75-11e9-b8e3-b03311fbbbfe_story.html.

[15] Interview with Professor Benny Tai, December 10, 2019.

[16] Jasmine Siu, "Hong Kong's High Court Unanimously Rejects Appeal against Occupy Convictions by Benny Tai, Eight Others," *South China Morning Post,* April 30, 2021, https://www.scmp.com/news/hong-kong/law-and-crime/article/3131704/hong-kongs-high-court-unanimously-rejects-appeal.

[17] Such effort started early with a pro-Beijing signature campaign to gain his ouster. "Petition to Oust Occupy Co-founder Benny Tai from University Post Attracts 80,000 Signatures," *South China Morning Post*, September 6, 2017, https://www.scmp.com/news/hong-kong/politics/article/2110047/petition-oust-occupy-co-founder-benny-tai-university-post. In 2020, the faculty senate refused to dismiss Tai, but the university council, whose members are mostly appointed by the government from outside the university, voted for his dismissal by an 18–2 vote. "University of Hong Kong Governing Council Sacks Legal Scholar Benny Tai over Convictions for Occupy Protests," *South China Morning Post*, July 28, 2020, https://www.scmp.com/news/hong-kong/politics/article/3095043/university-hong-kong-governing-council-sacks-legal-scholar.

[18] Their polemical oaths either included surplus language disparaging the government or, in one case, was stated at slow speed. "Success of Four Hong Kong Lawmakers Facing Expulsion Will Rest on Oath Solemnity Say Experts," *South China Morning Post*, December 8, 2016, https://www.scmp.com/news/hong-kong/politics/article/2052999/success-four-hong-kong-lawmakers-facing-expulsion-will-rest.

[19] Interpretation of Article 104 of the Basic Law of the Hong Kong Special Administrative Region of the People's Republic of China by the Standing Committee of the National People's Congress, November 7, 2016, https://www.basiclaw.gov.hk/en/basiclawtext/images/basiclawtext_doc25.pdf. See "China's Top Body Lays Down Law on Hong Kong Oath-Taking," *South China Morning Post*, November 8, 2019, https://www.scmp.com/news/hong-kong/politics/article/2043768/chinas-top-body-lays-down-law-hong-kong-oath-taking.

[20] Six candidates who were judged by electoral officers and then the Electoral Affairs Commission to favor independence or self-determination were barred from running for the Legislative Council in 2016. In 2019, umbrella activist Joshua Wong was barred from running for the district council. "Hong Kong Bars Democracy Activist Joshua Wong from Elections, Underscoring Fears over Freedoms," *South China Morning Post*, October 29, 2019, https://www.washingtonpost.com/world/asia_pacific/hong-kong-blocks-democracy-activist-joshua-wong-from-contesting-local-elections/2019/10/29/694b7df0-f632-11e9-b2d2-1f37c9d82dbb_story.html.

[21] "Journalist's Expulsion from Hong Kong 'Sends a Chilling Message,'" *New York Times*, October 8, 2018, https://www.nytimes.com/2018/10/08/world/asia/victor-mallet-hong-kong-financial-times.html. It is important that the Foreign Correspondents' Club is one of the august journalistic organizations in Hong Kong, with literally a who's who of media luminaries having passed through its doors. I have enjoyed the invitation to speak there on several occasions and found the events and the questions raised very balanced and professional. The more outspoken initiatives of the club have largely gone silent since the enactment of the NSL.

[22] NSL, articles 20 and 22.

[23] "Four Members of Hong Kong Pro-Independence Group Arrested by Police Officers from National Security Unit," *South China Morning Post*, July 29, 2020, https://scmp.com/news/hong-kong/law-and-crime/article/3095240/least-three-core-members-hong-kong-pro-independence; Jessie Pang, "Former Hong Kong Independence Group Leader Gets 43 Months under Security Law," *Reuters*, November 23, 2021, https://www.reuters.com/world/asia-pacific/former-hong-kong-independence-group-leader-gets-43-months-under-security-law-2021-11-23/.

[24] This often causes divisions in the pro-establishment camp as the Liaison Office may pick and choose among its favorites, though under the Basic Law, the Liaison Office should be barred from meddling in local politics. Dominic Chiu, "Why China's Supporters in Hong Kong are Divided," *The Diplomat*, January 20, 2017, https://thediplomat.com/2017/01/why-chinas-supporters-in-hong-kong-are-divided/. See also Eliza W. Y. Lee, "United Front, Clientelism, and Indirect Rule: Theorizing the Role of the 'Liaison Office' in Hong Kong," *Journal of Contemporary China* 29, no. 125 (September 2020), 763–775.

[25] Frank Chen, "Why Liaison Office Is Hong Kong's De Facto Government," *Ejinsight*, November 25, 2014, http://www.ejinsight.com/20141125-why-liaison-office-is-hks-de-facto-government/. The blurry line of command between the Liaison Office in Hong Kong and the higher-up Hong Kong and Macau Affairs Office (HKMAO) in Beijing makes it somewhat ambiguous whether to attach the label of "second Hong Kong government" to

HKMAO or to the local Liaison Office. See Sonny Shi-hing Lo, *The Dynamics of Beijing-Hong Kong Relations: A Model for Taiwan?* Hong Kong: Hong Kong University Press, 2008, 20–24.

[26] "China Sets Up Hong Kong Crisis Command Center in Mainland," *Reuters*, November 26, 2019, https://www.reuters.com/article/us-hongkong-protests-shenzhen-exclusive/exclusive-china-sets-up-hong-kong-crisis-center-in-mainland-considers-replacing-chief-liaison-idUSKBN1Y000P.

[27] Jeffie Lam and Willa Wu, "How to Understand the 'Elevation' of Beijing's Top Office for Hong Kong Affairs? Is the City More 'Special' Now? Analysts Unpack the Meaning behind the Move," *South China Morning Post*, March 19, 2023, https://scmp.com/news/hong-kong/politics/article/3214076/how-understand-elevation-beijings-top-office-hong-kong-affairs-city-more-special-now-analysts-unpack.

[28] "China Releases Plan on Reforming Party and State Institutions," *Xinhua*, March 16, 2023. http://english.www.gov.cn/policies/latestreleases/202303/16/content_WS6413be82c6d0f528699db58e.html

[29] Hong Kong and Macau Affairs Office in the State Council, http://english.www.gov.cn/state_council/2014/10/01/content_281474991090982.htm.

[30] "Why Did Beijing Appoint Trusted Xi Jinping Ally to Office Overseeing Hong Kong Affairs?" *South China Morning Post*, February 14, 2020, https://www.scmp.com/news/hong-kong/politics/article/3050548/why-did-beijing-appoint-trusted-xi-jinping-ally-office.

[31] This role included coordinating the underground Communist Party in Hong Kong. Christine Loh, *Underground Front: The Chinese Communist Party in Hong Kong*, Second Edition. Hong Kong: University of Hong Kong Press, 2017, 20–26.

[32] "Basic Law's Article 22 'Does Not Apply' to Beijing's Liaison Office, Hong Kong Justice Secretary Says," *South China Morning Post*, April 27, 2020, https://www.scmp.com/news/hong-kong/politics/article/3081816/basic-laws-article-22-does-not-apply-beijings-liaison.

[33] See Victoria Tinbor Hui, "Hong Kong's New Police State," *The Diplomat*, June 1, 2021, https://thediplomat.com/2021/05/hong-kongs-new-police-state/.

[34] "China's Communist Party Elite Wrap Up Meeting with Pledge to Safeguard National Security in Hong Kong," *South China Morning Post*, November 1, 2019, https://www.scmp.com/news/china/politics/article/3035818/chinas-communist-party-elite-wrap-meeting-pledge-safeguard.

[35] Natalie Wong and Lilian Cheng, "The Hong Kong Connection: Xi Jinpiing, 4 Other Top Chinese Leaders and an Ideologue Who Studied City from Afar," *South China Morning Post*, October 25, 2022, https://www.scmp.com/news/hong-kong/politics/article/3197106/hong-kong-connection-what-6-chinas-top-leadership-team-including-xi-jinping-have-common.

[36] Sunny Lo, Steven Hung and Jeff Loo, *China's New United Front Work in Hong Kong*. New York: Palgrave Macmillan, 2019.

[37] "Explainer: How Important is Hong Kong to the Rest of China?" *Reuters*, September 4, 2019, https://www.reuters.com/article/us-hongkong-protests-markets-explainer/explainer-how-important-is-hong-kong-to-the-rest-of-china-idUSKCN1VP35H. "Hong Kong 'Still Top Choice for China's Rich' Investing Outside the Mainland and Overseas," *South China Morning Post*, May 26, 2015, https://www.scmp.com/news/china/money-wealth/article/1808983/hong-kong-still-top-choice-chinas-rich-investing-outside.

[38] "How China Holds Sway over Who Leads Hong Kong," *Bloomberg*, February 28, 2017, https://www.bloomberg.com/graphics/2017-hk-election/; "Beijing Works the Phones in Secret Push to Pick Hong Kong's Next Leader," *Wall Street Journal*, February 28, 2017,

[39] "How Beijing Manipulates Legislative Elections in Hong Kong," *Hong Kong Free Press*, September 16, 2016, https://www.hongkongfp.com/2016/09/16/beijing-manipulates-legislative-elections-hong-kong/.

[40] Ibid.

[41] "Fueling the Hong Kong Protests: A World of Pop-Culture Memes," *New York Times*, August 2, 2019, https://www.nytimes.com/2019/08/02/world/asia/hong-kong-protests-memes.html.

[42] Hong Kong Journalists Association, Annual Reports on Freedom of Expression, https://www.hkja.org.hk/en/hkjas-news/publications/annual-report/.

[43] "Beijing Liaison Office Free to Do Its Own Thing, Hong Kong Leader Carrie Lam Says after Ownership of Leading Publisher Revealed," *South China Morning Post*, May 29, 2018, https://www.scmp.com/news/hong-kong/politics/article/2148274/beijings-liaison-office-free-do-its-own-thing-hong-kong.

[44] Francis L. F. Lee and Joseph Chan, "Organizational Production of Self-Censorship in the Hong Kong Media," *International Journal of Press/Politics* (November 3, 2008), https://journals.sagepub.com/doi/10.1177/1940161208326598. The *South China Morning Post* is the target of an exposé in the *Atlantic* in this regard. "A Newsroom at the Edge of Autocracy," *Atlantic*, August 1, 2020, https://www.theatlantic.com/international/archive/2020/08/scmp-hong-kong-china-media/614719/.

[45] Michael Steinberger, "An Apple a Day: Jimmy Lai's Tough Tabloid," *Columbia Journalism Review* 34, no. 6 (1996), 15; Jess Macy Yu, "Hong Kong Newspaper, Pro- and Anti-Beijing, Weigh In on Protests," *Sinosphere*, October 6, 2014, https://sinosphere.blogs.nytimes.com/2014/10/06/hong-kong-newspapers-pro-and-anti-beijing-weigh-in-on-protests/.

[46] "University of Hong Kong's Council Votes 12–8 to Reject Johannes Chan's Appointment as Pro-Vice-Chancellor," *South China Morning Post*, September 29, 2015, https://www.scmp.com/news/hong-kong/education/article/1862423/university-hong-kongs-council-votes-12-8-reject-johannes.

[47] William Yiu, "Hong Kong Was Not a British Colony as China Did Not Recognise Unequal Treaties Ceding City to Britain, New Textbooks Reveal," *South China Morning Post*, June 13, 2022, https://scmp.com/news/hong-kong/education/article/3181560/hong-kong-was-not-british-colony-china-did-not-recognise.

[48] Interview with Alan Leong, barrister and Civic Party chair, December 9, 2019.

[49] In early December 2019, Yeung reported that eighty teachers had been arrested for their involvement in the protests. "Advisers to Hong Kong's Leader Considered Collective Resignation over Ongoing Protests, Executive Council Member Regina Ip Reveals," *South China Morning Post*, December 29, 2019, https://www.scmp.com/news/hong-kong/politics/article/3043854/advisers-hong-kongs-leader-considered-collective.

[50] 2014 white paper.

[51] "Hong Kong Court Convicts Nine Activists behind Pro-Democracy 'Umbrella Movement,'" *Washington Post*, April 9, 2019, https://www.washingtonpost.com/world/hong-kong-court-convicts-nine-activists-behind-pro-democracy-umbrella-movement/2019/04/08/a16e524c-5a75-11e9-b8e3-b03311fbbbfe_story.html.

[52] "Hong Kong's Anti-terrorism Task Force Goes to Xinjiang to Study Local Methods," *South China Morning Post*, December 6, 2018, https://www.scmp.com/news/hong-kong/law-and-crime/article/2176737/hong-kongs-anti-terrorism-task-force-goes-xinjiang.

[53] "BHRC Publishes New Report on Judicial Independence in Hong Kong SAR Applying ABA Judicial Monitor Toolkit," *BAR Human Rights Committee of England & Wales*, April 2023, https://barhumanrights.org.uk/bhrc-publishes-new-report-on-judicial-independence-in-hong-kong-sar-applying-aba-judicial-monitor-toolkit/.

[54] Alan Leong, a barrister and Civic Party chair, laments the chipping away of the autonomy of the courts. Interview with Alan Leong, December 9, 2019.

[55] One leading barrister legislator, who preferred to remain anonymous for fear of retribution in the current post NSL climate, in 2019 offered praise for the judiciary so far as the most resilient branch of government, though he worried about the impact of the NPC Standing Committee's interpretations on long-term judicial independence. Interview with leading barrister, December 4, 2019.

[56] The group focused on providing community education, analysis, and support for Hong Kong's rule of law and civil liberties. Interview with lawyers Jason Ng, Angeline Chan, and Wilson Leung, Progressive Lawyers Group, December 8, 2019. Being among the groups later forced to disband, there is no longer a webpage for this group.

[57] See "Statement of ABA President Deborah Enix-Ross re: Arrest Warrants and Bounties on Hong Kong Lawyers," https://www.americanbar.org/news/abanews/aba-news-archives/2023/07/statement-of-aba-president-re-hong-kong-lawyers/

Chapter 6

[1] Hana Meihan Davis and Jeffrey Wasserstrom, "Hong Kong and 'The Hunger Games,'" The Millions, January 24, 2020. https://themillions.com/2020/01/hong-kong-and-the-hunger-games.html. "If We Burn, You Burn with Us," *Bloomberg*, August 17, 2019, https://www.bloomberg.com/news/newsletters/2019-08-17/if-we-burn-you-burn-with-us.

[2] There were 479 seats scattered across eighteen district councils, in which 452 seats were directly elected. The remaining twenty-seven seats were for the powerful chairpersons of rural committees, representing the indigenous villages. "Hong Kong Will Have Its

Only Truly Democratic Election This Weekend," *Quartz*, November 22, 2019, https://qz.com/1753318/what-you-need-to-know-about-hong-kongs-district-council-elections/.

³ "Hong Kong District Council Election: Chinese State Media Urges Citizens 'Vote to End Violence,'" *Hong Kong Free Press*, November 24, 2019, https://www.hongkongfp.com/2019/11/24/hong-kong-district-council-election-chinese-state-media-urges-citizens-vote-end-violence/.

⁴ "Hong Kong Elections: Pan-democrats Celebrating Landslide Win Vow to Keep Up the Pressure on City's Beleaguered Leader to Address Protesters' Demands," *South China Morning Post*, November 25, 2019, https://scmp.com/news/hong-kong/politics/article/3039306/hong-kong-elections-pan-democrats-celebrating-landslide-win.

⁵ World Justice Project Rule of Law Ranking Index 2019, February 28, 2019, https://worldjusticeproject.org/our-work/research-and-data/wjp-rule-law-index-2019.

⁶ Candice Chau, "Hong Kong Falls from Top 20 in Global Rule of Law Index," *Hong Kong Free Press,* October 26, 2022, https://hongkongfp.com/2022/10/26/hong-kong-falls-from-top-20-in-global-rule-of-law-index/. The city would fall one rank further in 2023. Irene Chan, "Hong Kong falls for 3rd year on global rule of law index, as gov't says ranking remains higher than 'some countries,'" *Hong Kong Free Press*, October 26, 2023. https://hongkongfp.com/2023/10/26/hong-kong-falls-for-3rd-year-on-global-rule-of-law-index-as-govt-says-ranking-remains-higher-than-some-countries.

⁷ Fugitive Offenders and Mutual Assistance in Criminal Matters Legislation (Amendment) Bill 2019 (hereinafter "extradition bill"), https://www.legco.gov.hk/yr18-19/english/bills/b201903291.pdf. Michael C. Davis, "Debate over Hong Kong's Extradition Law Devolves into a Scuffle in the Legislative Council," *Washington Post*, May 11, 2019, https://www.washingtonpost.com/politics/2019/05/11/debate-over-hong-kongs-proposed-extradition-law-devolves-into-scuffle-legislative-council/.

⁸ See Michael C. Davis and Victoria Tinbor Hui, "Will China Crush the Protests in Hong Kong? Why Beijing Doesn't Need to Send in Troops," *Foreign Affairs*, August 5, 2019, https://www.foreignaffairs.com/articles/china/2019-08-05/will-china-crush-protests-hong-kong.

⁹ "Special Report: How Murder, Kidnapping and Miscalculations Set Off Hong Kong's Revolt," *Reuters*, December 20, 2019, https://www.reuters.com/article/us-hongkong-protests-extradition-narrati/special-report-how-murder-kidnappings-and-miscalculation-set-off-hong-kongs-revolt-idUSKBN1YO18Q. Thomas Kellogg offered an analysis of how the proposed law stood up against international practice. Thomas Kellogg, "Hong Kong's Proposed Extradition Law and International Human Rights: Legalized Kidnapping," Lawfare Blog, June 6, 2019, https://www.lawfareblog.com/hong-kongs-proposed-extradition-law-and-international-human-rights-legalized-kidnapping.

¹⁰ "Bribery and Corruption, 2019, China," Global Legal Insights, section 5, https://www.globallegalinsights.com/practice-areas/bribery-and-corruption-laws-and-regulations/china.

¹¹ "Hong Kong Has Played an Outsized Role in Contributing to the Growth of China's Financial Markets," *South China Morning Post*, December 3, 2018, https://www.scmp.

com/business/article/2175980/hong-kong-has-played-outsize-role-contributing-growth-chinas-financial.

[12] James Palmer, "What Is Beijing Planning for Hong Kong?" *Foreign Policy*, November 6, 2019, https://foreignpolicy.com/2019/11/06/what-is-beijing-planning-for-hong-kong-protests-national-security-laws-carrie-lam-xi-jinping-mainland-china/.

[13] "Hong Kong Protesters Return to the Streets; Leader Apologizes but Doesn't Withdraw Extradition Bill," *Washington Post*, June 16, 2019, https://www.washingtonpost.com/world/large-scale-protests-return-to-hong-kong-despite-suspension-of-extradition-bill/2019/06/16/7ea7f9c6-8ee0-11e9-b6f4-033356502dce_story.html.

[14] Albert Chen, "A Commentary on the Fugitive Offenders and Mutual Legal Assistance in Criminal Matters Legislation (Amendment) Bill 2019," HKU Legal Scholarship Blog, May 3, 2019, http://researchblog.law.hku.hk/2019/05/albert-chens-commentary-on-proposed.html.

[15] Cap 383, Hong Kong Bill of Rights Ordinance (hereinafter "HKBORO"), https://www.elegislation.gov.hk/hk/cap383.

[16] "Hong Kong Security Law: China Hits Back in Extradition Row," *BBC News*, July 28, 2020, https://www.bbc.com/news/world-asia-53562437.

[17] See Edmund W. Cheng, Francis L. F. Lee, Samson Yuen, and Gary Tang, "Total Mobilization from Below: Hong Kong's Freedom Summer," *China Quarterly* 251 (September 2022): 629–659, https://www.cambridge.org/core/journals/china-quarterly/article/total-mobilization-from-below-hong-kongs-freedom-summer/92BA12D2EEA578 2B4330B0D07B389842; Thomas Yun-tong Tang, "The Evolution of Protest Repertoires in Hong Kong: Violent Tactics in the Anti-Extradition Bill Protests in 2019," *China Quarterly* 251 (September 2022): 660–682, https://www.cambridge.org/core/journals/china-quarterly/article/evolution-of-protest-repertoires-in-hong-kong-violent-tactics-in-the-antiextradition-bill-protests-in-2019/E59AC952FD5D818DB65F8043D4824A5F; Yan-ho Lai and Ming Sing, "Solidarity and Implications of a Leaderless Movement in Hong Kong: Its Strengths and Limitations," *Communist and Post-Communist Studies* 53, no. 4 (2020): 41–67, https://online.ucpress.edu/cpcs/article-abstract/53/4/41/114583/Solidarity-and-Implications-of-a-Leaderless?redirectedFrom=fulltext.

[18] "Hong Kong Protests Explained," Amnesty International, https://www.amnesty.org/en/latest/news/2019/09/hong-kong-protests-explained/.

[19] "Hong Kong Leader Carrie Lam Announces Formal Withdrawal of the Extradition Bill and Sets Up a Platform to Look into Key Causes of Protest Crisis," *South China Morning Post*, September 4, 2019, https://www.scmp.com/news/hong-kong/politics/article/3025641/hong-kong-leader-carrie-lam-announce-formal-withdrawal.

[20] Interview with Professor Sunny Lo, December 8, 2019.

[21] "Pro-establishment Allies of Hong Kong Leader Carrie Lam Lament to Her That Voters Punished Them at the Polls for Government's Handling of the Protest," *South China Morning Post*, November 26, 2019.

[22] "IPCC Probe into Hong Kong Police's Handling of Protests to Come under Legal Scrutiny," *South China Morning Post*, December 20, 2019, https://www.scmp.com/news/hong-kong/law-and-crime/article/3043041/ipcc-probe-hong-kong-polices-handling-protests-come.

[23] "Foreign Experts Quit Hong Kong Police Probe Questioning Its Independence," *Reuters*, December 10, 2019, https://www.reuters.com/article/us-hongkong-protests/foreign-experts-quit-hong-kong-police-probe-questioning-its-independence-idUSKBN1YF0AW.

[24] "Hong Kong: Impotent and Biased IPCC Report into Protests Fails to Bring Justice Any Closer," Amnesty International, May 15, 2020, https://www.amnesty.org/en/latest/news/2020/05/hong-kong-impotent-and-biased-ipcc-report-into-protests-fails-to-bring-justice-any-closer/.

[25] Interview with then Demosisto leader, Joshua Wong, December 6, 2019. Readers interested in the genesis of this phenomenal young activist might read his autobiographical book. Joshua Wong and Jason Y. Ng, *Unfree Speech: The Threat to Global Democracy and Why We Must Act Now*. New York: Penguin Books, 2020. In the introduction, mainland artist Ai Wei Wei describes Joshua Wong and his activist colleagues as a "new generation of rebels globalized in the post-internet era," who believe "by demonstrating their rights in a highly visible way, we can achieve justice and democracy in any society." Sadly, Joshua Wong has spent much of the last three years in jail facing NSL charges related to his participation in the June 2020 people's primary.

[26] "Special Report: How Murder, Kidnapping and Miscalculations Set Off Hong Kong's Revolt," *Reuters*, December 20, 2019.

[27] "How Hong Kong Got a Million Protesters Out on the Streets," *Bloomberg*, June 16, 2019, https://www.bloomberg.com/graphics/2019-hong-kong-protests-extradition-to-china/.

[28] "Hong Kong Protesters Storm Legislature, Dividing the Movement," *New York Times*, July 1, 2019, https://www.nytimes.com/2019/07/01/world/asia/china-hong-kong-protest.html.

[29] "Protesters Focus on Hong Kong's Airport, Snarling Transport Links after Day of Violence," *Washington Post*, September 1, 2019, https://www.washingtonpost.com/world/protesters-focus-again-on-hong-kongs-airport-snarling-transport-links-after-day-of-violence/2019/09/01/c21a43cc-cc97-11e9-87fa-8501a456c003_story.html.

[30] Antony Dapiran, *City on Fire: The Fight for Hong Kong*. Pontiac: Scribe Publications, 2020.

[31] "In Hong Kong, Unity between Peaceful and Radical Protesters. For Now," *New York Times*, September 27, 2019, https://www.nytimes.com/2019/09/27/world/asia/hong-kong-protests-violence.html.

[32] "Hong Kong Leader Carrie Lam Announces Formal Withdrawal of the Extraction Bill and Sets Up a Platform to Look into Key Causes of the Protest Crisis." *South China Morning Post*, September 4, 2019, https://www.scmp.com/news/hong-kong/politics/article/3025641/hong-kong-leader-carrie-lam-announce-formal-withdrawal. Editors of the *South China Morning Post* have prepared a compilation of the excellent daily reportage

of their reporters, several of whom, including one of the editors, I am pleased to note are among my former students of human rights. See Zuraidah Ibrahim and Jeffie Lam, *Rebel City: Hong Kong's Year of Water and Fire*. Hong Kong: South China Morning Post, 2020.

[33] "Hong Kong's 'Be Water' Protests Leave China Casting about for an Enemy," *The Guardian*, August 30, 2019, https://www.theguardian.com/world/2019/aug/30/hong-kongs-be-water-protests-leaves-china-casting-about-for-an-enemy; "'Be Water!': Seven Tactics that Are Winning Hong Kong's Democracy Revolution," *New Statesman*, August 1, 2019, https://www.newstatesman.com/world/2019/08/be-water-seven-tactics-are-winning-hong-kongs-democracy-revolution.

[34] Hana Meihan Davis and Jeffrey Wasserstrom, "Hong Kong and 'The Hunger Games,'" *The Millions*. "Fueling the Hong Kong Protests: A World of Pop-Culture Memes," *New York Times*, August 2, 2019, https://www.nytimes.com/2019/08/02/world/asia/hong-kong-protests-memes.html.

[35] There has been no formal determination whether he fell or was pushed. "From War Zone to 'Prison': Voices from Polytechnic University Siege, Site of Some of the Worst Violence amid Hong Kong's Protest Crisis," *South China Morning Post*, November 29, 2019, https://www.scmp.com/news/hong-kong/politics/article/3039838/war-zone-prison-voices-polytechnic-university-siege-site.

[36] Ibid.

[37] "Hong Kong Police Seize More than 3,800 Petrol Bombs from Polytechnic University, Saying Campus Siege Will End Friday," *South China Morning Post*, November 28, 2019, https://www.scmp.com/news/hong-kong/politics/article/3039681/hong-kong-police-team-enters-polytechnic-university-riot.

[38] Interview with Professor Benny Tai, December 10, 2019.

[39] "Nearly a Fifth of Hong Kong Voters Say They Support Violent Actions by Protesters, Such as Attacking Opponents or Hurling Petrol Bombs and Bricks," *South China Morning Post*, December 21, 2019, https://www.scmp.com/news/hong-kong/politics/article/3043073/nearly-fifth-voters-say-they-support-violent-actions.

[40] "Man Set Alight Hours after Hong Kong Protester Shot by Police as Clashes Erupt Citywide," CNN, November 19, 2019, https://www.cnn.com/2019/11/10/asia/hong-kong-protester-shot-intl-hnk/index.html.

[41] "Hong Kong Protests: Man Dies after Being Hit 'by Hard Object' during Protests," BBC News, November 15, 2020, https://www.bbc.com/news/world-asia-china-50428704.

[42] "Soul Searching among Hong Kong Protesters after Chaos at the Airport," *New York Times*, August 14, 2019, https://www.nytimes.com/2019/08/14/world/asia/hong-kong-airport-protests.html.

[43] Victoria Tin-bor Hui, "Crackdown: Hong Kong Faces Tiananmen 2.0," *Journal of Democracy* 31, no. 4 (October 2020), https://www.journalofdemocracy.org/articles/crackdown-hong-kong-faces-tiananmen-2-0/.

[44] There was a lot of discussion within the pan-democratic camp about organizing a primary to sort out optimal opportunity for democratic candidates in the proportional

representation system. Such a primary was in fact held in July 2020, organized by participants and subsequently the target of national security prosecutions. The election was subsequently delayed for a year. Many pan-democrats who had earlier won in the district council elections would later resign in the face of Beijing's patriots-only oath-taking requirements.

[45] "Hong Kong Elections: Mass Disqualification of Opposition Hopefuls Sparks Political Storm," *South China Morning Post*, July 30, 2020, https://scmp.com/news/hong-kong/politics/article/3095327/hong-kong-elections-12-opposition-candidates-disqualified.

[46] "Hong Kong Leader Delays Legislative Elections, Asks Beijing to Resolve Legal Questions, Citing Coronavirus Pandemic Dangers," *South China Morning Post*, July 31, 2020, https://scmp.com/news/hong-kong/politics/article/3095461/hong-kong-legislative-council-elections-be-postponed.

[47] Kenneth K.L. Chan, director and editor, "Election Observation Project Report: Democrats 35+ Civil Voting 11–12 July 2020 and LegCo 2020 Observation Update," English, July 25, 2020, https://hkeop.hk/en/democrats-35-civil-voting-11-12-july-2020-observation-report/.

[48] Interview with former vice convenor of the Hong Kong Civil Human Rights Front, Bonnie Leung, December 8, 2019.

[49] Ibid.

[50] Localists were usually viewed as being on the more radical end, though not the most extreme, of the pan-democratic camp in Hong Kong, advocating self-determination as opposed to full independence. For an account of the rise of the localist movement that identifies it with civic identification, see Sebastian Veg, "The Rise of 'Localism' and Civic Identity in Post-Handover Hong Kong: Questioning the Chinese State," *China Quarterly* 230 (2017): 323–347. See also Ho-fung Hung, *City on Edge: Hong Kong under Chinese Rule*, chapters 1 and 2.

[51] Interview with an anonymous group of HKIAD members, December 8, 2019.

[52] "New Hong Kong Police Chief Chris Tang Tells Top Beijing Officials 'Hard and Soft' Tactics Will Be Used to Thwart Protest Crisis," *South China Morning Post*, December 7, 2019, https://www.scmp.com/news/hong-kong/law-and-crime/article/3041102/new-hong-kong-police-chief-chris-tang-tells-top.

[53] "Our Research in Hong Kong Reveals What People Really Think of the Protesters—and the Police," *Independent*, October 16, 2019, https://www.independent.co.uk/voices/hong-kong-protests-police-violence-public-opinion-polling-support-a9158061.html. Their data showed around 70 percent of the people believed the police used excessive force, and 80 percent or more supported an independent investigation. Only around 40 percent felt the protesters used excessive force.

[54] Commissions of Inquiry Ordinance, Cap 86, Hong Kong Ordinances, https://www.elegislation.gov.hk/hk/cap86!en-zh-Hant-HK.

[55] Interviews with senior pan-democrats and with protest organizers or supporters appeared to repeat this view. Interview with Alan Leong, Civic Party chair, December 9,

2019; interview with anonymous representatives of student protest organization, Hong Kong Institutions International Affairs (HKIAD), December 8, 2019; interview with Bonnie Leung, December 8, 2019; interview with Joshua Wong, secretary general of Demosisto, December 6, 2019.

[56] "Police Reputation in Tatters across the Political Divide According to Online Survey of Hong Kong Voters," *South China Morning Post*, December 21, 2019, https://www.scmp.com/news/hong-kong/politics/article/3043030/police-reputation-tatters-across-political-divide-according. (The opinion poll in the article addresses both police support and political pessimism.)

[57] This includes "yellow shops" and "yellow consumption" in contrast to "blue shops." "'Buy Yellow, Eat Yellow': The Economic Arm of Hong Kong's Pro-Democracy Protests," *The Diplomat*, December 13, 2019, https://thediplomat.com/2019/12/buy-yellow-eat-yellow-the-economic-arm-of-hong-kongs-pro-democracy-protests/.

[58] "Daughter of Maxim's Founder Hits Out Again at Hong Kong Protesters, Saying She Has Lost Hope in the Next Two Generations," *South China Morning Post*, November 4, 2019, https://www.scmp.com/news/hong-kong/politics/article/3036260/daughter-maxims-founder-hits-out-again-hong-kong-protesters.

[59] Mary Hui, "A Cultural Revolution 2.0 Is Sweeping through Hong Kong Offices and Schools," *Quartz*, July 22, 2020, https://qz.com/1882496/cultural-revolution-2-0-political-repression-sweeps-hong-kong-workplaces/.

[60] Vivienne Chow, "I've Been Waiting for a Song Like 'Glory to Hong Kong" My Whole Life, I Just Didn't Realize it," *New York Times*, September 16, 2019, https://www.nytimes.com/2019/09/16/opinion/hong-kong-anthem.html.

[61] "Hong Kong Bans Protest Anthem in Schools as Fears over Freedoms Intensify," *Reuters*, July 8, 2020, https://www.reuters.com/article/us-hongkong-protests-education/hong-kong-bans-protest-anthem-in-schools-as-fears-over-freedoms-intensify-idUSKBN2490OE.

[62] Brian Wong, "Hong Kong's first person tried under the national anthem law sentenced to 3 months in jail for using protest song in a video," *South China Morning Post*, July 20, 2023. https://scmp.com/news/hong-kong/law-and-crime/article/3228325/hong-kongs-first-person-tried-under-national-anthem-law-sentenced-3-months-jail-using-protest-song

[63] "Hong Kong Arrests Harmonica Player at Queen Vigil for Sedition," *Guardian*, September 20, 2022, https://www.theguardian.com/world/2022/sep/20/hong-kong-arrests-harmonica-player-at-queen-vigil-for-sedition.

[64] "Hong Kong Jails First Person for Insulting the National Anthem," *Channel News Asia*, November 10, 2022, https://www.channelnewsasia.com/asia/hong-kong-jails-first-person-insulting-national-anthem-3060631.

[65] "'Liberate Hong Kong, Revolution of Our Times' Slogan is Illegal, Government Says," *Reuters*, July 3, 2020, https://www.huffpost.com/entry/liberate-hong-kong-revolution-of-our-times-slogan_n_5efefe8dc5b6acab284e7a88.

[66] The so-called "Fishball Revolution" arose out of a confrontation between police and hawkers over New Year's Day access to a popular area in Mong Kok. Some of the more radical localists called for supporters to show up to protect the hawkers. When the police showed up, the protesters, for the first time in Hong Kong, dug up street bricks to throw at the police. Edward Leung, who was then running for office, declared his presence was a campaign event, resulting in him being held responsible for the riot that ensued. "Hong Kong Independence Activist Edward Leung Jailed for Six Years," CNN, June 11, 2018, https://www.cnn.com/2018/06/11/asia/edward-leung-hong-kong-jailed-intl/index.html. Leung's conviction was upheld on appeal. "Hong Kong Court Quashes Appeal from Protest Movements 'Spiritual Leader,'" *Radio Free Asia*, April 29, 2020, https://www.rfa.org/english/news/china/appeal-04292020104253.html.

[67] "'Five Key Demands, Not One Less': Hong Kong Protesters Make Clear That Chief Executive Carrie Lam's Bill Withdrawal Is Not Enough," *South China Morning Post*, September 4, 2019, https://www.scmp.com/news/hong-kong/politics/article/3025750/five-key-demands-not-one-less-hong-kong-protesters-make.

[68] Interview with prominent pro-establishment business leader, who shall remain anonymous, December 10, 2019.

[69] "Hong Kong Investor David Webb Says City is Facing 'Brain Drain,'" *Bloomberg*, June 1, 2020.

[70] Interview with Regina Ip, legislator and former secretary for security, December 6, 2019.

[71] "Hong Kong Protesters Direct Anger at Police as Violence Flares," *Wall Street Journal*, November 11, 2019, https://www.wsj.com/articles/hong-kong-protesters-direct-anger-at-police-as-violence-flares-11573499473. "Hong Kong: Arbitrary Arrest, Brutal Beatings and Torture in Police Detention Revealed," Amnesty International, September 19, 2019, https://www.amnesty.org/en/latest/news/2019/09/hong-kong-arbitrary-arrests-brutal-beatings-and-torture-in-police-detention-revealed/.

[72] Interview with HKU Professor Puja Kapai, December 5, 2019 (reporting on the approval rating at the start of the Lam administration); "Police Reputation in Tatters across the Political Divide According to Online Survey of Hong Kong Voters," *South China Morning Post*, December 21, 2019, https://www.scmp.com/news/hong-kong/politics/article/3043030/police-reputation-tatters-across-political-divide-according.

[73] Such an independent investigation demanded by protesters would be carried out under the local Hong Kong ordinance on commissions of inquiry, which allows the chief executive to appoint one or more commissioners "to inquire into the conduct or management of any public body, the conduct of any public officer or into any matter whatsoever which is, in his opinion, of public importance." Cap 86, Hong Kong ordinances, Commissions of Inquiry, https://www.elegislation.gov.hk/hk/cap86.

[74] "In Hong Kong Crackdown the Police Repeatedly Broke Their Own Rules—and Faced No Consequence," *Washington Post*, December 24, 2019, https://www.washingtonpost.com/graphics/2019/world/hong-kong-protests-excessive-force/?fbclid=IwAR2_znXTd2chida3ExJ6s4X3R2PpcBpEYiZdjyxj3bbXrGxC2hy1Dt9N2ac.

[75] "Hong Kong Police Change Guidelines on Use of Force in Protest: Documents," *Reuters*, October 2, 2019, https://www.reuters.com/article/us-hongkong-protests-police/hong-kong-police-change-guidelines-on-use-of-force-in-protests-documents-idUSKBN1WI0TX.

[76] Interview with Mrs. Anson Chan, former chief secretary, December 10, 2019.

[77] "Statement from the Hong Kong Police in Response to Questions from the *Washington Post*," *Washington Post*, December 24, 2019, https://www.washingtonpost.com/world/asia_pacific/statement-from-the-hong-kong-police-in-response-to-questions-from-the-washington-post/2019/12/24/e91d3e96-25a9-11ea-b2ca-2e72667c1741_story.html.

[78] "Hong Kong Watchdog Panel Raises Doubts over Police Inquiry," *Bloomberg*, November 10, 2019, https://www.bloomberg.com/news/articles/2019-11-10/hong-kong-watchdog-panel-raises-doubts-over-lam-s-police-inquiry; Amy Gunia, "Hong Kong's Police Watchdog is Unable to Do Its Job, Experts Say," *Time*, November 11, 2019, https://time.com/5723615/hong-kong-ipcc-police-complaints/.

[79] See "A Thematic Study by the IPCC on the Public Order Events Arising from the Fugitive Offenders Bill since June 2019 and the Police Actions in Response," May 15, 2020, https://hongkongfp.com/wp-content/uploads/2020/05/IPCC.pdf. See also, "Hong Kong Police Watchdog Clears Force of Misconduct Citing Online 'Propaganda,' but Says 'Room for Improvement,'" *Hong Kong Free Press*, May 15, 2020, https://hongkongfp.com/2020/05/15/in-full-hong-kong-police-watchdog-releases-report-on-protest-conduct-but-no-evidence-of-yuen-long-mob-attack-collusion/.

[80] Kelley Ho, "Court Rules Hong Kong's Police Watchdogs 'Inadequate'; Failures in Displaying Officer IDs Breached Bill of Rights," *Hong Kong Free Press*, November 19, 2020, https://hongkongfp.com/2020/11/19/court-rules-hong-kongs-police-watchdogs-inadequate-failures-in-displaying-officer-ids-breached-bill-of-rights/.

[81] Peter Lee, "Hong Kong's High Court to Hear New Evidence in Challenge against Ruling That Police Breached Bill of Rights," *Hong Kong Free Press*, September 9, 2022, https://hongkongfp.com/2022/09/16/hong-kongs-high-court-to-hear-new-evidence-in-challenge-against-ruling-that-police-breached-bill-of-rights/.

[82] Interview with Legislative Counsellor Regina Ip, December 6, 2019.

[83] See Commission of Inquiry Ordinance, Cap 86.

[84] "Extradition Protesters in Hong Kong Face Tear Gas and Rubber Bullets," *New York Times*, June 12, 2019, https://www.nytimes.com/2019/06/12/world/asia/hong-kong-extradition-protest.html.

[85] "Hong Kong Journalism Groups Accuse Police of Assaulting Reporters and Photographers during Extradition Bill Clashes in Mong Kok," *South China Morning Post*, July 8, 2019. https://www.scmp.com/news/hong-kong/politics/article/3017673/hong-kong-journalism-groups-accuse-police-assaulting; "Arrest of Medical Staff during Hong Kong University Siege Sparks Furor," Radio Free Asia, November 22, 2019, https://www.rfa.org/english/news/china/medical-11222019130855.html.

[86] "Millions in Hong Kong Have Been Exposed to Tear Gas Since June," *Bloomberg Business Week*, November 5, 2019, https://www.bloomberg.com/news/articles/2019-11-05/up-to-88-of-hong-kong-population-exposed-to-tear-gas-since-june; "Hong Kong: Counting the Health Cost," *Lancet*, December 7, 2019, https://www.thelancet.com/journals/lancet/article/PIIS0140-6736(19)33049-1/fulltext. As of November 27, 2019, there had been ten thousand rounds of tear gas reportedly fired, as well as 4,800 rubber bullets and nineteen live rounds. "Over 2,000 Tear Gas Canisters Fired in a Single Day," Radio Television Hong Kong, November 27, 2019, https://news.rthk.hk/rthk/en/component/k2/1494810-20191127.htm.

[87] "Amnesty International Says Hong Kong Police Using 'Reckless and Indiscriminate Tactics,'" *Time*, September 20, 2019, https://time.com/5681906/amnesty-hong-kong-police-protests/.

[88] "Hong Kong Police Accused of Harassing Hospital Staff during Searches for Extradition Bill Protesters as Medical and Legal Professionals Call on Officers to Behave," *South China Morning Post*, June 23, 2019, https://www.scmp.com/news/hong-kong/law-and-crime/article/3015743/hong-kong-police-accused-harassing-hospital-staff.

[89] For a privately compiled online list of such abuse up until mid-October, see https://drive.google.com/drive/u/0/folders/1sdbhvxkWSvbECROtK1XXB8HR-s94vrKG?fbclid=IwAR2gYtJSkpkTfCEeTcZG3xE2HVW8nucbUaG4ihnJROTx28bgWa-X-fsMqNg. A couple recent clips include: https://www.dailymail.co.uk/video/news/video-2046534/Video-Police-beat-protester-Hong-Kongs-Holy-Cross-Catholic-Church.html; and https://www.scmp.com/news/hongkong/politics/article/3037135/shots-fired-hong-kong-anti-government-protesters-cause. For a summary of one week, see https://www.scmp.com/news/hong-kong/politics/article/3037135/shots-fired-hong-kong-anti-government-protesters-cause.

[90] "'No Difference': Hong Kong Police Likened to Thugs after Yuen Long Violence," *Guardian*, July 28, 2019, https://www.theguardian.com/world/2019/jul/28/hong-kong-police-likened-to-thugs-after-yuen-long-violence.

[91] His opposition colleagues speculate that Lam is being targeted by police due to his efforts to have the police investigated in respect to alleged police complicity in the horrific attacks made by the white-shirted thugs against the opposition protesters, who were returning to Yuen Long that day. "Police Now Claim Yuen Long Attacks Not Indiscriminate," *RTHK*, August 26, 2020, https://news.rthk.hk/rthk/en/component/k2/1546005-20200826.htm. A total of thirteen arrests, including several of the white-shirted attackers, were made. "Two Hong Kong Democrats Arrested over 2019 Protests; Lam Cheuk-ting Detained over Alleged 'Rioting' during Yuen Long Mob Attack," *Hong Kong Free Press*, August 26, 2020, https://hongkongfp.com/2020/08/26/two-hong-kong-democrats-arrested-over-2019-protests-lam-cheuk-ting-detained-over-alleged-rioting-during-yuen-long-mob-attack/.

[92] Brian Wong, "Ex-Hong Kong Lawmaker Cleared of Perverting the Course of Justice after Judge Finds He Was Trying to Calm a Tense Situation during the 2019 Protests," *South China Morning Post*, January 20, 2023, https://scmp.com/news/hong-kong/law-and-

crime/article/3207620/ex-hong-kong-lawmaker-cleared-perverting-course-justice-after-judge-finds-he-was-trying-calm-tense.

[93] Selena Cheng, "Ex-lawmaker Jailed for 4 Months for Revealing the Identity of Hong Kong Police Officer under Investigation," *Hong Kong Free Press*, January 26, 2022, https://hongkongfp.com/2022/01/26/ex-lawmaker-jailed-for-4-months-for-disclosing-identity-of-hong-kong-police-officer-under-investigation/.

[94] Caroline Kwok, "Hong Kong Lawmaker Charged with Rioting," *South China Morning Post*, August 28, 2020, https://www.scmp.com/video/hong-kong/3099239/hong-kong-lawmaker-charged-rioting-over-yuen-long-attack-accuses-police; James Lee, "Hong Kong democrat Lam Cheuk-ting pleads not guilty to rioting during 2019 Yuen Long mob attack," *Hong Kong Free Press*, October 16, 2023, https://hongkongfp.com/2023/10/16/former-pro-democracy-lawmaker-lam-cheuk-ting-pleads-not-guilty-to-rioting-during-2019-yuen-long-mob-attack/

[95] Interview with Legislator Lam Cheuk-ting, December 4, 2019. The August 2020 arrest appeared to reflect an effort by the police to change the narrative on what happened that day. A look at the video of events in the following *New York Times* story reveals a very different scenario from the police claim of justification for Mr. Lam's arrest. "With New Arrests, Hong Kong's Police Try to Change the Narrative," *New York Times*, August 26, 2020, https://www.nytimes.com/2020/08/25/world/asia/hongkong-arrests-lawmakers.html?campaign_id=7&emc=edit_MBAE_p_20200826&instance_id=21637&nl=morning-briefing&regi_id=81190950&section=topNews&segment_id=36973&te=1&user_id=28950c7fbc8795cb3bb3d311ae5b4a4e.

[96] Yuen Long Attack: Hong Kong Court Gives Seven Jail Time" BBC, July 22, 2021, https://www.bbc.com/news/world-asia-china-57925055; Hillary Leung, "Hong Kong Court Sentences Man to 4 Years and 3 Months over 2019 Yuen Long Mob Attacks," *Hong Kong Free Press*, October 27, 2022, https://hongkongfp.com/2022/10/27/hong-kong-court-sentences-man-to-4-years-and-3-months-over-2019-yuen-long-mob-attacks/.

[97] Tiffany May, "In Rare Victory for the Media, Hong Kong Court Overturns Conviction of Journalist," *New York Times*, June 5, 2023, https://www.nytimes.com/2023/06/05/world/asia/hong-kong-bao-choy-appeal.html

[98] Tsung-gan Kong, "Arrest and Trial of Hong Kong Protesters," on website tracking protests arrests based on police figures as supplemented, https://kongtsunggan.medium.com/arrests-and-trials-of-hong-kong-protesters-2019-9d9a601d4950.

[99] Pak Yiu, "Top Hong Kong Court Limits Scope of Riot Crimes," *Nikkei Asia*, November 4, 2021, https://asia.nikkei.com/Spotlight/Hong-Kong-security-law/Top-Hong-Kong-court-limits-scope-of-riot-crimes.

[100] Interview with Alvin Yeung, legislator and former Civic Party leader, December 4, 2019; interview with Legislator Chu Hoi-dik, December 5, 2019. Chu claimed then that four hundred people were already charged with rioting and was particularly concerned to remove the provision allowing anyone found in a rioting sight to be charged.

[101] Peter Lee, "Hong Kong Court Jails 13 for up to 4 Years for Rioting at 2019 Demo," *Hong Kong Free Press,* April 6, 2022, https://hongkongfp.com/2022/04/06/hong-kong-court-sentences-13-to-3-5-to-4-years-on-riot-charges-over-2019-sheung-wan-protest/.

[102] Three groups of lawyer volunteers raised substantial funds and were prominently involved in providing legal services pro bono: Civil Human Rights Front (150 lawyer volunteers), Civil Human Rights Observers (two hundred lawyer volunteers), and the Spark Alliance (unknown). Interview with leading barrister, December 9, 2019.

[103] These fees were presumably provided directly to the service provider by the 612 Humanitarian Relief Fund, which was a volunteer organization.

[104] The group identified itself as a "group of lawyers dedicated to promoting rule of law, democracy, human rights, freedom and justice," Progressive Lawyers Group, https://hkplg.org/. Core members Jason Ng, Wilson Leung, and Angeline Chan were interviewed on December 8, 2019.

[105] Interview with senior leading barrister, December 9, 2019. This prominent barrister noted that on the night of the siege of the Hong Kong Polytechnic University, the hotline received over one thousand calls.

[106] Interview with Hong Kong Bar Chair Philip Dykes, December 9, 2019.

[107] "China's Communist Party Elite Wrap Up Meeting with Pledge to Safeguard National Security in Hong Kong," *South China Morning Post,* November 1, 2019, https://www.scmp.com/news/china/politics/article/3035818/chinas-communist-party-elite-wrap-meeting-pledge-safeguard. Original of plenum communiqué can be found at: www.xinhuanet.com//2019-11/05/c_1125195786.htm. For an overview of China's national security concerns and article 23, see Hualing Fu, "China's Imperatives for National Security Legislation," in Cora Chan and Fiona de Londras, *China's National Security: Endangering Hong Kong's Rule of Law.* Oxford: Hart, 2010, available at https://ssrn.com/abstract=3452675.

[108] 2014 white paper.

[109] Interview with former Chief Secretary Mrs. Anson Chan, December 10, 2014.

[110] Ibid.

[111] Prohibition on Face Covering Regulation, Cap 241K, October 5, 2019, https://www.elegislation.gov.hk/hk/cap241K.

[112] Emergency Regulations Ordinance, Cap 241, February 28, 1922, https://www.elegislation.gov.hk/hk/cap241.

[113] *Kwok Wing Hang and Others v. Chief Executive in Council and Another,* HCAL2945A/2019, https://legalref.judiciary.hk/lrs/common/search/search_result_detail_frame.jsp?DIS=125452&QS=%2B&TP=JU&ILAN=en, press summary at https://legalref.judiciary.hk/doc/judg/html/vetted/other/en/2019/HCAL002945A_2019_files/HCAL002945A_2019ES.htm. See also "Hong Kong Court Rules Mask Ban Is Unconstitutional," *Wall Street Journal,* November 18, 2019, https://www.wsj.com/articles/hong-kong-court-rules-mask-ban-is-unconstitutional-11574057107.

114 "'No Other Authority Has Right to Make Judgements': China Slams Hong Kong Court's Ruling on Anti-mask Law as Unconstitutional," *South China Morning Post*, November 19, 2019, https://www.scmp.com/news/hong-kong/politics/article/3038325/hong-kong-judges-slammed-chinas-top-legislative-body.

115 Interview with a prominent barrister and legislator who prefers to remain anonymous due to the fear of retribution, December 4, 2019.

116 *Leung Kwok Hung v. Secretary for Justice and Chief Executive in Council*, 2020 HKCA 192, CACV 541/2019, April 9, 2020, https://legalref.judiciary.hk/lrs/common/search/search_result_detail_frame.jsp?DIS=127372&QS=%24%28mask%29&TP=JU.

117 *Leung Kwok Hung v. Secretary for Justice and Chief Executive in Council*, 2020 HKCFA 42, CACV Nos 542 and 583 of 2019, December 21, 2020, https://www.doj.gov.hk/en/notable_judgments/pdf/FACV_6_7_8_9_2020e.pdf.

118 "Hong Kong Asks China's Top Legislative Body to Resolve Legal Problems with Postponing Elections," *South China Morning Post*, July 31, 2020, https://scmp.com/news/hong-kong/politics/article/3095461/hong-kong-legislative-council-elections-be-postponed.

119 Michael C. Davis and Victoria T. Hui, "In Hong Kong, What Happens Now That Beijing Has Called the Protests a 'Color Revolution'? *Washington Post*, August 10, 2019, https://www.washingtonpost.com/politics/2019/08/10/hong-kong-what-happens-now-that-beijing-has-called-protests-color-revolution/.

120 Davis and Hui, "Will China Crush the Protests in Hong Kong? Why Beijing Doesn't Need to Send in Troops."

121 "Chinese Army's Hong Kong Garrison Releases Video Showing Anti-riot Drills," YouTube, August 1, 2019, https://www.youtube.com/watch?v=SwbbpStz5SY.

122 "Mainland Chinese Army, Police Not Part of Hong Kong Police Operations: Hong Kong Government," *Reuters*, October 10, 2019, https://www.reuters.com/article/us-hongkong-protests-pla/mainland-chinese-army-police-not-part-of-hong-kong-police-operations-hong-kong-government-idUSKBN1WP1PH.

123 Interview with prominent barrister and former legislator, December 10, 2019.

124 "Beijing Constructs an 'Independence' Plot for Hong Kong Protests through Information Operations," *Hong Kong Free Press*, November 5, 2019, https://www.hongkongfp.com/2019/11/05/beijing-constructs-independence-plot-hong-kong-protests-information-operations/.

Chapter 7

1 "Beijing's Hong Kong Office Warns Pro-democracy Poll Could Violate New Security Law," *Reuters*, July 13, 2020, https://www.reuters.com/article/us-hongkong-security/beijings-hong-kong-office-warns-pro-democracy-poll-could-violate-new-security-law-idUSKCN24F05Y.

[2] "Hong Kong Elections: Mass Disqualification of Opposition Hopefuls Sparks Political Storm," *South China Morning Post*, July 30, 2020, https://www.scmp.com/news/hong-kong/politics/article/3095327/hong-kong-elections-12-opposition-candidates-disqualified.

[3] "Protests Break Out in Hong Kong as First Arrests Made under New Security Law," CNN, July 1, 2020, https://www.cnn.com/2020/07/01/china/hong-kong-national-security-law-july-1-intl-hnk/index.html.

[4] "Hong Kong Police Arrest Four under New Security Law in Move Slammed by Rights Group," *Reuters*, July 29, 2020, https://www.reuters.com/article/us-hongkong-security/hong-kong-police-arrest-four-under-new-security-law-in-move-slammed-by-rights-group-idUSKCN24U3DQ.

[5] "Hong Kong University to Fire Law Professor Who Inspired Protests," *New York Times*, July 28, 2020, https://www.nytimes.com/2020/07/28/world/asia/benny-tai-hong-kong-university.html.

[6] "LegCo General Election Postponed for a Year, Press Release, Government of the Hong Kong SAR," July 31, 2020, https://www.info.gov.hk/gia/general/202007/31/P2020073100898.htm.

[7] "National Security Law: Hong Kong Media Mogul Jimmy Lai Freed as Activist Agnes Chow Calls Her Arrest 'Political Persecution and Suppression,'" *South China Morning Post*, August 11, 2020, https://www.scmp.com/news/hong-kong/politics/article/3096851/apple-daily-founder-jimmy-lai-taken-his-yacht-ing-hong.

[8] Mercedes Hutton and Hans Tse, "Closely-watched national security trial of Hong Kong's pro-democracy media magnate Jimmy Lai finally set to start," *Hong Kong Free Press*, December 17, 2023. https://hongkongfp.com/2023/12/17/closely-watched-national-security-trial-of-hong-kongs-pro-democracy-media-magnate-jimmy-lai-finally-set-to-start/

[9] "China's Arrest of a Free-Speech Icon Backfires in Hong Kong," *New Yorker*, August 14, 2020, https://www.newyorker.com/news/daily-comment/chinas-arrest-of-a-free-speech-icon-backfires-in-hong-kong.

[10] Ibid.

[11] "Jimmy Lai Shows Why the West Lost Faith in Hong Kong Courts," *Bloomberg*, August 11, 2020, https://www.bloombergquint.com/global-economics/jimmy-lai-arrest-shows-why-world-lost-faith-in-hong-kong-courts. The foreign ministry did not stop there, as it went on to signal its view of the Hong Kong Foreign Correspondents' Club, accusing it of trying to "whitewash" Lai and labeling it as an organization "siding with the forces sowing trouble in Hong Kong and China at large."

[12] Closely-watched national security trial of Hong Kong's pro-democracy media magnate Jimmy Lai finally set to start," *Hong Kong Free Press*, December 17, 2023. https://hongkongfp.com/2023/12/17/closely-watched-national-security-trial-of-hong-kongs-pro-democracy-media-magnate-jimmy-lai-finally-set-to-start/

[13] For a translation of Chow's letter describing her treatment see "2023 PSB to HK Activist:

Propaganda Trip Then Return Passport," David Cowhig's Translation Blog, posted December 3, 2023, https://gaodawei.wordpress.com/2023/12/03/2023-psb-to-hk-activist-propaganda-trip-then-return-passport/ Further weighing on her, she had also been arrested in 2020 for protest related activities and had served six months in jail. The scale of these police reeducation efforts is suggested by reports of another activist, who fled Hong Kong soon after, describing being targeted by similar reeducation efforts. Shibani Mahtani, "Hong Kong activist convicted under security law flees to U.K." *Washington Post*, December 28, 2023, https://www.washingtonpost.com/world/2023/12/28/hong-kong-security-law-asylum.

[14] Kelly Ho, "Hong Kong vows to pursue self-exiled activist Agnes Chow, leader says police 'leniency' resulted in 'deception,' *Hong Kong Free Press*, December 5, 2023, https://hongkongfp.com/2023/12/05/hong-kong-leader-vows-to-pursue-self-exiled-activist-agnes-chow-says-police-leniency-resulted-in-deception. As with other targeted human rights activist, Agnes Chow's parents were soon called in to talk to the police. Hans Tse, "Parents of Hong Kong self-exiled activist Agnes Chow questioned by police—local media," *Hong Kong Free Press*, December 29, 2023, https://hongkongfp.com/2023/12/29/parents-of-hong-kong-self-exiled-activist-agnes-chow-questioned-by-police-local-media.

[15] Legislation Law of the People's Republic of China, article 83 and 85, passed March 15, 2000, official English translation, Ministry of Defense of the People's Republic of China, http://eng.mod.gov.cn/publications/2017-03/02/content_4774201.htm.

[16] Johannes Chan, "Does the Decision of the National People's Congress on Enacting a National Security Law for Hong Kong Contravene the Basic Law?" University of Hong Kong Research Blog, June 1, 2020, https://researchblog.law.hku.hk/2020/06/johannes-chan-on-whether-npc-decision.html.

[17] Hualing Fu, "On the Relationship between Hong Kong's Basic Law and the National Security Law," Hong Kong Legal Scholarship Blog, August 12, 2020, http://researchblog.law.hku.hk/2020/08/hualing-fu-on-relationship-between-hong.html?utm_source=feedburner&utm_medium=email&utm_campaign=Feed%3A+HkuLegalScholarshipBlog+%28HKU+Legal+Scholarship+Blog%29.

[18] See, for example, Surya Deva, "Putting Byrnes and Hong Kong in a Time Machine: Human Rights in 2021 under the Shadow of Beijing's National Security Law," *Australian Journal of Human Rights* 27, no. 3: 467–486, https://www.tandfonline.com/doi/full/10.1080/1323238X.2021.2016021.

[19] PRC Legislation Law, articles 5, 36, and 37; Jamie P. Horsley, "Chinese Law Requires Public Consultation in Lawmaking: What Does It Mean for the Hong Kong National Security Legislation?" Order from Chaos, *Brookings*, June 8, 2020, https://www.brookings.edu/blog/order-from-chaos/2020/06/08/chinese-law-requires-public-consultation-in-lawmaking-what-does-it-mean-for-the-hong-kong-national-security-legislation/.

[20] Frank Ching offers a historical account of Xi Jinping's passion to bring Hong Kong and Taiwan under Beijing's control. Frank Ching, "Hong Kong and Taiwan Confront Rising Chinese Pressure," *Current History* (September 2020): 234–240.

[21] NSL, June 30, 2020, https://www.gld.gov.hk/egazette/pdf/20202444e/es220202444136.pdf.

[22] "National Security Law: Beijing Appoints Tough-Talking Party Official Zheng Yanxiong to Lead Powerful New Agency in Hong Kong," *South China Morning Post*, July 3, 2020, https://scmp.com/news/hong-kong/politics/article/3091664/beijings-top-hong-kong-official-luo-huining-will-be-city.

[23] Basic Law, article 23, stipulates that Hong Kong shall enact laws "on its own to prohibit any act of treason, secession, sedition, subversion against the Central People's Government, or theft of state secrets, to prohibit foreign political organizations or bodies from conducting political activities in the region."

[24] Michael C. Davis, "Controversy over the Role of Beijing's Offices in Hong Kong Shows Weight of 'One Country' Threatens the Scaffolding of 'Two Systems,'" *South China Morning Post*, April 24, 2020, https://www.scmp.com/comment/opinion/article/3081090/controversy-over-role-beijings-offices-hong-kong-shows-weight-one.

[25] NSL, articles 12 and 15.

[26] "Beijing Envoy Luo Huining Named National Security Adviser," *The Standard*, July 2, 2020, https://www.thestandard.com.hk/breaking-news/section/4/150264/Beijing-envoy-Luo-Huining-named-national-security-adviser.

[27] NSL, article 14.

[28] Ibid.

[29] NSL, article 19.

[30] "National Security Law: Beijing Appoints Tough-Talking Party Official Zheng Yanxiong to Lead Powerful New Agency in Hong Kong," *South China Morning Post*.

[31] NSL, articles 48 and 49.

[32] Basic Law Article 22 bars departments of the central government from interfering in Hong Kong's internal affairs.

[33] NSL, articles 55 and 56.

[34] Ibid., article 57.

[35] Ibid., articles 16, 17, and 18.

[36] Implementation Rules for Article 43 of the Law of the People's Republic of China on Safeguarding National Security in the Hong Kong Special Administrative Region, L.N. 139 of 2020, B2397, https://www.gld.gov.hk/egazette/pdf/20202449e/es220202449139.pdf; Operating Principles and Guidelines for Application for Authorization to Conduct Interception and Covert Surveillance, Issued Pursuant to Section 20 of Schedule 6 of the Implementation Rules for Article 43 of the Law of the People's Republic of China on Safeguarding National Security in the Hong Kong Special Administrative Region, G.N.(E.) 74 of 2020, https://www.gld.gov.hk/egazette/pdf/20202450e/egn2020245074.pdf. The ordinance, the regulation, and the operating principles carefully give law enforcement nearly unconstrained authority to conduct searches and surveillance.

[37] Basic Law, article 9.

[38] The participants in the letter include the special rapporteur on the promotion and protection of human rights and fundamental freedoms while countering terrorism; the Working Group on Arbitrary Detention; the special rapporteur on extrajudicial, summary, or arbitrary executions; the special rapporteur on the promotion and protection of the right to freedom of opinion and expression; the special rapporteur on the rights to freedom of peaceful assembly and of association; the special rapporteur on the situation of human rights defenders; and the special rapporteur on minority issues, Reference OL. CHN 17/2020, September 1, 2020 (hereinafter "special procedures letter"), https://spcommreports.ohchr.org/TMResultsBase/DownLoadPublicCommunicationFile?gId=25487.

[39] "Jimmy Lai's International Legal Team Files Urgent Appeal with United Nations," *Breadcrumb News*, April 8, 2022, https://www.doughtystreet.co.uk/news/jimmy-lais-international-legal-team-files-urgent-appeal-united-nations.

[40] "Hong Kong Media Tycoon Sentenced to Five Years in Prison," *New York Times*, December 10, 2022, https://www.nytimes.com/2022/12/10/world/asia/hong-kong-jimmy-lai-sentenced.html.

[41] Implementation Rules, schedule 1, section 3.

[42] NSL, article 43 and related implementation rules.

[43] NSL, article 16.

[44] Josh Chin and Liza Lin, *Surveillance State: Inside China's Quest to Launch a New Era of Social Control*. New York: St. Martin's Press, 2022, https://us.macmillan.com/books/9781250249296/surveillancestate.

[45] HRW notes further that some PRC detainees described being "restrained for days in so-called 'tiger chairs' (used to immobilize suspects during interrogations), handcuffs, or leg irons." Chinese official reports to international bodies have acknowledged that abuse in custody is a problem. See, "Tiger Chairs and Cell Bosses, Police Torture of Criminal Suspects in China," Human Rights Watch, May 13, 2015. https://www.hrw.org/report/2015/05/13/tiger-chairs-and-cell-bosses/police-torture-criminal-suspects-china.

[46] NSL, article 62.

[47] Pak Niu, "UN Expert Warns Hong Kong Security Law Compromising Judiciary," Nikkei, April 25, 2023, https://asia.nikkei.com/Spotlight/Hong-Kong-security-law/U.N.-expert-warns-Hong-Kong-security-law-compromising-judiciary. The Hong Kong Bar Association has raised special concern. "The Law of the People's Republic of China (PRC) on Safeguarding National Security in the Hong Kong Special Administrative Region ("HKSAR"): Statement of the Hong Kong Bar Association," July 1, 2020, https://www.hkba.org/sites/default/files/20200701%20HKBA%20statement%20on%20Safeguarding%20National%20%20Security%20in%20HKSAR.pdf.

[48] NSL, article 44.

[49] Ibid.

[50] NSL, article 65.

[51] NSL, article 42.

[52] *HKSAR v. Lai Chee Ying*, Final Appeal No. 1 of 2021, Hong Kong Court of Final Appeal, February 9, 2021, https://legalref.judiciary.hk/lrs/common/ju/ju_frame.jsp.

[53] NSL, article 46.

[54] NSL, article 41.

[55] In fact, the conduct of trials and secrecy requirements were the targets of severe criticisms in the special procedures letter.

[56] See "Explainer: Hong Kong's National Security Crackdown—Month 31," *Hong Kong Free Press*, January 28, 2023, https://hongkongfp.com/2023/01/28/explainer-hong-kongs-national-security-crackdown-month-31/?utm_medium=email.

[57] *HKSAR v. Lui Sai Yu*, Hong Kong Court of Final Appeal, Final Appeal No. 7 of 2023, HKCFA 26.

[58] NSL, articles 20, 22, 24, and 29.

[59] The case was, on an application for a writ of *habeas corpus*, denied. *Tong Ying Kit v. HKSAR*, Constitutional and Administrative Law List No. 1601 of 2020, in High Court, Court of First Instance, August 21, 2020, https://legalref.judiciary.hk/lrs/common/ju/ju_frame.jsp?DIS=130336&currpage=T; "Hong Kong National Security Law: First Person Charged under New Legislation Is Motorcyclist Arrested during July 1 Protest," *South China Morning Post*, July 3, 2020, https://www.scmp.com/news/hong-kong/law-and-crime/article/3091710/hong-kong-national-security-law-first-person-charged.

[60] NSL, articles 20, 24, and 25.

[61] "Hong Kong Security Law: New Police Powers to Surveil Lawyers a 'Major Threat,' Barristers and Legal Scholars Say," *Hong Kong Free Press*, July 9, 2020, https://hongkongfp.com/2020/07/09/hong-kong-security-law-new-police-powers-to-surveil-lawyers-a-major-threat-barrister-and-legal-scholars-say/.

[62] "Australia Suspends Hong Kong Extradition Treaty," BBC, July 9, 2020, https://www.bbc.com/news/world-australia-53344013.

[63] NSL, articles 20, 22, 24, and 29.

[64] NSL, article 6.

[65] Susan Finder, "How China Classifies State Secrets," *The Diplomat*, December 23, 2014, https://thediplomat.com/2014/12/how-china-classifies-state-secrets/.

[66] NSL, article 22.

[67] NSL, article 24.

[68] NSL, article 29.

[69] Tom Blackwell, "Hong Kong Says It Can Target Anyone in the World after Canadian Journalists Charged," *National Post*, August 31, 2022, https://nationalpost.com/news/canada/hong-kong-national-security-law-victor-ho.

[70] The Johannesburg Principles on National Security, Freedom of Expression and Access to Information, *Article 19*, November 1996, https://www.article19.org/wp-content/uploads/2018/02/joburg-principles.pdf; special procedures letter.

71 Margaret Satterthwaite, Letter to Chinese Government, "Mandate of the Special Rapporteur on the Independence of Judges and Lawyers," Ref.:OL CHN 2/2023. https:// spcommreports.ohchr.org/TMResultsBase/DownLoadPublicCommunicationFile

72 NSL, articles 21, 22, 23, 26, 27, and 30.

73 NSL, article 29.

74 Mary Hui, "A Cultural Revolution 2.0 is Sweeping through Hong Kong's Offices and Schools," *Quartz*, July 22, 2020, https://qz.com/1882496/cultural-revolution-2-0-political-repression-sweeps-hong-kong-workplaces/.

75 "Hongkongers Waving Independence Flags or Chanting Slogans Risk Arrest under National Security Law—Report," *Hong Kong Free Press*, July 1, 2020, https://hongkongfp.com/2020/07/01/hongkongers-waving-independence-flags-or-chanting-slogans-risk-arrest-under-national-security-law-report/.

76 "Protests Break Out in Hong Kong as First Arrests Made under New Security Law," CNN, July 1, 2020, https://www.cnn.com/2020/07/01/china/hong-kong-national-security-law-july-1-intl-hnk/index.html.

77 "'Hidden Language': Hongkongers Get Creative against Security Law," *Guardian*, July 4, 2020, https://www.theguardian.com/world/2020/jul/04/hidden-language-hong-kong-security-law-residents-wordplay.

78 Kanis Leung and Zen Soo, "China Virus Protests Hit Hong Kong after Mainland Rallies," *The Diplomat,* November 29, 2022, https://thediplomat.com/2022/11/china-virus-protests-hit-hong-kong-after-mainland-rallies/.

79 "Hong Kong Changed Overnight, Navigates its New Reality," *New York Times*, July 13, 2020, https://www.nytimes.com/2020/07/05/world/asia/hong-kong-security-law.html.

80 "Facebook Temporarily Stops Hong Kong Data Requests," *New York Times*, July 6, 2020, https://www.nytimes.com/2020/07/06/technology/facebook-temporarily-stops-hong-kong-data-requests.htm; "Facebook, Twitter, Google Face Free-Speech Test in Hong Kong," *Wall Street Journal*, July 3, 2020, https://www.wsj.com/articles/facebook-twitter-google-face-free-speech-test-in-hong-kong-11593790205.

81 NSL, article 54.

82 "Hong Kong Press Freedom Hits Record Low, among Fears of Uncertainty over National Security Law," *South China Morning Post*, July 7, 2020, https://scmp.com/news/hong-kong/article/3092208/hong-kongs-press-freedom-hits-record-low-amid-fears-uncertainty-over.

83 "National Security Law: Hong Kong Journalists Association Survey Reveals 98 Per Cent Oppose Legislation amid Fears over Personal Safety, Self-Censorship," *South China Morning Post*, June 21, 2020, https://scmp.com/news/hong-kong/politics/article/3089563/national-security-law-hong-kong-journalists-association.

84 "Hong Kong's Free Media Fears Being Silenced by China's National Security Law," *Reuters*, June 5, 2020, https://www.reuters.com/article/us-hongkong-protests-media-insight/hong-kongs-free-media-fears-being-silenced-by-chinas-national-security-law-

idUSKBN23C0J6; "When Will They Come for Journalists?: Hong Kong Press Freedom under New National Security Law," *Hong Kong Free Press*, July 4, 2020, https://hongkongfp.com/2020/07/04/when-will-they-come-for-journalists-hong-kong-press-freedom-under-the-new-national-security-law/.

[85] See Jean-Pierre Cabestan and Lawrence Daziano, "Hong Kong: The Second Handover," *Fondation pour L'Innovation Politique*, July 2020, http://www.fondapol.org/en/etudes-en/hong-kong-the-second-handover/.

[86] NSL, article 10.

[87] "Hong Kong Pupils Banned from Political Activity," BBC News, July 8, 2020, https://www.bbc.com/news/world-asia-china-53336191.

[88] Power, Lam, and Cheung, "National Security Law: For Hong Kong Scholars a Fear of the Unknown."

[89] "Council of Eight Universities in Hong Kong Back New Security Law," *South China Morning Post*, June 1, 2020, https://www.scmp.com/news/hong-kong/education/article/3086955/five-hong-kong-university-heads-cite-stability-supporting.

[90] "What HSBC and Cathay Pacific's Bow to Beijing on Hong Kong's National Security Law Tells Investors about Management in Political Crisis." *South China Morning Post*, June 9, 2020, https://www.scmp.com/business/companies/article/3088056/what-hsbc-and-cathay-pacifics-bow-beijing-hong-kong-national.

[91] Ibid.

[92] "Hong Kong Elections: Mass Disqualification of Opposition Hopefuls Sparks Political Storm," *South China Morning Post*, July 30, 2020, https://scmp.com/news/hong-kong/politics/article/3095327/hong-kong-elections-12-opposition-candidates-disqualified.

Chapter 8

[1] "China's Top Judge Warns Courts on Judicial Independence," *Reuters*, January 16, 2017, https://www.reuters.com/article/us-china-policy-law/chinas-top-judge-warns-courts-on-judicial-independence-idUSKBN1500OF.

[2] State Council of the PRC, "The Practice of the 'One Country, Two Systems' Policy in the People's Republic of China," http://english.www.gov.cn/archive/white_paper/2014/08/23/content_281474982986578.htm.

[3] Decision of the National People's Congress on Improving the Electoral System of the Hong Kong Special Administrative Region, English Translation, March 13, 2021, available at https://www.chinalawtranslate.com/en/hkelectoralreformdecision/.

[4] Suzanne Pepper, "Beijing's Hard Sell of 'Hong Kong-Style Capitalist Democracy," *Hong Kong Free Press*, January 22, 2022, https://hongkongfp.com/2022/01/22/beijings-hard-sell-of-hong-kong-style-capitalist-democracy/.

[5] Sino-British Joint Declaration on the Question of Hong Kong, January 1, 1984, available at https://digitalcommons.lmu.edu/cgi/viewcontent.cgi?article=1071&context=ilr.

[6] Basic Law of the Hong Kong Special Administrative Region, 1990, available at https://www.legco.gov.hk/general/english/procedur/companion/chapter_15/mcp-part3-ch15-n1-e.pdf.

[7] Ibid, articles 45 and 68.

[8] Natalie Wong, "Hong Kong's national security law: 3 years on, more that 160 prosecutions, 8 bounties later, what else can the city expect? *Hong Kong Free Press*, July 17, 2023. https://hongkongfp.com/2023/07/17/hong-kong-security-law-article-23-would-target-modern-day-espionage-and-internet-loopholes-security-chief-says. For a detailed breakdown, see Lydia Wong, Eric Yan-ho Lai, Charlotte Yeung, and Thomas Kellogg, "Tracking the Impact of Hong Kong's National Security Law," *ChinaFile*, April 13, 2023, https://www.chinafile.com/tracking-impact-of-hong-kongs-national-security-law.

[9] Jerome Cohen, "Hong Kong's Transformed Criminal Justice System: Instrument of Fear," *Academia Sinica Law Journal*, Special Issue (2022), http://publication.iias.sinica.edu.tw/60105122.pdf. The Hong Kong Rule of Law Monitor, which includes many Hong Kong lawyers in exile, has published an excellent overview of the many political prosecutions over 2022. HKRLM, Hong Kong Rule of Law Report 2022, October 23, 2023, https://hkrlm.org/2023/10/23/rol-report-2022/.

[10] *HKSAR v. Tong Ying-Kit*, Hong Kong Court of First Instance 2200, July 27, 2021, https://legalref.judiciary.hk/lrs/common/ju/ju_frame.jsp?DIS=137456&currpage=T. See also Thomas E. Kellogg and Eric Yan-ho Lai, "The Tong Ying-Kit NSL Verdict: An International and Comparative Law Analysis," Georgetown Center for Asian Law Briefing Paper, October 2021, https://www.law.georgetown.edu/law-asia/wp-content/uploads/sites/31/2021/10/TongYingKitVerdictGCAL.pdf.

[11] For a comprehensive analysis of human rights concerns in the case, see Yan-ho Lai and Thomas E. Kellogg, "Departure from International Human Rights Law and Comparative Best Practices: HKSAR v. Tong Ying-Kit," *Hong Kong Law Journal* 52, no. 2: 465–486, September 2022, https://web.law.hku.hk/hklj/2022-Vol-52.php#part2.

[12] Michael C. Davis, "National Security Trial Ruling a Setback for Human Rights in Hong Kong," *South China Morning Post* (Hong Kong), August 4, 2021.

[13] The Johannesburg Principles on National Security, Freedom of Expression and Access to Information, article 19, November 1996, https://www.article19.org/wp-content/uploads/2018/02/joburg-principles.pdf.

[14] See, for example, *Brandenburg v. Ohio*, 395 U.S. 444, United State Supreme Court, 1969.

[15] Peter Lee, "Hong Kong Orders First Person Convicted under Security Law to Pay HK$1.38 Million for Failed Legal Bids," *Hong Kong Free Press*, July 18, 2022, https://hongkongfp.com/2022/07/18/hong-kong-orders-first-person-convicted-under-security-law-to-pay-hk1-38-million-for-failed-legal-bids/.

[16] Hillary Leung, "Man jailed under security law says he was swayed by society's atmosphere in Hong Kong police-promoted TV show," *Hong Kong Free Press*, December 14, 2023, https://hongkongfp.com/2023/12/14/man-jailed-under-security-law-says-he-was-swayed-by-societys-atmosphere-in-hong-kong-police-promoted-tv-show/ Others were similarly included in the twelve episodes of the police TV series.

[17] Johannes Chan, "National Security Law 2020 in Hong Kong: One Year On," *Academia Sinica Law Journal*, Special Issue (2022), http://publication.iias.sinica.edu.tw/30109022.pdf.

[18] The other arrestees ultimately included Editor in Chief Ryan Law and staff members Chow Tat-keun, Cheung Kim-hung, Chan Pui-man, Cheung Chi-wai, Yeung Ching-kee, Fung Wai-kong, and Lam Man-Chung, *Association of Overseas Hong Kong Media Professionals*, press release, November 12, 2022, https://www.aohkmp.org.uk/trial_presser/.

[19] *HKSAR v. Lai Chee Ying*, Final Appeal No. 1 of 2021, Hong Kong Court of Final Appeal, February 9, 2021, https://legalref.judiciary.hk/lrs/common/ju/ju_frame.jsp?DIS=133491.

[20] Candice Chau, "Justice Sec: Those Found Not Guilty under Security Law at Hong Kong High Court Could Be Detained Again if Gov't Appeals," *Hong Kong Free Press*, May 23, 2023, https://hongkongfp.com/2023/05/23/people-acquitted-under-security-law-at-hong-kong-high-court-could-be-remanded-if-govt-appeals-says-justice-sec/

[21] Candice Chau, "Hong Kong Media Tycoon Jimmy Lai's Bid to Hire UK Lawyer for National Security Case Opposed by Justice Minister," *Hong Kong Free Press,* September 30, 2022, https://hongkongfp.com/2022/09/30/hong-kong-media-tycoon-jimmy-lais-bid-to-hire-uk-lawyer-for-national-security-case-opposed-by-justice-minister/.

[22] Hillary Leung, "National Security Trial for Hong Kong Media Mogul Jimmy Lai to Proceed without a Jury—Reports," *Hong Kong Free Press*, August 17, 2022, https://hongkongfp.com/2022/08/17/national-security-trial-for-hong-kong-media-mogul-jimmy-lai-to-proceed-without-jury-reports/.

[23] Brian Wong, "Hong Kong National Security Law: 6 Ex-Apple Daily Staff to Admit Collusion, Jimmy Lai to Stand Trial without Jury after Pleading Not Guilty," *South China Morning Post*, August 22, 2022, https://scmp.com/news/hong-kong/law-and-crime/article/3189736/hong-kong-national-security-law-6-former-apple-daily.

[24] Brian Wong, "Hong Kong National Security Law: Appeal Court Upholds Move to Allow Top UK Lawyer to Join Jimmy Lai's Defense Team in Light of 'Clear Public Interest,'" *Hong Kong Free Press*, November 9, 2022, https://scmp.com/news/hong-kong/law-and-crime/article/3198997/hong-kong-national-security-law-appeal-court-upholds-move-allow-top-uk-lawyer-join-jimmy-lais.

[25] Lilian Cheng, "How Will Beijing Deal with Hong Kong Leader John Lee's Query about Foreign Lawyers in National Security Cases?" *South China Morning Post,* December 4, 2022, https://scmp.com/news/hong-kong/politics/article/3201995/how-will-beijing-deal-hong-kong-leader-john-lees-query-about-foreign-lawyers-national-security-law.

[26] NPCSC"S Interpretation of Hong Kong National Security Law over Jimmy Lai's Foreign Defense Counsel," *NPC Observer*, December 30, 2022, https://npcobserver.com/2022/12/explainer-npcscs-interpretation-of-hong-kong-national-security-law-over-jimmy-lais-foreign-defense-counsel/

[27] Candice Chau, "Hong Kong Lawmakers Unanimously Vote to Let City Leader Restrict Overseas Lawyers from National Security Cases," *Hong Kong Free Press*, May 10, 2023.

https://hongkongfp.com/2023/05/10/hong-kong-lawmakers-unanimously-vote-to-let-city-leader-restrict-overseas-lawyers-from-national-security-cases/.

28 Candice Chau, "Hong Kong Court Rejects Media Tycoon Jimmy Lai's Bid to Challenge National Security Committee Decision," *Hong Kong Free Press*, May 19, 2023, https://hongkongfp.com/2023/05/19/breaking-hong-kong-court-rejects-media-tycoon-jimmy-lais-bid-to-challenge-nat-security-committee-decision/.

29 James Pomfret and Sarah Cheng, "Hong Kong Apple Daily Founder and Staff Face New Sedition Charge," *Reuters*, December 28, 2021, https://www.reuters.com/world/asia-pacific/hong-kong-apple-daily-founder-staff-face-new-sedition-charge-2021-12-28/.

30 Jimmy Lai's legal team in the U.K. request United Nations to investigate his imprisonment and multiple criminal charges filed against him," Dimsum Daily, April 12, 2022, https://www.dimsumdaily.hk/jimmy-lais-legal-team-in-u-k-requests-united-nations-to-investigate-his-imprisonment-and-multiple-criminal-charges-filed-against-him/

31 "Hong Kong Charges 47 Democracy Supporters with Violating the Security Law," *New York Times*, February 28, 2021, updated July 30, 2021, https://www.nytimes.com/2021/02/28/world/asia/hong-kong-security-law-arrests.html.

32 "Explainer: Hong Kong's National Security Crackdown—Month 32," *Hong Kong Free Press*, March 6, 2023, https://hongkongfp.com/2023/03/06/explainer-hong-kongs-national-security-crackdown-month-32/; Kelly Ho, "Hong Kong 47: Benny Tai Intended to 'Politicise District-Level Work, Democrat Tells Court in National Security Trial," *Hong Kong Free Press*, March 29, 2023, https://hongkongfp.com/2023/03/29/hong-kong-47-benny-tai-intended-to-politicise-district-level-work-democrat-tells-court-in-national-security-trial/.

33 Brian Wong, "Hong Kong's Stability and Livelihood Could Have Been 'Gravely Affected' by 2020 Unofficial Primary Scheme, Court Hears," *South China Morning Post*, February 7, 2023, https://scmp.com/news/hong-kong/law-and-crime/article/3209404/hong-kongs-stability-and-livelihood-could-have-been-gravely-affected-2020-unofficial-primary-scheme.

34 Kelly Ho, "Hong Kong 47: Ex-Lawmaker Au Nok-hin Testifies against Fellow Democrats during National Security Trial," *Hong Kong Free Press*, February 13, 2023, https://hongkongfp.com/2023/02/13/hong-kong-47-ex-lawmaker-au-nok-hin-testifies-against-fellow-democrats-during-national-security-trial/.

35 "Hong Kong: 47 Lawmakers, Activists Face Unfair Trial," Human Rights Watch, August 22, 2022.

36 Editorial, "Backlog of Hong Kong Cases Must Be Cleared so Justice Is Not Delayed or Denied," *South China Morning Post*, April 29, 2022, https://scmp.com/comment/opinion/article/3175902/backlog-hong-kong-cases-must-be-cleared-so-justice-not-delayed-or.

37 Samuel Bickett, "The Court of Final Appeal Must End Indefinite Pre-Trial Detentions," Samuel Bickett on Hong Kong Law and Policy, January 13, 2022, https://samuelbickett.substack.com/p/the-court-of-final-appeal-must-end.

38 Brian Wong, "Hong Kong National Security Law: 5 Teens from Pro-independence Group Get up to 3 Years' Detention for Abetting 'Armed Revolution,'" *South China Morning Post*, October 8, 2022, https://scmp.com/news/hong-kong/law-and-crime/article/3195275/hong-kong-national-security-law-5-teens-pro.

39 "Alarm by Sentencing under National Security Law," UN Office of the High Commissioner for Human Rights, October 11, 2022, https://www.ohchr.org/en/press-briefing-notes/2022/10/alarm-sentencing-under-national-security-law.

40 Brian Wong, "29 of 47 Hong Kong Opposition to Plead Guilty to Subversion Charges over Unofficial Primary Election," *South China Morning Post*, August 18, 2022, https://www.scmp.com/news/hong-kong/law-and-crime/article/3189327/national-security-law-29-47-hong-kong-opposition; Michael Bristow, "Denial of Bail Is Silencing Hong Kong's Democrats," BBC News, April 27, 2022, https://www.bbc.com/news/world-asia-china-61235777.

41 Jun Chan, Eric Yan-ho Lai, and Thomas E. Kellogg, T*he Hong Kong 2019 Protest Movement: A Data Analysis of Arrests and Prosecutions*, October 23, 2023, https://www.law.georgetown.edu/law-asia/wp-content/uploads/sites/31/2023/10/GCAL-HK-2019-ARREST-DATA-REPORT-FINAL-OCT-2023.pdf . This excellent report provides a comprehensive analysis and supportive date to document the government's aggressive posture toward the protests.

42 Based on data on political prisoners compiled by Brian Kern for the Hong Kong Democracy Council. Yojana Sharma, "Student Arrest Related to the 2019 Campus Siege Raises Alarm," *University World News*, May 26, 2023, https://www.universityworldnews.com/post.php.

43 HKDC, "Hong Kong Political Prisoners Database," https://www.hkdc.us/political-prisoner-database.

44 Brian Wong, "Hong Kong Protests: 7 Fugitives Jailed for 10 Months Each for Thwarted Escape to Taiwan," *South China Morning Post*, July 15, 2022, https://www.scmp.com/news/hong-kong/law-and-crime/article/3185412/hong-kong-protests-7-fugitives-jailed-10-months-each.

45 Kelly Ho, "Hong Kong Activist, Paralegal to Both Face Sentencing after Jimmy Lai's National Security Trial in December." *Hong Kong Free Press*, September 16, 2022, https://hongkongfp.com/2022/09/16/hong-kong-activist-paralegal-to-both-face-sentencing-after-jimmy-lais-national-security-trial-in-december. "Andy Li's Confession Used to Incriminate Jimmy Lai," *Citizen News*, August 29, 2021, https://www.hkcnews.com/article/44806/jimmy_lai-andy_li李宇軒-national_security_law-45001/andy-lis-confession-used-to-incriminate-jimmy-lai.

46 Shibani Mahtani, "Witness against Hong Kong media mogul was mistreated, Post examination finds," *Washington Post*, December 17, 2023. https://www.washingtonpost.com/world/2023/12/17/jimmy-lai-trial-witness-treatment-hong-kong

47 Hayley Wong, "Hong Kong Supercharges 1938 British Sedition Law to Curb Dissent," *Bloomberg*, August 23, 2022, https://www.bloomberg.com/news/articles/2022-08-23/hong-kong-supercharges-1938-british-sedition-law-to-curb-dissent#xj4y7vzkg.

[48] Thomas E. Kellogg, "How a Ruling by Hong Kong's Top Court Opens the Door to a More Intrusive Security Law," *Hong Kong Free Press*, December 17, 2021, https://hongkongfp.com/2021/12/17/how-a-ruling-by-hong-kongs-top-court-opens-the-door-to-a-more-intrusive-security-law/.

[49] Michael C. Davis, "Children's Books Branded Seditious in Hong Kong," *The Diplomat*, September 12, 2022, https://thediplomat.com/2022/09/childrens-books-branded-seditious-in-hong-kong/.

[50] Editorial Board, "In Hong Kong, Even Children's Books about Sheep Are Deemed 'Seditious,'" *Washington Post*, September 9, 2022, https://www.washingtonpost.com/opinions/2022/09/09/hong-kong-children-books-sedition/.

[51] Kelly Ho, "2 Hong Kong Speech Therapists Apply to Challenge Conviction over 'Seditious' Children's Books," *Hong Kong Free Press*, September 29, 2022, https://hongkongfp.com/2022/09/29/2-hong-kong-speech-therapists-apply-to-challenge-conviction-over-seditious-childrens-books/.

[52] "Hong Kong Arrest over 'Seditious' Children's Books from the UK," *Times*, March 16, 2023, https://www.thetimes.co.uk/article/hong-kong-seditious-childrens-books-mailed-uk-2023-0kjdfd9rq.

[53] The court encouraged the government to enact new reform legislation during the suspension. Hari Kumar and Sameer Yasir, "India's Top Court Suspends Colonial-Era Sedition Law," *New York Times,* May 11, 2022, https://www.nytimes.com/2022/05/11/world/asia/india-sedition-law-suspended.html.

[54] *HKSAR v. Tam Tak Chi* [2022] HKDC 208; Angeline Chan, "After Hong Kong Activist Tam Tak-chi's Conviction, We Still Don't Know What Is or Is Not Seditious," *Hong Kong Free Press*, March 6, 2022, https://hongkongfp.com/2022/03/06/after-hong-kong-activist-tam-tak-chis-conviction-we-still-dont-know-what-is-or-is-not-seditious/.

[55] As summarized, Brian Wong, "Hong Kong Protests: Judge Rules Insulting City's Government 'A Challenge to Beijing's Authority' as Ex-Radio Host Tam Tak-Chi Found Guilty under Sedition Law," *South China Morning Post*, March 2, 2022, https://www.scmp.com/news/hong-kong/law-and-crime/article/3168913/hong-kong-protests-judge-rules-insulting-hong-kong.

[56] Brian Wong, "Hong Kong opposition activist Tam Tak-chi appeals against sedition conviction, court hear colonial-era law falls short of global standards. South China Morning Post, July 4, 2023. https://scmp.com/news/hong-kong/law-and-crime/article/3226521/hong-kong-opposition-activist-tam-tak-chi-appeals-against-sedition-charges-court-hears-colonial-era

[57] Natalie Wong, "Stricter Bail Conditions to Apply to Offenders under Hong Kong's Future National Security Law, Justice Minister Says," *South China Morning Post*, July 17, 2022, https://scmp.com/news/hong-kong/politics/article/3185585/stricter-bail-conditions-apply-offenders-under-hong-kongs.

[58] "Hong Kong security law Article 23 would target modern day 'espionage' and 'internet loopholes,' security chief says," *Hong Kong Free Press*, July 17, 2023. https://hongkongfp.

com/2023/07/17/hong-kong-security-law-article-23-would-target-modern-day-espionage-and-internet-loopholes-security-chief-says/

59 Reporting from the content of a pro-Beijing magazine. Pak Yiu, "Hong Kong Judicial Independence Fears Threaten City's Business Case," *Nikkei*, June 14, 2022, https://asia.nikkei.com/Spotlight/Asia-Insight/Hong-Kong-judicial-independence-fears-threaten-city-s-business-case.

60 Dennis Kwok, "Look to Hong Kong, Not Ukraine, for Signals about China's Taiwan Plans," *The Diplomat*, April 5, 2022, https://thediplomat.com/2022/04/look-to-hong-kong-not-ukraine-for-signals-about-chinas-taiwan-plans/.

61 The Practice of the "One Country, Two Systems" Policy in the Hong Kong Special Administrative Region (white paper, 2014), Information Office of the State Council, June 2014, http://english.www.gov.cn/archive/white_paper/2014/08/23/content_281474982986578.htm.

62 Su Di, "Observer: Approving Jimmy Lai's Bail Harmful to Hong Kong's Rule of Law," *People's Daily* (Beijing), December 28, 2020.

63 Michael Holden and Greg Torode, "UK Judges Resign from Hong Kong Court over China's Crackdown on Dissent," *Reuters*, March 30, 2022, https://www.reuters.com/world/uk-judges-quit-hong-kong-court-over-new-security-law-2022-03-30/; Austin Ramsy, "Two U.K. Judges Quit Hong Kong Court, Citing Lost Freedoms," *New York Times*, March 30, 2022, https://www.nytimes.com/2022/03/30/world/asia/hong-kong-british-judges.html.

64 William Xu and Li Bingcun, "Justices' Decisions 'Vote of Confidence' in HK's Legal System," *China Daily, HK Edition,* April 2, 2022, https://s.chinadailyhk.com/mqEzIz https://www.chinadailyhk.com/article/266298#Justices'-decisions-'vote-of-confidence'-in-HK's-legal-system.

65 Patrick Wintour, "Hong Kong Judicial Independence under Systematic Attack, Legal Figures Warn," *Guardian*, May 26, 2022, https://www.theguardian.com/world/2022/may/26/hong-kong-judicial-independence-overseas-judges.

66 Chris Lau, "Hong Kong's Secretary for Justice: 'I Intend to Speak Up about City's High Degree of Rule of Law," *South China Morning Post*, August 5, 2022, https://scmp.com/news/hong-kong/politics/article/3187750/hong-kongs-secretary-justice-i-intend-speak-about-citys.

67 Report, "Business Not as Usual: International Companies in the New Authoritarian Hong Kong," Hong Kong Democracy Council, October 25, 2022, https://twitter.com/hkdc_us/status/1584973278359486464.

68 "Moody's Downgrades Hong Kong's Ratings Outlook to Negative," *Agence France-Presse* (as published by VOA), December 6, 2023, https://www.voanews.com/a/moody-s-downgrades-hong-kong-rating-outlook-to-negative/7386403.html

69 "Commissioners Ask President to Sanction Hong Kong Prosecutors," Congressional-Executive Commission on China, https://www.cecc.gov/media-center/press-releases/%EF%BB%BF-commissioners-ask-president-to-sanction-hong-kong-prosecutors.

The letter to the president was backed up by a staff research report. See "Hong Kong Prosecutors Play a Key Role in Carrying Out Political Prosecutions," Staff Research Report, Congressional-Executive Commission on China, July 1, 2022, https://www. cecc.gov/sites/chinacommission.house.gov/files/CECC%20Staff%20Report%20July%20 2022%20-%20Hong%20Kong%20Prosecutors.pdf.

[70] Report, "One City, Two Legal Systems: Hong Kong Judges' Role in Rights Violations under the National Security Law," Congressional-Executive Commission on China, May 10, 2023, https://www.cecc.gov/publications/commission-analysis/one-city-two-legal-systems-hong-kong-judges'-role-in-rights.

[71] Chris Lau and Natalie Wong, "Hong Kong Accuses US Commission of 'Cheap, Bullying Behaviour' after Report Calls for Sanctions on New Justice Chief, 15 of City's Prosecutors," *South China Morning Post*, July 13, 2022, https://scmp.com/news/hong-kong/law-and-crime/article/3185152/hong-kong-bar-association-chief-deplores-us-commission; see also Press Release, "HKSAR Government Strongly Condemns US Congressional-Executive Commission on China's Despicable Attempt to Intimidate Hong Kong Prosecutors," July 13, 2022, https://www.info.gov.hk/gia/general/202207/13/P2022071300618.htm.

[72] Rhoda Kwan, "Hong Kong Justice Sec. Warns Law Societies to Steer Clear of Politics after Chinese State Media Blast Barristers," *Hong Kong Free Press*, August 16, 2021, https://hongkongfp.com/2021/08/16/hong-kongs-justice-sec-warns-law-societies-to-steerclear-of-politics-after-chinese-state-media-blasts-barristers.

[73] Kari Soo Lindberg and Olivia Tam, "Hong Kong Ex-Bar Association Chair Flees after Police Probe, Media Says," *Bloomberg*, March 1, 2022, https://www.bloomberg.com/news/articles/2022-03-02/hong-kong-ex-bar-chair-flees-city-after-police-probe-media-says.

[74] "Carrie Lam Delays Filling Post, Raising Questions about the Judiciary's Independence," *The Standard/Reuters*, January 31, 2022, https://app.thestandard.com.hk/article/48813362.

[75] Kelly Ho, "Hong Kong Bar Association Should Not Discuss Politics, New Chairman Says," *Hong Kong Free Press*, January 21, 2022, https://hongkongfp.com/2022/01/21/hong-kong-bar-association-should-not-discuss-politics-new-chairman-says/.

[76] Cannix Yau, "Hong Kong Bar Association to Go on 'Ice-Breaking' Trip to Beijing after Being Frozen out for 5 Years," *South China Morning Post*, March 16, 2023, https://scmp.com/news/hong-kong/society/article/3213667/hong-kong-bar-association-go-ice-breaking-trip-beijing-after-being-frozen-out-five-years.

[77] Chris Lau, "Prominent Human Rights Lawyer Loses Seat on Hong Kong Law Society's Governing Council as Ex-president Wins Re-election," *Hong Kong Free Press*, August 24, 2022, https://scmp.com/news/hong-kong/law-and-crime/article/3189938/prominent-human-rights-lawyer-loses-seat-hong-kong-law.

[78] Hong Kong disqualifies legislators for 'endangering security,'" Al Jazeera, November 11, 2020, https://www.aljazeera.com/news/2020/11/11/hong-kong-disqualifies-four-opposition-legislators

[79] Michael C. Davis Testimony: US-China Economic and Security Review Commission, September 8, 2021, https://www.uscc.gov/sites/default/files/2021-08/Michael_Davis_Testimony.pdf.

[80] "Hong Kong: Prominent Democracy Advocates Arrested," Human Rights Watch, May 13, 2022, https://www.hrw.org/news/2022/05/13/hong-kong-prominent-democracy-advocates-arrested.

[81] Kelly Ho, "Cardinal Zen and 5 Others to Stand Trial in Sept. over Alleged Failure to Register Protester Relief Fund as Society," *Hong Kong Free Press*, August 9, 2022, https://hongkongfp.com/2022/08/09/cardinal-zen-and-5-others-to-stand-trial-in-sept-over-alleged-failure-to-register-protester-relief-fund-as-society/.

[82] "Hong Kong: Arrests of Activists, including 90-Year-Old Cardinal, a 'Shocking Escalation' of Repression," Amnesty International, May 11, 2022, https://www.amnesty.org/en/latest/news/2022/05/hong-kong-arrests-of-activists-including-90-year-old-cardinal-a-shocking-escalation-of-repression/.

[83] Christy Leung and Chris Lau, "Hong Kong National Security Police Lodge Complaint against Lawyers Who Allegedly Took Fees from Legal Defence Fund Despite Claims of Pro Bono Services," *South China Morning Post*, May 12, 2022, https://scmp.com/news/hong-kong/law-and-crime/article/3177540/hong-kong-national-security-police-lodge-complaint.

[84] Peter Lee, "Some 35 Lawyers Linked to Protester Relief Fund being Probed by Hong Kong Bar Association—Reports," *Hong Kong Free Press*, July 5, 2022, https://hongkongfp.com/2022/07/05/some-35-lawyers-linked-to-protester-relief-fund-being-probed-by-hong-kong-bar-association-reports/.

[85] Chris Lau, "Why Proposed Overhaul to Hong Kong's Legal Aid Has Some Lawyers Worried and Raised Fears Opposition Figures Will Suffer," *South China Morning Post*, October 22, 2021, https://scmp.com/news/hong-kong/politics/article/3153400/why-proposed-overhaul-hong-kongs-legal-aid-has-some-lawyers.

Chapter 9

[1] RSF—Reporters Without Borders, Hong Kong, Index 2022, https://rsf.org/en/country/hong-kong. In 2023, this ranking rose slightly to 140th. Candice Chau, "Hong Kong Ranks 140th on 2023 Int'l RSF Press Freedom Index below Colombia, and Cameroon," *Hong Kong Free Press*, May 3, 2023, https://hongkongfp.com/2023/05/03/just-in-hong-kong-ranks-140th-on-2023-intl-press-freedom-index-below-colombia-cameroon. At the same time Hong Kong, long considered one of the freest territories in the world, also dropped dramatically in the Human Freedom Index to 46th in the world, Hans Tse, "Hong Kong drops to 46th place in global freedom ranking, as think tanks cite China's 'increasing interference,'" Hong Kong Free Press, December 20, 2023, https://hongkongfp.com/2023/12/20/hong-kong-drops-to-46th-place-in-global-freedom-ranking-as-think-tanks-cite-chinas-increasing-interference.

[2] Candice Chau, "Satisfaction with Hong Kong's Press Freedom Drops to Record Low, Poll Finds," *Hong Kong Free Press*, April 1, 2022, https://hongkongfp.com/2022/04/01/satisfaction-with-hong-kongs-press-freedom-drops-to-record-low-poll-finds/; Almond Li, "Hong Kong Media Credibility Drops to a New Low, Study Finds," *Hong Kong Free Press*,

August 26, 2022, https://hongkongfp.com/2022/08/26/hong-kong-media-credibility-drops-to-new-low-study-finds/.

[3] Hillary Leung, "'Shrinking News Industry': Hong Kong Press Freedom Index Sinks to New Low as Media Outlets Disappear," *Hong Kong Free Press*, September 24, 2022, https://hongkongfp.com/2022/09/24/shrinking-news-industry-hong-kong-press-freedom-index-sinks-to-new-low-as-media-outlets-disappear/. The HKJA ranking has gone down every year over the last four years. Hillary Leung, "Hong Kong press freedom index dips further a journalists say they are hesitant to criticise Beijing," Hong Kong Free Press, July 7, 2023. https://hongkongfp.com/2023/07/07/hong-kong-press-freedom-index-dips-further-as-journalists-hesitant-to-criticise-beijing/

[4] Hong Kong Crimes Ordinance, cap 200, section 10, https://www.hklii.hk/eng/hk/legis/ord/200/s10.html. Clare Jim and Sara Cheng, "Hong Kong court denies bail to former Stand News editors charged with sedition," Reuters, December 30, 2021, https://www.reuters.com/business/media-telecom/hong-kong-leader-says-stand-news-arrests-not-aimed-media-industry-2021-12-30.

[5] Candice Chau, "Veteran Hong Kong Journalist Allan Au Arrested by National Security Police—Reports," *Hong Kong Free Press*, April 11, 2022, https://hongkongfp.com/2022/04/11/breaking-veteran-hong-kong-journalist-allan-au-arrested-by-national-security-police-reports/.

[6] "Explainer: Hong Kong's National Security Crackdown—Month 32," *Hong Kong Free Press*, March 6, 2023, https://hongkongfp.com/2023/03/06/explainer-hong-kongs-national-security-crackdown-month-32/.

[7] "Hong Kong: 'Sedition Arrests after Clapping in Court a New Low for Human Rights,'" Amnesty International, April 6, 2022, https://www.amnesty.org/en/latest/news/2022/04/hong-kong-sedition-arrests-after-clapping-in-court-a-new-low-for-human-rights/.

[8] Thomas E. Kellogg, "Crimes Ordinance Sedition versus Hong Kong's National Security Law: Different Legal Tools, Same Outcome?" *China Collection*, January 6, 2022, https://thechinacollection.org/crimes-ordinance-sedition-versus-hong-kongs-national-security-law-different-legal-tools-outcome/.

[9] Jeffie Lam, "Hong Kong Online Portal Citizen News to Shut Down on Tuesday," *South China Morning Post*, January 2, 2022, https://scmp.com/news/hong-kong/politics/article/3161872/hong-kong-online-portal-citizen-news-cease-operations.

[10] Viola Zhou, "They Were Reporters in Hong Kong. Now They Drive Cabs and Sell Fried Chicken," *Vice World News*, January 25, 2022, https://www.vice.com/en/article/akvjd8/hong-kong-journalists-cabbies-fried-chicken.

[11] Hillary Leung, "Hong Kong Investigative News Platform Factwire Disbands—4th Outlet to Shutter in under a Year," *Hong Kong Free Press*, June 10, 2022, https://hongkongfp.com/2022/06/10/breaking-hong-kong-investigative-news-platform-factwire-disbands/?utm_medium=email.

[12] Clifford Lo and Ng Kang-chung, "Hong Kong National Security Police Tell Funder of Digital Media Outlet Passion Times to Remove 'Sensitive' Online Posts," *South*

China Morning Post, May 18, 2022, https://scmp.com/news/hong-kong/law-and-crime/article/3178249/hong-kong-national-security-police-tell-founder.

[13] Candice Chau, "Explainer: The Decline of Hong Kong's Press Freedom under the National Security Law," *Hong Kong Free Press*, January 5, 2022, https://hongkongfp.com/2022/01/05/explainer-the-decline-of-hong-kongs-press-freedom-under-the-national-security-law/.

[14] Tom Grundy, "Hong Kong Again Bars Several Registered Media Outlets from Gov't Event, Repeatedly Evades Questions as to Why," *Hong Kong Free Press*, April 21, 2023, https://hongkongfp.com/2023/04/21/hong-kong-again-bars-several-registered-media-outlets-from-govt-event-repeatedly-evades-questions-as-to-why/.

[15] Willa Wu, "Hong Kong Leader Says Media Coverage Should Avoid 'False, Biased, Defamatory or Misleading' Information after Cartoonist Zunzi Dropped by Ming Pao," *South China Morning Post*, May 12, 2023, https://scmp.com/news/hong-kong/politics/article/3220389/hong-kong-leader-john-lee-says-media-coverage-should-avoid-false-biased-defamatory-or-misleading; Mandy Cheng, "Books of a Satirical Cartoonist Zunzi Disappear from Hong Kong Public Libraries after Paper Axes Comic," *Hong Kong Free Press*, May 12, 2023, https://hongkongfp.com/2023/05/12/books-by-satirical-cartoonist-zunzi-disappear-from-hong-kong-public-libraries-after-paper-axes-comic.

[16] Peter Lee, "Explainer: Small Chinese-Language Media Outlets Spring Up as Hong Kong's Big Names Disappear," *Hong Kong Free Press*, May 9, 2022, https://hongkongfp.com/2022/05/09/explainer-small-chinese-language-media-outlets-spring-up-as-hong-kongs-big-names-shut-down/.

[17] "The Dismantling of Hong Kong's Civil Society," Congressional-Executive Commission on China Hearing, July 12, 2022, https://www.cecc.gov/events/hearings/the-dismantling-of-hong-kongs-civil-society.

[18] Kelly Ho, "Fewer Hongkongers Trust Public Broadcaster RTHK as Press Freedom Fears 'Become Reality'—Survey," *Hong Kong Free Press*, June 15, 2022, https://hongkongfp.com/2022/06/15/fewer-hongkongers-trust-public-broadcaster-rthk-as-press-freedom-fears-become-reality-survey/.

[19] "Hong Kong Names New Broadcasting Chief," *The Standard*, August 5, 2022, https://www.thestandard.com.hk/breaking-news/section/4/193146/Hong-Kong-names-new-broadcasting-chief.

[20] "RTHK Issues New Editorial Guidelines," Radio Television Hong Kong, September 29, 2021, https://news.rthk.hk/rthk/en/component/k2/1612799-20210929.htm.

[21] Kelly Ho, "Hong Kong's RTHK Fires Veteran Radio Phone-In Host as More Shows Are Axed," *Hong Kong Free Press*, June 29, 2021, https://hongkongfp.com/2021/06/29/hong-kongs-rthk-fires-veteran-radio-phone-in-host-as-more-shows-are-axed/.

[22] Rhoda Kwan, "Hong Kong's RTHK Will Become State Media after Partnership with China's CCTV, Says Press Group Chief," *Hong Kong Free Press*, August 11, 2021, https://hongkongfp.com/2021/08/11/hong-kongs-rthk-will-become-state-media-afterpartnership-with-chinas-cctv-says-press-group-chief.

[23] Vivian Wang, "Hong Kong Broadcaster's Swift Turn from Maverick Voice to Official Mouthpiece," *New York Times*, November 12, 2021, https://www.nytimes.com/2021/11/12/world/asia/hong-kong-rthk-crackdown-china.html.

[24] Jeffie Lam, "Hong Kong's Largest Journalist Group Faces Scrutiny from Authorities, Asked to Justify Activities Amid Media Crackdown Fears," *South China Morning Post*, January 21, 2022, https://scmp.com/news/hong-kong/politics/article/3164269/hong-kongs-largest-journalist-group-faces-scrutiny; Rachel Yeo and Denise Tsang, "Beijing Accuses Hong Kong's Foreign Correspondents' Club of 'Sowing Discord' over State of Press Freedom," November 5, 2021, https://scmp.com/news/hong-kong/society/article/3154909/hong-kong-journalists-urge-government-drop-plans-fake-news.

[25] William Yu, "Hong Kong's Largest Journalist Group Holds Meeting to Discuss Possibility of Disbandment, Says It Will Still Operate for 'Forseeable Future,'" *South China Morning Post*, April 23, 2022, https://scmp.com/news/hong-kong/politics/article/3175305/hong-kongs-largest-journalist-group-holds-meeting-discuss.

[26] Rhoda Kwan, "Beijing-Controlled Paper Labels Hong Kong Press Union an 'Anti-Govt Political Organisation,'" *Hong Kong Free Press*, August 13, 2021, https://hongkongfp.com/2021/08/13/beijing-controlled-paper-labels-hong-kong-press-union-an-anti-govtpolitical-organisation.

[27] Danny Mok, "Hong Kong's largest journalist group to consider disbanding in response to mounting government pressure for more transparency," *South China Morning Post*, April 13, 2022, https://www.scmp.com/news/hong-kong/article/3174173/hong-kongs-largest-journalist-group-consider-disbanding-response.

[28] Peter Lee, "Head of Hong Kong Journalist Group Ronson Chan Charged with Obstructing Police Officers during Reporting," *Hong Kong Free Press*, September 19, 2022, https://hongkongfp.com/2022/09/19/head-of-hong-kong-journalist-group-ronson-chan-charged-with-obstructing-police-officers-during-reporting/.

[29] Candice Chau, "Hong Kong Court Quashes Decision to Enforce Reporting Ban on Activist's National Security Case in Landmark Ruling," *Hong Kong Free Press*, August 3, 2022, https://hongkongfp.com/2022/08/02/hong-kong-court-quashes-decision-to-enforce-reporting-ban-on-activists-national-security-case-in-landmark-ruling/.

[30] Natalie Wong and Ng Kang-chung, "Hong Kong Activist Detained for Inciting Subversion of State Wins Judicial Review to Lift Reporting Restrictions on Case," *South China Morning Post*, August 2, 2022, https://scmp.com/news/hong-kong/politics/article/3187435/hong-kong-activist-detained-inciting-state-subversion-wins.

[31] Candice Chau, "Hong Kong Court Bars Activist Chow Hang-Tung from Saying 'Tiananmen Massacre' in National Security Trial," *Hong Kong Free Press*, October 26, 2022, https://hongkongfp.com/2022/10/26/hong-kong-court-bars-activist-chow-hang-tung-from-saying-tiananmen-massacre-in-national-security-trial/.

[32] "New York Times Will Move Part of Hong Kong Office to Seoul," *New York Times*, July 14, 2020, https://www.nytimes.com/2020/07/14/business/media/new-york-times-hong-kong.html.

[33] Timothy McLaughlin, "Where Foreign Correspondents Capitulated to Autocracy: Hong Kong's Main Press Club Has Given Up in The Face of a New, Repressive Regime," *The Atlantic*, April 27, 2022, https://www.theatlantic.com/international/archive/2022/04/hong-kong-foreign-correspondents-club-awards/629685/.

[34] Lillian Cheng, "Hong Kong FCC Axed Human Rights Press Awards to Avoid Risks of Jail, Chief Cites Concerns about Independence of Courts under National Security Law," *South China Morning Post*, June 12, 2022, https://www.scmp.com/news/hong-kong/politics/article/3181360/hong-kong-fcc-chief-axed-human-rights-press-awards-avoid; Almond Li, "Hong Kong Press Club Chief Apologises to Judges of Axed Human Rights Press Awards," *Hong Kong Free Press*, April 27, 2022, https://hongkongfp.com/2022/04/27/hong-kong-press-club-chief-apologises-to-judges-of-axed-human-rights-press-awards/.

[35] Tom Grundy, "Hong Kong Ousts Economist Journalist Sue-Lin Wong with Explanation, in Latest Blow to Press Freedom," *Hong Kong Free Press*, November 13, 2021, https://hongkongfp.com/2021/11/13/hong-kong-ousts-economist-journalist-sue-lin-wong-without-explanation-in-latest-blow-to-press-freedom/.

[36] Dewey Sim, et al., "Hong Kong Expats Are Relocating at a Faster Pace than Before, but Singapore Isn't Their Only Destination," *South China Morning Post*, January 8, 2022, https://scmp.com/week-asia/people/article/3162495/hong-kong-expats-are-relocating-faster-pace-singapore-isnt-their.

[37] Mercedes Hutton, "Amid Exodus and Societal Shifts, Hong Kong's Independent Bookstores Offer Freedom of Thought, Community," *Hong Kong Free Press*, July 18, 2022, https://hongkongfp.com/2022/07/17/amid-exodus-and-societal-shifts-hong-kongs-independent-bookstores-offer-freedom-of-thought-community/?utm_medium=email.

[38] Hong Kong publishers excluded from book fair over politically sensitive material," *The Guardian*, July 22, 2022, https://www.theguardian.com/world/2022/jul/22/hong-kong-publishers-excluded-from-book-fair-over-politically-sensitive-material.

[39] Lea Mok, "Independent 'Hongkongers Book Fair' Axed after Organizers Allegedly Accused of Lease Violation," *Hong Kong Free Press*, July 14, 2022, https://hongkongfp.com/2022/07/13/independent-hongkongers-book-fair-axed-after-organisers-allegedly-accused-of-lease-violation/.

[40] "'Indie' book show hosts publishers excluded from Hong Kong Book Fair, but organizer is pessimistic about the future," *Hong Kong Free Press*, July 26, 2023. https://hongkongfp.com/2023/07/26/indie-book-show-hosts-publishers-excluded-from-hong-kong-book-fair-but-organiser-is-pessimistic-about-future

[41] Chris Lau, "End of Story or New Chapter? How Hong Kong's Independent Booksellers Are Adapting to Life under National Security Law," *South China Morning Post*, July 21, 2022, https://scmp.com/news/hong-kong/politics/article/3185996/end-story-or-new-chapter-how-hong-kongs-independent.

[42] Harvey Kong, "Hong Kong's Audit Commission Demands City Libraries Step Up Efforts to Root Out Books 'Manifestly Contrary' to National Security," *South China Morning Post*, April 26, 2023, https://scmp.com/news/hong-kong/politics/article/3218437/hong-kongs-audit-commission-demands-city-libraries-step-efforts-root-out-books-

manifestly-contrary: Mandy Cheng, "Hongkongers 'welcome' to report library books that may endanger national security," *Hong Kong Free Press*, July 6, 2023. https://hongkongfp.com/2023/07/06/hongkongers-welcome-to-report-library-books-that-may-endanger-national-security/

[43] Candice Chau, "Books Removed from Hong Kong Public Libraries Still Accessible in Shops, Says Chief Executive John Lee," *Hong Kong Free Press*, May 16, 2023, https://hongkongfp.com/2023/05/16/books-removed-from-hong-kong-public-libraries-still-accessible-in-shops-says-chief-executive-john-lee/.

[44] Kelly Ho, "Hong Kong Passes Bill to Censor Films 'Contrary' to China's National Security—HK$1m Fine, 3 Years Jail for Offenders," *Hong Kong Free Press*, October 27, 2021, https://hongkongfp.com/2021/10/27/hong-kong-passes-bill-to-censor-films-contrary-to-chinas-national-security-hk1m-fine-3-years-jail-for-offenders/.

[45] Oliver Young, "Latest Targets of Hong Kong Censorship include Films, Publishers, and Pro-transparency Social Media Pages," *China Digital Times*, August 18, 2022, https://chinadigitaltimes.net/2022/08/latest-targets-of-hong-kong-censorship-include-films-publishers-and-pro-transparency-social-media-pages/.

[46] Gary Cheung and Chris Lau, "National Security Law: Documentary on Hong Kong's 2019 Protests Getting Screen Time Overseas, but Is It Illegal to Download or Watch in the City?" *South China Morning* Post, June 1, 2022, https://scmp.com/news/hong-kong/politics/article/3180059/national-security-law-documentary-hong-kongs-2019-protests; Ian Young, "Audiences Sing, Sob, Chant as Hong Kong 'Revolution' Film Is a Sold-Out Success in Protest Stronghold Vancouver," *Hong Kong Free Press*, March 8, 2022, https://www.scmp.com/news/china/diplomacy/article/3169741/audiences-sing-sob-and-chant-hong-kong-revolution-film-sold.

[47] Oliver Young, "Latest Targets of Hong Kong Censorship include Films, Publishers, and Pro-transparency Social Media Pages," *China Digital Times*.

[48] Jess Ma, "No More 'Secrets' in Hong Kong? Facebook Pages for Anonymous Rants, Comments Shut Following National Security Law Arrests," *South China Morning Post*, August 14, 2022, https://scmp.com/news/hong-kong/politics/article/3188821/no-more-secrets-hong-kong-facebook-pages-anonymous-rants.

[49] Judge Rejects Hong Kong's Bid to Ban Pro-democracy Song From Internet," New York Times, July 28, 2023, https://www.nytimes.com/2023/07/28/business/glory-to-hong-kong-injunction.html.

[50] Natalie Wong, "Hong Kong technology chief says Google told officials it would only remove protest song under court order, sparking injunction bid," *South China Morning Post*, July 1, 2023. https://www.scmp.com/news/hong-kong/politics/article/3226219/hong-kong-technology-chief-says-google-told-officials-it-would-only-remove-protest-song-under-court

[51] *Secretary for Justice v. Persons Conducting Themselves in Any of the Acts Prohibited Under Paragraphs 1 (a), (b), (c) or (d) of the Endorsement of Claim*, ACA 855/2023, (2023) HKCFI 1950 https://legalref.judiciary.hk/lrs/common/ju/ju_frame.jsp?DIS=154086&currpage=T. "Judge Rejects Hong Kong's bid to Ban Pro-Democracy Song from Internet," New York

Times, July 28, 2023. https://www.nytimes.com/2023/07/28/business/glory-to-hong-kong-injunction.html

[52] Kelly Ho, "Hong Kong Passes New Anti-Doxxing Law—Violators Face HK$1m Fine and 5 Years Jail." *Hong Kong Free Press*, September 30, 2021, https://hongkongfp.com/2021/09/30/hong-kong-passes-new-anti-doxxing-law-violators-face-hk1m-fine-and-5-years-jail/.

[53] Almond Li, "Hong Kong Watchdog Told 14 Social Media Sites to Remove 3,900 Doxxing Items in 8 Months," *Hong Kong Free Press*, June 14, 2022, https://hongkongfp.com/2022/06/14/hong-kong-watchdog-told-14-social-media-sites-to-remove-3900-doxxing-items-in-8-months/.

[54] "Journalists Warn of Chilling Impact of Hong Kong's Planned 'Fake News' Law," *Radio Free Asia*, February 15, 2022, https://www.rfa.org/english/news/china/hongkong-media-02152022111200.html.

[55] Mercedes Hutton, "Website of NGO Hong Kong Democracy Council Partially Blocked in City amid Fears over Erosion of Open Internet," *Hong Kong Free Press*, October 26, 2022, https://hongkongfp.com/2022/10/26/website-of-ngo-hong-kong-democracy-council-partially-blocked-in-city-amid-fears-over-erosion-of-open-internet/.

[56] Chris Lau and Nadia Lam, "Hong Kong Law Reform Commission Proposes 5 New Offenses to Rein in Cybercrime, with Tougher Penalties of Up to Life in Prison," *South China Morning Post*, July 20, 2022, https://www.scmp.com/news/hong-kong/law-and-crime/article/3185994/hong-kong-law-reform-commission-proposes-5-new.

[57] The Law Reform Commission of Hong Kong, "Cyberdependent Crimes and Jurisdiction Issues," July 2022, https://www.hkreform.gov.hk/en/publications/cybercrime.htm. See also Charles Mok, "Hong Kong's New Cybercrimes Law Consultation," *The Diplomat*, July 22, 2022, https://thediplomat.com/2022/07/hong-kongs-new-cybercrime-law-consultation/.

[58] Tony Cheung, "Proposed Cybercrime Law Needs Long Reach to Cover Offences Outside Hong Kong, Compel Tech Giants to Cooperate: Legislators," *South China Morning Post*, November 7, 2022, https://scmp.com/news/hong-kong/law-and-crime/article/3198751/proposed-cybercrime-law-needs-long-reach-cover-offences-outside-hong-kong-compel-tech-giants.

[59] Charles Mok, "Teardown of Hong Kong's Internet Freedom," *Dialogues on Digital Rights*, April 22, 2022, https://www.linkedin.com/pulse/dialogues-digital-rights-teardown-hong-kongs-internet-freedom-optf/.

[60] "The Charter of Human Rights and Principles for the Internet," The UN Internet Governance Forum, August 2014, https://www.ohchr.org/Documents/Issues/Opinion/Communications/InternetPrinciplesAndRightsCoalition.pdf.

[61] Hong Kong Students and Residents Reject National-Education Classes, 2012, Global Non-violent Action Database, July 29 to September 8, 2012, https://nvdatabase.swarthmore.edu/content/hong-kong-students-and-residents-reject-national-education-classes-2012.

[62] Michael C. Davis, *Making Hong Kong China: The Rollback of Human Rights and the Rule of Law*. New York: Columbia University Press, 2020, chapter 5.

[63] See the HKSAR's official education circulars of February 4, 2021, https://applications. edb.gov.hk/circular/upload/EDBC/EDBC21002E.pdf and https://applications.edb.gov. hk/circular/upload/EDBC/EDBC21003E.pdf. Added to this mainland imposition, the NPCSC in late October 2023 passed a national law on patriotic education which has been extended to Hong Kong, whose implications are yet unclear. Mercedes Hutton, "Hong Kong 'welcomes' passing of China's patriotic education law, which covers city and Macau," *Hong Kong Free Press*, October 25, 2023, https://hongkongfp.com/2023/10/25/hong-kong-welcomes-passing-of-chinas-patriotic-education-law-which-covers-city-and-macau/

[64] William Yiu, "Hong Kong Schools Encouraged to Play Patriotic Music Video ahead of National Day," *South China Morning Post*, September 21, 2022, https://scmp.com/news/ hong-kong/education/article/3193329/hong-kong-schools-encouraged-play-patriotic-music-video.

[65] Carston A. Holz, "Hong Kong's Contested Academic Freedom," *The Diplomat*, January 27, 2022, https://thediplomat.com/2022/01/hong-kongs-contested-academic-freedom/; Mimi Leung and Yojana Sharma, "Universities Pressed to Implement 'Security Law' Education," *University World News*, March 24, 2021, www.universityworldnews.com/post. php?story=20210324074153521.

[66] Natalie Wong, "Revealing Evidence of Foreign Forces Undermining Hong Kong's National Security Is Not Needed, Just as Proof of Coronavirus Is Not Shown to Require Wearing of Face Masks: CY Leung," *South China Morning Post*, July 22, 2022, https://scmp.com/news/hong-kong/politics/article/3186305/revealing-evidence-foreign-forces-undermining-hong-kongs.

[67] Suzanne Pepper, "White Papers, Fact Sheets and Colour Revolutions: Beijing's New Narrative to Justify Hong Kong's National Security Regime," *Hong Kong Free Press*, May 28, 2022, https://hongkongfp.com/2022/05/28/white-papers-fact-sheets-and-colour-revolutions-beijings-new-narrative-to-justify-hong-kongs-national-security-regime/.

[68] Chris Lau and Sum Lok-kei, "Four of Nine Occupy Leaders Jailed for up to 16 Months over Roles in Hong Kong's 2014 Umbrella Movement," *South China Morning Post*, April 24, 2019, https://www.scmp.com/news/hong-kong/law-and-crime/article/3007414/ occupy-sentence-hong-kong-lawmaker-tanya-chan-be.

[69] "Academic freedom under vicious attack says Chan," Foreign Correspondence Club Hong Kong, February 2, 2016, https://www.fcchk.org/correspondent/academic-freedom-under-vicious-attack-says-chan/

[70] Nadia Lam, "Hong Kong Social Scientist from Pollster Group Pori Flees City, Citing 'Threats from Powerful Bodies,' Fear of 'Moving Red Lines,'" *South China Morning Post*, April 25, 2022, https://scmp.com/news/hong-kong/politics/article/3175394/hong-kong-social-scientist-pollster-group-pori-flees-city.

[71] Kang-Chung Ng, "Political Scientist Brian Fong Leaves Education University of Hong Kong after Pro-Beijing Attacks," *South China Morning Post*, February 13, 2022, https://

www.scmp.com/news/hong-kong/politics/article/3166902/political-scientist-brian-fong-leaves-education-university.

[72] Hillary Leung, "Baptist University Professor Leaves Hong Kong after Police Allegedly Contacted over 2019 Protest Article," *Hong Kong Free Press*, January 7, 2023, https://hongkongfp.com/2023/01/07/baptist-university-professor-leaves-hong-kong-after-police-allegedly-contacted-over-2019-protest-article/. Ho-him Chan, "Hong Kong universities under pressure as academics head for the exits," *Financial Times*, October 24, 2023. https://www.ft.com/content/1b9de404-d8c3-4cf9-bdec-cc4349140e11

[73] Peter Baehr, "Hong Kong Universities in the Shadow of the National Security Law," Society 59 (June 2022): 225-239, https://link.springer.com/article/10.1007/s12115-022-00709-9

[74] Sammy Heung, "US human rights professor denied visa by Hong Kong immigration authorities for university teaching position," South China Morning Post, February 2, 2022, https://www.scmp.com/news/hong-kong/education/article/3165584/us-human-rights-professor-denied-visa-hong-kong. Ho-him Chan, "Hong Kong denies visa to scholar of China's 1989 Tiananmen crackdown," *Financial Times*, October 27, 2023, https://www.ft.com/content/c58cebc8-1c88-4ba7-affe-1eb212990c2f.

[75] Mimi Leung and Yojana Sharma, "University 'Purge' Continues Apace as Another Leader Departs," *University World News*, February 18, 2022, https://www.universityworldnews.com/post.php?story=2022021808255472; Peter Baehr, "Hong Kong Universities in the Shadow of the National Security Law," *Society* 59 (June 2022): 225–239, https://link.springer.com/article/10.1007/s12115-022-00709-9.

[76] Carsten A. Holz, "Hong Kong's Contested Academic Freedom," *The Diplomat*, January 27, 2022, https://thediplomat.com/2022/01/hong-kongs-contested-academic-freedom/.

[77] Yojana Sharma, "Academics from Mainland China Outnumber Hong Kong Faculty," *University World News*, May 19, 2023, https://www.universityworldnews.com/post.php?story=20230519105129722.

[78] Mimi Leung and Yojana Sharma, "University 'Purge' Continues Apace as Another Leader Departs," *University World News*.

[79] Cannix Yau, "Head of Chinese University of Hong Kong 'evading' overruling council revamp plans," *South China Morning Post,* August 4, 2023. https://scmp.com/news/hong-kong/politics/article/3230016/head-chinese-university-hong-kong-evading-grilling-lawmakers-over-council-reform-plans

[80] Thomas Chan, "The Death of Hong Kong's University Student Unions," The Diplomat, April 14, 2022. https://thediplomat.com/2022/04/the-death-of-hong-kongs-university-student-unions/

[81] Lea Mok, "Two Universities in Hong Kong Plan to Restructure Politics Departments amid Security Law Chill," *Hong Kong Free Press*, May 30, 2022, https://hongkongfp.com/2022/05/30/two-universities-in-hong-kong-to-restructure-politics-departments-amid-security-law-chill/.

82 "Hong Kong Police Arrest Students over 'Advocating Terrorism,'" *New York Times*, August 18, 2021, https://www.nytimes.com/2021/08/18/world/asia/hong-kong-university-arrests.html. They would later plead guilty to a different charge of inciting others to wound.

83 Lea Mok, "National Security Case against Four HKU Students Adjourned as 'New Development' Emerges," *Hong Kong Free Press*, August 11, 2022, https://hongkongfp.com/2022/08/11/national-security-case-against-four-hku-students-adjourned-as-new-development-emerges/.

84 Hillary Leung, "University of Hong Kong ex-student leaders jailed for 2 years over mourning death of man who stabbed police officer," *Hong Kong Free Press*, October 30, 2023. https://hongkongfp.com/2023/10/30/breaking-university-of-hong-kong-ex-student-leaders-jailed-2-years-each-over-mourning-death-of-man-who-stabbed-police-officer/

85 Peter Lee, "University of Hong Kong Students Protest Removal of Tiananmen Monument with 'Invisible' Flash-Mob Using Airdrop," *Hong Kong Free Press*, January 18, 2022, https://hongkongfp.com/2022/01/18/university-of-hong-kong-students-organise-flash-mob-protest-against-removal-of-tiananmen-massacre-monument/.

86 William Yu, "University of Hong Kong Proposes Disciplining Students for 'Bringing Disrepute' to Institution, Fuelling Concerns over Freedom of Speech," April 26, 2022, https://scmp.com/news/hong-kong/education/article/3175599/university-hong-kong-proposes-disciplining-students.

87 Candice Chau, "University of Hong Kong Makes National Security Law Course a Mandatory Graduation Requirement," *Hong Kong Free Press*, July 25, 2022, https://hongkongfp.com/2022/07/25/university-of-hong-kong-makes-national-security-law-course-a-mandatory-graduation-requirement/.

88 Peter Lee, "HKU National Security Course: 10 Hours of Video Viewing and a Multiple-Choice Test to Pass and to Graduate," *Hong Kong Free Press*, August 16, 2022, https://hongkongfp.com/2022/08/19/hku-national-security-course-10-hours-of-video-viewing-and-a-multiple-choice-test-to-pass-and-to-graduate/.

89 Dawna Fung, "HKU's National Security Course Explains the Law but Fails to Answer Where the Red Line Is Drawn, Students Say," *Hong Kong Free Press*, October 4, 2022, https://hongkongfp.com/2022/10/04/hkus-national-security-course-explains-the-law-but-fails-to-answer-where-the-red-line-is-drawn-students-say/.

90 Candice Chau, "6 Hong Kong Teachers Disqualified over Complaints Linked To 2019 Protests," *Hong Kong Free Press*, April 13, 2022, https://hongkongfp.com/2022/04/13/6-hong-kong-teachers-disqualified-over-complaints-linked-to-2019-protests/.

91 Rachel Wong, "Second Hong Kong Teacher Sacked, This Time for Opium War Blunder as Lawmaker Says Punishment Too Harsh," November 13, 2020, https://hongkongfp.com/2020/11/13/second-hong-kong-teacher-sacked-this-time-for-opium-war-blunder-as-lawmaker-says-punishment-too-harsh/.

92 Hillary Leung, "Hong Kong Schools Should Set Up CCTV Cameras in Classrooms, Police Say," *Hong Kong Free Press*, May 22, 2023, https://hongkongfp.com/2023/05/22/hong-kong-schools-should-set-up-cctv-cameras-in-classrooms-police-say/.

[93] Hillary Leung, "Exclusive: Some Foreign English Teachers Employed by Gov't Must Swear Allegiance to Hong Kong or Their Job," *Hong Kong Free Press*, June 10, 2022, https://hongkongfp.com/2022/06/10/exlcusive-some-foreign-english-teachers-employed-by-govt-must-swear-allegiance-to-hong-kong-or-risk-their-job/.

[94] Irene Chan, "Over 100 Hong Kong gov't-subsidized further education providers asked to safeguard national security," Hong Kong Free Press, September 21, 2023, https://hongkongfp.com/2023/09/21/over-100-hong-kong-govt-subsidised-further-education-providers-asked-to-safeguard-national-security/

[95] Lilian Cheng and Chris Lau, "Hong Kong's Biggest Teachers' Union 'Seeks to Speed Up Dissolution by Changing Its Rules' as Beijing Attack Continues," *South China Morning Post*, August 11, 2021, https://www.scmp.com/news/hong-kong/politics/article/3144711/hong-kongs-biggest-teachers-union-seeks-speed-dissolution.

[96] William Yiu, "Hong Kong Schools Must Infuse Civic, Moral Values into All Subject under the New Framework to Be Revealed Soon," *South China Morning Post*, November 30, 2021, https://www.scmp.com/news/hong-kong/education/article/3157811/hong-kong-schools-must-infuse-civic-moral-values-all.

[97] Guidelines on Teachers' Professional Conduct, Education Bureau, 2022, https://www.edb.gov.hk/en/teacher/guidelines_tpc/index.html.

[98] Theodora Yu, "Under Pressure from Beijing, Hong Kong's Schools Become More Patriotic," *Washington Post*, June 22, 2022, https://www.washingtonpost.com/world/2022/06/22/hong-kong-education-beijing-colony/.

[99] William Yu, "New History Textbooks for Hong Kong Students 'Compress Details of Tiananmen Square Crackdown, with No Mention of Commemorative Vigil,'" *South China Morning Post*, June 3, 2022, https://scmp.com/news/hong-kong/education/article/3180388/new-history-textbooks-hong-kong-students-compress-details.

[100] Ian Johnson, *Sparks—China's Underground Historians And Their Battle For The Future* (Oxford University Press, 2023) https://www.amazon.com/Sparks-Chinas-Underground-Historians-Battle/dp/0197575501

[101] William Yiu, "What You Need to Know about Hong Kong's New School Subject Focused on National Security, Sense of Belonging," *South China Morning Post,* October 16, 2022, https://scmp.com/news/hong-kong/education/article/3196123/what-you-need-know-about-hong-kongs-new-school-subject.

[102] Kang-chung Ng, "Patriotism, National Security Education Should Make Up a Quarter of Primary Schools' Teaching Time, Hong Kong Education Bureau Says," *South China Morning Post*, September 8, 2022, https://scmp.com/news/hong-kong/education/article/3191871/hong-kong-education-bureau-suggests-primary-schools-spend SAR. See also Guardian Staff, "Hong Kong to restructure primary education to make it more 'patriotic,'" *The Guardian*, November 24, 2023. https://www.theguardian.com/world/2023/nov/24/hong-kong-to-restructure-primary-education-to-make-it-more-patriotic

[103] Ho-him Chan, "Four in 10 Hong Kong Teachers Want to Leave the Profession, Most of Them Blame Political Pressure, Survey Finds," *South China Morning Post*, May 9, 2021,

https://www.scmp.com/news/hong-kong/education/article/3132809/four-10-hong-kong-teachers-want-leave-profession-most-them?module=hard_link&pgtype=article.

104 Hilary Leung, "Hong Kong Schools See over 5,000 Teachers Leave This Academic Year, Marking 50% Increase in 'Drop-Out' Rate," *Hong Kong Free Press*, April 14, 2022, https://hongkongfp.com/2022/04/14/hong-kong-schools-see-over-5000-teachers-leave-this-academic-year-marking-50-increase-in-drop-out-rate/.

105 David Cowhig, "Half of Hong Kongers Want to Leave, Even Those with Poor English," *Oriental Daily Hong Kong Chinese,* March 20, 2023, https://gaodawei.wordpress.com/2023/03/20/2023-hong-kong-survey-many-want-to-leave/.

106 Irene Chan, "Over 27,000 Hong Kong students left city's schools last year amid emigration wave," *Hong Kong Free Press*, July 12, 2023. https://hongkongfp.com/2023/07/12/over-27000-hong-kong-students-left-citys-schools-last-year-amid-emigration-wave/

107 Krystal Chia, "Expat Students at Hong Kong Schools Decline by 12% Amid Exodus," *Bloomberg*, April 18, 2023, https://www.bloomberg.com/news/articles/2023-04-18/expat-students-at-hong-kong-schools-decline-12-amid-exodus.

108 Theodora Yu and Christian Shepherd, "Hong Kong Schools Tread Cautiously in Push to Make Students Love China," *Washington Post*, October 7, 2022, https://www.washingtonpost.com/world/2022/10/07/hong-kong-schools-education-china.

109 Oliver Young, "Hong Kong Opens Youth 'Deradicalization' Programs and Closes Student Unions," *China Digital Times*, April 21, 2022, https://chinadigitaltimes.net/2022/04/hong-kong-opens-youth-deradicalization-programs-and-closes-student-unions/.

110 William Yiu, "Record 24 per cent jump in Number of Students Leaving Hong Kong's Government-Funded Universities in Past Academic Year," *South China Morning Post*, January 21, 2022, https://scmp.com/news/hong-kong/education/article/3164318/record-24-cent-jump-number-students-leaving-hong-kongs.

111 William Yiu, "Record Admission Rates, New Low in Applicant Numbers at Hong Kong Universities," *South China Morning Post*, August 10, 2022, https://scmp.com/news/hong-kong/education/article/3188332/record-admission-rates-new-low-applicant-numbers-hong-kong.

112 Rhoda Kwan, "Explainer: Over Fifty Groups Gone in 11 Months—How Hong Kong's Pro-Democracy Forces Crumbled," *Hong Kong Free Press*, November 28, 2021, https://hongkongfp.com/2021/11/28/explainer-over-50-groups-gone-in-11-months-howhongkongs-pro-democracy-forces-crumbled.

113 Xinqi Su, "The Shadowy Messengers Delivering Threats to Hong Kong Civil Society," *AFP*, as republished in *Hong Kong Free Press*, February 21, 2022, https://hongkongfp.com/2022/02/21/the-shadowy-messengers-delivering-threats-to-hong-kong-civil-society/.

114 Ng Kang-chung and Natalie Wong, "National Security Law: Hong Kong's Biggest Opposition Trade Union Votes by Overwhelming Majority to Disband," *South China Morning Post*, October 3, 2021, https://scmp.com/news/hong-kong/politics/

article/3151047/national-security-law-hong-kongs-biggest-opposition-trade; Peter Lee, "Hong Kong National Security Police Quiz Ex-Leaders of Disbanded Pro-Democracy Union—Reports," *Hong Kong Free Press*, March 31, 2022, https://hongkongfp. com/2022/03/31/hong-kong-national-security-police-quiz-ex-leaders-of-disbanded-pro-democracy-union-reports/.

[115] Medium.com, "Albert Ho Chun-yan—The First Imprisoned Human Rights Lawyer in Hong Kong," *The 29 Principles,* January 24, 2022, see note 1, https://medium.com/@ the29principles/albert-ho-chun-yan-the-first-imprisoned-human-rights-lawyer-in-hong-kong-228654a2dd92.

[116] Brian Wong, "Hong Kong National Security Law: Former Vice-Chairwoman of June 4 Group Fails to Block Transfer of Subversion Case to High Court," *South China Morning Post*, September 9, 2022, https://scmp.com/news/hong-kong/law-and-crime/ article/3191904/hong-kong-national-security-law-former-vice-chairwoman. Chow Hang-tung's statement in court regarding the subversion charge has been translated and published by *China Change*. Chow Hang-tung, "Chow Hang-tung's Testimony during Preliminary Court Inquiry in the Hong Kong Alliance 'Incitement to Subversion' Case," *China Change*, September 7, 2022, https://chinachange.org/2022/09/07/chow-hang-tungs-testimony-during-preliminary-court-inquiry-in-the-hong-kong-alliance-incitement-to-subversion-case/.

[117] Cannix Yau and Jasmine Siu, "National Security Police Freeze Assets of Hong Kong Group behind Annual Tiananmen Vigil," *Hong Kong Free Press*, September 29, 2021, https://scmp.com/news/hong-kong/politics/article/3150594/national-security-police-freeze-all-assets-hong-kong-group.

[118] Clifford Lo and Ng Kang-chung, "Unionist Wife of Jailed Hong Kong Opposition Politician Lee Cheuk-Yan Arrested by National Security Officers after Prison Visit," *South China Morning Post*, March 9, 2023, https://scmp.com/news/hong-kong/law-and-crime/ article/3212918/wife-jailed-hong-kong-opposition-politician-arrested-national-security-officers-after-prison-visit.

[119] "China: No Justice 33 Years after Tiananmen Massacre," Human Rights Watch, June 2, 2022, https://www.hrw.org/news/2022/06/02/china-no-justice-33-years-after-tiananmen-massacre.

[120] Hillary Leung, "Ex-Organiser Of Hong Kong Tiananmen Vigil Chow Hang-Tung Wins Appeal against Conviction and Sentencing," *Hong Kong Free Press*, December 14, 2022, https://hongkongfp.com/2022/12/14/breaking-ex-organiser-of-hong-kong-tiananmen-vigil-chow-hang-tung-wins-appeal-against-conviction-and-sentencing/.

[121] Brian Wong, "Hong Kong National Security Law: Former Vice-Chairwoman of June 4 Group Fails to Block Transfer of Subversion Case to High Court," *South China Morning Post*, September 9, 2022, https://scmp.com/news/hong-kong/law-and-crime/ article/3191904/hong-kong-national-security-law-former-vice-chairwoman.

[122] "Hong Kong Arrests under Security Law Are Serious Concern, UN Experts Call for Review," United Nations Human Rights Office of the High Commissioner, October 12, 2021, https://www.ohchr.org/EN/NewsEvents/Pages/DisplyNews.aspx.

[123] Candice Chau, "3 Hong Kong Tiananmen Vigil Group Activists Appeal against National Security Conviction and Sentence," *Hong Kong Free Press*, March 23, 2023, https://hongkongfp.com/2023/03/23/3-hong-kong-tiananmen-vigil-group-activists-appeal-against-national-security-conviction-and-sentence/.

[124] Candice Chau, "Hong Kong Ex-lawmaker Albert Ho Arrested by National Security Police While on Bail," *Hong Kong Free Press*, March 21, 2023, https://hongkongfp.com/2023/03/21/hong-kong-ex-lawmaker-albert-ho-arrested-by-national-security-police-while-on-bail-reports.

[125] Clifford Lo, "Hong Kong Police Launch Series of Raids on Civil Human Rights Front Following Missed Deadline for Disclosing Financial, Other Records," *South China Morning Post*, October 28, 2021, https://scmp.com/news/hong-kong/law-and-crime/article/3153981/hong-kong-police-launch-series-raids-civil-human.

[126] Hillary Leung, "Trade Unions Must Now Declare They Will Not 'Endanger National Security' to Register," *Hong Kong Free Press*, September 16, 2022, https://hongkongfp.com/2022/09/16/trade-unions-must-now-declare-they-will-not-endanger-national-security-to-register-in-hong-kong/.

[127] Ibid.

[128] Hong Kong Watch launches groundbreaking new report on threats to freedom of religion or belief in Hong Kong," https://www.hongkongwatch.org/all-posts/2023/11/7/hong-kong-watch-launches-groundbreaking-new-report-on-threats-to-freedom-of-religion-or-belief-in-hong-kong

[129] Greg Torode, "Vatican Envoy in Hong Kong Warns Catholic Missions to Prepare for China Crackdown," *Reuters*, July 5, 2022, https://www.reuters.com/world/asia-pacific/vatican-envoy-hong-kong-warns-catholic-missions-prepare-china-crackdown-2022-07-05/.

[130] Greg Torode, "Historica conclave: Chinese bishops, priests brief Hong Kong clerics on Xi's religious views," Reuters, December 30, 2021, https://www.reuters.com/world/china/exclusive-historic-conclave-chinese-bishops-priests-brief-hong-kong-clerics-xis-2021-12-30/

[131] "'Evil Forces' Push Hong Kong Pro-Democracy Clothes Shop to Shut," *Reuters*, November 18, 2021, https://www.reuters.com/world/asia-pacific/evil-forces-push-hong-kong-pro-democracy-clothes-shop-shut-2021-11-18/.

[132] "Hong Kong Adds Security Law Clauses to All Land Sales, Property Stocks Drop," *Reuters*, February 13, 2023, https://www.reuters.com/world/asia-pacific/hong-kong-adds-security-law-clauses-to-land-sales-property-stocks-drop-2023-02-13/.

[133] "Deloitte and KPMG ask staff to use burner phones for Hong Kong trips," Financial Times, November 27, 2023. https://on.ft.com/3N7pVEj

[134] Tony Cheung, "Beijing to 'Improve' System for Ruling Hong Kong, Devise 'Legal Weapons' to Counter Foreign Forces," *South China Morning Post*, March 8, 2022, https://www.scmp.com/news/hong-kong/politics/article/3169648/beijing-improve-system-ruling-hong-kong-devise-legal.

[135] "Fact Sheet on the National Endowment for Democracy," Ministry of Foreign Affairs of the People's Republic of China, May 7, 2022, https://www.fmprc.gov.cn/eng/zxxx_662805/202205/t20220507_10683090.html.

[136] Tony Cheung and Chris Lau, "Hongkongers with Ties to the US-Backed Group Slammed by Beijing Report Could Risk Censure, Analysts Warn," *South China Morning Post*, May 12, 2022, https://scmp.com/news/hong-kong/politics/article/3177383/hongkongers-ties-us-backed-group-slammed-beijing-report.

[137] Helen Davidson, "Amnesty International to Close Hong Kong Offices Due to National Security Law," *Guardian*, October 25, 2021, https://www.theguardian.com/world/2021/oct/25/amnesty-international-to-close-hong-kong-offices-due-to-national-security-law.

[138] Hang-tung Chow, "Amnesty International has Left Hong Kong but There Will Still Be Candles in the Darkness," *Amnesty International*, May 18, 2022, https://www.amnesty.org/en/latest/news/2022/05/amnesty-international-has-left-hong-kong-but-there-will-still-be-candles-in-the-darkness/.

[139] Hong Kong Public Order Ordinance, Cap 245. https://www.elegislation.gov.hk/hk/cap245!en.pdf

[140] Ezra Cheung and Elizabeth Cheung, "Number Tags for Marchers but No Masks, Hong Kong Police Tell Organisers for First Protest Since Lifting of All Covid-19 Curbs," *South China Morning Post*, March 24, 2023, https://scmp.com/news/hong-kong/politics/article/3214798/number-tags-marchers-no-masks-hong-kong-police-tell-organisers-first-protest-lifting-all-covid-curbs.

[141] Tim Hamlett, "Hong Kong's new protest regulations are designed by those who don't like protests," *Hong Kong Free Press*, March 31, 2023. https://hongkongfp.com/2023/03/31/hong-kongs-new-protest-regulations-are-designed-by-those-who-dont-like-protests/

[142] Lea Mok, "'Emotional meltdown': Hong Kong Labour Day demo cancelled, as activist says security law prevents disclosing why," *Hong Kong Free Press*, April 26, 2023. https://hongkongfp.com/2023/04/26/emotional-meltdown-hong-kong-labour-day-demo-cancelled-as-activist-says-security-law-prevents-disclosing-why/

[143] Tim Hamlett, "Hong Kong's freedom to protest comes back to life … or does it?" *Hong Kong Free Press*, March 19, 2023. https://hongkongfp.com/2023/03/19/hong-kongs-freedom-to-protest-comes-back-to-life-or-does-it/

[144] Xinqi Su, "Hong Kong Police Step Up Surveillance to 'Tame' Activists," Barrons, September 28, 2023, https://www.barrons.com/news/hong-kong-police-step-up-surveillance-to-tame-activists-d946b2f0

[145] Special Report, *Hong Kong's Civil Society: From Open City to a City of Fear*, Congressional Executive Commission on China, October 2022, https://www.cecc.gov/sites/chinacommission.house.gov/files/documents/Hong%20Kong%20Civil%20Society%20Report.pdf.

[146] Concluding Observations on the Fourth Periodic Report on Hong Kong, China, UN Human Rights Committee, July 27, 2022, https://tbinternet.ohchr.org/Treaties/CCPR/Shared%20Documents/HKG/CCPR_C_CHN-HKG_CO_4_49295_E.pdf.

[147] HKSAR Government Vehemently Opposes Comments by the US Congressional-Executive Commission on China, October 5, 2022, https://www.info.gov.hk/gia/general/202210/05/P2022100500692.htm.

[148] Amelia Loi, "Hong Kong Rights Review Marred by Crackdown on Civil Society Groups," RFA, July 11, 2022, https://www.rfa.org/english/news/china/hongkong-un-07112022080337.html.

[149] Jerrine Tan, "Protest Hides in Plain Sight in Hong Kong," *Wired*, August 4, 2022, https://www.wired.com/story/protest-hides-in-plain-sight-in-hong-kong/.

[150] In their recent books, Louisa Lim and Karen Cheung offer excellent further elaborations on the many ways Hong Kong's hidden voices poke through official repression. Louisa Lim, *Indelible City: Dispossession and Defiance in Hong Kong*. New York: Riverhead Books, 2022; Karen Cheung, *Impossible City: A Hong Kong Memoir*. New York: Random House, 2022.

[151] Selina Cheng, "Hong Kong's Top Court Rejects Bail for Group Charged with Sedition over Children's Picture Book," *Hong Kong Free Press*, December 11, 2021, https://hongkongfp.com/2021/12/11/hong-kongs-top-court-rejects-bail-for-group-charged-with-sedition-over-childrens-picture-books/.

[152] Office of the UN High Commissioner for Human Rights, "Civil Society: Resources for NGOs, Human Rights Defenders and Other Actors in Civic Space," July 19, 2022, https://perma.cc/T6PT-7E2X.

[153] "How China's Civil Society Collapsed under Xi," Radio France Internationale, April 10, 2022, https://www.rfi.fr/en/international-news/20221004-how-china-s-civil-society-collapsed-under-xi.

[154] "An Anatomy of Erasure: How a Free and Open Hong Kong Became a Police State," *Economist*, July 1, 2022, https://www.economist.com/interactive/essay/2022/07/01/how-hong-kong-became-a-police-state.

[155] Christine Loh, *Underground Front: The Chinese Communist Party in Hong Kong*, second edition. Hong Kong: Hong Kong University Press: 2019.

[156] Harsh words fly in 'loyal rubbish' row," The Standard, March 16, 2021, https://www.thestandard.com.hk/section-news/section/21/228385/Harsh-words-fly-in-%27loyal-rubbish%27-row.

[157] Ho-fung Hung, *City on the Edge: Hong Kong Under Chinese Rule*, chapter 4.

[158] Irene Chan, "National security police 'take away' family members of wanted Hong Kong activists for questioning," *Hong Kong Free Press*, July 20, 2023. https://hongkongfp.com/2023/07/20/national-security-police-take-away-family-members-of-wanted-hong-kong-activists-for-questioning.

[159] In December 2023 the Hong Kong government added the HK$1 million bounty to five other overseas activists, including Simon Cheng, Francis Hui, Joey Siu, Johnny Fok and Tony Choi.

[160] S1838, Hong Kong Human Rights and Democracy Act of 2019, https://www.congress.gov/bill/116th-congress/senate-bill/1838. Regarding these earlier arrest warrants see Helen Regan and Angus Watson, "Hong Kong Issues Arrest Warrants for Six Overseas Democracy Activists Including US Citizen, State Media Reports," CNN, August 1, 2020, https://www.cnn.com/2020/08/01/china/hong-kong-activists-arrest-warrant-intl-hnk/index.html.

[161] UK Foreign Secretary, press release, "Hong Kong Watch: Foreign Secretary's Statement," March 14, 2022, https://www.gov.uk/government/news/foreign-secretary-statement-on-hong-kong-watch-march-2022.

[162] "Security Bureau Threatens UK-Based Hong Kong Watch Founder with Life Imprisonment: NGO Says It Won't Disband," *Hong Kong Free Press*, March 14, 2022, https://hongkongfp.com/2022/03/14/security-bureau-threatens-uk-based-hong-kong-watch-founder-with-life-imprisonment-ngo-says-it-wont-disband/.

[163] Jojo Man and Amelia Loi, "Hong Kong to Pursue Canada-Based Political Activists under National Security Law," Radio Free Asia, August 3, 2022, https://www.rfa.org/english/news/china/hongkong-exiles-08032022123706.html.

[164] "Hong Kong Security Law: Hong Kong Police Seek Activist Nathan Law and 5 Others for Inciting Secession and Collusion, Insider Says," *South China Morning Post*, August 1, 2020, https://scmp.com/news/hong-kong/law-and-crime/article/3095615/national-security-law-hong-kong-police-said-seek.

[165] Mandy Cheng, "Treat Hong Kong's 8 wanted democrats like 'street rats' who are to be 'avoided at all costs,' leader John Lee says," *Hong Kong Free Press*, July 11, 2023. https://hongkongfp.com/2023/07/11/treat-hong-kongs-8-wanted-democrats-like-street-rats-who-should-be-avoided-at-all-costs-leader-john-lee-says/

[166] Ng Kang-chung, "Hong Kong justice chief lodges professional misconduct complaints against two activist lawyers on police wanted list," *South China Morning Post*, July 10, 2023. https://scmp.com/news/hong-kong/law-and-crime/article/3227226/hong-kong-justice-chief-lodges-professional-misconduct-complaints-against-two-activist-lawyers

[167] The bounty attracted international condemnation from e.g., "Statement of ABA President Deborah Enix-Ross Re: Arrest warrants and bounties on Hong Kong Lawyers," July 17, 2023. https://www.americanbar.org/news/abanews/aba-news-archives/2023/07/statement-of-aba-president-re-hong-kong-lawyers; "IBAHRI expresses concern over arrest warrants for overseas pro-democracy figures," July 14,2023. https://www.ibanet.org/Hong-Kong-IBAHRI-expresses-concern-over-arrest-warrants-for-overseas-pro-democracy-figures; Commonwealth Lawyers Association, Statement Concerning Hong Kong, July 28, 2023. https://www.commonwealthlawyers.com/statement/statement-concerning-hong-kong/ The Hong Kong government dismissed these concerns as groundless slander. "HKSAR Government strongly opposes and condemns," Press Release, August 1, 2023. https://www.info.gov.hk/gia/general/202308/01/P2023080100651.htm

[168] Clifford Lo, "'Dozens of Hong Kong residents" on police national security 'wanted' list, including for crowdfunding drives," *South China Morning Post*, July 4, 2023.

https://scmp.com/news/hong-kong/law-and-crime/article/3226559/dozens-hong-kong-residents-police-national-security-wanted-list-including-crowdfunding-drives-post

169 Kelly Ho, "Hong Kong national security police arrest one more man over alleged conspiracy to fund self-exiled activists," *Hong Kong Free Press*, July 6, 2023. https://hongkongfp.com/2023/07/06/hong-kong-national-security-police-arrest-one-more-man-over-alleged-conspiracy-to-fund-self-exiled-activists/

Chapter 10

1 Kinling Lo and Tony Cheung, "Western-Style Democracy 'Would Doom Hong Kong to Chaos,' Chinese Officials Say," *South China Morning Post*, January 11, 2022, https://scmp.com/news/china/politics/article/3162986/western-style-democracy-would-doom-hong-kong-chaos-chinese.

2 "Hong Kong elections: 30.2 per cent turnout in first Legislative Council poll since Beijing overhaul," South China Morning Post, December 20, 2021, https://www.scmp.com/news/hong-kong/politics/article/3160336/hong-kong-elections-all-eyes-final-turnout-first-big-test

3 *China: Democracy That Works*, The State Council Office of the People's Republic of China, December 4, 2021, http://www.news.cn/english/2021-12/04/c_1310351231.htm.

4 *Hong Kong: Democratic Progress under the Framework of One Country, Two Systems*, The State Council Office of the People's Republic of China, December 20, 2021, http://www.china-embassy.org/eng/zgyw/202112/t20211220_10471806.htm.

5 Joint Report to the European Parliament and the Council, "Hong Kong Special Administrative Region: Annual Report for 2012," *Eur-Lex*, JOIN/2022/16 final, May 20, 2022, https://eur-lex.europa.eu/legal-content/EN/ALL/?uri=JOIN:2022:16:FIN.

6 ICCPR Human Rights Committee, General Comment No. 25, 1996, https://www.equalrightstrust.org/ertdocumentbank/general%20comment%2025.pdf.

7 "Hong Kong, Its Elections Upended, Reconsiders Its Dream of Democracy," New York Times, September 24, 2021, https://www.nytimes.com/2021/03/20/world/asia/hong-kong-elections-democracy.html.

8 "Hong Kong Is Holding Elections. It wants Them to Look Real," New York Times, September 24, 2021, https://www.nytimes.com/2021/09/24/world/asia/hong-kong-elections.html.

9 Chris Lau, "Democratic Party Expels 2 Members for Breaking Ranks by Backing Centrist Candidate in Hong Kong's Revamped Legislative Poll," *South China Morning Post*, February 17, 2022, https://scmp.com/news/hong-kong/politics/article/3167329/democratic-party-expels-2-members-breaking-ranks-backing.

10 Peter Lee, "Hong Kong's Democratic Party Urges Next Leader to Clarify National Security Boundaries and Pardon 2019 Protesters," *Hong Kong Free Press*, June 1, 2022, https://hongkongfp.com/2022/06/01/hong-kongs-democratic-party-urges-next-leader-to-clarify-national-security-boundaries-pardon-2019-protesters/.

[11] Hillary Leung, "Hong Kong's Democratic Party calls for 'open' society as it omits mention of voting rights in annual policy proposal," Hong Kong Free Press, September 13, 2023. https://hongkongfp.com/2023/09/13/hong-kongs-democratic-party-calls-for-open-society-as-it-omits-mention-of-voting-rights-in-annual-policy-proposal.

[12] Candice Chau, "Hong Kong's Pro-Democracy Civic Party Could Disband If No One Takes Up Executive Committee Roles," Hong Kong Free Press, October 5, 2022, https://hongkongfp.com/2022/10/05/hong-kongs-pro-democracy-civic-party-could-disband-if-no-one-takes-up-executive-committee-roles/.

[13] Hillary Leung, "'No Voice': Without an Opposition, Hong Kong's 'Patriots Only' Legislative Council Leaves Marginalised Groups Behind," Hong Kong Free Press, January 15, 2023, https://hongkongfp.com/2023/01/15/no-voice-without-an-opposition-hong-kongs-patriots-only-legislative-council-leaves-marginalised-groups-behind/.

[14] Brian Wong, "2 Plead Guilty to Inciting Others to Cast Invalid Ballots in Hong Kong's Legislative Council Poll," South China Morning Post, February 15, 2022, https://scmp.com/news/hong-kong/law-and-crime/article/3167135/2-plead-guilty-inciting-others-cast-invalid-ballots; Lilian Cheng, "Hong Kong's Graft-Buster Charges 4 for Allegedly Urging Others to Cast Blank Ballots by Sharing Posts from Fugitive Activists in 2021 Legco Election," South China Morning Post, November 9, 2022, https://scmp.com/news/hong-kong/law-and-crime/article/3199014/hong-kongs-graft-buster-charges-4-allegedly-urging-others-cast-blank-ballots-sharing-posts-fugitive.

[15] Almond Li, "Ex-Student Leader Charged over 'Inciting Others to Cast Blank Votes' in Hong Kong Election," Hong Kong Free Press, July 27, 2022. https://hongkongfp.com/2022/07/27/ex-student-leader-charged-with-inciting-others-to-cast-blank-votes-in-hong-kong-election/.

[16] Chen Zifei, "Hong Kong Pro-Democracy Lawmaker in Exile Vows to Keep Speaking Out for the City," Radio Free Asia, October 3, 2022, https://www.rfa.org/english/news/china/hongkong-ted-hui-10032022133152.html.

[17] SCMP Reporters, "Hong Kong Elections: 30.2 Percent Turnout in First Legislative Council Poll Since Beijing Overhaul," South China Morning Post, December 20, 2021, https://www.scmp.com/news/hong-kong/politics/article/3160336/hong-kong-elections-all-eyes-final-turnout-first-big-test.

[18] Candice Chau, "Explainer: 7 Charts Showing Voter Demographics in Hong Kong's First 'Patriots-Only' Legislative Election," Hong Kong Free Press, May 1, 2022, https://hongkongfp.com/2022/05/01/explainer-7-charts-showing-voter-demographics-in-hong-kongs-first-patriots-only-legislative-election/?utm_medium=email.

[19] Anthony J. Blinkin, Secretary of State, Joint Statement on Hong Kong Legislative Council Elections, December 20, 2021, https://www.state.gov/joint-statement-on-hong-kong-legislative-council-elections/. (It included Canada, Australia, New Zealand, and the United Kingdom.)

[20] Kang-Chung Ng, "Hong Kong's Democratic Party Plans to Mount Comeback Bid in Next Year's District Council Election," South China Morning Post, September 14, 2022,

https://scmp.com/news/hong-kong/politics/article/3192515/hong-kongs-democratic-party-plans-mount-comeback-bid-next.

[21] Kahon Chan, "How Will Hong Kong's District Council Overhaul Change Neighbourhood Political Life? Direct Voting Curbed, Lines Redrawn in 'Patriots-Only' Revamp," *South China Morning Post*, May 3, 2023, https://scmp.com/news/hong-kong/politics/article/3219182/how-will-hong-kongs-district-council-overhaul-change-neighbourhood-political-life-direct-voting.

[22] Kelly Ho, "All 399 Hong Kong District Council election candidates pass patriotism test," Hong Kong Free Press, November 10, 2023. https://hongkongfp.com/2023/11/10/all-399-hong-kong-district-council-candidates-pass-patriotism-requirement/

[23] Kelly Ho, "Lowest-ever turnout for Hong Kong District Council election; 6 arrest during opposition-free polls, " Hong Kong Free Press, December 11, 2023, https://hongkongfp.com/2023/12/11/breaking-poorest-ever-turnout-for-hong-kongs-district-council-election-6-arrests-during-opposition-free-polls/

[24] Kahon Chan, "Hong Kong Democratic Party endorses 8 hopefuls for first district council election since 'patriots-only' overhaul," *South China Morning Post*, September 20, 2023. https://www.scmp.com/news/hong-kong/politics/article/3235239/hong-kongs-democratic-party-endorses-8-hopefuls-run-first-district-council-election-patriots-only. Kelley Ho, "Opposition shut out of Hong Kong's 'patriots-only' District Council race; leader John Lee hails 'fierce competition,'" *Hong Kong Free Press*, October 31, 2023. https://hongkongfp.com/2023/10/31/opposition-shut-out-of-hong-kongs-patriots-only-district-council-race-leader-john-lee-hails-fierce-competition/. Sadly it is reported that 75 percent of the candidates nominated for the directly elected seats were members of the committee doing the nominating.

[25] Kelley Ho, "Deciding whether to join Hong Kong's next District Council election 'Tough and painful,' says Democratic Party vice-chief," *Hong Kong Free Press*, July 20, 2023. https://hongkongfp.com/2023/07/20/deciding-whether-to-join-hong-kongs-next-district-council-election-tough-and-painful-says-democratic-party-vice-chief/

[26] Shibani Mahtani, "Hong Kong's Carrie Lam Won't Seek Second Term as Chief Executive," *Washington Post*, April 4, 2022, https://www.washingtonpost.com/world/2022/04/04/hong-kong-carrie-lam/.

[27] Candice Chau, "Explainer: Hong Kong's first small-circle leadership race since Beijing's 'patriots-only' electoral overhaul," Hong Kong Free Press, May 5, 2022, https://hongkongfp.com/2022/04/15/explainer-hong-kongs-first-small-circle-leadership-race-since-beijings-patriots-only-electoral-overhaul.

[28] Lilian Cheng, Nadia Lam, and Tony Cheung, "Hong Kong Chief Executive Election 2022: John Lee Submits 786 Nominations to Stand for the City's Top Job, Representing More Than Half of Election Committee Members," *South China Morning Post*, April 13, 2022, https://scmp.com/news/hong-kong/politics/article/3174082/hong-kong-chief-executive-election-2022-john-lee-submits.

[29] Hillary Leung, Tom Grundy, Kelly Ho, and Almond Li, "1,416 Elite Voters Select Sole Candidate John Lee as Hong Kong's Next Leader," *Hong Kong Free Press*, May 8, 2022,

https://hongkongfp.com/2022/05/08/breaking-sole-candidate-john-lee-selected-as-hong-kongs-next-leader/.

[30] Pak Yiu, "Hong Kong Fears Run Deep as John Lee Aims to Take Charge," *Nikkei Asia*, April 12, 2022, https://asia.nikkei.com/Spotlight/Asia-Insight/Hong-Kong-fears-run-deep-as-John-Lee-aims-to-take-charge; Charles Mok, "China's Choice of Hong Kong's Chief Executive Reveals Its Own Insecurity," *The Diplomat*, April 9, 2022, https://thediplomat.com/2022/04/chinas-choice-for-hong-kongs-chief-executive-reveals-its-own-insecurity/.

[31] Shibani Mahtani and Theodora Yu, "Beijing's Handpicked Candidate for Hong Kong Signals Tighter Control," *Washington Post*, April 8, 2022, https://www.washingtonpost.com/world/2022/04/08/hong-kong-chief-executive-beijing-china.

[32] Lau Siu-kai, "Lee Meets Beijing's Criteria for HK's Next CE," *China Daily HK Edition*, April 11, 2022, https://www.chinadailyhk.com/article/267198#Lee-meets-Beijing's-criteria-for-HK's-next-CE.

[33] John Burns, "What John Lee as Chief Executive Might Mean for Hong Kong," *Hong Kong Free Press*, April 6, 2022, https://hongkongfp.com/2022/04/06/what-john-lee-as-chief-executive-might-mean-for-hong-kong/.

[34] Wang Xiangwei, "Upholding Common Law, Tackling Vested Interests: Xi's Vision of Hong Kong Strikes a Chord," *South China Morning Post*, July 9, 2022, https://scmp.com/week-asia/opinion/article/3184573/upholding-common-law-tacking-vested-interests-xis-vision-hong.

[35] Austin Ramzy and Tiffany May, "For Hong Kong's Beijing-Backed Officials, Xi's All That," *New York Times*, July 27, 2022, https://www.nytimes.com/2022/07/27/world/asia/xi-jinping-hong-kong.html.

[36] William Yiu and Ng Kang-chung, "Hong Kong Sectors Rush to Hold Seminars to Study Xi Jingping's Speech, Sparking Debate on Effectiveness of Such "Mainland-Style' Forums," *South China Morning Post*, July 6, 2022, https://scmp.com/news/hong-kong/politics/article/3184242/hong-kong-sectors-rush-hold-seminars-study-xi-jinpings.

[38] Hillary Leung, "Number of People Resigning from Hong Kong Government Jobs Doubles from Previous Year," *Hong Kong Free Press*, July 29, 2022, https://hongkongfp.com/2022/07/29/number-of-people-resigning-from-hong-kong-government-jobs-doubles-from-previous-year/.

[38] Hillary Leung, "Hong Kong to allow university students to apply for gov't jobs up to 2 years ahead of graduation," Hong Kong Free Press, June 1, 2023, https://hongkongfp.com/2023/06/01/hong-kong-to-allow-university-students-to-apply-for-govt-jobs-up-to-2-years-ahead-of-graduation/

Chapter 11

[1] This is well illustrated by the dramatic growth in population from 1,860,000 in 1949—the year of the communist revolution—to 6.5 million in 1997, the year of the handover. Fan Shuh Ching, *The Population of Hong Kong*. Committee for International

Coordination of National Research in Demography, 1974, 1–11, http://www.cicred.org/Eng/Publications/pdf/c-c21.pdf; *Demographic Trends in Hong Kong, 1986–2016*. Census and Statistics Department, Hong Kong SAR, 2017, https://www.statistics.gov.hk/pub/B1120017042017XXXXB0100.pdf.

[2] The British recorded the Hong Kong population when they took the colony in 1841 as a mere 7,500 people. See Louisa Lim, *Indelible City*.

[3] Richard Hughes, *Hong Kong: Borrowed Place, Borrowed Time*.

[4] "2022 Hong Kong Policy Act Report," DOS Bureau of East Asian and Pacific Affairs, March 31, 2022, https://www.state.gov/2022-hong-kong-policy-act-report/.

[5] 2023 Hong Kong Policy Act Report, DOS Bureau of East Asian and Pacific Affairs, March 31, 2023, https://www.state.gov/2023-hong-kong-policy-act-report/; "HKSAR Government Strongly Disapproves and Firmly Rejects the US Hong Kong Policy Act Report," Press Releases, HKSAR Government, April 1, 2023, https://www.info.gov.hk/gia/general/202304/01/P2023040100058.htm.

[6] ICCPR, Human Rights Committee, Concluding Observations on the Fourth Periodic Report of Hong Kong, China, advanced unedited version, July 27, 2022, chrome-extension: //efaidnbmnnnibpcajpcglclefindmkaj/https://tbinternet.ohchr.org/Treaties/CCPR/Shared%20Documents/HKG/CCPR_C_CHN-HKG_CO_4_49295_E.pdf; for a background on this HRC report, see Carole J. Petersen, "Hong Kong's Rights Reckoning: What We Can Expect from the UN Human Rights Committee," *USALI Perspectives* 2, no. 24 (June 9, 2022), https://usali.org/usali-perspectives-blog/hong-kongs-rights-reckoning.

[7] Chris Lau, "UN Human Rights Committee Grills Hong Kong Officials Overuse, 'Dramatic Scope' of National Security Law," *South China Morning Post*, July 7, 2022, https://scmp.com/news/hong-kong/politics/article/3184519/un-human-rights-committee-grills-hong-kong-officials-over.

[8] Michael C. Davis, "Why Hong Kong Should Heed UN Condemnation of Its Failure to Protect Basic Rights," *South China Morning Post*, August 2, 2022, https://www.scmp.com/comment/opinion/article/3187157/why-hong-kong-should-heed-un-condemnation-its-failure-protect-basic.

[9] Tony Cheung, "'Abandon Arrogance, Face Fact That National Security Law Has Restored Stability in Hong Kong," *South China Morning Post*, July 29, 2022, https://scmp.com/news/hong-kong/politics/article/3187006/abandon-arrogance-face-fact-national-security-law-has.

[10] Hilary Leung, "Hong Kong Tells the UN Democracy Took 'Quantum Leap Forward' amid Grilling over Press Freedom, Disbanded NGOs." *Hong Kong Free Press*, July 13, 2022, https://hongkongfp.com/2022/07/13/hong-kong-tells-un-democracy-took-quantum-leap-forward-amid-grilling-over-press-freedom-disbanded-ngos/.

[11] Hans Tse, "Crime in Hong Kong rises by 34.6 % in first 8 months of 2023, security chief says, led by over 50% spike in fraud, Hong Kong Free Press, September 27, 2023, https://hongkongfp.com/2023/09/27/crime-in-hong-kong-rises-by-34-6-in-first-eight-months-in-2023-security-chief-says-led-by-over-50-spike-in-fraud/

[12] "'Every Person on the Planet' Affected: Hong Kong Security Law More Draconian Than Feared, Say Analysts," *Hong Kong Free Press*, from AFP, July 2, 2020, https://hongkongfp.com/2020/07/02/every-person-on-the-planet-affected-hong-kong-security-law-more-draconian-than-feared-say-analysts/.

[13] NSL, articles 29, 36, 37, and 38.

[14] NSL, articles 29 and 34.

[15] Hong Kong Public Opinion Research Institute, People Ethnic Identity Survey (Random Sample ~1,000), https://www.pori.hk/pop-poll/ethnic-identity.html.

[16] "House Foreign Affairs Committee Holds Hearing on Hong Kong National Security Law," Lawfare Blog, July 1, 2020, https://www.lawfareblog.com/house-foreign-affairs-holds-hearing-hong-kong-national-security-law.

[17] "Hong Kong: Lee Cheuk-yan Given Further Jail Sentences for Pro-Democracy Protests," *International Trade Union Confederation Report*, May 28, 2021, https://www.ituc-csi.org/hong-kong-lee-cheuk-yan-sentence.

[18] "Hong Kong Tiananmen Vigil Organizers Charged under the National Security Law," BBC News, September 10, 2021, https://www.bbc.com/news/world-asia-china-58522326.

[19] Hong Kong Human Rights and Democracy Act of 2019, Public Law 116-76, November 27, 2019, https://www.congress.gov/116/plaws/publ76/PLAW-116publ76.pdf.

[20] "China's Top Diplomat Wang Yi Lashes Out at US for 'Seriously Damaging' Mutual Trust," *South China Morning Post*, December 13, 2019, https://www.scmp.com/news/china/diplomacy/article/3041990/chinas-top-diplomat-wang-yi-lashes-out-us-seriously-damaging; "China's Foreign Minister Calls US the 'Troublemaker of the World,'" *Washington Post*, December 13, 2019, https://www.washingtonpost.com/world/asia_pacific/chinese-foreign-minister-calls-us-the-troublemaker-of-the-world/2019/12/13/ce58a184-1d77-11ea-977a-15a6710ed6da_story.html.

[21] By Representative Joaquin Castro, vice-chair of House Foreign Affairs Committee, during the committee hearing on Hong Kong on July 1, 2020, https://foreignaffairs.house.gov/hearings?ID=878C9D04-7712-47A7-BC92-86E4C028F749, available on YouTube, https://youtu.be/W6Byt9dcG-k.

[22] The 2017, 2018, and 2019 reports appear to have been taken down, but the 2016 report is sufficiently representative. Hong Kong Policy Act Report 2016, US Department of State, https://2009-2017.state.gov/p/eap/rls/reports/2016/257085.htm.

[23] "Hong Kong Has Lost Autonomy, Pompeo Says, Opening Door to US Action," *New York Times,* June 29, 2020, https://www.nytimes.com/2020/05/27/us/politics/china-hong-kong-pompeo-trade.html.

[24] The President's Executive Order on Hong Kong Normalization, July 14, 2020, https://hk.usconsulate.gov/2020071403/. Subsequently, the US halted the extradition agreement, abandoning agreements to surrender fugitive offenders, transfer sentenced persons, and grant reciprocal tax exemptions on income derived from international shipping. "US Suspends Its Extradition Treaty with Hong Kong over China's National Security Law," *South China Morning Post*, August 20, 2020, https://www.scmp.com/news/world/united-

states-canada/article/3098043/us-suspends-its-extradition-treaty-hong-kong. China retaliated by suspending the Hong Kong agreement on mutual legal assistance. "National Security Law: US Stands to Lose Just as Much or Even More by Suspending Three Bilateral Treaties Hong Kong Warns," *South China Morning Post*, August 20, 2019, https://www.scmp.com/news/hong-kong/politics/article/3098097/national-security-law-hong-kong-government-slams-us.

[25] "Trump Administration Penalizes Hong Kong Officials for Crackdown on Protesters," *New York Times*, August 7, 2020, https://www.nytimes.com/2020/08/07/world/asia/trump-china-hong-kong-sanctions.html.

[26] "'Shameless and Despicable': Hong Kong Decries US Sanctions on Hong Kong Officials over National Security Law," *South China Morning Post*, August 8, 2020, https://www.scmp.com/news/hong-kong/politics/article/3096577/hong-kong-national-security-law-us-sanctions-11-individuals.

[27] Shannon Tiezzi, "US Becomes the Latest Country to Suspend Extradition Treaty with Hong Kong," *The Diplomat*, August 20, 2020, https://thediplomat.com/2020/08/us-becomes-latest-country-to-suspend-extradition-treaty-with-hong-kong/.

[28] "Pursued for Life—HK's Hunt for Fugitives Using the National Security Law," *Safeguard Defenders*, January 13, 2022, https://safeguarddefenders.com/en/blog/pursued-life-hks-hunt-fugitives-using-national-security-law.

[29] Christian Shepherd, "China's Aggressive Efforts to Bring Back Fugitives Grow More Brazen," *Washington Post*, April 29, 2022, https://www.washingtonpost.com/world/2022/04/29/china-deportation-cyprus-uyghur/.

[30] Constitution of the International Criminal Police Organization—Interpol, Article 3, I/CONS/GA/1956 (2021), https://www.interpol.int/en/Who-we-are/Legal-framework/Legal-documents.

[31] Case of *Liu v. Poland, European Court of Human Rights,* October 6, 2022, chrome-extension://efaidnbmnnnibpcajpcglclefindmkaj/https://safeguarddefenders.com/sites/default/files/ECtHR%20Poland%20-%20Liu%20case.pdf. For analysis see, "Landmark Decision Could Herald End to Europe's Extraditions to China," *Safeguard Defenders*, November 3, 2022, https://safeguarddefenders.com/en/blog/landmark-decision-could-herald-end-europe-s-extraditions-china.

[32] Ng Kang-chung and Chris Lau, "Call by US Lawmakers for Sanctions against Hong Kong Judges and Prosecutors Handling National Security Law Dismissed by Judiciary as 'Absolutely Unacceptable,'" *South China Morning Post*, May 11, 2022, https://scmp.com/news/hong-kong/politics/article/3177367/call-us-lawmakers-sanctions-against-hong-kong-judges-and.

[33] Staff Report, "Hong Kong Prosecutors Play a Key Role in Carrying Out Political Prosecutions," Congressional-Executive Commission on China (CECC), July 2022, https://www.cecc.gov/publications/commission-analysis/hong-kong-prosecutors-play-a-key-role-in-carrying-out-political. These issues were discussed at a CECC-related hearing. CECC Hearing: The Dismantling of Hong Kong's Civil Society, CECC, July 14, 2022, https://www.youtube.com/watch?v=dac5hYkcq0k.

[34] Primrose Riordan, "US Law Firm Denounced for Joining Event to Mark Hong Kong National Security Law," *Financial Times*, May 20, 2022, www.ft.com /content/efc91e6f-b990-40bb-bab0-6ff1dfbea5ee.

[35] HR7440, 116th Congress (2019-2020), Public Law No. 116-140, 7-14-2020, https://www.congress.gov/bill/116th-congress/house-bill/7440.

[36] "UK Unveils New Special Visa for Hong Kong's BNO Holders," BBC News, July 22, 2020, https://www.bbc.com/news/world-asia-china-53503338.

[37] "National Security Law: EU Proposes Cutting Off Hong Kong's Access to Goods Used in Surveillance and 'Internal Repression,'" *South China Morning Post*, July 24, 2020, https://scmp.com/economy/china-economy/article/3094637/national-security-law-eu-proposes-cutting-hong-kongs-access.

[38] Ibid.

[39] Interviews with legislators who prefer to remain anonymous due to the fear of retribution. Interviews with anonymous members of HKIAD, December 8, 2019. The latter group was reportedly active in promoting the Hong Kong cause in capitals abroad, with special attention to the UK and Germany. Very early in the protest, the German Green Party submitted a motion demanding that the German government call China out on most of the matters included in reports of the then evolving protester treatment, though it was doubtful substantial action would clear a Beijing-friendly German government. Keine weitere Eskalation in Hongkong—Das Prinzip „Ein Land, zwei Systeme" wahren ("No further escalation in Hong Hong—on the principle of 'one country, two systems,'" German Bundestag, June 11, 2019, http://dipbt.bundestag.de/doc/btd/19/148/1914823.pdf.

[40] Mrs. Anson Chan notes that, as chief secretary in the early years, she was herself often sent abroad to sell the one country, two systems policy. In those early years, when China was more restrained, she was happy to do so. Interview with former chief secretary, Mrs. Anson Chan, December 10, 2019.

Chapter 12

[1] Yan-ho Lai, "Securitisation or Autocratisation? Hong Kong's Rule of Law under the Shadow of China's Authoritarian Governance," *Journal of Asian and African Studies* 58, no. 1 (October 8, 2022): 1–18, https://journals.sagepub.com/doi/10.1177/00219096221124978.

[2] Michael C. Davis, "To Go or Not to Go," *Far Easter Economic Review* (1989). The full citation for this article is long lost, along with the demise of the *Far Eastern Economic Review*.